MW00561534

REFOCUSED PSYCHOTHERAPY AS THE FIRST LINE INTERVENTION IN BEHAVIORAL HEALTH

Written by father-daughter psychologists Nicholas (Nick) and Janet Cummings, this text provides proven patient-responsive interventions by practitioners who together have nearly a century of hands-on practice and innovation between them. *Refocused Psychotherapy* responds directly to the recent decline of psychosocial services and helps to put psychotherapy back as the first line intervention in mental health.

The authors teach psychotherapists how to work side by side with primary care physicians to provide efficacy, effectiveness, and efficiency—the standards psychotherapeutic intervention is held up to. Detailed case studies are followed up by discussions of diagnosis, personality type, homework, and therapeutic techniques that show readers how to form their own case conceptualizations. The authors also teach readers how to treat their patients individually and to diagnose effectively through their onion/garlic conceptualization. Finally, they provide lists of common abbreviations that are helpful to know when reading prescriptions, and lists of drugs, drug interactions, dosage, and side effects that expand readers' vocabulary and allow them to be more knowledgeable as they work with primary care physicians. These innovative and revealing techniques will help readers develop the skills necessary for cost-effective therapeutic results.

Nicholas A. Cummings, PhD, ScD, is a past President of the American Psychological Association who for the past half century has been predicting the course of psychology and forming organizations designed to meet the challenges as each occurred. He holds an extensive psychotherapy practice, is the author of 49 books and over 400 journal articles, and has had a profound effect on the course of the profession.

Janet L. Cummings, PsyD, has authored nine books with her father, Nicholas Cummings, and is currently Founder's Professor in the Doctor of Behavioral Health program at Arizona State University. A cutting-edge practitioner, she also finds time to serve as President of the Nicholas and Dorothy Cummings Foundation.

REFOCUSED PSYCHOTHERAPY AS THE FIRST LINE INTERVENTION IN BEHAVIORAL HEALTH

*Nicholas A. Cummings and
Janet L. Cummings*

Routledge
Taylor & Francis Group

NEW YORK AND LONDON

First published 2013
by Routledge
711 Third Avenue, New York, NY 10017

Simultaneously published in the UK
by Routledge
27 Church Road, Hove, East Sussex BN3 2FA

Routledge is an imprint of the Taylor & Francis Group, an informa business

Library of Congress Cataloging in Publication Data
Cummings, Nicholas A.
Refocused psychotherapy as the first line intervention in behavioral health/
by Nicholas A. Cummings and Janet L. Cummings.
  p. cm.
Includes bibliographical references and index.
  1. Psychotherapy—Practice. 2. Managed mental health care. I. Cummings,
Janet L. II. Title.
RC465.5.C86 2012
616.89'140068—dc23
2012003799

ISBN: 978-0-415-89301-5 (hbk)
ISBN: 978-0-203-10681-5 (ebk)

Typeset in Bembo
by Florence Production Ltd, Stoodleigh, Devon

Printed and bound in the United States of America by Sheridan Books, Inc. (a Sheridan Group company)

BLACK BOX WARNING

If you suffer from a fear of innovation,
adhere to a therapeutic psycho-religion,
or believe that psychotherapy is ineffective,

DO NOT READ THIS BOOK.

CONTENTS

ACKNOWLEDGMENTS

The authors express their gratitude to Linda Goddard, our Executive Assistant, for her tireless and dedicated participation in the execution of this new edition and its update. Fortunately, when our computers crashed or our data were misplaced, her files remained intact. Several times, her vigilance guaranteed the completion of this volume.

A note of thanks goes to our 14-year-old daughter/granddaughter, Mary Amy-Janelle Cummings, for suggesting that *Focused Psychotherapy* should be renamed *Refocused Psychotherapy* in this update. Previously, while in the 4th grade, she read the first edition, understood it, and gave a report and demonstration in her class that astounded her teacher.

The psychotherapy model described as applicable for extensive delivery systems is exemplified in the Arizona State University's Nicholas A. Cummings Doctor of Behavioral Health program. Special acknowledgments are due to Dr. Ronald O'Donnell, Director, for his bringing it to unprecedented successful fruition when psychology departments of three other major universities failed to do so. His tenure was made possible by the innovations of prescient ASU President Michael Crow, the boldness of Provost Elizabeth Capaldi in making the DBH program independent of the psychology department by creating a new doctoral degree, and the day-by-day incisive oversight and support of Dean Frederick Corey.

Finally, and importantly, the bold, insightful support of Dr. John Caccavale and the National Alliance of Professional Psychology Providers (NAPPP) has successfully launched the DBH training and degree as those of the behavioral health practitioner of the future.

PREFACE

He who studies medicine without books sails an uncharted sea. But he who studies medicine without patients does not go to sea at all.

(Sir William Osler)

This is as true for the practice of psychotherapy as it is for the practice of medicine, but unfortunately too many books on the practice of psychology are written by academic clinicians who may be good teachers and researchers, but they do not see patients. Unfortunately, these same academics train our future psychotherapists, thus psychotherapy today may be more efficacious, but is less effective and efficient than it might otherwise be. This book is committed to providing proven patient responsive interventions for patient responsive practitioners, by patient and practitioner responsive authors with nearly a century of proven hands-on practice and innovation with literally thousands of patients, trainees, and supervisees. Taking our lead from the unsurpassed cardiac surgical experience of the Cleveland Clinic, one is not a successful practitioner without having successfully treated at least 1,000 patients, no matter how many excellent books have been read or even written.

The precursor to this volume was titled *Focused Psychotherapy*. It was to aid psychotherapists in response to rapidly growing managed care, teaching them extraordinary skills that would enable them to form delivery systems that would lift them beyond the limitations of the managed care reimbursement panels. Since it was written in 1995, managed care has become pro forma in mental health and the new threat is the medicalization of mental health. This has resulted in the decline of psychotherapy services, for medications have replaced psychosocial services as the dominant treatment modality.

With the failure of antidepressants and other psychotropic meds to cure mental illness as initially expected, there arises the opportunity for psychotherapy to be restored as the first line intervention in behavioral care. But it will require efficient and effective psychotherapists within the healthcare setting whose skills can demonstrate therapeutic results as well as cost-effectiveness. To this end, the revised 1995 edition of *Focused Psychotherapy* has been renamed *Refocused Psychotherapy* so as to reflect these changes.

The Authors
March 1, 2012
Reno, Nevada

INTRODUCTION

How it Was: The Golden Age of Psychotherapy

Let us turn back the clock to the late 1950s and early 1960s and magically recall what the delivery of mental health services was like. Psychiatry was well established, psychology was flexing its muscles and growing rapidly, and social work was well respected, but very few social workers were in the private practice of psychotherapy as were psychiatrists and psychologists. Counselors and marriage/family therapists did not yet exist as independent professions, and there was a shortage of psychotherapists as Americans clamored for services. No one could even conceive of what later came to be known as managed care, for psychotherapy was a stated exclusion in health insurance policies. Paying out of pocket did not deter prospective patients, as fees were nominal: $15 per 50-minute hour for established psychiatrists and $10 for emerging psychologists.

Society was enamored of psychotherapy. Movies, radio, early television, and regular articles in the print media glamorized it. For two decades, polls among young women listed psychologists as potentially the most desired mates, and people did not shy away from referring to their own psychotherapy when among friends. It was generally accepted that psychotherapy was long term, and celebrated psychoanalysts maintained months-long waiting lists of eager patients waiting to be called. Psychotherapy came of age during World War II under the guidance of psychiatrist and wartime general William Menninger, co-founder of the late famous Menninger Clinic in Topeka, Kansas. The successes of military psychiatrists and psychologists had become legendary by 1960 through several best-selling books and popular movies, and the public's demand for psychotherapy was seemingly insatiable. The senior author entered independent practice in California in 1948 as a newly minted psychologist and rode this surge along with young colleagues who were also World War II veterans who were trained under the auspices of the GI Bill.

When a patient wanted to be seen, he/she would call the psychiatrist or psychologist directly and would be granted an appointment over the phone. He/she would be instructed to sit in the waiting room until called, which was always, with very rare exception, precisely at the appointed time, and would terminate exactly 50 minutes later. This allowed the psychotherapist 10 minutes to write notes, answer phone calls, and prepare for the next patient at the top of the next hour. Very few psychotherapists had receptionists, the overwhelming majority were in solo practice, and children and psychotic patients would be accompanied by a responsible person. Couples and families in therapy were, of course, seen together. Approximately 60 percent of patients were referred by their physicians, while a surprising 40 percent were self-referred, having obtained the psychotherapist's name usually from a friend, and occasionally from the Yellow Pages. Play therapy for children was in vogue, pediatricians made frequent referrals, and many psychologists maintained a playroom for that purpose. Psychological testing was a very large part of any psychologist's practice, and psychiatrists made frequent referrals for testing of their own patients. Likewise, psychologists would refer to a collaborating psychiatrist any psychotic patients in need of medication.

In this golden age, psychologists flourished. Psychotropic medications were infrequent and were always preceded by a visit to a psychotherapist (psychologist or psychiatrist), whose treatment plan would invariably be psychotherapy first and medication a relatively rare accompaniment to psychotherapy.

However, two problems existed and persisted during this era. One was that psychotherapy was essentially sought by the middle and affluent classes, with degree of education highly correlated with the seeking of these services. The working or so-called blue-collar classes were only slightly represented among those seeking psychotherapy. The second problem was the over-hospitalization of psychotic patients, and the serious over-crowding of state hospitals. Both were in the process of being effectively addressed through modifications in the delivery of behavioral health services when the golden age of psychotherapy was replaced by the medicalization of mental health, which made medication, not psychotherapy, the first-line intervention.

Expanding Psychotherapy to the General Population

The first of these problems was addressed by the Kaiser Permanente healthcare system, when in the late 1950s it began making psychotherapy a covered benefit. The senior author demonstrated (Follette & Cummings, 1967; Cummings & Follette, 1968) through medical cost offset research that psychotherapy was not only economically feasible, but its introduction saved medical/surgical dollars far beyond the cost of providing the behavioral care services. On the basis of this research, Nick Cummings wrote the nation's first prepaid psychotherapy benefit insurance policy in 1959, which became the basis for the healthcare industry to regard psychotherapy as not only feasible, but economically desirable (Cummings & VandenBos, 1981). The Kaiser Permanente medical outreach research was spectacularly replicated in the randomized, controlled Hawaii Project, which involved the entire Medicaid population of Hawaii as well as all of that state's federal employees (Cummings, Dorken, Pallak, & Henke, 1991; 1993). These two delivery systems (Kaiser Permanente and the Hawaii Project) became the basis for the launching of a capitated, prepaid managed behavioral care delivery system in the 1980s, which in 10 years grew to 25 million enrollees in all 50 states. Called American Biodyne, it was psychologist driven, and although each state had a medical director, he/she reported to a clinical director who was a psychologist.

The three delivery systems (Kaiser Permanente, Hawaii Project, American Biodyne) spanned over 40 years and involved tens of millions of covered lives, untold millions of treatment episodes, delivered by thousands of psychotherapists, all without a single malpractice suit. Such a record remains unduplicated in the healthcare industry where lawsuits are rife. The engine that drove the Biodyne model was prepaid psychotherapy provided exclusively by psychologists and social workers, and always as the first line intervention, rather than medication. In the relatively infrequent instances in which medication might secondarily be required, the psychotherapist was trained in psychopharmacology, not to prescribe, but to request an appropriate prescription from a psychiatrist on the staff. The prescription would be written and handed to the psychotherapist who would then give it to the patient, along with stated instructions and a discussion of possible side effects. This was so the prescribing would not interfere with the psycho-therapeutic transference or detract from the fact that psychotherapy was the primary treatment modality, not medication. This procedure has worked for five decades at Kaiser Permanente, and was challenged only once. In 2001, a disgruntled physician who failed to make the cut and was let go filed a suit in Oakland, California charging that at Kaiser Permanente psychologists and social workers were de facto prescribing. The court took cognizance that this procedure had been ongoing for over 40 years without a single hint of harm to any patient and threw the case out.

In the early days of the Biodyne model, psychiatrists (e.g., Kaiser Permanente) were psychotherapists along with psychologists and social workers. In the 1980s, however, after psychiatry had medicalized and psychotherapy was no longer included in their training, no psychiatrist thus untrained was allowed to do psychotherapy at American Biodyne. In fact, these newly minted psychiatrists disdainfully referred to psychotherapy as "talk therapy," stressing that behavioral problems were the result of chemical imbalances in the brain for which psychotherapy was irrelevant. When the senior author caught one psychiatrist doing psychotherapy and who then refused to abstain, he was promptly fired.

Meeting the Challenge of the Over-hospitalization of Psychotic Patients

While the Kaiser Permanente program led the way to the almost universal third-party payment of psychotherapy, which extended its use to the working classes and to minorities, and while the Hawaii Project convinced the government to include extensive psychotherapy services as a part of Medicaid, the problem of the over-hospitalization of psychotic patients, along with the serious over-crowding of state hospitals, was not so deftly resolved. Eventually, it led to deinstitutionalization, which by the 1980s rendered the street the de facto mental health hospital, with the prison system not far behind.

Prior to that, however, the National Institute of Mental Health (NIMH) was earnestly addressing the problem through research into community-based behavioral care services. The community mental health system, designed under the Kennedy administration and enacted during President Johnson's term after President Kennedy's assassination, was designed to keep patients out of mental hospitals by providing extensive outpatient behavioral interventions right in the patient's community. Additionally, NIMH was funding bold research programs such as the Soteria Project in California in the 1960s and 1970s. Headed and designed by forward-thinking psychiatrist Loren Mosher at NIMH, the two Soteria Houses, named for the Greek word "deliverance," were behaviorally oriented alternatives to hospitalization. In its random, controlled research design, every third patient presenting for mental hospitalization in Santa Clara County, California was remanded instead to one of the Soteria Houses. The program was behaviorally based, using milieu therapy, community self-governance, psycho-therapy, family therapy, and other appropriate behavioral techniques, with less than 10 percent receiving psychotropic medication, and then only for short periods (Mosher and Hendrix, 2008).

During three of the dozen years of the Soteria Project, the senior author was privileged to be director of Palo Alto's prestigious Mental Research Institute (MRI) that administered the Soteria Houses. He spent considerable time on their premises observing the rapid abatement of psychotic symptoms without medication, with several years of follow-up revealing no recurrence of symptoms. The program was so remarkably effective in eliminating hospitalization and without reliance on medication that NIMH was planning extensive replications in other regions of the United States. This threatened the rapidly emerging medicalization of psychiatry, whose events are described in Chapter 1. New leadership at NIMH (such as Gerald Klerman, head of the Alcohol, Drug Abuse and Mental Health Administration or ADAMHA, and now renamed SAMHSA) sought to devalue psychotherapy and replace it with medication based on brain chemical imbalance theories. Loren Mosher was fired by NIMH, the funding for Soteria was withdrawn literally overnight, and the project was shut down. NIMH saw to it that the final report was never written, so that now data on the Soteria

Project and its remarkable effectiveness is next to impossible to obtain. Mental health historian Robert Whitaker, however, has extensively chronicled this debacle (Whitaker, 2010). Shortly thereafter, deinstitutionalization, based on the assumption that the new medications would replace the need for mental hospitalization, moved rapidly forward.

A surprisingly simple method of effectively reducing mental hospitalization was to begin outpatient psychotherapy in the emergency room, whatever the night hour. The standard and mostly ineffective procedure that is generally employed is the following: when a patient with severe emotional distress presents to the ER, usually late at night, the emergency room physician calls the psychiatrist on duty. After a brief phone discussion between them, the psychiatrist advises that the patient should be admitted and he/she will examine the hospitalized patient in the morning. By the time the psychiatrist shows up, the patient has spent the night in a "crazy place," decides "I must be crazier than I thought," and is so overwhelmed that extended hospitalization is almost inevitable. By a simple, almost obvious method, this sequence is interrupted to the benefit that most such patients do not have to be hospitalized. A specially trained doctoral-level psychologist or psychiatric nurse practitioner, rather than a psychiatrist, goes immediately to the ER no matter how late at night. There, outpatient psychotherapy is begun, and if the patient responds positively, it is apparent that inpatient care is unnecessary and the patient is sent home with the responsible relative who brought the patient to the ER. Then the patient is seen the next day at an appropriate time that has given him/her a chance to sleep, and may be seen daily for several days. All of this is decidedly less expensive than even one day in the hospital. This procedure was adopted successfully by Kaiser Permanente and later by American Biodyne. The latter was able to reduce psychiatric hospitalization by a startling 90 percent, and shifted an impressive portion of this saving to a never-before-seen array of outpatient psychotherapy coverage, which included such usual exclusions as marital and occupational counseling (Cummings, 2011).

The Take-over of Mental Health by Managed Care

By the early 1990s, managed care had extended its industrialization to the point it now controlled psychotherapy, determining its practice through its own networks which prescribed the number of sessions, what interventions would be reimbursed through its approval of treatment plans by mostly non-professional case managers, and essentially cutting costs by artificial limitations of services. The American Psychological Association (APA) failed to heed warnings that healthcare was industrializing (Cummings, 1986), while the American Psychiatric Association (ApA) more or less welcomed it as long as it could exert its influence over it. The APA is now facing the decline as a behavioral science and practice by the replacement of psychotherapy through the dominance of medication, something the ApA finds quite compatible with its own medicalization.

Throughout the 1980s and 1990s, the only managed care company that maintained its behavioral fidelity was psychology-driven American Biodyne. It flourished as a delivery system in a manner that the Wall Street-controlled managed care companies lacked the practice knowledge to replicate, relying instead on psychiatry and its emphasis on psychotropic medication. Challenged several times by the ApA, it won every skirmish, proving that effective behavioral care services could succeed in the legal sphere as well as the economic. Tired of incessantly fighting both the ApA and his own APA, the senior author, who was founding CEO, along with his colleagues, sold the company in the mid-1990s with the proviso that the fidelity of the delivery system would be maintained. Erosion, however, began almost immediately, and the promise was totally shattered within six months.

Restoring Psychotherapy as the First Line Intervention

This book addresses the need for psychotherapy to once again assume its rightful place as the first line intervention in behavioral health, and provides a roadmap for doing so. Having lost that role to medication, with resulting unintended consequences, the public is now ready for change if the behavioral care professions appropriately rise to the occasion. However, by abandoning its foundation in psychopathology, psychology has lost its way, inadvertently fostering the rise of medication as the immediate treatment for all anxiety and depression, now prescribed without regard for the behavioral causes of such feelings. Arbitrary collections of symptoms are given scientific-sounding names, and have replaced any validity to actual diseases or conditions. As will be seen in Chapter 1, these same arbitrary collections of symptoms are reshuffled and renamed from one DSM to the next. The intervention for all of these reshuffled syndromes is always the latest in psychotropic medications whose efficacy is being seriously challenged and whose alarming side effects are mounting.

This calls for a new emphasis in behavioral healthcare, grounded in psychopathology and dispensed as an integral part of mainstream healthcare. Recognizing that the vast majority of emotionally distressed patients are found in primary care, the National Health Reform Act of 2010 has essentially placed the primary care physician (PCP) in charge of the delivery of mental health, emphasizing the need for the behavioral care provider (BCP) to emerge from the solo practice office and work side by side with the physician. In this role, the BCP would not only function as a primary care psychotherapist, but would also educate the physician on the need, timeliness, and appropriateness of various behavioral interventions. This calls for efficacy (i.e., proven interventions) that works beyond the clinical trials (i.e., effectiveness) and finally efficiency (e.g., the 50-minute hour is not sacrosanct). In other words, the BCP would learn to function more like a physician without compromising grounding in behavioral health. In short, the primary care system would assume the complexion projected by the British mental health pioneer Michael Balint more than half a century ago: "Psychologists need to become more like physicians, while physicians need to become more like psychologists" (Balint, 1957: 43).

The system to be described, which has come to be known as the Biodyne Model, is not only evidence-based, but it has been field-tested for over four decades with cohorts numbering over 30 to 40 million covered lives and in actual delivery systems throughout the United States. It has its roots beginning in 1959 at Kaiser Permanente where its prescient founding physician, Sidney Garfield, saw the value of psychology over psychiatry, and where his successor and protégé, Morris F. Collen, himself also a physician, accorded N. Cummings the freedom to develop the model with its then four million covered lives (Cummings & VandenBos, 1981). It was then tested in the prospective, randomized government Hawaii Medicaid Project with 120,000 subjects from 1980 to 1987 (Cummings et al., 1991; 1993). In 1985, it became the foundation for the national proprietary delivery system called American Biodyne, where it addressed all mental health needs of 25 million covered lives in all 50 states over 10 years. As was previously mentioned, in this experience, there was not a single malpractice suit or patient complaint that had to be adjudicated, a feat never duplicated before or since by any national healthcare company. With this history, the Biodyne Model is a one-of-a-kind exemplar in efficacy, effectiveness, and efficiency, and is the behavioral treatment model described in this book.

About the Authors

Who are the authors? We are father and daughter psychologists, and this is our ninth book together. Nick is a past president (1979) of the American Psychological Association who was head of mental health for Kaiser Permanente, principle investigator for the Hawaii Project, founder of the professional psychology movement with the four campuses of the California School of Professional Psychology (now Alliant University), director of the Mental Research Institute in Palo Alto, and the founding CEO of American Biodyne. More recently, he is the architect of the Nicholas A. Cummings Doctor of Behavioral Program at Arizona State University where Janet was founding co-director and continues in the role of adjunct associate professor. Janet, an authority on psychopharmacology, psychopathology, and pathophysiology, studied molecular biology before becoming a psychologist. She was named Alumna of the Year by Wright State University where she obtained her doctorate. Both of us are on the faculty of the University of Nevada, Reno, where Nick is distinguished professor and Janet is adjunct professor. We have treated thousands of patients, supervised hundreds of psychotherapists, and have taught scores of doctoral students in graduate schools. We are dedicated hands-on practitioners who, in spite of whatever else we were doing, have also maintained an extensive independent practice in psychotherapy and behavioral care.

For more extensive biographies, log on to www.thecummingsfoundation.org.

1

A RETURN TO PSYCHOPATHOLOGY AND PATHOPHYSIOLOGY

Validity and Effectiveness

Much of what passes as psychotherapy today is crippled by the absence of real cause-and-effect psychopathology. Symptoms are taken at face value, regardless of whether they are found in an Axis I versus an Axis II patient, and both are treated the same way by cognitive therapy, with motivational interviewing substituting for a real understanding of the patient's resistance and how to therapeutically respond to it. Consequently, our mental health services are bogged down by borderline personality patients who, year after year, manipulate the system to achieve their own ends or even to get out of trouble.

By opting out of mainstream healthcare and isolating ourselves in our psychotherapy offices, even the term patient has been replaced by the word client. Physicians, dentists, nurses, optometrists, podiatrists, veterinarians, and even chiropractors all have patients, while lawyers, accountants, stockbrokers, and financial advisers, along with psychologists, counselors, and social workers, have clients. Does this seem odd, or have we gone down this path so far that today any suggestion that someone might have more than just faulty learning or ineffective attitudes borders on the politically incorrect? We no longer "treat" patients; we "advise" clients. In fact, the most highly touted psychotherapy approach as of this writing is acceptance commitment therapy (ACT), which teaches that unhappiness is the natural human condition, and the sooner the client accepts this, the better. Started originally by Steven Hayes (2000), a radical behaviorist who 30 years ago would not espouse even cognitive behaviorism, we have seen ACT gravitate toward and copy now out-of-fashion gestalt therapy and go even beyond, rendering it at times indistinguishable from pop psychology. This is only one of too many psychotherapeutic fads in an era in which validity to psychopathology and pathophysiology is non-existent.

At one time, all medicine was symptom-oriented. The medical profession progressed rapidly in the twentieth century in discovering actual diseases, their causes, and their treatment, while the twenty-first century sees psychiatry as the only remaining branch of medicine that remains symptom-oriented wherein syndromes (arbitrary clusters of symptoms that have no validity to actual diseases) are named and "treated" as if they are diseases. To illustrate, the psychopathologist and the pathophysiologist would assert the following:

- Fever is not a diagnosis, but a symptom that accompanies a number of different diseases.
- Likewise, depression is a symptom that can accompany a number of diseases.
- Similarly, anxiety is also a symptom, not a diagnosis.
- Bereavement is not pathology, but nature's healing response to severe loss.
- It is likely that real Post Traumatic Stress Disorder (PTSD) is not a disorder, but nature's healing process for severe, intolerable stress. Like bereavement, a reliving of the stress takes one to two painful years of healing and should not be prolonged with interference from medication (Konigsberg, 2011).
- It is probable that ADHD and autism are not diseases but symptoms of a yet-to-be-determined disease or diseases. The recent questionable DSM extensions of these conditions has created a lot of false positives.

Today, symptoms are disorders, and for every symptom there is a medication. This is tantamount to diagnosing a headache as a disorder for which aspirin is the prescribed treatment regardless of whether the headache is the symptom of an array of causes, such as eye strain, tension, migraine, or a rapidly growing brain tumor. Whereas the first two might experience temporary relief with the aspirin, the migraine patient is not helped at all and continues to suffer until the migraine attack passes, but in the fourth instance the patient will likely die.

There was a time when psychotherapists would not merely assess the patient's beliefs and frustration, but would help the patient delve into the path that led to these (i.e., causation). How did we get from the golden age of psychotherapy to the present absence of all psychopathology? It is a process that spanned 30 years, slowly but steadily eroding validity in favor of arbitrary clusters of symptoms for which there is always a medication and without the need for skilled psychotherapy. In the present era:

1. It is rare to find a psychiatrist under age 50 who performs psychotherapy.
2. Psychiatry has become an "every 15 minute per patient pill pushing" profession (Shorter, 2010) that has proven unattractive to medical school graduates who shun it as a career. Consequently, there is a severe shortage of psychiatrists.
3. As a result, 85 percent of all psychotropic drugs are prescribed by non-psychiatric physicians, an inevitable outcome predicted by psychiatrist Stan Lesse over 30 years ago (Lesse, 1982).

4. The vast majority of mental health simply involves the dispensing of psychotropic medications, with the portion attributable to behavioral care services continuing to shrink.
5. Masters-level psychotherapists have proliferated to where they far outnumber doctoral psychologists. Because their fees are less, "counselors" now perform the vast majority of psychotherapy in America. Since psychiatrists, by virtue of being physicians, are in control of most of mental health, they supervise these masters-level providers in the "talk therapy" they long ago gave up, and in which they are no longer experts. The vast majority of mental health involves the dispensing of psychotropic medications, with the portion attributable to behavioral care being often cynically regarded as a way of handling unresponsive or troublesome patients.

A Brief Historical Perspective

How did we awaken like Rip van Winkle to find that the profession for which we were trained no longer existed or had been severely curtailed? Interestingly, the successive DSMs provide benchmarks on the progression of what has been termed the "medicalization of psychiatry," along with the subsequent and thereby inevitable loss of validity in mental health practice.

The Diagnostic and Statistical Manuals of Mental Health Disorders, known as the DSMs for short, have undergone a series of iterations in the past half century since the inception of DSM-I by the American Psychiatric Association in the 1950s. Known colloquially as the "psychiatric bible," it is the basis for reimbursement for services, as well as the nomenclature by which government and other agencies collect statistical data on aspects of mental and emotional illness. In spite of its seemingly universal utility, however, it has been fraught with controversy. As the DSM proceeded through its iterations, the controversy increased steadily, reaching a crescendo with the construction of DSM-V.

Few, if any, mental health professionals practicing today are aware of the void, better described as incredulity, that existed in diagnosis prior to the inception of the first DSM. The senior author entered independent practice in California in 1948, and thumbing through some early diagnostic reports he gleaned a host of archaically colorful diagnoses that were once accepted parlance. Consider, for example, "anal retentive personality culminating in rectal cancer." Or, if you can look at one that would be resented by every woman living today: "exaggerated female masochism, conveniently married to a sadistic husband who emotionally rewards her by becoming contrite after each occasion in which he beats her." Often, these atavistic diagnoses sought to embody causation, such as "severe Oedipus complex inevitably resulting in homosexuality and effeminate personality." And, of course, there is the all-time favorite, "idiot, imbecile grade."

The now apparent absurdity of these diagnoses reflects the fact that each school of psychiatry (and even of then budding clinical psychology) used its own esoteric nomenclature. In other words, diagnoses were parochial, with each "system" disdaining all others. That this was hampering interchangeability among various practitioners soon became subordinate to the greater problem that emerged in the 1950s as government and private insurance began to reimburse for psychiatric services. (Note that reimbursement of psychiatric services preceded that for services of psychologists for a number of years, with that for social workers and counselors occurring much later.) Diagnoses were so diverse that third-party payers struggled to discern which claims were proper and deserving of reimbursement. Hence, the real impetus for DSM-I was unmistakably economic, which in time propelled the DSM to the status of the "psychiatric bible." As will be seen, the economic purpose remains the dominate impetus inasmuch as the so-called diagnostic categories are actually collections of symptoms rather than reflective of actual disease processes as those seen in medical diagnoses.

DSM-I: The Age of Anxiety

Published in 1952, the first Diagnostic and Statistical Manual was a relatively succinct and simple document compared to its most recent successors. In the 1950s and 1960s, when psychiatry was still under the influence of the European scientific tradition, there was a striving for reasonably accurate diagnoses, as reflected in the DSM-I (Shorter, 2010). Furthermore, it must be remembered that, although it has become more difficult to believe in the last two decades, psychiatry was still psychotherapeutically oriented. "Psychoneurosis" was the principal diagnosis of the day, where simply put, if a patient complained of being "blue, uneasy or generally jumpy, 'nerves' was the common diagnosis. To the psychotherapeutically oriented psychiatrists of the day, 'psychoneurosis' was the equivalent of nerves" (Shorter, 2010: 1). There was no reason to delineate this further, as both doctor and patient understood "a case of nerves."

The DSM-I was not widely used in the 1950s, which is in sharp contrast to the must-use dictum since the 1980s. It did serve as a centrifugal force, bringing order to the jumble of nomenclatures proffered by what this author long ago named the "psycho-religions," for its simplicity seemed to satisfy widely divergent practitioners. The notion that anxiety was central to all psychological conditions was the subject of two widely read and generally highly regarded books of that era: Rollo May's *The Meaning of Anxiety* (1950, 1977) and Hans Selye's *The Stressors of Life* (1956). In coining the term "stressor," Selye added a word universally invoked by the psychiatrists (and psychologists) of the era (Menand, 2010).

The then universal nature of anxiety fostered the fiasco of the earliest psychotropic medications. In 1955, meprobamate with the brand name Milltown was introduced as an anxiolytic, and soon it became the largest-selling drug in American history up to that time (Tone, 2009). In fact, it accounted for one-third of all prescriptions written by American physicians. It is startling to recall that Milltown was soon eclipsed by two other anxiolytics, Librium and Valium, introduced in 1960 and 1963. By 1968, Valium became the most prescribed drug in the Western world, and the stock of its manufacturer, Hoffman-La Roche, increased in 1972 to $73,000 a share (Tone, 2009).

Marketed with FDA approval as non-addictive, the senior author became alarmed as a legion of patients heavily addicted to these anxiolytics filled his practice. His early attempts to sound an alarm were dismissed by both the manufacturer and the FDA, but by 1980 the research findings were incontrovertible and the FDA issued a warning label, only the second in history after the fetus-crippling drug Thalidomide. The warning stated that the stressors of everyday life did not warrant the use of such addictive drugs (Tone, 2009). The crash of Librium and Valium sales marked the end of the age of anxiety, but there was an overlap with the introduction of DSM-II.

DSM-II: A Freudian Document While Personality Disorders Become Mental Illnesses

The second DSM was more complicated and was based on the concepts put forth by Sigmund Freud and Adolph Meyer, with the latter having come to the United States from Switzerland (Menand, 2010). Thus, it was based on psychoanalytic theory, but it reflected Adolph Meyer's persistence, which led to the inclusion of a vast population (i.e., then known as character disorders) that had not been previously regarded as patients.

Introduced in 1968 as Axis II disorders, the second DSM gave character disorders the new name of personality disorders, and made them the province of psychiatric treatment. Heretofore, they were termed "characterological" because they were regarded as enduring aspects of one's character and impervious to treatment. By changing the designation, it added millions of new potential paying patients to psychiatry, and forever cluttered the field with intractable but demanding patients to the detriment of non-Axis II patients and the severely mentally ill, both of whom do not bombard the besieged system with vociferous demands for immediate attention. But this was only the beginning of the now self-serving expansion of psychiatric diagnoses into aspects of life's daily vicissitudes.

DSM-III: The End of Psychopathology

The publication of the third iteration in 1980 brought about a sea change and destined mental health to the eventual crisis in which it now finds itself. With energetic and engaging psychiatrist Rene Spitzer at the helm, it was determined to solve the problem of reliability so that every practitioner given a set of symptoms would come out with the same diagnosis. In so doing, however, the manual did not address an even greater problem, namely validity, defined as the correspondence of symptoms to organic conditions (Greenberg, 2010; Menand, 2010). In other words, rather than diseases, the end result was a set of "conditions" or "syndromes" characterized by common signs and symptoms, often loosely woven, whose existence and validity could not be proven.

Spitzer did accomplish one positive reform: he purged the DSM of the Freudian jargon that had plagued the previous editions. In so doing, however, he threw out the baby with the bathwater. Psychoanalysis at least struggled to base itself on psychopathology (i.e., cause and effect), but Spitzer inadvertently omitted psychopathology altogether. Consider where medicine would be without pathophysiology—exactly where it was over a century ago, dealing with conditions and syndromes rather than diseases. This is perhaps why psychiatry has gone overboard in espousing psychopharmacology before it has any known diseases to medicate (Kirsch, 2010).

To illustrate further the arbitrary nature of the diagnostic system, DSM-III began the process of "diagnosis by ballot," perfected in the next iteration. Just imagine for one minute if the diagnosis of pancreatic or ovarian cancer was rendered by vote rather than blood tests or biopsy.

DSM-IV and IV-TR: Our Beleaguered Present

Not surprisingly, this iteration is comprised of a series of controversial and arbitrary positions that have not abated, but have increased the questionable aspects of its predecessors by incorporating diagnosis by ballot, first by elimination of homosexuality as a diagnosis and with the substitution of dystonic homosexuality to satisfy dissent. Then silently and without explanation that compromise (i.e., dystonic homosexuality) was dropped. The question is not whether homosexuality should be a diagnosis (these authors believe it should not), but the issue is the egregious concept of diagnosis by ballot rather than by research validating psychopathology. The process has been amplified by DSM committees, often deliberating in secret, voting on adding or subtracting diagnoses in the absence of validity.

The current DSM has resulted in the age of depression similar to the age of anxiety with its Milltown, Librium, and Valium in the 1960s. Now with the over-diagnosing of depression for which only antidepressants are prescribed, there are predictions we may be heading for the same train wreck with antidepressants (Greenberg, 2010; Herzberg, 2008; Kirsch, 2010). In addressing the propensity to prescribe antidepressants for the problems of daily living, Wakefield and Horwitz (2007) deplore the elimination of sadness as a normal and informative emotion in daily living. These same authors have summarized the growing body of literature that reveals the relative ineffectiveness of antidepressants, especially in milder cases, along with the startling array of harmful side effects, many of them quite serious. Psychiatrist Carlat (2010) concludes flatly that psychotherapy might be more effective and less physically destructive than antidepressants, a position espoused by an ever-increasing number of critics both inside and outside the profession (Whitaker, 2010).

The series of signs and symptoms that comprise our syndromes do not lead to behavioral interventions, but rather facilitate the prescribing of medication. For every symptom, there is ostensibly a medication. Although there exists a large inventory of psychotropic drugs, there is a limited number of different classes, and often the same medication is prescribed for a variety of different conditions. For example, antidepressants may not only be prescribed for depression, but also may be prescribed off-label for obsessive-compulsive disorder, smoking cessation, job dissatisfaction, low libido, premature ejaculation, eating disorders, or whatever else the diverse but questionable literature might suggest. Furthermore, anxiety and depression are not diagnoses any more than is headache or fever, but manifestation of any number of diseases. Because DSM-IV constitutes a reshuffling of the same old symptoms to describe conditions with new names, this has led critics such as Menand (2010) to ask if we may not be dealing with one disease (mental illness) with a variety of stages and symptoms.

Diagnosis by Consensus Rather than Science

In the absence of validity, and with the emphasis on reliability alone, determination of diagnosis by consensus is perhaps as good as it can get. Thus, everyone looking at a set of symptoms concludes the same "diagnosis," even if the agreement has nothing to do with an actual disease. This is far from scientific validity, bringing with it flaws that expose the consensus to well-meaning biases that reflect more the social and political beliefs of the time than actual diseases that require specific medicating. To be sure, the consensus may be the result of extensive clinical experience, but vast experience with just diagnosing a fever gives only limited knowledge (e.g., a fever is seen when present, but its etiology remains unknown).

By 2010, non-psychiatric physicians, who when it comes to physical illness are scrupulously disease-oriented, have completely bought into the DSM-IV nomenclature and have become the main source of psychotropic prescribing, with 85 percent of all such dispensing being done by them. Not so in China, where, as of this writing, the Biodyne Model is being imported. For decades, Chinese healthcare providers and the general population used the Chinese-language equivalent of neurasthenia to define somatizers. With the advent of DSM-III and the invasion of pharmaceutical reps in China, psychiatry abandoned the concept in favor of symptoms/depression, just as their counterparts in the United States have done, with the same validity problems and over-use of medications now extant there. In contrast to America, however, in China, both the physicians and the general public prefer neurasthenia and approach somatization accordingly (Lee, 1997; Lee & Kleinman, 2007). This explains why the rampant over-prescribing by Chinese psychiatrists has not been emulated by non-psychiatric physicians.

Accompanying the abandonment of psychoneurosis has been a rapid de-emphasis of both the taking of extensive patient histories and the administration of psychological tests. The brief paper-and-pencil screening tests used now principally to determine depression are so transparent that they are readily skewed, especially by the plethora of manipulating Axis II patients who can look profoundly depressed when they seek hospitalization to escape trouble, and then look normal when the subterfuge has worked, the trouble has passed, and they want to leave the hospital. Let us look at some of the more flagrant unscientific decisions that have resulted from capitulation to concurrent social and political biases.

In formulating DSM-III, there was considerable horse-trading. The younger biology-oriented psychiatrists were able to dump some of the previous designations that sounded like psychoanalytic mumbo-jumbo with the new term major depression, but as a concession to their older colleagues they coined the addition of dysthymia. To the psychoanalysts, this sounded like their beloved neurotic depression, and the compromise was affected. With the further addition to bipolar of a separate unipolar, there were now enough categories for nearly everyone to qualify as a depressive, even though all of these "depressions" may be the same condition with slightly varying symptom formation (Shorter, 2010). Anxiety was finished, and the stage was set for almost everyone to be eligible for treatment with antidepressants. Greenberg (2010) goes so far as to accuse the profession of a conspiracy to render sadness a chemical disease of the brain.

With consensus and compromise determining diagnoses, it was inevitable that political correctness would insert itself in the process. In 1973, the American Psychiatric Association removed homosexuality as a treatable aberrant condition. The question here is not the right or wrong of that decision, but rather the way it was done. A political firestorm had been created by lesbian and gay activist groups within psychiatry, with intense opposition to normalizing homosexuality coming from a few outspoken psychiatrists who were demonized and even threatened, rather than scientifically refuted. Psychiatry's House of Delegates sidestepped the conflict by putting the matter to a vote of the membership, marking the first time in the history of healthcare that a diagnosis or lack of a diagnosis was decided by popular vote rather than by scientific evidence. Similarly, a number of issues sensitive to feminists and other activists were determined politically (for a comprehensive delineation, see Wright and Cummings, 2005), underscoring the arbitrary nature of psychiatric diagnoses. Could this have occurred with the diagnoses of pancreatic cancer, or tuberculosis, without the physical and laboratory tests to corroborate? Yet, the trend continues, one example being the disturbing effort to normalize some pedophilias in the forthcoming DSM-V.

The preliminary history of the proposed DSM-V emphasizes the arbitrariness of psychiatric diagnoses. After deliberating secretly for almost three years, enough disturbing information as to what was being contemplated by the task force was leaked, creating a firestorm of controversy. As a result, the completion was delayed for two years while widespread comment is being solicited. At best, the outcome can only be consensus, not validity.

Since new diagnoses are based on votes of committees rather than neurobiological testing, the field is vulnerable to "disease mongering" (Carlat, 2010), defined as the expansion of "disease" definitions in order to pump up the market for medication treatment. We have already seen how the inclusion of personality disorders more than doubled our potential patients. The redefinition in 2001 of ADHD quadrupled the number of children eligible to be so diagnosed (Cummings & Wiggins, 2001), while the increase in the number of categories of depression eliminated sadness and rendered almost anyone eligible to be prescribed antidepressants. At times, the expansion became colorful, with seasonal affective disorder (SAD) to be followed by reverse seasonal affective disorder (reverse SAD) for people who are depressed in the summer rather than the winter. Not only have diagnoses been expanded so that they encroach upon the responses to daily living, but the number of categories has proliferated remarkably. Consider that the DSM has increased from its original 50 pages to 900, and the number of diagnostic categories has exploded from 100 to 800 (Follette & Houts, 1996). These are just some examples of why some critics have referred to our psychiatric diagnostic system as *psychosprawl* (Carlat, 2010). To add a bit of consumer humor, a very knowledgeable former patient weighed in with her own suggested addition to DSM-V. She and her fellow octogenarian or near octogenarian wives were discussing the fact that men become debilitated before their wives do, and are unable to perform sexually. She, herself, had not had sex for eight years, and in an extended discussion with her friends she and they would submit to the DSM-V committee that any wife who had gone over two years without sex be designated the new syndrome *Born Again Virgin* (Janet Simpson, personal communication, January 2011). Fanciful? Perhaps, but it fulfills today's criteria for new DSM syndromes: consensus by an arbitrarily appointed committee, a definition that is readily identifiable and recognizable by all clinicians, and one that can be treated by a new drug yet to be developed that might be called "unviagra."

Finally, it is important to reiterate that symptom-oriented diagnosis not only has no efficacy to actual diseases, but it misses and even obscures the ability to relate the patient's symptoms to any possible underlying or even readily existing behavioral psychopathology. Just as the Biodyne Model met managed care head-on in 1980 to 1995 and succeeded, it is now prepared to address the limitations of the biomedical revolution and restore psychotherapy to its rightful place as the first line intervention in behavioral health. It can do this through efficacy, effectiveness, and efficiency, all reflected in the bold innovations to be described.

Summary

Psychiatry is the last branch of medicine that is still *intuitive*. This means that diagnoses are determined by symptoms/syndromes rather than by actual diseases derived through objective tests such as blood draws, X-rays, imaging, laboratory analyses, and the many determinants currently available to all other branches of medicine. There once was a time prior to the twentieth century when all medicine was intuitive, an era characterized by not questioning the only procedures available, as then there would be nothing else. A prime example was bloodletting: when the patient died, it was always attributed to the disease and not the bloodletting. Similarly, in psychiatry today when there are deleterious side effects, with some as serious as death or suicide, the tendency is to attribute these outcomes to the patient's syndrome, and not the medication. Why? Because psychiatry has nothing in its therapeutic armamentarium other than psychotropic medications, and to otherwise question such adverse outcomes is to leave the psychiatrists virtually without an arrow in their quiver.

Restoring psychotherapy as the first line intervention, which would include a battery of objective tests and a comprehensive history, would also restore the importance of cause-and-effect relationships, which would address the root cause of the patient's anxiety or depression, and make it possible to address these in psychotherapy. The question remains whether increases or decreases in anxiety and depression are caused by fluctuations in levels of serotonin and dopamine, or are these symptoms that accompany job stress, marital unhappiness, legal difficulties, and severe loss, along with other symptoms such as headache, fever, rise in blood pressure, or suppressed breathing that are *symptoms* of a disease, but not the disease itself?

To the extent the psychotherapist is not well-grounded in therapeutic address of cause-and-effect relationships, failures in psychotherapy are blamed on the patient. One hears such excuses as the patient was not motivated, or he/she was not "psychologically minded" (whatever that is), or he/she was uncooperative. In the Biodyne Model, there are no such excuses, as the therapist is trained to recruit the patient's resistance as an ally.

2

CAUSE-AND-EFFECT PSYCHOTHERAPY

Treating More than Just Symptoms

Unfortunately, in the two decades during which psychotherapy was relegated to secondary status by the ascendancy of psychotropic medication, the definition of what constitutes psychotherapy has been muddied and left in need of clarification. Primary care physicians have been dispensing 85 percent of the mental health in the United States, mostly through prescribed medication and occasionally through counseling that accompanies the prescription. It has been a stopgap necessitated by the shortage of psychiatrists, but this counseling by primary care physicians, no matter how skillful or even appropriate, falls far short of being psychotherapy. First of all, psychotherapy is a *behavioral health procedure* that is therapeutic. Many things are therapeutic, but they are not a procedure: a good night's sleep, getting a job, reading a good book, making love, going out with friends, and even prayer (the latter shown to be therapeutic in summaries by Cooper, 1995 and Cummings & Cummings, 1997). The distinction between an intervention and a procedure is obvious in medicine, but it was not seen as a distinction until Manaster and Corsini (1982) defined a behavioral care procedure.

To continue the distinction further, not all procedures are therapeutic. Applying leeches to remove "bad blood" was a past procedure in medicine, but it was never therapeutic. Eye movement desensitization response (EMDR) is a procedure, but it remains controversial whether it is therapeutic, although recent research suggests that what accompanies the eye movements may be therapeutic. Holding on to crystals during psychotherapy, as was once a fad among now disgraced New Age psychologists in Sedona, Arizona, is neither psychotherapy nor a procedure. On the other hand, biofeedback is a procedure that has been shown to be highly therapeutic with migraine headaches, but it is not psychotherapy. In short, psychotherapy is "talk therapy" between psychotherapist and patient (or patients, as in group therapy), preferably face-to-face, in which there is a deliberate effort to determine a cause-and-effect relationship with the intent of improving the patient's behavior and well-being. In short, psychotherapy fulfills the definition of a *therapeutic procedure*.

Procedures in healthcare are generally reimbursed for the event, not by the clock. For example, a gastroenterologist who performs a colonoscopy is paid for the procedure, whether it is rapidly completed because the colon is clear, or it takes longer because several polyps were discovered and had to be snipped off. A century and a half ago, someone (perhaps it was Sigmund Freud) determined that psychotherapists should be paid by the hour much like we pay a plumber who repairs our faucet. This has led to two unfortunate consequences. The first is that the psychotherapist is incented to perform longer-term therapy, especially if all of his/her hours are not filled. The second is that the third-party payer (e.g., insurance, health plan) is incented to arbitrarily limit the number of sessions allowed. In either case, the motive is monetary and not therapeutic. There have been plans that have instituted a "case rate" with a set rate to be paid for conclusion of the therapy. The size of the fee is predetermined by the nature of the case and its severity. Thus, a skillful psychotherapist will do well financially, while an unskilled one will expend an otherwise needless amount of time, thus impacting negatively on income. In case rate reimbursement, cutting corners and declaring a case as concluded when it is not leads to dismissal of the therapist from the referral roster, as the third-party payer keeps meticulous records of patient satisfaction and dissatisfaction, as well as those of patients returning with the same or continuing problem. By and large, behavioral practitioners dislike case rate reimbursement, as their inefficiency curtails their income.

The Biodyne Model of Psychotherapy

Focused psychotherapy is based on determining causality and thereby effecting change of sufficient magnitude to improve one's life. Hence the word Biodyne, which is composed of two classical Greek words, *bio* meaning "life," and *dyne* (or *dyna*) meaning "change." Therefore, the goal of the Biodyne Model is life change. The term for this causal relationship is psychopathology, and the response to it is psychotherapy. Before getting into the nuts and bolts of process and technique, two overriding principles require not only understanding, but a full commitment from the psychotherapist. Without a gut-level appreciation and application of these two guiding principles, the techniques often required in helping the patient may seem to range from artistry to tough love, and may erroneously appear to be harsh or even disingenuous at times. Before moving on to the actual interventions, take time to ponder and fully digest these. If they do not resonate, you need not read further.

Principle 1: Therapist's Obligation

The patient is entitled to relief from pain, anxiety, and depression in the shortest time possible, with the least intrusive intervention, and without harm. To accomplish this, the psychotherapist is obligated to hone one's skills so as to make this possible.

Principle 2: The Patient Bill of Rights

I will never abandon you as long as you need me, and I will never ask you to do anything until you are ready. In return for this, you must join me in a partnership to render me obsolete as soon as possible.

The actual phraseology is altered to be responsive to the patient's vernacular and level of education, but in all cases these principles are thoroughly discussed until the patient not only understands what is involved, but agrees with and accepts these guiding principles. In the very rare instance in which the patient disagrees, the interview is terminated and the patient is offered a referral. The effect here is to establish a relationship in which patient and therapist are partners in affecting the patient's recovery or life change.

In this current psychological climate, the concept that the patient has obligations is startling to many practitioners, if not to most patients. Such requirements of the patient are not new, but over two thousand years old. They are a cornerstone of the Hippocratic oath. Most readers are aware that Hippocrates cautioned, "first, do no harm." They are unaware that, along with the commitments of the doctor, Hippocrates promulgated a list of patient obligations, not the least of which was the obligation to cooperate in the treatment. Failure to do so, according to Hippocrates, freed the doctor from the obligation to treat the patient.

In the Biodyne Model, the practitioner is actually required to terminate treatment if the patients fail to live up to their obligations. This is done with determination as well as with sensitivity and concern, and, as will be shown later, it actually motivates the patient to get well. It is particularly useful in the treatment of personality disorders, very often catapulting the patient to positive outcomes, and ending the otherwise endless game of manipulating a hapless, passive, and overly accepting therapist.

The Biodyne Model is also efficient. Just because a treatment is successful is not reason to utilize it if that treatment is more intrusive or it takes longer than another effective, evidence-based treatment. The partnership between psycho-therapist and patient further eliminates "therapeutic drift," the situation in which nothing is happening in the sessions. But since a third party is paying for them, and as long as something positive might occur in the future, why not just continue session after session?

And finally, it will be noted that the recipient is unabashedly called the patient, underscoring that this is not self-exploration/fulfillment, remediation, self-improvement, or the ever elusive self-actualization, but rather there is a diagnosable psychological condition for which the individual is receiving a *treatment* called psychotherapy by a *doctor* called a psychotherapist.

Characteristics of the Biodyne Model

It is an Amalgam

For the past one hundred years, our profession has been characterized by competition among the various "schools of psychology," what we refer to as "psycho-religions" because of the insistence of each as having a monopoly on the truth. The controversy has been fueled by the ability of each psycho-religion to demonstrate effectiveness in some, even though most often limited, areas while ignoring the wider range where it is not effective. Our model has been able to tap into the effective aspects of behavioral, cognitive, psychodynamic systems and strategic therapies, not arbitrarily, but through persistent, ongoing research in both the laboratory and the delivery system. For a detailed discussion of these 40 years of ongoing research, see Appendix II.

The past two decades have witnessed evidence-based research directed only at cognitive therapy, leaving the erroneous impression that only cognitive approaches were efficacious. Much of this limited research simply reflected the fact that cognitive variables are easy to quantify. During this one-sided era, psychodynamics fell into near disgrace in most training programs, resulting in the throwing out of the baby with the bathwater. The conclusion was drawn that the absence of evidence reflected an absence of validity rather than the absence of research performed. The recent expanded investigations of Jonathan Shedler have demonstrated that psychodynamic therapy has powerful benefits (Shedler, 2010a; 2010b). Not surprisingly, these findings vindicate the selective use of psychodynamics that has consistently been a part of the Biodyne Model.

It is Brief, Intermittent Psychotherapy throughout the Life Cycle

As an individual traverses the various stages of life (infancy, childhood, adolescence, early adulthood, middle age, and old age, with transitions in school, college, marriage, parenthood, and eventual decline such as described first by Erikson, 1950), difficulties often arise that could be helped by the services of a psychotherapist. There was a time when it was believed one stayed in psycho-therapy interminably until all facets of present anxieties and any potential future problems had been eliminated for all time. Consequently, therapy grew longer and longer until the fallacy of this notion became apparent. Our approach is rather like that of the physician. A patient treated for the flu does not continue in treatment once the influenza infection has passed. But the patient may come back in a year with a sprained ankle, an allergy rash, or any number of physical ailments.

Likewise, a patient who had difficulty adjusting to leaving home for college may not return for years until there is a pending divorce, as merely an illustration of innumerable possible sequences.

Rather than preparing the patient for termination, there is mere interruption as the patient is encouraged to return as needed. It has been found that:

1. termination anxiety is eliminated;
2. return episodes tend to be brief inasmuch as the patient builds on preceding therapy; and
3. knowing there is always access to the therapist, the patient learns to "talk" to the therapist in one's own head, thus often arriving at a solution without actually being seen. It is frequently reported by patients, "I knew it was time to see you again because I did not find an answer talking to you in my head" (Cummings & Cummings, 2000).

Taking the Patient's History for Diagnostic Evaluation is Imperative

Over two thousand years ago, Hippocrates stated it is more important to know what kind of person has a disease than to know what disease a person has. This could not be truer than when treating emotional problems, as our interventions are not a one-size-fits-all address of mere faulty thinking. As shall be seen, patients are approached differently whether they are psychoneurotic, psychotic, or personality disordered. Furthermore, there are patients who cannot be successfully treated, but need to be managed. An additional differentiation is whether a patient is capable of real insight, or what is termed analyzable versus non-analyzable. All of these will be expanded in later sections, but at this point it is important for the reader to anticipate the view that life experiences have molded the patient, for better or for worse, and these need to be understood by the patient in arriving at a corrective experience.

A skilled therapist does not delay treatment until a complete history has been taken. Rather, treatment begins immediately, even while greeting the patient in the waiting room, or on the phone while making the appointment if this is done by the therapist. As the session unfolds, the therapist notes the cause-and-effect relationships in the patient's life and adroitly asks pertinent questions without seeming to be taking a formal history. Rather than scribbling notes, the exceptional psychotherapist knows how to make memory markers so that the information can be transcribed after the patient has left so that note-taking does not become a distraction during the interview.

Cost/Therapeutic Effectiveness

Healthcare costs are escalating at an alarming rate, and are coincident with the growing scarcity of resources. Currently, only 2 percent of US medical school graduates go into primary care, and nurse practitioners have been steadily moving toward becoming the de facto primary care physicians of the future. Rationing of healthcare takes many forms to hide its existence, and is seldom, if ever, honestly so labeled. In the US, the healthcare industry employs a host of artificial cost-saving techniques: preauthorization, session limits, therapist profiling, eligibility hurdles, and so-called case management. These "bean-counter techniques," as we have called them, are fall-back positions because the healthcare industry simply does not know how to control over-utilization through effective practice. Because the healthcare industry knows even less how to reduce mental health costs through effective practice, bean-counter restrictions on psychotherapy are particularly prevalent, with the ultimate one being that drugs are a much cheaper solution, even though their effectiveness is questionable with many patients.

Costs reflect supply and demand. If Florida experiences a cold winter that ravages the citrus crop, the shortage of oranges will manifest itself in a higher price for your frozen orange juice. On the other hand, a bumper crop of citrus will result in a lower price at the grocery store. Because healthcare is perennially limited, healthcare companies attempt to solve the consequent steady rise in costs by limiting demand through artificial means, making it difficult or even impossible for the patient to access services. This is a flagrant attempt to circumvent need by purposely *reducing supply*, otherwise known as rationing. One of the most bald-faced rationings of recent years was in regard to the frequency of mammograms. Since less than 1 percent of women in their forties develop breast cancer, those who favor rationing use this as justification to eliminate routine mammograms until age 50. Thus, the savings in millions of dollars is chosen over the lives of a few thousand women who may die.

In contrast to artificially limiting demand by making it less available, the Biodyne Model reduces demand by increasing the availability (supply) of rapidly effective psychotherapy, which both eliminates interminable or ineffective psychotherapy and equally ineffective drug therapy, and dramatically reduces medical/surgical costs by as much as 40 percent and more by addressing the 60 percent of medical patients who are really translating emotional problems into somatic complaints. This phenomenon, called "medical cost offset," was first discovered by Cummings and Follette (Follette & Cummings, 1967; Cummings & Follette, 1968) and confirmed by a plethora of NIMH sponsored research (Jones & Vischi, 1979). The reason the healthcare industry continues to employ artificial suppression of demand is because it is run by business interests rather than healthcare professionals. Nonetheless, medical cost offset is available for extensive use by practitioners who create their own incented delivery arrangements within healthcare, as is discussed in Chapter 5 and Appendix II.

Outreach of High Utilizers of Medical/Surgical Care

The first three considerations in regard to healthcare in the current era are cost, cost, and cost. This concern is mostly concentrated in medicine and surgery, as in recent years all of the fat has been cut from psychotherapy, and the mental health system is down to the bone. Additionally, the majority of mental health costs have been shifted to psychotropic medication, and the managed care companies have now embarked on cost-cutting techniques there. However, when patients' psychological issues are not appropriately addressed, they surface in the form of somatic complaints, over-burdening the medical/surgical system so that the apparent savings in mental health expenditures have merely been shifted.

The Biodyne Model has employed a High Utilizer Outreach Program that is not only readily implemented, but is highly effective in reducing medical visits, surgical procedures, ER visits, prescriptions for medications, and, of special interest to primary care physicians, eliminates the frequent emotional breakdowns in the doctor's office that disrupt practice. The savings in medical care are considerably above the cost of implementing the outreach program and delivering the subsequent psychotherapy, which averages between 5.4 and 6.2 sessions depending on the setting (for a summary of studies, see Cummings, O'Donohue, & Ferguson, 2002).

The procedure is simply conducted. The medical records of the 15 percent highest utilizers of healthcare are elicited, and are arranged first as to those suspected of translating emotional problems into somatic complaints because no physical cause can be determined in spite of repeated tests. Then, there are those who have a physical disease such as hypertension, asthma, diabetes, ischemic heart disease, COPD, etc. but whose emotional problems interfere with healing and are often manifested in non-compliance with medical regimen. Within this 15 percent of high utilizers are the substance abusers, both alcohol and drugs, who also manifest a disproportionate share of doctor visits, especially after the halcyon days of addiction have passed and the health consequences begin manifesting themselves but with no interest on the part of the addict to quit. The Biodyne Model has protocols that readily discern these different types within the high utilizing 15 percent.

Each psychotherapist in a practice setting is assigned a share of these high utilizers to begin calling on the telephone during their time not devoted to seeing patients. They do not challenge the person's somatizing, but rather say with concern, "Someone who is having so much physical illness must be upset about it. Perhaps I can help you with this." And, as a last resort, "Perhaps I can help you find a more sympathetic physician," a statement that resonates, as these patients have more than experienced their doctor's exasperation. If properly done, 80 percent to 85 percent of these patients will make an appointment, doubtlessly spurred with being offered their favorite activity: seeing another doctor.

Practitioners seeing these patients must be skilled in motivating them to take the next step and enter treatment. It must be remembered that in none of this is the patient's belief that there is a physical disease challenged. The addicted patient is offered a compromise, what we call a pre-addiction group, but one in which the patients can prove to their own satisfaction that "I am a social user and not addicted." With skilled psychotherapists, usually 90 percent of patients so interviewed take the next step and enter treatment, with the addicts surprisingly included in this percentage.

Mitigating the ability to conduct this outreach is that in many, if not most, of our health systems, medical and mental health records are in separate computer programs and do not relate to each other. Special effort has to be made to overcome this handicap, which requires a degree of sophistication that is usually absent in the top business echelons that administer healthcare. But the research findings are indeed robust, spanning many years, and involving a variety of large delivery systems. The following summary is from Cummings, Cummings, & Johnson (1997: 19–20):

> Over 35 years of medical cost offset research, spanning three generations of activity, reveal that the cost offset is greater (1) in organized settings where (2) behavioral health and primary care are completely integrated, and where (3) the behavioral delivery system is based on field proven efficacy, effectiveness and efficiency.

3

THE BIODYNE MODEL OF REFOCUSED PSYCHOTHERAPY

To fulfill the Biodyne Patient Bill of Rights by providing relief from pain, anxiety, and depression in the shortest time possible and with the least intrusive intervention, the therapist must be highly skilled in dispensing not only effective, but also efficient psychotherapy. It must be emphasized that this does not mean the usual perfunctory skills training inasmuch as conventionally in psychology this involves only evidence-based interventions. Hopefully, on rare occasions, it also addresses the thorny question of whether "evidence-based" transcends the laboratory into the real world of co-morbidities and other complexities that were not an issue in the need for pure cases to fulfill the research design. The issue of "the shortest time possible" is, if at all, a response to the limited number of sessions currently approved for reimbursement by managed care.

In the Biodyne Model, the therapist acquires specific skills that result in effectiveness and efficiency, not only on an individual psychotherapy level, but also in group therapy. Ultimately, it pervades every aspect of the delivery system itself, rendering it uniquely effective and efficient on a large scale. The following attributes will be discussed in detail:

- 15 percent of the therapist's time is devoted to ongoing quality assurance, which includes a perpetual honing of the psychotherapist's skills as well as a never ceasing improvement in the armamentarium of therapeutic interventions.
- The Biodyne-trained therapist makes resistance a therapeutic ally rather than seeing it as an impediment to therapeutic progress.
- Before arriving at a treatment plan, the operational diagnosis must be determined. This is defined as the reason why the patient is coming in now instead of last week, last year, or next month.

- Also, before arriving at a treatment plan, the psychotherapist determines the real reason why the patient is present. Called the implicit contract, it differs often markedly from the explicit contract proffered only by the patient. To proceed on the basis of this explicit contract prolongs psychotherapy, while therapist and patient flounder because they have missed the real reason the patient is coming in.
- Thus, a pertinent history is imperative, but the skilled therapist obtains this without seemingly taking a formal history. Imperative information is adroitly gleaned in the course of the patient–therapist interaction.
- Who is presenting is often more important than what is being presented. It is imperative that personality disorders are treated in a different manner. When this is not followed, treatment is almost assured to fail.
- Efficiency is determined by skill, not by employing cost-cutting "bean-counter" restrictions.

The Biodyne Model is cognitive/behavioral, psychodynamic, strategic, and humanistic, but it is not eclectic. Which of these therapies is employed is determined by years of research indicating specific interventions in particular kinds of cases, not an over-arching commitment to a psycho-religion. Our armamentarium includes incisive and timely application of free association, interpretation of transference, interpretation of inner conflicts, prescribing the resistance, interpretation of projections, mimicking the transference, and joining the delusion, all of which are psychodynamic. It also includes such behavioral interventions as relaxation, systematic desensitization, schedules of reinforcement, exposure treatment, homework assignments, cognitive restructuring, and role playing. It further includes such strategic interventions as reframing, paradoxical intention, double bind, prescribing the resistance, humoring the resistance, overwhelming the resistance, doing the unexpected (novel), and, the most difficult intervention for most therapists, the denial of treatment. Many patients manifest problems of will and responsibility for which humanistic or existential psychotherapy is indicated. The re-evaluation of meaning in one's life is not an uncommon experience in mid-life, after a jolting event, or following a heart-rending tragedy. Such popular techniques as motivational interviewing are often used to bring around resistive or difficult patients, but the therapist must be cognizant that all techniques, even if appropriate, may be useless with Axis II or psychotic patients that require their own interventions.

The Anatomy of Refocused Psychotherapy

There are certain ingredients that make up focused psychotherapy, but first and foremost it is important to stress what psychotherapy is not, or should not be, inasmuch as the following characteristics are contrary to the profession's widely held beliefs.

Psychotherapy is Not Paid Compassion

Psychotherapists are by necessity compassionate people, but psychotherapy is far more than compassion, a nicety that is available through family, friends, the clergy, charities, and the many persons of goodwill in our environment. It often goes against the grain of our warm-hearted colleagues to dispense tough love; for example, to say what needs to be said to the 52-year-old man who has shed tears to six ineffective but compassionate therapists that "my mother didn't love me," to encourage a grieving widow to cry and be all alone because that enhances the work of mourning and shortens its duration, to ask a person whose aggressive behavior has left him with no friends whether he has ever considered he might be obnoxious, to enforce the homework assignment for the patient who plays upon the therapist's sympathy, and to challenge the patient's rationalization "that I was just too upset to do it," and even to dismiss the patient who comes in not for treatment, but to manipulate the system.

These are not examples of non-compassion, but rather of effective psycho-therapists who show their compassion by effectively treating the patient. The many years of education and training were not intended to prepare the psychotherapist to be merely a "paid friend," to replicate the Salvation Army that is already there doing its fine work, but to be an incisive, effective psychotherapist. *There is no place for the squeamish psychotherapist.* A patient who needs intensive surgery would never seek out a surgeon who cannot stand the sight of blood. So why seek out a psychotherapist who fears "psychic blood," the discomfort and sometimes emotional pain that the patient might have to endure in effective treatment?

Not only have individual psychologists often blunted their effectiveness by misplaced compassion, but there are instances in which the entire profession of psychology has fallen prey to the unintended consequences of well-meaning understanding. A prime example is the misplaced compassion called "victimology" that was widespread until recently. It reflected the good intention to not blame the victim, but it had the effect of convincing the victim he/she was helpless (Zur, 2005). It resulted in the deleterious effect of encouraging the victim to just give up and remain victimized. Fortunately, research demonstrating the abject failure of victimology has led to an emphasis on resiliency, a far more effective thrust led surprisingly by the military, which has had to treat a combat epidemic of PTSD (Konigsberg, 2011).

Psychotherapy is Not Protracted

Psychotherapy is neither long term nor short term; it is the right length to treat the patient's condition. If it is long term, it should be because of the patient's condition needing it, not because of the therapist's psycho-religion. Furthermore, if it is short term, it should be a combination of the patient's condition and the therapist's skill, not the managed care company's arbitrary restrictions on session limits.

Garfield (1998) has traced the transition during the past century of long-term therapy to brief therapy, which occurred in spite of massive resistance from most privately practicing psychotherapists. It is startling to note that, before 1937, psychoanalysis was usually concluded in six months, and rarely exceeded one year. With the death of Freud, psychoanalysis rapidly became more and more protracted, eventually lasting five, 10, and even 15 years, with the movie actor/director Woody Allen reputedly topping 25 years with seemingly no demonstrable positive effect. In the latter part of the twentieth century, books on brief therapy proliferated to an amazing extent, while those dealing with long-term therapy dwindled to nothing. Because the profession failed to address adequately the parameters of appropriate length, managed care stepped in and arbitrarily set the rules. Caught napping, a beleaguered profession blamed the senior author of providing the insurance industry with the rationale to ration psychotherapy sessions, when all along the Biodyne Model championed appropriate length according to the patient's condition. As early as three decades ago, Cummings (1977) found in his research that at least 10 percent of patients need and should get long-term therapy, 85 percent do better with brief but intermittent psychotherapy, while 5 percent are interminable and efficient schedules must be devised that will treat them for life.

Psychotherapy is Not Just Insight

Insight can be an important accompaniment of psychotherapy, and can often precede progress, so much so that both the therapist and the patient stack insight upon insight, prolonging therapy, and avoiding the awareness that little or no change is occurring. In fact, so-called insight becomes an end in itself, indulging the patient's narcissism and assuaging the therapist's guilt that the treatment is unnecessarily protracted. Again, the ongoing joke is Woody Allen, who after 25 years of psychoanalysis is a fountain of insight, translating it into entertaining and engaging motion pictures but seldom reflecting it as he conducts his personal life. Similarly, our colleague and friend Dr. Leonard Blank stated recently, "After twenty years of psychoanalysis, I found out in my first session in group therapy that I was simply obnoxious, and I finally did something about it" (personal communication, July 2005).

It cannot be overly emphasized: in the Biodyne Model, therapeutic progress is reflected in positive behavioral change, not by expressed insight. Symptom reduction that accompanies these behavioral changes is not only deemed as desirable, but it encourages and even hastens positive changes in behavior. Much has been written regarding symptom substitution, defined as the sudden cropping up of a new symptom when an old one disappears. In our experience, this occurs only if the patient's armor and defensive symptomatology are yanked away suddenly, and without behavioral change as seen in symptom removal by such abrupt methods as hypnosis, so-called "amytal therapy" in which the twilight sleep is purposely drug-induced by the psychiatrist, or a sudden catapulting of the patient into a severely restrictive environment such as so-called sweat boxes in New Age "motivational centers" as in Sedona, Arizona. The disclosure of so-called shameful experiences before an audience of like-minded susceptible patients, or military-style "bootcamps," as have at times off-and-on been popular for delinquent youth or defiant children, are all examples of the forceful removal of symptomatology without accompanying behavioral change, and will invariably result in symptom substitution and frequently even in a later return of the original symptom.

A special case in point is the use of painkillers for the reduction of severe pain, usually back pain or other such debilitating symptoms. The danger of addiction is always present, and once the patient is addicted, withdrawal of the opioid invariably replicates the exact original pain that prompted the medication use in the first place. It is as if the addictive process is using this now addiction-induced pain as opposed to the original pain as a way of justifying continuous renewals of prescriptions of the painkiller by the sympathetic physician. The give-away, of course, is the continued escalation of dosage as occurs in all opioid addictions, and the patient must either convince the unaware physician that the pain is getting worse, or resort to multiple physicians and multiple prescriptions.

Psychotherapy is Not Catharsis, but a Corrective Emotional Experience

Our patients either come from a dysfunctional background, or they have created an environment for themselves that is dysfunctional. In most of our patients, both are true. Catharsis is usually an emotionally discharged complaint about this condition, and much different than the one in which the patient grew up and probably continues to reside. This does not mean, however, that it is incumbent upon the therapist to make up for the unfortunate things that happened to the patient or to excuse the patient for the self-imposed misfortunes. As indicated before, the new atmosphere stresses resilience over victimhood.

The Therapist Can and Must Act as a Catalyst

The so-called "repetition compulsion," the propensity to repeat responses to early trauma, has baffled research psychologists for decades. Reinforcement theory, stemming from the original Pavlovian doctrine, postulates that a response is repeated because it is rewarded. After a certain period in which it is not rewarded, the response suffers extinction. A dog salivates because it learned under certain conditions to anticipate food. But if the food ceases to arrive, the dog will, in time, stop salivating to previous precursors to the food. Yet, the response to early trauma is repeated over and over in spite of punishment rather than reward. It was not until Skinnerian theory (Skinner, 1938) discovered that behaviors learned in the very early developmental stages of an organism are not subject to extinction. A puppy that in its infancy is severely and repeatedly beaten by a sadistic man may very likely shy away from males for the rest of its life.

There is another dynamic that drives the repetition compulsion. Not only anxiety, but the striving for growth, compels us to repeat scenarios or scripts that are symbolic equivalents of early trauma upon which we are fixated. This repetition is an attempt to achieve mastery. To the extent that our energies are fixated on early trauma, even though we may not even remember it, they are not available for growth. Therefore, we are compelled to repeat the experience of the original trauma in order to free our energies to grow. When the repetition occurs in relation to the therapist, the skillful practitioner will respond in a way to bring insight and closure, thus freeing the patient for the next step to growth. Often, it is surprising how a lifetime of repeating a scenario can be telescoped into one catalytic event with the therapist, resulting in rapid understanding and progress.

Case Illustration: Lester, the Limpid Librarian

A 28-year-old single man came into treatment because he was unable to finish his doctoral dissertation in mathematics. He was an obsessional man whose high intelligence was being crippled by ruminative thinking that never arrived at a conclusion. During his course work, he excelled, probably because mathematics has a definite answer on either side of an equation. Now faced with a dissertation in which he was required to engage in speculative thinking, his behavior was one of paralysis; he was unable to move ahead and equally unable to walk away from the task. This had been going on for over two years, during which time he took a job in the local library for which he was markedly overqualified. In the first three sessions, he was stilted in his speech, grossly over-intellectualizing trivia revolving around his flunky job, and unable to discuss anything of importance. Emotional tone was nonexistent.

During these sessions, the therapist learned that Lester's father was a controlling man who hid his own emotions in over-intellectualization. The home resembled a library. Each of the children was regularly assigned books to read that were chosen by the father, who began each dinner with, "In accordance with your assigned reading, the topic for discussion at the table tonight is Homeric scholarship as seen through the differing eyes of the English versus German classicists" (or some other such utterly esoteric subject that was far removed from anything in the family's real life). Lester complained bitterly about his father's controlling intellectualizations, but he continued living his life according to the "library" rules in which he was brought up. At the end of the third session, the therapist assigned three books, one each on Freud, Jung, and Adler. As he removed them from his bookcase, he asked that the patient read these before the next session. The patient brightened up, as here was something he could easily do.

The therapist began the fourth session by stating, "Our topic for today pertains to who was the better therapist, Freud, Jung, or Adler." Lester was startled but he complied. When he asked for feedback on his discussion, he seemed perplexed to hear the therapist mouth a series of platitudes. This was repeated for two more sessions, with books on Carl Rogers, Milton Erickson, Erik Erikson, Karen Horney, Frieda Fromm-Reichman, and Jay Haley. In session five, when Lester asked what the relevance of all this was to his inability to complete his dissertation, the therapist's response mimicked the father's usual cryptic coldness: "I'll be the judge of that."

Halfway through session six, during which the therapist asked the patient to compare Erikson's life stages to Freud's psychosexual development, Lester broke. He began to yell and shake as can only an obsessional who has lost his isolation. He screamed, "I don't have to do this shit!" The therapist screamed back with equal volubility, "I know you don't have to do this shit, but do you really know it? Your whole life is shit!" Lester sank back into his chair stunned. His behavior was remarkably different from then on. Gone was the stilted, over-intellectualized, and emotionless Lester. There emerged a new Lester who did not know exactly how to walk, talk, or think, but who was no longer terrified of leaving both libraries—one the place of employment and the other the place of emotional paralysis. He finished his dissertation with unprecedented rapidity, and he continued in therapy to complete other unfinished aspects of his life.

Understanding and Utilizing the Transference in Psychotherapy

By its very nature, the psychotherapist–patient relationship will more or less, depending on the intensity of the treatment, resemble the parent–child relationship. It is fertile ground for all manner of childhood and adolescent emotions to appear, and these can range from differentiation through dependency. With the dominance of cognitive/behavioral therapy in the last several decades, the psychotherapist–patient transference is not only most often overlooked, but young practitioners entering the field today reveal both oblivion and discomfort with it. Consequently, the therapist tries to be a "good figure," often resulting in over-protection and even indulgence. This is countertransference, and reflects lack of skill in the therapist, or even indicates the therapist has not resolved his/her own parent–child relationship. In refocused psychotherapy, the transference is a virtual gold mine of opportunity to propel therapy forward, and it was seen how, in the case of Lester, the therapist skillfully simulated the father–son relationship with a rapid, positive abatement of the patient's emotional paralysis.

Simulating the patient's transference is an extremely effective technique, but it is one that should be undertaken only after careful deliberation and only by a very skilled psychotherapist. Will it intensify the relationship? Yes. Will it decrease the dependency? Absolutely.

Therapists should be cautioned against and trained to refrain from counter-transference behavior, defined as a loss of objectivity in which the patient is seen in terms of the therapist's own needs. The punitive therapist is rare; rather, the most frequent countertransference today is reflected in a determination to be helpful—indeed, not only to "do good," but to save the world. "I want to become a psychologist to be helpful, not to make money," is a phrase all too frequently heard from students today. Unfortunately, this may presage a therapist who will neither do good nor make a decent living. Acceptance of the patient's behavior does not mean indulgence. For example, continuing a session in which the patient had consumed alcohol or smoked marijuana just before coming in is futile, and the patient should be sent home with the admonition that such sabotage of therapy will not be tolerated. If the therapist wants to be effective rather than do the ethereal "good," this dose of reality may be the most therapeutic thing that can be done for this patient who, by coming in intoxicated, is signaling disdain and noncooperation. The skilled therapist uses the countertransference as well as comfort with his/her own feelings as therapeutic information. For example, when experiencing feelings of anger arising, the psychotherapist would do well to ask "Why is the patient trying to make me angry?" Posing the question frequently leads to the answer. Also, it can often move therapy when the therapist poignantly asks the question, "You seem unusually annoying today. What have I done that has made you angry with me?" This is the conscious, positive use of counter-transference, as opposed to the negative countertransference of which the therapist is unaware.

Summary

The ideal first session with a patient will encompass the following interventions by the psychotherapist. It cannot be overly emphasized that a treatment plan cannot be made until all of these have been determined. Furthermore, if an ineffective treatment plan has been erroneously or prematurely made, it is imperative that the therapist change course, and if necessary even explain to the patient why the treatment is changing in direction.

• Do something novel or unexpected in the first session. Before seeing you, the patient has reflected and even mentally rehearsed the session, and may even have made the wrong self-interpretation of why psychotherapy is being sought. Our personality disordered patients will especially plan how to control the course of the first interview. A surprising number of first interviews are by patients who have been in previous ineffective treatment, and are returning because they want to accomplish or even manipulate a predetermined outcome. Affectionately termed "trained seals" in our model, it is incumbent upon the therapist to skillfully guide the session toward a therapeutic outcome. Doing something novel in the first session for all patients is a skill that directly addresses both resistance and manipulation.

- Do not strong-arm the resistance. Every patient has a right to his/her resistance because to the troubled patient the symptoms or faulty behaviors are regarded as a painful but necessary clinging to the edge of an abyss, and without them the patient faces falling into this terrifying, unknown abyss. The skillful psychotherapist enlists the resistance as an ally in the treatment plan.

- Determine the operational diagnosis, which tells the therapist why the patient is coming in now instead of last week, last year, or next month. Knowing the real reason the patient is seeking help, instead of the rationalized reason the patient will most often present, will determine the treatment plan. For example, the patient may proffer that "I am drinking too much." But the patient has been an alcoholic for several years, and this statement does not reveal *why now?*

- Determine the implicit contract as opposed to the explicit contract. The latter is the patient's rationalized or face-saving reason for coming in and will just lead the therapy into meaningless, ineffective directions. This concept on the surface seems obvious, but until the skill is acquired, the therapist will miss the implicit contract and accept one of a number of explicit contracts. Caution: this is one of the most decisive skills the Biodyne Model has to offer, and the most difficult to master.

- Neurotic patients (Axis I) are treated very differently than are personality disordered patients (Axis II). Furthermore, there are corresponding differences among psychotic patients. Surprisingly, the vast number of patients who plague the mental health system by never benefitting from repeated or interminable psychotherapy are diagnostically Axis II. Neurotic patients are treated; personality disordered patients cannot be treated, but are managed.

Each of these will be discussed in depth in the following chapters. The learning of these skills can turn a good clinician into an incisive and effective master psychotherapist.

4

PSYCHOJUDO

Staying One Step Ahead of the Patient's Resistance

The Japanese martial art of judo can serve as an apt metaphor for psychotherapeutic intervention. The patients before us are in conflict with themselves. They cling to the neurotic modus operandi that has seemingly served them well in the past, yet this past salvation traps them in the present suffering. As time and events have progressed in their lives, the capacity to resolve developmental tasks and their accompanying tensions require new behaviors. The emerging problems of life require not only new resolutions, but usually more currently adaptive modes of curtailing anxiety. As a simple example, it is not unusual for infants to use their more advanced oral capacity to abate anxiety or discomfort. Thumb sucking is so appropriate in infancy that many parents provide pacifiers. But the growing child that is fixated in thumb-sucking behavior soon becomes the object of derision among his/her peers. If this child remains trapped in oral modes of address to the problems of growing older (e.g., school, puberty, peer relationships), he/she may discover sniffing glue or smoking pot. Not only does this escalation of oral behavior temporarily pacify, but it may increase self-esteem, as many peers regard this as "cool." This only strengthens and furthers the fixation until one day you are confronted with treating a heroin addict or an alcoholic.

By the time our patients are referred to us, their now very advanced modes of meeting anxiety are so fixated they cannot imagine survival without them. These are no longer working, but they cannot fathom an alternative. To deprive them of their admittedly ineffective fixations is anticipated by the patient as the precursor to falling into the abyss of permanent anxiety and despair. This propensity is sometimes referred to in the clinical literature as the repetition compulsion because of its tenacity. The therapist may correctly identify the fixation, but even when the patients agree with the therapist's effort to change their lifestyle, they feel trapped and will fight the therapy tooth and nail. They will seek solace, not change, from their psychotherapy. This is resistance, and the patient is entitled to it. The Biodyne Model refocuses the resistance and makes it an ally in the patient's treatment. Instead of prolonged treatment, made even longer by the well-intended therapist–patient struggle, the therapeutic process is catapulted toward resolution. This is psychojudo.

Case Illustration: Persistent Paula

A woman in her early twenties is living with the type of man who could aptly be termed "ver Stunken." She works from 8:00 a.m. to 5:00 p.m. supporting both of them, then comes home, cooks dinner, and cleans the house while ver Stunken lies on the couch all day, smoking pot and pretending to be writing poetry. He has convinced her one day he will be heralded as a great poet. Unfortunately, this is not an uncommon relationship. In the first session, she declares, "I'm tired of this."

Her therapist asks, "Do you want to get out of the relationship?"

She says, "I can't stand it any longer."

Unfortunately, her psychotherapist misinterprets this to mean she is ready to leave him and begins to work on helping this woman leave ver Stunken. The more he tries to help her leave him, the more she digs her heels in because the therapist has overlooked Paula's low self-esteem. In the back of her mind, this woman feels this is the only man she is worthy of, and her fantasy is that, through loving him, she can make him better. She dislikes herself so much that the only alternative she sees to ver Stunken is the abyss of eternal loneliness. The psychotherapist has missed what she is really saying: "Help me become more lovable so he'll get a job and we'll have a nice relationship." She is not coming to leave him. The psychotherapist who personally sees this as such an obviously one-sided and undesirable living arrangement does not realize he and his patient are far from being on the same page when he leaps to help her extricate herself.

If you listen to the patient's unconscious dialogue with your third ear, you will come up not only with the patient's context, but also with the patient's own words. Then you will be amazed how fast therapy can move, as the therapist can utilize resistance in the service of growth. After locking horns with the therapist for three sessions, Paula quit and sustained a painful three-month hiatus before deciding to try again with a different therapist, this time at Biodyne. He said to her on their first session what she had been saying to herself all along: "I know you think you have tried everything, but next week I want you to do three things you have never done before to make this man love you."

She returned the following week, recited what she had done, but it hadn't worked. Ver Stunken continued to lie on the couch smoking pot. In spite of her protestations, her new therapist insisted, "I'm not convinced you have done everything that you can do to make him love you. I want you to go out next week and do three other things you have never done before to make him love you." This sequence was repeated for the third session, whereupon Paula came into the fourth session stating she had left ver Stunken. To her amazement, it was only two days before he moved in with another woman and totally forgot about Paula. Now it was time to work on Paula's low self-esteem, which already had gotten a boost following her courage to leave ver Stunken, parlaying her amusement that he had found another woman so quickly. Paula began to realize, as she understood herself, that there are so many women with low self-esteem that there is literally a shortage of ver Stunkens.

This is an illustration of the effectiveness of psychojudo. It can never be repeated often enough: never, never, never strong-arm the resistance. Rather, make it your ally. This is one of the cornerstones of the Biodyne Model and its refocused psychotherapy.

The Ideal First Session

As has become apparent in preceding chapters, the refocused psychotherapist hits the ground running. The first session is crucial, as whether or not bonding with the patient occurs is determined here. It also often determines whether the patient will continue in therapy.

Doing Something Novel in the First Session

Doing something novel and unpredictable in the first session cuts through the expectations of the "trained patient." Affectionately called "trained seals," there are far too many patients today who are in and out of therapy, using it to personal advantage rather than for change. Especially, this is true of personality disorders who come in when in difficulty, and promptly quit when the "therapy" has been successful in having charges dropped or in otherwise getting their way. Most often, for the first-time patient, the experience of someone truly listening is itself novel, but therapists have a tendency to rely on this far too much. Doing something novel catapults the patient into treatment in spite of the resistance.

Case Illustration: Amazing Grace

Grace was referred by a colleague who, after seeing her for three years, felt such hostility toward her that he disqualified himself from treating her. He warned me (the senior author) that Grace, a "schizoholic," would generally alternate among three behaviors. She would appear drunk in one session, urinate in the chair on the next session, and finally do some semblance of therapeutic engagement in the third. One never knew which session would be the urination session. To protect himself from the consequences, he put the kind of rubber sheet used in a baby's crib over the therapy chair. All attempts to stop this erratic behavior resulted in Grace's falling to the floor, stopping breathing, turning blue, and becoming cyanotic, at which point the therapist was obliged to call the paramedics to resuscitate her, literally saving her life.

With this in mind, I decided to assume certain educated risks and became an authority on cyanosis during the next couple of weeks, after which I was scheduled to see her. I learned, of course, what every defiant child learns early in life: you cannot kill yourself by just holding your breath. If you do so long enough to pass out, normal breathing will resume while you are unconscious. When Grace arrived for her appointment, even though forewarned about her appearance, no one could be prepared. She was beyond slovenly. It was as if Grace had turned ugliness into her own peculiar art form. After all, what kind of person would urinate through her own clothing on purpose?

At the first session, I warned Grace that urinating in the chair would end our therapeutic relationship. From her previous therapist, a Jungian psychiatrist, I had learned that she worked for the Post Office and that she was such a poor employee that the only way she was keeping her job was by claiming her seemingly overly liberal civil service "rights" as a sick employee under treatment. Thus, her psychotherapy appointments were imperative. But I gave her this warning on the grounds that it would be deleterious to continue treating a patient who was behaving in a most regressed, anti-therapeutic fashion, and to impotently expect change in the face of extreme opposition. Her previous therapist had already made that mistake. Grace's reaction to my warning was to clear her throat and spit on the carpet. When I handed her a box of Kleenex and asked her to clean it up, she countered that I had not told her she could not spit on the carpet. I explained that there were many unacceptable kinds of behavior, as she was quite aware, and I had no intention of warning her about every one of them. Any recurrence of such incidents would result in our terminating therapy.

Grace stared at me without saying a word for several minutes before falling to the floor. She stopped breathing and began to turn blue, which is a symptom of cyanosis. Instead of calling the paramedics, I did what I had prepared and planned to do, and went to my desk to retrieve my camera. I discovered to my dismay, in this era of pre-cellphone cameras, that it was empty of film. While I searched frantically for the film, I talked excitedly to Grace, encouraging her to keep up the performance so it could be recorded for medical history. Every once in a while, Grace would open one eye and stare at me in disbelief.

Finally, when I got the camera loaded and began to take pictures, my flash did not work. Before I could get the flash attachment working with a new battery, Grace was back in her chair, apparently ready to begin a more constructive relationship. I saw Grace four times before going to the next step in her therapy.

Grace's behavior frequently brought her to San Francisco's various hospital emergency rooms, and her cyanotic attacks had often been repeated there. At our fourth session with Grace, I obtained her permission to have my telephone number at the various ERs, with instructions that I should be called if her behavior became troublesome. As expected, Grace did subsequently become cyanotic during an ER intervention, and I was summoned to deal with her. This first time, the fact of my physical presence was enough to cause her to stop the behavior. Subsequently, a brief exchange between us by telephone sufficed. Within three weeks, Grace had stopped the behavior completely.

Real therapy could now begin. Grace was born an unwanted child whose mother reminded her every day of her childhood that her arrival had ruined her mother's life. The little girl's response was to become the "awful" child she was accused of being. She worked at being ugly and obnoxious. As an adult, her ultimate self-deprecation and contempt for the world was to urinate in the chair of any authority figure.

The case of Grace illustrates how the "primary patient" can sometimes be the therapist. The primary patient was very obviously the psychiatrist who had referred Grace; the ER staff that repeatedly dealt with her "cyanosis" were secondary patients. Her previous therapist was deeply disgusted with her, but he made himself the brunt of her abuse by falling victim to his misguided notion that a therapist must be kind and all-accepting of patients, no matter what. After a further 18 sessions, Grace and I terminated. During this time, she changed from looking like an angry, defiant homeless person to that of a self-respecting human being. She was grooming herself and had stopped drinking. Although she was still schizophrenic, she was no longer a "schizoholic" who felt compelled to go through life getting attention by exhibiting antisocial behaviors.

It may be that other interventions may have had a therapeutic effect on Grace, but it is doubtful that anything but a very novel approach could have so rapidly cut through the stonewall resistance of this thoroughly "trained" patient. Grace's regression into infancy was profound. She was willing to sink into any depth of self-deprecation to prove her mother, the therapist, and the world unworthy and unloving. She was a prime candidate for psychojudo, as well as for other Biodyne techniques that will follow.

Prescribing the Resistance

Prescribing the resistance can also fulfill the goal of doing something novel. By directing the patient to continue behavior that seems anti-therapeutic, the therapist surprises the patient's defenses, engages the patient in a positive working relationship, and forces oppositional patients to adopt the position of the therapist. We saw this in the case of Persistent Paula, who readily accepted the therapist's prescription to continue to do more to make ver Stunken love her. Variations of prescribing the resistance are seen in such techniques as treating premature ejaculation in men. The tension that the patient experiences in beginning the sexual encounter often misleads psychotherapists to prescribe relaxation techniques, usually dooming the intervention attempt to fail. Confronted with the act of love-making, trying to relax heightens the tension. Directing the patient to satisfy his partner through oral or manual approaches, and then go ahead and have his premature ejaculation, results in time in the gradual disappearance of the symptom in a surprising number of patients. It is as if the patient, now not under the push to perform, is finally able to relax. At that point, the therapy can proceed to other possible underlying psychopathology, such as the fear of, or anger toward, women.

In the following case of Patricia, a very intelligent registered nurse and single mother, the resistance is manifested by the manner in which she thwarted all attempts to treat her young son. Not until later was it discovered that stonewalling the current therapist was only the latest in a series of such behaviors. The resistance in each situation may have differed slightly in its expression, but the end result was the same. After an array of different therapists, her son was still not getting the treatment he needed. Prescribing the resistance is particularly useful in patients who manage to prevent treatment for even themselves, unless their demands are met. These demands, if acceded to, would essentially nullify any attempts at change. On the other hand, strong-arming the resistance would guarantee therapeutic failure. By prescribing the resistance, the therapist also joins the resistance and slowly, as if one were turning around an ocean liner rather than making the abrupt turn capable of a motorcycle, the resistance is transformed into a valid treatment procedure.

Case Illustration: Patricia, the Overprotective Co-therapist

A social worker had arranged with the patient's mother to allow the visiting psychologist (the senior author) to sit in on the next session. This is how Patricia and the identified patient, her son Billy, were seen jointly by the therapist and the visiting psychologist.

Billy, age 10, was referred by a beleaguered school system that was unable to deal with the boy's attacks on other students, his abusiveness toward his teachers, and his truancy. The center had interviewed the mother and the son and, in keeping with good practice, had asked the mother to enter therapy for herself while Billy was being seen by the child psychologist. She flatly refused to enter treatment or for Billy to be seen unless she was in the room. Her position was that Billy was the patient and she knew more about him than anyone else. The center stood firm and essentially denied treatment. The school was up in arms and demanded something be done by the center. It was at this point that Patricia agreed to be seen with Billy by the visiting psychologist and the social worker.

Just before going into the session, the visiting psychologist was handed a 40-page, nicely bound and indexed case history of Billy. It was written by Patricia, a registered nurse with several years of pediatric nursing experience. It was a remarkable document that professionally identified all the variables in Billy's case. The boy had never known his father, who had disappeared shortly after Billy was born. Patricia suffered a postpartum psychosis, and Billy was in foster homes for the first three years of his life. Once Patricia recovered, she returned to nursing while Billy was being cared for by a series of day care centers or reluctant relatives. At the present time, he is what is known as a "latch-key kid." During the time between the end of school and the return of his mother from work, he is on his own. But there are many days Billy does not show up at school at all. There was an abusive, alcoholic stepfather who was in and out of the house, as Patricia seemed to always take him back. All of the information was there, presented by Patricia without any defensiveness.

In contrast to her written material, Patricia was very defensive. Once in the social worker's office, and before sitting down, she demanded that certain conditions be understood. "Billy is the patient, not me, and no one sees Billy without me." She stated flatly that, if the visiting psychologist did not agree with those conditions, she and Billy were leaving immediately. It was obvious to everyone except Patricia that she felt so guilty and responsible for Billy's difficulties that she had plunged into extreme defensiveness and denial. The resistance could not be strong-armed. It was time to do something novel and unexpected.

The visiting psychologist responded unequivocally that Billy was the patient. Not only would he not be seen without her, but he insisted that Patricia join in the treatment plan as the social worker's co-therapist. "I just had the opportunity to read this brilliantly presented case history. You really understand Billy's problems better than any of us can, and I ask you to come on board as his co-therapist." Patricia was stunned, but pleased. She had so prepared herself for a battle and then walking out that she was speechless for several minutes. During that time, the psychologist continued to extol the accuracy and the professionalism of the document she had written. The social worker, who had not anticipated this approach, was also stunned. When she recovered, she not only was cooperative, but she acknowledged that she would welcome Patricia as her co-therapist.

It was now necessary to work out the details. Recovered from her surprise, Patricia enthusiastically entered into the planning. The social worker would be in charge of the case, and Patricia, as co-therapist, would be a resource and the person who would implement at home what was discovered in therapy. Because Patricia would be the co-therapist, she would not be able to use any of Billy's time on her own tensions and problems. This would contaminate the role of co-therapist. Patricia expressed her concerns: what if she needed help at some point? The psychologist replied, "You'll just have to tough it through, unless you have a better idea." After some silence, Patricia asked why she could not be seeing someone else separately. The psychologist pondered the question, and then agreed that would work, but only if Patricia made certain it did not in any way contaminate her role as Billy's co-therapist. While seeing her own therapist, she must clearly be the patient, not Billy. She agreed this would be of paramount importance.

The arrangement proceeded better than the best expectations. In her role as patient, Patricia learned in her own therapy she felt so guilty that she had become an ineffectual and over-protective mother. As the co-therapist who implemented insights from therapy, she became an engaged, effective parent. She stuck by her decision to separate from Billy's stepfather, and she allowed her son to return to the Cub Scouts. She had defensively pulled him out of there when the adult leader spoke with her about Billy's problems. The real reason is that Billy had begun to relate to this man, as this boy really needed a male surrogate.

Billy steadily improved. After a number of sessions, the therapist and co-therapist agreed that Billy could profit from seeing a male therapist. Patricia insisted that Billy be transferred to a male social worker "and both of us women co-therapists bow out." Patricia ended her career as co-therapist and over-protector.

Humoring the Resistance

Unfortunately, too many practitioners take their role as psychotherapists so seriously that they believe humor has no place in treatment. The old saying, "Humor is good for the soul," might suggest that it is also good for the psyche. To be sure, humor can be destructive, especially if it is mocking or ill-conceived and ill-timed. Suffering patients cannot tolerate being kidded about their painful condition, and a well-meaning but ill-timed sense of humor can come across as insensitivity. Humoring the resistance is an effective intervention that requires great skill, and if properly conveyed it can be received as empathic. It can give a frightened or resistant patient just enough distance to allow them to engage in therapy.

While generally useful in establishing rapport and disarming the patient's initial protective shield, humor is especially effective with borderline patients. The more a patient plays psychological games, the more likely that person will enjoy therapeutic or constructive humor. How outrageous the therapist can be is established by the degree to which the patient behaves outrageously. The constructive humor will be understood just below the surface of the patient's consciousness, just as the patient realizes in the very accessible preconscious level when he/she is "pulling someone's leg." This process is clearly demonstrated in the following case of Mona.

It will also become apparent, as with Mona, the therapist not only can be, but must be, as outrageous as the patient in applying the technique of humoring the resistance. Listen carefully to the patient and adjust the therapeutic response accordingly. If the therapist is too reserved, the intervention will fall flat. If the therapist exceeds the patient's intensity, anger will result. In either situation, over- or underplaying the humor, the patient will quit therapy. Mona not only responded to the appropriate level of humoring her resistance, she was relieved of the highly eroticized lesbian transference to the therapist, which up to that point had been preventing treatment. Humoring was the successful point of entry for this "woman scorned."

Case Illustration: Mona—Lay that Pistol Down

A petite social worker originally from Turkey was entangled with a woman of 6'2" who was threatening to kill her with a gun. This patient had a history of assault, and she had a pistol. You can imagine the therapist's countertransference at this point. So she asked the senior author to see the patient.

We went into the office and in the introduction I extended my hand to this woman who was wearing aviator dark glasses. She said, "I don't shake hands."

I said, "You're very wise. Do you know how many germs are transmitted by people shaking hands? And I feel particularly infectious today. You're very wise."

She looked at me skeptically, and I motioned her to sit down. She went across the room to a chair that was farthest away from me and the social worker who was sitting next to me.

We sat thus across the room looking at each other until she finally asked, "Aren't you going to say something?"

I said. "I can't."

She asked, "Why can't you?"

"I can't see your eyes. I never talk to people if I can't see their eyes. Because I talk to people's eyes."

"Oh," she said. "What do you mean?"

"Well, if you take off your glasses we can talk."

She took of her glasses. Though she rejected shaking hands, we had established enough rapport for this. Now that she had taken off her glasses, we talked. It became apparent to me that this woman was very much in love with the therapist. She was a borderline woman whose homosexuality was getting in the way because of her erotic transference to her therapist. I said, "I would like you to name three things you like about your therapist and three things you don't like about her. And you can do it in whatever order you want, but I want three of one and three of the other."

She replied, "Fine, let me do what I like first. She listens to me, she's always there for me, and she helps me."

"I would give that therapist an A, as she can't do any better than that. Three things you don't like."

She struggled and struggled. She couldn't think of anything. I began to realize how profoundly in love this person was with the therapist. I said, "You've got to give me three." She said again, "I can't."

I repeated, "You've got to give me three."

She said, "Okay. She has a dark complexion, she was born in Turkey, and she's short."

I said, "I can't accept any of those three."

She asked, "Why not?"

I replied, "Because she can't help those. She can't change her complexion, she can't change her birthplace, and she can't suddenly stretch herself to six feet tall. I can't accept those. I want you to name three things you don't like about her that she can change."

This was a useful intervention in that the patient, in her eroticized transference, was ambivalent. She wanted to make the therapist look bad only because she sensed her love was rejected. Basically, she liked the way the therapist looked. She struggled, and finally said, "I can only think of one."

"And what is that?"

She hesitantly replied, "She wears baggy pants." The therapist had on a skirt that day, but apparently she frequently wore those Middle East pants that bloom out. I said, "Okay, thank you. Now, have you noticed that the more you like your therapist, the more you want to kill her?"

She exclaimed in surprise, "You know that?"

I replied, "Yes, it's very obvious. When you feel like killing her, can you leave the room for 10 minutes and just walk down the hall?"

She said, "I can do that."

I said, "Yes. That's a rule."

She said, "What is she going to do?"

I said, "She's going to quit wearing baggy pants."

Smilingly, she said, "Fine, it's a deal."

"Okay, in order to do this you have to temporarily give up your pistol. We'll lock it up in the center's safe until you're finished with your therapist."

She handed me her pistol. Near the end of the session, she asked, "Dr. Cummings, this Biodyne stuff, does it really work?"

When a patient asks that, you know something has happened, and something has connected. But the patient is still wary or frightened and needs some distancing. I looked up and asked, "Do you want the truth?"

She said, "Yeah."

I said, "It's a scam."

She did not flinch at this, and only asked, "Why do you do it then?"

I replied, "Very simple. It's a great living and I give a livelihood to all those therapists. You may not know, but this center is only one of many centers we have throughout all 50 states. We give a lot of jobs to a lot of therapists."

Intently she asked, "Can I join the scam?"

"Of course. We have to have some people pretending to be therapists and others pretending to be patients."

She was really intent at this point. "How do I do that? Be a patient, I mean?"

I said, "Very simply. To join the scam and be a patient in the scam, you have to keep every appointment. You can't call after hours. You can't threaten your therapist, and you can't show up at emergency rooms. And you have to leave your pistol in the Biodyne safe."

She said, "I can do that." She continued her treatment and became a model patient. At the end of every session she said, "This scam is really something. You know, sometimes I really think I'm a patient." Thinking of therapy as a scam gave this paranoid personality just enough distance to work on herself without feeling overwhelmingly vulnerable. The rules of being a model patient gave her the boundaries she needed, all the while also propping up her ego as she was, indeed, that model patient.

Mobilizing Rage in the Service of Health

Rage is a more galvanizing emotion than love. Love may ultimately be the stronger emotion, but love takes longer. Rage is immediate and can be utilized to empower change in the patient. Frieda Fromm-Reichmann (1929/1950) called this "the mobilization of rage in the interest of health." The compassion that is part of being a psychotherapist makes it difficult for most to cope with the tough love that is inherent in mobilizing rage in the service of health. Yet, employed judiciously, and especially in critical situations, it has been shown to save lives.

Just as one would not trust a surgeon who fears the sight of blood, why trust a psychotherapist who cannot stand the sight of "psychic blood" when an intervention that might be termed psychological surgery is in the best interest of the patient? Mobilization of rage in the interest of health is a powerful technique in the hands of a compassionate therapist. It is deadly in the hands of a non-compassionate therapist. Similarly, the surgeon's scalpel in the wrong hands would be inappropriate, sadistic, or fatal.

The following case of Elaine justified the use of this technique in that the therapist on call who had never seen her had to first keep her on the phone long enough to ascertain the facts and then establish a therapeutic bond so as to intervene effectively and prevent her from committing suicide. She was going to kill herself because she was in a rage against her regular therapist. She saw him as abandoning her when she most needed him. By mobilizing that rage in the service of the patient's health, the therapist was able to save her life by taking the added step of paradoxical intention.

Case Illustration: Elaine—Death by Drowning

In a busy practice, one is frequently called upon to handle emergencies on the telephone. These are usually difficult cases made even more difficult by the absence of visual cues. Often, these cases are suicidal. The practitioner should bear in mind that, beneath all of the determination to destroy oneself, there is a part of the patient that wants to be talked out of it. Otherwise, the patient would not have telephoned. But conventional interventions often replicate everything that has been said to the patient by relatives, friends, and lovers. Such talk has already been discounted, so it is not effective. When all else fails, the appropriate mobilization of rage in the interest of health is very effective.

In this case, shortly after the center in Hawaii opened one morning, Elaine telephoned asking for her therapist who was out of town and unavailable, but would be back the day after tomorrow. She informed the receptionist this was too late. She had promised her therapist she would not commit suicide until she talked with him. She believed that she had fulfilled that promise by calling, and would now proceed to kill herself. This, of course, had been a poorly constructed nonsuicide pact. The therapist should have obtained believable assurance that the patient would not attempt suicide until patient and therapist had their next scheduled session. The agreement must also be within the ability of the patient and in accordance with the dictum that a patient is not asked to do what he/she is not able to do.

Elaine agreed to talk with the therapist's supervisor, who was visiting from the mainland. This psychologist took the position that, to really fulfill her promise to talk to her therapist before she committed suicide, she had the obligation to talk to his surrogate. She agreed. In the meantime, the receptionist had given the psychologist Elaine's psychological chart. Unfortunately, the writing was illegible, so the psychologist would have to obtain the pertinent information from the patient herself.

He began by asking Elaine why she planned to kill herself. She replied that the building she and her three children were living in had been condemned and she was being forced to move. The four of them had been living in one room, with a shared bath and toilet down the hall. They slept, ate, and lived in this one room that had been home for two years. With the deadline for leaving the condemned building rapidly approaching, Elaine had found a three-room apartment with its own bath and toilet. She and her daughter could have their own room separate from the two boys, but the welfare office could not give her the extra money required for the higher rent. She had decided that her three children could be taken better care of by the state than by her. "As orphans, they will get the things I can't give them."

The psychologist expressed admiration for Elaine's dedication to her children, and lamented that the loss of such a good mother would be a tragedy. Had she considered other ways of helping her children short of having to kill herself? She recounted six things she had thought of doing, and one by one she discounted each as ineffective. The psychologist agreed with her that, sadly, she was right: committing suicide would be the best assurance her children would be properly cared for. Again, he expressed admiration for her dedication as a mother.

Then Elaine was asked to relay more about herself. She was born and grew up in Puerto Rico and moved to Hawaii for better opportunity. It was also ascertained that she had been married twice, and each of the three children had a different father. She had not married the father of the third child. In her conversation, the patient sounded both childish and hysterical. The psychologist asked how she planned to commit suicide. She said she was going to ingest the contents of a bottle of Valium and then walk into the surf and drown. This form of suicide is frequent where the ocean is warm, but rare in colder climates. She had decided that, at 11:00 that morning, when the children would be with a friend, she would walk out into the ocean. She could not state how much Valium she had, so the psychologist asked her to count the pills. She did so, and reported there were 27. Then she was asked to look on the label and report whether they were 1, 3, or 5 mg. She responded they were each 1 mg. The therapist then advised her she did not have enough Valium. "You have just enough so you will be rescued but not drown, and end up alive and probably disfigured for life." (This latter was stated authoritatively for, already having determined the patient's hysterical personality, the therapist was connecting with that part of a hysteric that would rather be dead than disfigured.) The patient owed it to her children to do this right and he recommended at least 100 mg and certainly never less than 75 mg. She wondered where she could obtain the additional Valium and the psychologist pointed out she had already demonstrated she could get small amounts from each of several physicians. She might not be able to obtain the additional medication by 11:00 a.m., but it was certainly doable by the end of the day.

The patient was silent. The psychologist interrupted the silence by saying he had noticed that she was scheduled to see her therapist at 2:00 p.m. the day after tomorrow. He wanted her permission to cancel that appointment as she would be dead anyway. "The center has three patients waiting for a cancellation. If you do not cancel, the hour will go to waste and a needy patient will be deprived." There followed a long silence, after which the patient said she did not want to cancel the appointment unless she acquired the requisite amount of Valium. If she obtained the extra pills, she would call and cancel.

The patient did not cancel. As the psychologist expected, she kept her appointment with her therapist two days later. But before entering the office, she stuck her head through the doorway and asked the receptionist, "Has that awful Dr. Cummings gone back to the mainland?" Assured that he had, she entered the center. But every week before entering the waiting room, she would ask if Dr. Cummings was still on the mainland. She also never again threatened suicide. Rage had been mobilized in the interest of her health.

In contrast to Linda that follows, Elaine was in a rage at a therapist who not only was present for her, but was knocking himself out to successfully treat her. He was unable, however, to please her because he was not able to obtain for her what she was demanding. Again, rage at the therapist was making Elaine suicidal. In spite of this, it must be remembered that the greater the intensity of the rage, the greater the energy that can be mobilized in the service of saving the patient's life. In the following case, the senior author purposely allowed himself to be scapegoated by the patient in the interest of restoring the primary patient's credibility.

Case Illustration: Linda, the Infatuated

A 22-year-old overweight woman who was on welfare consulted the therapist for weight control. Treatment proceeded well. Linda lost a significant amount of weight and had enrolled in a community college course in practical nursing. She showed promise of soon being a thin, self-supporting, and self-respecting young woman.

Her history revealed turmoil. Her mother had committed suicide and the father, inexplicably blaming Linda, had not spoken to her in several years. The patient responded with depression, obesity, failure in school, and an inability to support herself without welfare. Although she came in for weight control, her depression became the focus of the therapy. Amazingly, the depression lifted rapidly and Linda manifested the aforementioned behavioral changes.

Suddenly, Linda regressed back into depression. She regained her weight and began to fail in her nursing course. She was on academic probation and she actively declared that suicide was the only solution. She had amassed a large cache of prescription drugs, which she would use to overdose and kill herself. So critical were her threats that the therapist appropriately got her to surrender her pills while therapy continued for 30 days. She insisted on the contract that, at the end of 30 days, if she wanted her pills back the psychologist would return them. He agreed.

At the end of the 30 days, Linda was even more depressed and she demanded her pills back. She would not enter into a therapeutic contract to not commit suicide before her next visit, and her therapist was properly concerned. He refused to return her pills. The therapeutic relationship had come to a standstill. The psychologist called his supervisor, who at the time was the senior author. The therapist realized the therapeutic breach and was painfully aware that an angry, determined patient could find other ways to kill herself if she were denied her cache of pills. As Linda was still in the office, she agreed to speak with Dr. Cummings. Patient and supervisor talked for about 20 minutes. The patient reiterated her decision to commit suicide, especially now that her therapist had "lied" to her. She responded to the supervisor's request that she give herself one more week, at which time the supervisor would be visiting the center and could meet with her to attempt to resolve her angry complaint against the therapist. If the circumstances warranted, her therapist would be properly chastised. She eagerly agreed, and seemed to look forward to her "day in court."

The following week, it took less than 15 minutes to ascertain that Linda was totally infatuated with her therapist, who was a young and eligible psychologist. He made up for the father who rejected her and he could be the lover she never had and always wanted. Her therapist had been blind to her many signs of infatuation, and she interpreted this as rejection. Her suicide would be that of a woman scorned.

The visiting supervisor confided that he was convinced that she would kill herself, and apologized for his colleague who had broken his therapeutic contract with her. He said he would be returning her pills and he wanted to be notified as soon as she had committed suicide. He would then fire her therapist for incompetence. Linda was shocked and began to extol the virtues of the therapist.

She said she had tried several therapists before, but no one understood her until now. The supervisor scoffed at this and interjected that he was not able to prevent a simple suicide and, therefore, indeed he was incompetent. She began to plead for him, even bursting into tears. The supervisor brushed her entreaties aside and added that he was not going to wait until several more of his patients killed themselves before he got rid of this incompetent. Finally, distraught and desperate, Linda promised she would not commit suicide and would continue in her therapy if only the therapist was not fired. The supervisor grudgingly agreed, but voiced his skepticism that she could be helped.

Linda continued with her therapist, who now made analysis and resolution of her eroticized transference the first therapeutic priority. With this new emphasis in treatment, Linda was able to settle into a realistic transference and recapture her previous progress.

Since the dynamic of reactive depression is anger turned inward to the introjected hated object, mobilizing rage can be particularly useful in expelling the introject, as will be seen later in the cases of John and Lenore presented later in the discussion of depression.

Denying Treatment

For somebody who only pretends to be your patient for ulterior or non-therapeutic reasons, the best course can well be to deny treatment. Often, when you deny treatment to a patient who is not there for any legitimate reason, he/she will return later legitimately. One such patient remarked, "Well, if I am here just to bullshit you, I may as well not come in at all. Later, when I really needed help, I said to myself that's the guy I want to see."

Denying treatment is especially effective when engaging an addict who is in denial. This technique is extensively presented in the book describing the Biodyne Model with addictions (Cummings and Cummings, 2000). It is used in the most effective inpatient addiction centers, but drug rehab has become a huge business in the United States, so much so that most centers would rather become so-called revolving doors than miss the income from someone who is not serious about cleaning up. In applying the technique of denying treatment, it is important that the therapist verbalize what the patient is secretly saying to himself/herself. By becoming the resistance, the patient is placed in the position of assuming the role of the therapist. This is illustrated by the case of Kevin to be presented later.

The case of Glenda illustrates the appropriate usefulness of denying treatment. What made this approach the treatment of choice overriding Glenda's arrogance and manipulation was the underlying figure of a terrified little girl who had been orphaned by the untimely deaths of two irresponsible, substance-abusing parents. Denying treatment to Glenda meant that the therapist was even more powerful than the grandmother whom he was willing to defy if necessary. Glenda's demeanor toward the therapist, once he denied treatment, was to emotionally grab him as if he were a lifeline. Without this clinging, desperate transference, the denial of treatment would have accorded her the excuse to leave and never return. On the other hand, to have only temporarily and even slightly accepted any of Glenda's manipulations in the interest of establishing rapport would have relegated the therapist to the category of irresponsibility she reserved for her deceased parents.

Case Illustration: Glenda's Grandmother

Glenda's indolent lifestyle in San Francisco was made possible by a regular monthly check from her wealthy grandmother in New Jersey. This 20-year-old woman was ostensibly attending nursing school, but actually she was not doing much of anything as she dabbled in San Francisco's drug culture and pretended to paint. Her grandmother had grown suspicious and, checking with the nursing school, she learned that Glenda had not attended classes beyond the first week almost two years ago. Her grandmother was furious since she had received regular letters from Glenda describing her nursing classes and indicating how well she was doing. She consulted a psychologist in New Jersey who advised her to make the monthly checks contingent upon the granddaughter's being in psychotherapy. The psychologist also recommended Nick Cummings in San Francisco.

The patient breezed in on the first therapy session as one who is used to getting her own way. She was confident that she could talk her way out of anything, and immediately initiated an ingratiating manner designed to draw the psychologist into a plot to appease her grandmother. The psychotherapist sidestepped this thrust and sought to learn as much as he could about Glenda. It was a tale of a sordid lifestyle made possible by too much money in the hands of parents who lacked stability. Her mother had been married and divorced seven times. Her father had died of a combination of cocaine and alcohol when Glenda was 11. The patient was deposited in a series of expensive boarding schools from New England to Switzerland, and managed to get thrown out of several of them. Three years ago, her mother was killed in a head-on collision while driving at 90 miles an hour. Her blood alcohol level was 0.21 according to the autopsy. The grandmother, long ago having realized the destructive effect money had on her daughter (Glenda's mother), had arranged to take charge of the family fortune. Glenda inherited nothing until her grandmother died, so she was completely dependent on the very generous checks, which were to keep her more than comfortable while she was ostensibly attending nursing school.

Succinctly, Glenda was a spoiled brat. But at 20 she was also a lonely, frightened, abandoned little girl who had not one clue as to how she might conduct an adult life. It was with this latter that the psychologist connected. The patient latched onto the therapist in her needy, frightened fashion, but it was evident in her cynical smugness that she had conned the therapist and was about to manipulate him. So she was stunned when she was told the psychologist would not see her because she had no intention of giving up drugs and entering school. "You have to see me. If you don't, grandmother will be furious." The psychologist replied, "I am a psychotherapist, not a babysitter hired by your grandmother." There followed a series of rationalizations in which Glenda escalated her volubility, all of which were deflected by the psychologist. Little by little, the patient began to talk as if she were the therapist, culminating with her sobbing, "I don't want to die like my drug-ridden father and my drunken mother." By the end of the first session, Glenda entered treatment subject to a series of conditions as part of the therapeutic contract. Her $6,500 monthly allowance was cut to $2,500 and she would also have to pay for her therapy sessions out of that. She would refrain from all mind-altering substances. She would resume school at the beginning of the next semester, which was to be in three weeks, and she would succeed in school. Any violation of the therapeutic contract would result in the suspension of both her therapy and her allowance. If her grandmother did not agree, the therapist would not see the patient.

An amazed grandmother eagerly agreed, but was properly skeptical. The patient entered an incredibly turbulent treatment. She alternately soaked up like a sponge the parenting of which she had been deprived and heaped upon the therapist all of the hostility intended for her parents who had betrayed her. She was seen for more than two years, illustrating that our goal is not brief therapy, but effective and efficient therapy. If the latter two are present, the length will take care of itself.

Joining the Delusion

In today's medicalized treatment era, the presence of delusions or hallucinations requires immediate antipsychotic medication. In fact, schizophrenia is defined as the presence of delusions and/or hallucinations rather than as a thought disorder that exists most often without the presence of either delusions or hallucinations. Schizophrenics develop delusions as a way of trying to restore their mental and emotional thought-disordered equilibrium when stress or circumstances have disrupted it. Thus, delusions, as well as hallucinations, are attempts at restitution inasmuch as they are the schizophrenic's way of trying to understand and explain what is happening. If the breakdown continues, delusions and hallucinations intensify, fighting off the threat. The real pathology of schizophrenia is withdrawal. When delusions and hallucinations fail, the schizophrenic is reduced to an unfortunate being who has completely withdrawn from the world.

Antipsychotic medications in various ways disrupt delusions and hallucinations, mostly by reducing their intensity so that they may be described as "background noise." But because the patient has lost this attempt at restitution, the psychotic period of schizophrenia may continue indefinitely, and thus require lifelong medication (Whitaker, 2010). Once the medication is withdrawn, delusions and hallucinations return with full intensity. In the Biodyne Model, the restitution to reality, with the decline and even total disappearance of delusions, are accomplished by the psychotherapist's exceptional skill and training. The patient no longer needs these symptoms. The therapist has accomplished this improvement by interventions that resulted in the patient admitting the therapist into his/her inner delusional life. In the future, when stress occurs, instead of resorting to delusions, the patient readily seeks the therapist's guidance. Because of the rapport that has been established, the therapist is able to intercede rapidly and rectify the problem before the delusions reoccur.

The senior author was trained by the late, great Frieda Fromm-Reichmann, an exceptional psychoanalyst who began practicing in the late 1920s and the decades beyond. This was the era before medications, when mental hospitals were noisy and fecal smearing by regressed schizophrenics was common. When seeing such a behavior, psychiatrists would avoid the patient and then would merely order the attendants to clean up the mess. Not so Dr. Fromm-Reichmann. She wore a white smock, which was usually several days beyond needing to go to the laundry, and in one pocket she kept packages of surgical gloves, and in the other candy bars. When making her rounds and seeing a patient smearing, she would kneel on the floor, put on a pair of rubber gloves, and begin smearing feces with the patient. After a few minutes of this, she would discard the soiled gloves, reach in the other pocket for a candy bar which she would offer to the patient, saying: "I would like for you to try this candy bar. You may like it better than feces. I'll be by here about this same time tomorrow and if you are not smearing feces, I'll know you prefer the candy bar and I'll have another one for you. But if you are smearing, I'll know you prefer feces and I won't bother you."

Invariably, the patient the next day would be clean and awaiting the candy bar. I witnessed this over two dozen times, and it never failed once. Fromm-Reichmann (1929/1950) makes the point over and over again that just because a schizophrenic patient is seemingly attentive to the therapist does not mean one iota that the therapist has been accepted. With schizophrenics, the therapist has no influence until the patient lets the therapist into his/her life space. The patient does not accord this unless the therapist has demonstrated eligibility, as defined by the patient, to be let in. At Patton State Hospital in the mid-1940s, I used this technique several times until Thorazine stopped fecal smearing. Though admittedly I did so with great inner revulsion, I was always amazed how such regressed schizophrenics would make the recognition and let me into their inner world.

Fortunately today we are not asked to do this to be admitted by the patient. But the same psychological factors are operative when the therapist deftly joins the patient's delusion and is subsequently accepted by the patient. In the following case of delusional Sam, calling the police would have completely alienated him not only from the present therapist, but probably subsequent therapists as well. On the other hand, the therapist's joining the delusion was the entry into the patient's inner world. It was helpful that the therapist had studied chemistry and knew that LSD, being an acid, would be completely neutralized in the great quantity of water in the reservoir. Delusions occupy psychological "space" in which there is room for only one person. Once the therapist is let in, the patient invariably abandons the delusion, but only after learning that the therapist can be trusted and relied upon, a process that begins only after the therapist successfully joins the delusion.

Case Illustration: Sam—LSD for the City Reservoir

A very concerned psychologist consulted the senior author by telephone. He had just seen a patient for the second time who threatened to dump several pounds of LSD into the city reservoir. He had been making LSD in his home laboratory for months and had now accumulated this large quantity. When a certain combination of lights, sounds, colors, and numbers came together in the universe in a prescribed order, it would be the signal for him to back his pick-up truck to the city reservoir and throw in the LSD. The patient, though psychotic, had an advanced degree in chemistry and could talk scientifically far beyond the comprehension of the therapist.

The therapist had diagnosed the patient as paranoid schizophrenic, and he was not certain that the cache of LSD was not also a part of the delusional system and did not exist. But if it did exist, he did not wish to take the chance that the city's water supply would be poisoned. Interestingly, during the 1960s and 1970s, it was an often expressed fantasy of hippie patients that through the city reservoir an entire population would simultaneously "flip out on acid." The therapist wanted to call in the police, which would destroy any potential therapeutic relationship. The senior author assured him over the telephone that LSD, being an acid, would be quickly diluted and neutralized in the water. It would require an enormous amount of any kind of acid to have a significant effect on such a large supply of water, a fact the patient as a chemist would know well were it not for his delusion.

A treatment plan was devised in which the therapist would join the delusion. Since the therapist could make no sense of the system in which lights, sounds, colors, and numbers would come together in the universe, the entry point was obvious. The patient, over the next several sessions, would teach this "coming together in the universe" to the therapist so both of them would recognize the signal when it occurred. The therapist agreed, but still feared the consequences of a poisoned city water supply. He called a friend who was a chemistry professor for the accuracy of the information he had been given in the telephone consultation and was completely reassured.

Over the next several weeks, the therapist listened intently as the patient used all kinds of didactic means to teach him the "system," as the anticipated coming together in the universe came to be called. During this time, the therapist was also providing a refuge from a world with which the patient no longer could cope. After eight sessions, the therapist still did not understand the "system," but he telephoned the senior author to tell him the patient had completely abandoned the delusion and they were discussing the real issues of independent living outside the hospital and within the limitations of his schizophrenia.

In joining a delusion, the therapist also has to effectively humor the resistance. This is true in the case of Sam, and is even better illustrated in the case of Dennis. The latter case also underscores the importance that, in joining the delusion, the therapist never states an untruth. A paranoid patient is especially sensitive to hearing a lie, and the therapist must tailor the response to something the therapist can personally believe. Declaring to a paranoid, "I believe you" will result in the patient's fleeing from the psychotherapy. Note how, in the case of Dennis, the therapist retained his integrity without contradicting the patient's belief. The ultimate rapport was the result of the therapist's refusal to be told, for his own safety, the content of the delusion.

Case Illustration: Dennis, the CIA Menace

A smiling, friendly, 31-year-old single man consulted the psychologist on referral from his dentist. In spite of Dennis' affability, there seemed something guarded in his demeanor. He volunteered, "My dentist thinks I'm crazy because I want him to remove all my teeth." The patient went on to state that, even though the dentist cannot find anything wrong with his teeth, they do give him a great deal of trouble. "He says if you say I am not crazy, he will go ahead. Do you think I'm crazy?" Every psychotherapist recognizes that such a question is not just rhetorical. It is a key question, the answer to which is critical as to whether the patient develops any trust. A perfunctory negative response or some kind of reassurance will be seen as mechanical and raise a warning flag to the paranoid patient. Most often, the best approach is to follow the cues presented by the patient, both in content and behavior.

Duplicating the patient's affability, the therapist responded, "I had an uncle who had all of his teeth removed and he was crazy. But I knew why he was crazy, and it had nothing to do with his teeth. Why should I think you are crazy?" The patient relaxed somewhat as he laughed along with the therapist. Then, without responding to the question, he talked of his background. The patient had graduated from a prestigious university with a degree in engineering. After college, he married a woman he had occasionally dated, but the marriage lasted only eight months. He confided that she had left because she found the patient to be boring. His father, also an engineer, died of a heart attack three years ago. His widowed mother lived alone in the family home in the Midwest. A sister, two years older than Dennis, had committed suicide by jumping off a building about three years ago. After graduation from college and again until about three years ago, Dennis worked in a defense plant in a highly classified position.

Abruptly, Dennis asked the therapist if he believed a tooth could act as a radio receiver. The therapist responded genuinely that he had heard that certain fillings could behave like a crystal set, but he was not an expert on the subject. He added, "You're the engineer and you would know better than I. Other than that I've heard of the possibility, I would defer to you." The patient reflected for a minute or two, seemed satisfied, and proceeded to tell his story. In his employment in the defense plant with a super-secret project, he began to discover certain irregularities. He reported these to his supervisor, and shortly thereafter he began to be singled out for discrimination. At first, he was denied a well-deserved promotion. Then he was transferred to a relatively menial job since his supervisor continued to rate his performance as unsatisfactory. Finally, a little over two years ago, he was discharged. With his firing, his security clearance was revoked. He had not worked since, living on modest savings and a small inheritance from his father.

Then the patient fell silent for about two or three minutes, during which time he stared intently at the psychologist. He broke the silence abruptly, "What would you say if I told you I discovered a classified document which would have international repercussions if revealed, and might even lead to World War III, and that's why they're after me?" The therapist replied, "I would not want anyone after me, so please don't tell me the rest." This was the right answer. It enabled the patient to tell the rest of his story.

This man had an elaborate delusion, and as in all such psychotic cases, doubting the authenticity of the patient's belief is tantamount to strong-arming the resistance in a neurotic or personality disordered patient. It is imperative that the therapist show no skepticism. On the other hand, the paranoid patient's hypersensitivity to insincerity will detect any posturing on the part of the therapist. It will be noted that the therapist's responses to critical questions not only did not challenge the patient's beliefs, but also were limited statements he could genuinely defend. They had been carefully selected to fulfill both criteria. The decisive response was the therapist's declaration that he did not wish to know the international secret. This is convincing to a paranoid, whereas any attempt to imply "I believe you" would be rejected.

Dennis became very intense as he recounted a sequence of events beginning over three years ago in which "they" attempted to intimidate him so as to curtail his pursuing the irregularities he had discovered. He believed his father did not die of natural causes, but was murdered by the CIA with a drug that would simulate a heart attack. He also believed that his sister was pushed out of an eighteen-story window. The reason they did not murder him was because the CIA, finding itself under constant congressional scrutiny for overstepping its authority in the past, could not risk another scandal. It developed the strategy of driving him insane. They sent constant threatening messages through the bridgework in his teeth and they followed him 24 hours a day to prevent his passing on the international secret. Once he was declared insane and was omitted to a mental hospital, he could talk about the international secret and no one would believe him. It was an effective strategy. The patient feared it was succeeding.

This is a brilliant delusion devised by an intelligent man to account for his gradual decompensation into psychosis. The delusion was restitutive. It enabled the patient to cling to some explanation of reality, and therefore must not be attacked. But this delusion could also cause the patient to turn against the therapist. One error and the therapist would become one of "them." Therapy requires that the therapist join the patient in the delusion in a therapeutic manner. Just because a psychotic talks about the delusion does not mean the therapist has been allowed into the patient's life space. It is only after the therapist has been permitted into that space that the patient's psychosis can be treated. The eventual outcome will be that, since all delusions occupy psychological space in which there is room for only one person, the patient abandons the delusion. This is how it worked with Dennis.

The psychologist stressed that he was not an expert in international intrigue, although he had been engaged in one covert operation in World War II and recognized many of the characteristics in what was ostensibly being done to Dennis. What, then, would be the goal of psychotherapy? Almost as if the therapist had put words in the patient's mouth, Dennis replied, "But you are an expert on mental illness. You could help to keep me from succumbing and becoming insane." The therapist indicated he would very much like to work with the patient in that regard, but the patient would have to promise that, in the course of therapy, he would never reveal the international secret. Even more reassured, the patient agreed and eagerly accepted the homework assigned to him.

The therapist asked whether the patient had noticed that the CIA frequently changed operatives, so whenever he looked back there was a different person following him. The patient replied in the affirmative, and was amazed that the therapist knew this. This was "standard operating procedure," designed to escape detection. The patient was to keep a precise log, describing each CIA agent, recording the exact time he (they were always males) began following and the exact time he was replaced. Then the patient would do the same with the second operative, and so on through the entire day and the entire week. The patient enthusiastically agreed.

The patient was a meticulous, scientifically trained engineer. He arrived the following week with an extensive log that was the epitome of precision. The therapist congratulated the patient on his work and expressed confidence that, with this kind of material, in time they would discover the CIA pattern and be able to neutralize its effects on the patient's emotional health. From the patient's log, they constructed color-coded charts that were taped to the wall. The patient was as pleased as the therapist. Dennis left, thanking the therapist, "I already feel more confident knowing there is someone on my side." During the third session, while translating the log into color-coded charts to hang on the office wall, the therapist abruptly stopped. "Dennis, look at your description of this new man following you. Your excellent log has noted how well dressed he is in an expensive suit. That man is not CIA, he is FBI. The FBI agents are the best dressed operatives in the world; J. Edgar Hoover used to demand it. Not only is the CIA watching you, so is the FBI. You must have some international secret. Please, please! Do not ever reveal it to me." The patient was amazed and impressed.

By the fourth session, the psychologist's office began looking like a Pentagon war room. As more color-coded charts were being taped to the now fully covered wall, the therapist again abruptly noted a discrepancy. "Dennis, look at this guy who fell in behind you at 3:03 p.m. on Tuesday. He is neither CIA nor FBI. By your notes, he is short, stocky, and heavy-faced. This is KGB. That description fits every KGB agent in the world. You must have some secret. Even the Russians are watching you. I never want to be privy to that secret you hold." The patient nodded in amazement.

During the fifth session, while the therapist was at the height of his animation, the patient embarrassingly interrupted: "Nick, while you were discovering the KGB agent last week, it occurred to me that this is all my imagination. I didn't want to say anything because you were having such a good time with it." The delusion had imploded. The psychological space could no longer contain the patient and the therapist, to say nothing about an ever-expanding premise. Now, psychotherapy in the regular sense could begin.

Over the next several sessions, Dennis talked about the impact on him of his father's fatal heart attack and his sister's suicide, which occurred the same year. It had always been difficult for him to face, much less express emotions. His engineer father was an undemonstrative man who created a sterile atmosphere more akin to a laboratory than to a home. His sister, who had just gone through a very emotional divorce, became even more depressed when the father died. Within months, she ended her life. The patient now recognized that he too had snapped, but his response was to slide gradually into the psychosis that began the year of his father's death. Many times, the patient thanked the therapist for not attacking his delusion the way other therapists had done. "I never went back after the one session with them." Then, in admiration, he added, "You should get an Oscar for that performance." The therapist had to confess to the patient, "Dennis, I had so put myself in your shoes that I no longer felt it as a performance." Dennis smiled, "I know. That's why I hated to stop you. No one had ever done that for me before."

Overwhelming the Resistance

In certain cases, the resistance must be overwhelmed, but these are rare and very severe cases. Overwhelming the resistance as a conscious, deliberate, and necessary strategy must not be confused with strong-arming the resistance in unplanned and nonstrategic psychotherapy. This was the case with Beth, the most severe case of rage depression that the senior author had encountered in 60 years of practice. Because she was willing to die in order to kill the interject (her husband), she required drastic therapeutic risks, which I would never recommend to either a supervisee or a colleague. The reader has doubtlessly already ascertained that the cases presented are chosen because they are difficult and severe. They are intended not only to illustrate the technique, but also to be remembered because of their severity. If one can master the most difficult, the easy ones fall into place. The case is presented as an extreme illustration of how the most profound determination to punish by slow, torturous suicide can respond to equally profound and determined confrontation. Overwhelming the resistance can be a useful but difficult technique, but we emphasize: a response of this magnitude and danger should not ever be undertaken.

Being older and wiser, the senior author would never undertake such a procedure again. The therapist, once he embarked on this course, deeply regretted ever undertaking it. But once begun, it could not be abandoned without remanding the patient to certain and determined death. We repeat that it is something that should never have been undertaken, but it illustrates beyond any other possible example the power of highly skillful psychotherapy to save a life. Whenever a trainee falters or fears performing one of the other far less difficult techniques in the Biodyne repertoire, he/she would be reminded of this case. Think of Beth and all else becomes reasonable and doable and, once learned, not difficult by comparison.

Furthermore, the case of Beth does demonstrate three important points:

1. The same psychodynamics and therapeutic entry points prevail in other rage depressions. The introject, which is the object of the now internalized rage against the person with whom the patient is furiously angry, must be expelled.
2. Only the intensity of the person's determination in this case differs. In this case, the intensity is extreme.
3. For the treatment to be successful, the intensity of the therapeutic response must equal the intensity of the patient's resistance. In fact, the matching of the intensity is a necessary condition, and the therapist must derive therapeutic cues and take direction from the intensity of the patient's behavior.

And perhaps this case illustrates that there are fewer hopeless cases than we believe, and that some so-called hopeless cases may actually reflect the therapist's lack of experience or determination. In fulfilling the therapist's side of the therapeutic contract, it is our responsibility to continue to hone our skills until each of us is a master psychotherapist.

Case Illustration: Beth—Death by Neurodermatitis

Beth was a woman in her mid-fifties who was referred by her son's therapist in a distant city. For five years, she had suffered from a progressive, intractable, morbid neurodermatitis that, if it continued to progress, would eventually claim her life. Her distraught husband had taken her to every conceivable medical and psychiatric setting, but the neurodermatitis progressively got worse until her eyes were shut and her entire body was covered with giant hives. Only the soles of her feet remained free and she avoided pain by standing. Eventually, even the soles of her feet succumbed to the skin eruptions. The family was told that, eventually, Beth would develop these sores in her trachea and would choke herself to death. Her son was beside himself, and prevailed upon his therapist to call to make the referral.

The husband came in alone since Beth had not agreed to be seen. He asked if the psychologist wanted his wife's medical and psychiatric records and, upon receiving an affirmative reply, the next day delivered 11 file boxes of records. The events leading up to the illness were frankly presented by the husband, a nationally recognized economist whose almost 10-year affair with his secretary was discovered five years ago by his wife. Beth was enraged by the betrayal and vowed to punish her husband. An active woman all of her life, she quickly lapsed into depression and indolence. Soon, the neurodermatitis appeared and rapidly grew worse. Her husband took her from physician to physician and from psycho-therapist to psychotherapist, but all attempts to help her were thwarted by this angry woman.

After two weeks, Beth agreed to come in, an event that required considerable logistics. The husband had equipped a station wagon with a collapsible gurney upon which Beth was wheeled in by the husband and a male nurse. Beth lay upon thick pads of foam rubber and she was swathed in layers of cotton. Her eyes were closed, but she examined the therapist by prying one set of swollen eyelids open with her thumb and forefinger. Even through this small slit, one could see the contempt and defiance in Beth's eye. She had been hospitalized many times, both medically and psychiatrically, and she challenged the new therapist right off by asking, "And what do you think you can do that hasn't already been tried?"

There was not anything one could say that would make an impression on her. Beth frankly admitted her rage and her determination to die, but according to her own schedule and only when she was convinced her 63-year-old husband had been punished enough. She readily described herself as a witch, bitch, and monster. What if her 63-year-old husband, who had already suffered two heart attacks, should die first? She quietly responded, "That would be nice." Every inventive, innovative paradox, double bind, and reframing that the therapist could conjure would receive the contemptuous response, "That's cute, but it won't work, Doctor." To the suggestion that she was also hurting her innocent adult son, she shrugged, "The Bible says the sins of the father are visited upon the third and fourth generation." The sores were engulfing Beth's mucous membranes and she was already wheezing. She let everyone know she would not accept the insertion of a tube into her trachea. She was determined to die. Her eight sessions with the psychologist were nothing more than a funeral dirge.

The therapist was baffled and spent a great deal of time reflecting on the case. He finally decided to fall back upon his war experiences when untried, high-risk heroics were applied as all else failed to save a life. A plan evolved in the psychologist's mind, but it was a drastic strategy that could be justified only by the fact that otherwise the patient would die. He explained the plan to the husband and son; in desperation, they agreed to proceed with it. They signed a legal consent, a document that was not worth anything under the circumstances, but it at least made husband, son, and psychologist feel somewhat better.

A search for a psychiatric hospital that would cooperate was not easy to find. Finally, a small facility agreed, and Beth was hospitalized some distance from her home city. She was kept comfortable and medically stabilized, but in isolation. She was allowed no visitors, no therapeutic activities, and no television, radio, or reading material. Every Friday, she would have a bedside session with the psychologist, who would be her only mental health professional as well as her only visitor.

In the first such session, the psychologist spent fifteen minutes explaining to Beth that he was going to put a cyanide capsule on her bedside table. It was real cyanide and had been taken from a high-ranking German prisoner in World War II and kept as a war souvenir. He would then leave the room for fifteen minutes, during which time the patient had the option of ending it all. He then added that this might be a relief for all concerned, but he doubted that she had the courage. After all, she was too much of a coward to end her life quickly, which was why she had chosen the neurodermatitis. Then the psychologist left the room for fifteen minutes.

Only his most intense war experiences could match the emotions of that quarter of an hour. He sweated clear through his suit as he experienced strong chest pains. At the appointed time, the therapist re-entered the room, found Beth alive and defiant, and put the cyanide back in his pocket. He then spent fifteen minutes telling Beth she was indeed a coward, and a fraud as well. He would be back next Friday when the procedure would be repeated. This ritual was repeated on four additional Fridays.

During the intervening days between the Fridays, the therapist slept poorly and ate little. He lost several pounds and experienced almost constant hyperidrosis and frequent chest pains. He questioned over and over the wisdom of what he was doing. He felt the constant terror that the next Friday would be it. But each time he reviewed the case, he arrived at the same conclusion and was determined to press on. Those Friday fifteen-minute episodes outside Beth's hospital room never got easier. His suit would be as wet as if he had stood under a shower. Had the psychologist chosen to use a harmless capsule, claiming it was cyanide, Beth would have seen through the ruse.

The therapist's emotions left no doubt but that the game was real and deadly. On the sixth Friday, the psychologist immediately noticed that one eye was open and the swelling on her face was down considerably. Beth no longer scowled defiantly, but rather berated the psychologist for what must be the worst therapeutic maneuver of all time. Therapy had begun: she was beginning to expel the introject. Thereafter, Beth was seen daily and in some of the stormiest sessions this psychologist had ever seen. As her anger rose in crescendo, her neurodermatitis subsided, leaving only the permanent scars and disfigurement that were to be her depression's legacy. Yes, she divorced her husband and she rebuilt her life in other directions. But at least she had a life to rebuild.

Following the dramatic first phase of treatment, Beth and her therapist discussed at some length and at her initiation the dangers involved in challenging her to end her life. She confided that actually what saved her life was the realization that, should she kill herself in the manner she had prescribed, the therapist's career would at the least be over, and at worst there would be a prison sentence. "That someone would take that chance with me forced me to really look at the hate and venom that was inside me." This was also a profound experience for the therapist, and since that time he has realized that the greatest therapeutic ingredient is the therapist's courageous commitment to the patient. Traditional, wimpy do-gooders often just increase the patient's sick resolve. Even Beth, who was determined to eventuate her slow death, could discern this.

Psychojudo with a Family

The following case illustrates how the principle of psychojudo can be applied to family therapy. This dysfunctional family collectively had over 50 years of psychotherapy, with no end in sight. From the beginning, it was apparent to the therapist he would need to skillfully apply psychojudo. It was also important to employ interventions that were novel so these "trained" patients would not have a rehearsed response.

In applying psychojudo to a family, it must be kept in mind that the family is a system that supports the collective pathology. The identified patient is not necessarily the primary patient, for all will be patients to one extent or the other. Often, one member of the family is chosen to represent the entire family pathology. To complicate matters, along with the family system, each family member will have his/her individual reason for being there (to be later defined as the "operational diagnosis"), and an equally individual expectation from therapy (to be described later as the "implicit contract"). The therapist must determine each of these personalized responses, along with understanding the family's overall pathological system that binds all the players together. Finally, the therapist, who behaved in this case in a seemingly outrageous fashion, derived his cues from the outrageousness of this dysfunctional family.

Case Illustration: Marlene and Her "Schizophrenogenic" Family

Marlene was 29 when she first came into treatment. She had her big "3-0," as she called it, during the family therapy series. It was Irene, the mother, who initially called for Marlene's appointment, but shortly thereafter there was another call from Marvin, the father. The family was thought to consist only of two other persons: Carol was Irene and Marvin's second daughter and Marlene's sister, and Robin was Marvin's second wife.

The choice of family therapy in this case may be surprising to some, but the reasons become apparent in the description of the case. In treating families, it is important to utilize within the systems approach the same techniques and concepts that are useful in individual therapy.

Marlene had suffered four psychotic episodes for which she had been hospitalized. She had been diagnosed as suffering from bipolar disorder and had been on lithium carbonate for three years. Three of her four hospitalizations occurred while she was taking lithium. Carol had just graduated from high school and would begin college in the fall. Marvin was trained as a lawyer, but rather than practicing law he founded and managed a large and successful publishing company that specialized in legal books. Marvin and Irene were divorced when Marlene was 13 years old. Robin, whom he married shortly after his divorce, had been having a secret affair with Marvin for a number of years. This disclosure left Irene hurt and angry, and she pursued and obtained a substantial settlement that included regular monthly payments as a combination of alimony and child support.

It was not until Marlene was seen that it was learned there was a 33-year-old brother who had been committed over 25 years ago to a private institution, the bill for which was being paid by a trust fund created by Marvin. This brother, Dick, was diagnosed as autistic in his first year of life, and Irene and Marvin kept him at home until he was age 6. With the beginning of school, it became apparent that Dick would require far greater therapeutic management than could be provided at home. Marlene was about 3 years old when Dick was institutionalized, and did not remember the event that was so painful to both parents.

As stated, the first contact came from Irene, who attempted to make an appointment for her daughter. The psychologist advised her that Marlene would have to make her own appointment, which she did within an hour. Two days after Marlene's appointment had been scheduled, Marvin called, stating he had pertinent information and wanted to come in before his daughter had her appointment. The father was advised that Marlene would have to give her consent and within the context of what would take place in her appointment. Marvin seemed angry, but accepted it. After another two days, the psychologist received a large manila envelope from Irene. It was close to 60 typed pages of history, very professionally done since Irene was a master's level counselor. In this treatise, Irene noted that Robin was a psychiatric social worker. As the treating psychologist speculated about the number of unsolicited "co-therapists," he made the decision to explore family therapy if the session with Marlene seemed to warrant it.

Marlene arrived precisely on time for her appointment. She was a short, plain, 29-year-old who immediately announced that her occupation was that of a waitress. She then went on to explain with a paradoxical mixture of both defensiveness and defiance, "No one in my family wants me to be a waitress. They think it's terrible." The psychologist replied, "So I've heard," and then he explained he had received a phone call from her father and the equivalent to the collected papers of Sigmund Freud from her mother. Marlene laughed and said, "Well, that's my family."

In the ensuing session, Marlene's subtle and most often well-hidden thought disorder became apparent. She manifested many of the signs of pseudoneurotic schizophrenia. If, in fact, she had been misdiagnosed, it was no wonder the lithium regimen had not prevented re-hospitalizations. As she talked, her isolation became clear. Her sole activity, outside work, was watching baseball games on television and reading about baseball. She was a walking encyclopedia of baseball statistics. This was the only real interest in her life. Work, on the other hand, gave her the illusion of having a family. The regular customers were assigned mythical roles as cousins, aunts, uncles, and even grandparents. The restaurant owner, sensing her limitations, benevolently protected her. Talking with Marlene during the first session was like talking to an 8-year-old. When asked about her parents, her life, her feelings, she would childishly and laconically answer, "Fine," or "Good," or "Okay."

The psychologist discussed with her the possibility of family therapy. She responded, "Do you really want to be in the same room with my family?" When asked if they were really that bad, she laughingly replied, "Yeah, yeah. We're pretty bad." She was asked to think about the possibility and told a decision would be postponed until the second session.

Marlene came in the following week and announced, "I haven't been able to think about anything but family therapy." Then she paradoxically began to talk about baseball. The therapist interrupted, "We were going to decide about family therapy." She replied, "Oh, yeah. I think that would be fine." The therapist did not just accept this, but asked on what basis she made her decision. She said cogently, "Well, I can't talk to my family because they won't listen to me. So if we get them all in the same room with you, maybe they will listen to me." Together, we called the family members and everyone readily agreed except Carol. Since she had just turned 18, she believed she had a choice to refuse. She was told she certainly had that right, but her presence might be helpful to Marlene. On that basis, she agreed to come in. Robin had expected to be excluded, as she was the stepmother. She was delighted to be included.

So, the cast of characters assembled. Irene turned out to be a very attractive, statuesque woman of 52 with long hair and penetrating blue eyes. She was one of these remarkable women who, in her fifties, looks as good as she did in her thirties. Marvin, on the other hand, was short like Marlene, and he came in with his legal brief case. Robin turned out to be a Southern belle, peroxide blond, flashy, articulate, and hysterical. Carol was the perfect child with straight As through the city's premier academic high school.

Being institutionalized, Dick was never seen by the therapist. Irene and Marvin separately visited him no less than two or three times a month. Robin participated in the visits with Marvin and was very much a part of the family. As might be expected, there was considerable rivalry between Irene and Robin, a situation that Marvin seemed to encourage. The session began with Irene distributing copies of her treatment plan. It was very well written, but Robin questioned its validity. She criticized it as being too rigid and insisted that what everyone should do is hug each other. She announced, "Love will overcome all adversity," and then she walked across the room and dramatically hugged the therapist's favorite plant, a beautiful 5-foot rubber tree. She broke it in three places. The tension between Irene and Robin was at a critical point.

Then Carol began to talk. As if she had reconsidered after witnessing strange behaviors that opened the first family session, she stated she had a right not to be there. The therapist reiterated that everyone's presence was voluntary and he would appreciate her participation. Marvin launched into a 10-minute speech justifying Carol's position and ending with a comprehensive definition of patients' rights. At this point, Carol decided to stay.

Irene again seized the floor, demanding that they get back to her treatment plan. The interplay between Irene and Robin was not what it seemed. Marvin cleverly set Irene and Robin against each other as he had evidently been doing for 17 years. It was apparent that Irene and Robin had much to like in each other, and would have resolved their differences had not Marvin actively prevented it.

When they finally seemed to run down, they looked to the therapist to proceed. He talked baseball with Marlene. The reaction was instantaneous. Irene was furious, screaming, "What kind of treatment is this?" Marvin protested that he was paying for all this and he was not going to pay for talk about baseball. Robin attempted to be the peacemaker, but was drowned out by Irene who demanded to know why we had arrived at the end of the session without engaging her treatment plan. She accused the psychologist of incompetence, whereupon Robin defended him, saying, "I think Dr. Cummings is wonderful. We all need to hug each other." Then she caught a glimpse of the rubber tree, which was now a heap of rubble, and abruptly stopped talking.

The therapist took advantage of the pause and assigned homework. "Irene, your treatment plan is incomplete and lacking authenticity. Your assignment is to write a new treatment plan." He then instructed Marvin to write a brief about parliamentary procedures in therapy and be prepared to chair the meeting. Embarrassed, Marvin confessed, "I'm not really an authority on patients' rights." The therapist then asked, "How about divorce. Are you an authority on why you are paying such high alimony?" Irene became furious all over again.

At this moment, Carol interjected, "What am I going to do?" The therapist replied, "Well, I want you to tell us what you are doing to get ready for college and where you will be going to college." This was based on Irene's initial 60-page treatise, which revealed that Irene was determined that Carol would stay home, attending college via the subway, while Carol was just as adamant that she would go away to school.

Robin asked, "What do you want me to do?" The therapist quickly responded, "I want you to bring me a new rubber tree." By this time, everyone except Marlene, who was enjoying seeing her family "out-kooked," thought the therapist was very strange. The identified patient was the only one who really understood what the therapist was doing.

Marlene asked, "What do you want me to do?" She was told her job would be to grade everyone on how well they did their respective homework. Marlene stood up smiling, as if having gotten the cue she was ending the session. She appeared to be much taller than her five-foot stature.

During the ensuing week, both Marvin and Robin called the psychologist to ask what he was doing and what he hoped to accomplish. They were instructed to ask at the second session. Unless it was an emergency, the psychologist wanted everyone present whenever there was any communication whatsoever. They seemed annoyed, but resigned. Irene called, left a message, then called back to cancel it.

Marlene came in the next session looking absolutely smashing. She was totally different from the first session in which she looked drab, as if she had just been waiting on tables for eight hours. She was well dressed, well groomed. She brought a compilation of the batting averages of her favorite players because the therapist had confessed ignorance. She brought this in a chart and she was prepared to criticize everybody's homework.

It was learned at this point that Marlene and Marvin once had a very close relationship to the point where Irene used to complain about it and said, "I want to have another daughter and that one is going to be mine." So, she had Carol. It was part of the family understanding that Marlene would be Marvin's daughter and Carol would be Irene's daughter. Following the divorce, Irene had both children. With the beginning of adolescence, Marlene showed no rebelliousness, but began to do poorly in school. She would daydream in school and disappear after recess or between class changes, only to be found later just wandering around the hall. She was constantly accused of playing hooky as she would just wander away in a kind of daze. As soon as Marlene was 18, she left home, got a job as a waitress, and did not speak to her mother until three years ago.

It was also learned at this time that her mother had been in psychotherapy for 22 years. Marvin was in orthodox psychoanalysis with a very well known psychoanalyst since the year before his divorce." So, that made eighteen years. Robin was in treatment with about six people, as she was one of the growth circuit people who are constantly pursuing therapy fads.

Marlene had been in treatment with four psychiatrists. After each psychotic break, the family changed her psychotherapist. Thus, the current therapist was number five. One of the things he did immediately was to have a psychopharmacologist physician colleague change Marlene's medication. The physician put her on Melaril, discontinued the lithium, and started the appropriate blood tests.

Irene and Marvin said, "Of course we can continue our other therapy while we're being seen in family therapy here?" The therapist turned to Marlene, "Marlene, what do you think about that?" She said, "I think that's crazy." So he then replied, "Okay, you can't. You don't have to terminate your therapy, just interrupt it for a while. I'm only going to have a few sessions with you." Marvin said, "A few sessions?" He replied, "Yes," and turned to Marlene and said, "Do you think I could stand any more than that?" She said, "Of course you couldn't. Nobody could." Then he said, "I think that we can make the sacrifice for Marlene's family therapy here." It was so stated because they had each called and referred to it as "Marlene's family therapy." The therapist then concluded, "You can make that sacrifice and not see your shrinks for a few weeks." At this point, Robin made the biggest protest. She was not in therapy just weekly, she was in something every day. Eventually, they all agreed.

The therapist then turned to the homework and called upon Irene first. She had condensed her treatment plan to five pages. Marvin, on the other hand, had prepared an extensive legal brief that concluded that only the therapist could chair the meeting. "You are the doctor and you are responsible because you are the expert." Robin had brought in a gorgeous new rubber tree, complete with ceramic vase. The psychologist ignored it until Robin, unable to stand it any longer, asked, "Where do you want the new plant?" She was told she could put it anywhere. She replaced the old tree in the exact same spot and took the remains of the old tree out into the waiting room. Then she returned and stood admiring the new tree, but she made no attempt to hug it.

Marlene rated Robin's rubber plant an "A" and she flunked Irene and Marvin. As she failed them she said, "All my life my father only knows two ways to talk to me. Either as a lawyer or he talks baby talk." The therapist then said, "Marvin, we've seen the law side of you, now talk baby talk with Marlene." He was very embarrassed. Marlene started talking baby talk with him. Indeed, they had a language. They did talk baby talk. It was quite remarkable.

Irene was flunked by Marlene because she said, "My mother has always tried to be my psychologist and I resented it. This is why, after I left home at 18, I never talked to her until my first hospitalization." It was during Marlene's psychoses that her mother was in her glory. She arranged the hospitalizations, and she chose the psychiatrist and every subsequent psychiatrist.

Why, after years of stabilized crazy behavior, did this family fall apart as represented by Marlene's four psychotic breaks? During those years, Irene made a monument of her divorce, vowing to never recover from it while making Marvin pay for his leaving her. Marvin responded by pitting Irene and Robin against each other as they both fought for Marvin's attention. So, what had changed? The answer to that would be the operational diagnosis. Carol had changed and, by so doing, she changed all the family dynamics.

Carol was about to leave home and Irene could not tolerate this. She had lost Dick to the institution. Marlene, who was Marvin's favorite, at least had been with her until age 18. Since that time, Marlene had refused to see or talk with her mother. If, indeed, she ever had Marlene, she definitely lost her when she left home at age 18. Now there was the threat she would lose Carol.

Two days before the third family session, Irene called the therapist's answering service late at night, stating it was an emergency as she had just killed someone. The therapist called her back and obtained the following story from Irene. "I was thinking this afternoon about my father's partner in business and I said, 'I wonder if the old goat is still alive?' And as I was going to bed and having my cup of hot chocolate and reading the newspaper, I saw on the obituary page that he had just died. I killed him."

It was now clear that Irene's own latent schizophrenia could decompensate and become overt. The therapist calmed her and then stated emphatically, "No, no, Irene, you didn't kill him. You can't kill people by thoughts and also I want you to read that obituary carefully. You will find out that he died yesterday and you only had the thought this afternoon." "Oh," she said. "Oh, okay." Then she settled down and we terminated the phone call.

At the next session, the whole family discussed where Carol was going to go to college. She had done her homework on time but the family had not gotten to it the previous week. Carol was very adamant about the fact that she was going to go away to college. She was not going to commute to college from home. Her mother brought up every possible objection. Her father had given her, for high school graduation, a compact car. Her mother was saying that, if she ever had a wreck in a small car, she'd be killed because it lacked the protection of size. And what are the ground rules going to be, what time will she have to be in the dormitory at night?

Well, it became very clear that this mother was having a very difficult time letting go of Carol. So, it was hypothesized that if we could settle Irene's empty nest syndrome, it would not only help Carol get to college, but Marlene would not have to continue having psychotic breaks. Mother seemed to be precipitating Marlene's active psychosis in a pathetic plea that, if she could not have Carol, she would get Marlene back. At this time, everyone recalled Marlene's first break at age 13 to 14 in school. Irene came through for Marlene and helped her regain some semblance of stability. But Marlene intuitively realized that her future was that of being mother's dependent invalid, and she fled as soon as she could. Irene, on the other hand, was saying that, if she lost Carol, she would settle for a "crippled" Marlene. She would be Marlene's real therapist and, since she hired and fired the psychiatrists, she would thwart their helping Marlene.

All of this was openly discussed at the third family session. Marvin was amazed and said, "I do think you're right." Robin was quietly sympathetic as she silently and genuinely reached out to Irene.

Irene began to talk of her own mother's divorce and remarriage. Irene's father disappeared after her mother left him to marry the very wealthy stepfather. There was then a half-sister who was her mother's favorite. The mother died first, and when the wealthy stepfather died, all the money went to the half-sister. Irene got nothing and she saw this as the story of her life. She lost Marvin to Robin, Dick to the institution, and now Carol to her independence. She would at least have Marlene. She wept profusely. The family wept in empathy.

Irene's homework at this point was to include what she would do with her loneliness because Carol and Marlene, indeed, were going to stand on their own two feet. The therapist gently said, "I don't want your treatment plan for Marlene. I want your treatment plan for Irene."

The family came to the fourth session and, by this time, everybody had stopped being "kooky." They were being cooperative human beings. Robin and Irene had grown close. Robin was feeling empathic toward Irene, saying, "I know how you feel. When Marvin and I got married, I immediately wanted to have a child and Marvin said no, that he already had three children and he didn't want any more. I felt alone and left out."

So, at this point, everything focused on Irene's treatment plan for herself. It was quite remarkable. She agreed in her treatment plan that Carol should indeed go away to college, Marlene should indeed do what she wanted, and if it suited her to be a waitress, she should continue to be a waitress.

It was also evident that Marvin was the one who most objected to Marlene's being a waitress. Her mother was perfectly happy and realized it was Marvin who wanted her to go to college. He said, "When she was a little girl, I fantasized that she would become a lawyer." Within several weeks of termination, Marlene went out and got a waitress job, but she also enrolled in an A.A. program at the community college to become a paralegal.

With full family consent, the family therapy was terminated after the five sessions, and Irene began individual sessions with the psychologist.

5

INCISIVE, EFFECTIVE INTERVENTION

The title of this chapter forewarns that we have just begun to define incisive, effective psychotherapy. The usual and solely cognitive behavioral therapist (CBT) of today who is used to merely addressing and changing the patient's value system may already be reeling from the startling interventions of the preceding chapter. As a reminder, refocused psychotherapy, in its mission to restore psychosocial interventions as the first line intervention in behavioral health, must be more cost- and therapeutically effective than medication. This requires active, incisive, and effective interventions that are not for the faint of heart.

Now that we have addressed how to render the patient's resistance an ally for change, we will look more directly at the individual characteristics of each patient: who, for what, and why? Therapists regularly beguile themselves into believing they have addressed these questions, and to some extent they may have, but the intensity of the techniques to follow will reveal that the address may have been partial at best. At the completion of this exploration, the reader will be taken back to the case illustrations of Chapter 4, and each will be defined in accordance with these new insights.

In brief, intermittent, and refocused psychotherapy, it is anticipated that patients will have episodes of treatment throughout the life cycle. For each treatment episode, the refocused psychotherapist must answer four questions.

1. Who is presenting? The psychotherapist makes a differential diagnosis, which will reveal the psychodynamics of the patient and the consequent *entry points*.
2. Why now? The psychotherapist makes an *operational diagnosis* that reveals the precipitating incident that brings the patient to seek psychotherapy at this particular time. Caution: what seems obvious is most often the wrong conclusion.

3. What for? The psychotherapist determines the *implicit contract* of the patient, which differs often markedly from the stated or *explicit* request for help. Caution: just when you think you have the real reason for coming in, it will most often not be correct. This is one of the most elusive concepts in psychotherapy.
4. How? The psychotherapist formulates a *treatment plan*, operationalizes the *therapy contract*, and plans *homework*. The therapeutic contract states the obligations of both therapist and patient. The treatment plan can only be formulated after the differential diagnosis, the operational diagnosis, and the implicit contract have all been correctly determined.

Answering these questions will enable the therapist to structure effectively the episode of psychotherapy. There will be occasions when the therapist arrived at the wrong operational diagnosis, or the wrong implicit contract, thus an ineffective treatment plan was formulated. In such instances, the psychotherapist apologizes to the patient and reformulates the treatment plan. The differential diagnosis may be stable over time, but personality is layered and different dynamics may be at play at different times. Clearly, "why now," "what for," and "how" are questions that must be answered specific to the current episode. To a certain extent, these questions should be considered not only in each episode, but also for each session of psychotherapy.

Who is Presenting? The Differential Diagnosis

There are two broad categories that can usefully differentiate patients according to implications for treatment. Defense mechanisms can be divided into two kinds: onion and garlic. After eating onions, one suffers their aftertaste with each burp or swallow. On the other hand, after eating garlic, one no longer is aware of the garlic odor, but everyone around suffers the smell. Similarly, there are patients who suffer (onion) and patients who cause others to suffer (garlic). As a general therapeutic axiom: always treat garlic before onion. Denial is at the core of garlic psychodynamics and cannot be broken by onion therapy, which is guilt reduction. Reducing guilt in a garlic patient is like pouring gasoline on a fire, but psychotherapists do it because training in psychotherapy has been mainly onion therapy. Garlic patients may feign guilt, but they are actually upset about the trouble they are in. When you reduce the anxiety in a garlic patient, they will lose their motivation for treatment and leave, saying, "Goodbye, Doc, I didn't need you in the first place." With onion patients, it is legitimate to relieve some of their pain as soon as possible.

If you remember garlic before onion, you can reduce your therapeutic failures significantly. Because so many garlics have onion underneath, they will sense your vulnerability as a caring, empathic person and dangle onion in front of you. You must work through the garlic defenses before doing onion therapy.

In addition to the onion–garlic dimension, patients must be differentiated as to whether they are analyzable or not. Analyzable patients can benefit from uncovering therapy, understand through reasoning, and obtain change through insight into their behavior. Non-analyzable patients deteriorate with uncovering therapy and learn by action and consequences rather than by reason or insight. The narcissistic and borderline personalities straddle the analyzable–non-analyzable line because, while they share many similarities, they present very different therapeutic challenges. Both show low ego strength, low self-control, the tendency to perversions, addictions, and acting out. The narcissistic personality, however, has a pervasive sense of vulnerability so that, at the point when they are ready to plunge the knife and destroy you as a therapist, they pull their arm back because they feel terrified of having to live without you. The borderline will go ahead and destroy you, hang your scalp on his/her belt, and go on to the next therapist. The narcissistic personality will eventually respond to insight. The borderline personality will deteriorate with uncovering therapy.

In Chapters 6–9 of this book, "Onion/Garlic Psychodynamics," 14 diagnostic categories are presented on a four-fold table created along these two dimensions. The objective of the differential diagnosis is to determine which diagnostic category most aptly fits the psychodynamics of the patient. This simple chart, however, belies the complexity of fully assessing the interplay of psychodynamics and life events that are impacting the patient's personality at any time. The following case of Marla illustrates this.

One of the most difficult therapeutic decisions is that of threatening the garlic while postponing treatment on the onion's guilt and suffering. The more onion the basic personality, the greater the therapist's difficulty. The epitome of onion is the all-suffering agoraphobic. For this reason, the 10 percent to 15 percent of agoraphobics who become addicted to either tranquilizers or alcohol as a way of surviving in the face of restricting phobias are almost always missed by the psychotherapist. Addictions are denial, thus always garlic. It is as if the therapist cannot face the therapeutically painful task at hand. It is easier to overlook the garlic.

The case of Marla demonstrates the futility of treating the underlying onion before addressing the overlay of garlic, in this instance chemical dependency. This also illustrates the technique of being prepared to deny treatment if the patient is not willing to make a commitment to abstinence.

Case Illustration: Marla—Garlic over Onion

Such a case was that of Marla, a housebound agoraphobic who failed to make even the slightest gains in her desensitization program. In contrast to the people-pleasing compliance of the agoraphobic, Marla was belligerent and highly resistive, with scores of excuses why she had not done her homework. After over eight months of therapeutic standoff, her highly skilled psychologist, who specialized in phobias, referred Marla in total exasperation. The psychologist had completely missed the severe garlic overlay. The psychologist was blinded not only by the severe phobias, but also by the tragedy the patient had suffered.

Marla was a 33-year-old single woman who lived with her 35-year-old lover, Dave. She had created a unique and successful public accounting business serving small businesses, the majority of which could be characterized as mom-and-pop operations. Marla had a well equipped van she would drive to her clients' places of business, where she would either work on their business books on the spot or take the more complicated work with her. Her agoraphobia threatened the loss of her highly successful practice.

The patient eagerly accepted the referral to the new psychologist and she spent the first part of the session complaining that her former psychologist had actually exacerbated her condition. Marla's phobias began 19 months earlier following a severe auto accident that necessitated two plastic surgeries to repair scars on her face. The initial phobia was the fear of driving, which became so intense that she could not service her clients. Dave, an insurance adjuster who had total control of his own schedule, literally saved Marla's bookkeeping practice by becoming her chauffeur. Recently, Dave had begun to protest, and was threatening to leave the relationship of four years.

Dave and Marla had set three different dates to be married, but each was postponed at Marla's insistence. This was the real reason why Dave was about to break off the relationship. At the present time, Marla made it clear she could not marry until she had recovered from her severe phobias, which had grown to the point that she could not leave the house without Dave. She resisted any insight into her ambivalence in her love life, and denied in advance that her phobias had anything to do with her not wanting to get married right now.

The greatest denial was reserved for her Valium and alcohol addictions. Marla's phobias began about four years ago when her relationship with Dave became serious. Shortly after the setting of the first marriage date, Marla began to experience panic attacks while driving. She was prescribed Valium by her physician and this enabled her to continue her itinerant bookkeeping business. On especially difficult days, she added alcohol to the Valium, and soon Marla was self-medicating herself to the point of nearly perpetual intoxication. The day of the auto accident, she had had considerable wine to drink on top of her Valium, a fact that Marla reluctantly admitted to her therapist only after several sessions and after she became totally abstinent. The matter of her alcohol/Valium blood level at the time of the accident had become a significant issue in her pending lawsuit against the driver who hit her.

From the first session, Marla's addiction was obvious to the psychologist. Her hands were tremulous, her eyes were bloodshot, her speech was slurred, and her patience was thin. Her behavior would become belligerent whenever her denial was threatened. Marla did not give up her alcohol and Valium without a fight. After explaining that treatment was futile as long as she relied on her addiction, abstinence was made a condition for continuing treatment. "All insight is soluble in alcohol" and, until she was "clean," therapy would continue to be the same waste of time the previous eight months had been with her first psychologist.

Once abstinent, Marla lost her garlic demeanor. She became timid, guilt-ridden, and self-effacing, but her treatment proceeded in earnest. She faced her fear of marriage, eagerly performed her homework, and had desensitized herself within two months. She accepted her responsibility to say either "Yes" or "No" to Dave regardless of the consequences, and in time she said "Yes." Dave and Marla are married. She remains sober, and has learned to retreat and then desensitize herself whenever her phobias threaten her during difficult times in her life.

LEGEND

Psychological mechanism	Denial, displacement
Diagnosis	Agoraphobia, alcohol dependence
Operational diagnosis	Previous therapist gave up
Implicit contract	Don't treat my drinking
Personality type	Onion attempting to hide garlic
Therapeutic techniques	Addictive therapy (abstinence) followed by desensitization

---

Why Now? The Operational Diagnosis

In addition to bonding, the ideal goal for the first session is to determine the operational diagnosis and the implicit contract. Without these two, the effectiveness of a treatment plan will be based on luck. The operational diagnosis tells you why the patient is coming in now instead of last week, last year, or next month. Patients respond in many different ways to the seemingly simple question, "What brings you in for treatment now?"

A patient may say, "I'm here because I drink too much, and I want to stop." Accepting that overlooks the fact that this patient has probably been drinking too much for years. So why is he seeking treatment now? Finding out that, after ten years of threatening, his wife finally kicked him out of the house gets you closer to the operational diagnosis.

The operational diagnosis assesses the motivation of the patient. By identifying the event precipitating the treatment episode, the therapist can more clearly understand the pain that leads the patient to seek psychotherapy at this particular time. In this example, the patient may not want to stop drinking. The pain is the impending loss of his marriage, and the patient may want psychotherapy solely to patch things up with his wife. A treatment plan to achieve abstinence will be met with resistance unless the implicit contract of the patient is addressed and a therapeutic contract agreed to.

When it is difficult to determine the operational diagnosis, this simple question is often useful: "What were you thinking the precise moment you picked up the phone and called for an appointment? Don't tell me what you were thinking last week, last year. Tell me what you were thinking the moment you decided to pick up the phone."

Many patients have thought of making an appointment many times before, but they never called. What was pushing them to go through with it this time?

The importance of the operational diagnosis is clear in the case below. The wrong operational diagnosis would have resulted in initiating bereavement counseling, with the strong possibility that the patient would have committed suicide.

Case Illustration: Arthur to Ashes

I was asked to sit in on an intake session with an elderly man who was in tears. He had been widowed about eleven months ago. The therapist immediately started bereavement counseling. I interrupted, saying, "Whoa, we don't have an operational diagnosis." I began interviewing the man and asked, "If your wife died eleven months previously, why are you coming in now?"

"Well," he said, "I have one more thing to do. I have to scatter my wife's ashes in the Atlantic." He had them in an urn. His wife had been cremated.

I asked, "You cremated your wife?"

He started crying, "Yes, I never should have done it."

I said, "Aren't you Jewish? Isn't that against your religion?"

He said, "Yes. I never should have done it. I never should have done it."

I kept probing. His wife had terminal cancer. She was in excruciating pain. They made a pact that he would poison her. He would have her cremated so, in case anybody got suspicious, they wouldn't be able to detect the poison and have him stand trial for murder. They also agreed that, within a year, he would scatter her ashes into the Atlantic and then poison himself. I said, "When is the year?"

He said, "A week from Monday."

If we had continued bereavement counseling with this depressed man, he would be dead today. Do not assume just because somebody is widowed that bereavement is the issue. Listen for self-recrimination and loathing, which signals depression. In bereavement, what you hear is longing: "I keep looking for my husband." "I keep looking for my wife." "When I hear footsteps, I think my husband's coming home; he walked like that." "Oh, I hear my wife's high heels coming." You're missing the person. If you have uncomplicated bereavement, do bereavement counseling. If you have depression mixed in with the bereavement, stop the bereavement counseling, treat the depression, and then at some point you can go back to the bereavement counseling.

I spoke very bluntly to him: "It's very obvious from everything you're feeling right now, that you really feel you did wrong in cremating your wife." He was an Orthodox Jewish man and felt guilty about the cremation. The poisoning, he felt, was compassionate and humanitarian. She apparently was in terrible pain. So I said to him: "Look, you say you did wrong. Now you're going to compound the wrong? By poisoning yourself and leaving instructions to be cremated and having your ashes scattered in the Atlantic? You're going to do two wrongs. Two wrongs make a right, huh?"

While we are talking like this, he is crying the whole time. He made a nonsuicide pact, and we nullified the agreement with his wife. We went over it again and again as if I were his lawyer making a contract. God only knows why they made the pact for him to kill himself. They had been married 44 years. At the moment that they made the decision to use poison, he may have said, "I don't think I could live without you." She may have said, "Then why don't you join me?" Who knows? There were very intense emotions when they made that pact.

LEGEND

Psychological mechanism	Introjection covered by denial
Diagnosis	Rage depression primary to bereavement
Operational diagnosis	It is time to kill myself
Implicit contract	Do I deserve to die?
Personality type	Onion
Therapeutic technique	Rewrite death contract

What for? The Implicit Contract

The implicit contract, in contrast to the operational diagnosis, which tells you why the patient is coming in now, tells you what the patient is coming into treatment for. The implicit contract always bears the resistance. If the difference between the implicit contract and the explicit contract is too great, therapy will be sabotaged. Therapy might sometimes proceed well without having ferreted out the implicit contract, but it will take longer.

Returning to the example of the patient whose explicit contract is "Help me stop drinking," if the operational diagnosis is, "My boss said that he'll fire me if

I have liquor on my breath after lunch one more time," he really does not want to become abstinent. Even though the explicit contract is, "Help me quit drinking," the implicit contract might be, "Show me how not to drink during the day except on the weekends so that I can drink every day after 5:00 p.m. and all weekend." Or, if the patient is the kind of alcoholic who never makes it to work on Monday because he has been on a weekend binge, the implicit contract may be: "Show me how to stop early enough Sunday night so I can get to work on Monday morning." The implicit contract of the alcoholic whose wife threatened to kick him out might be, "Gee, maybe if I come into therapy, my wife will be impressed and take me back home, and I won't have to quit drinking." Each, however, will say, "Help me stop drinking." Most therapists accept the explicit contract at face value, even though it is the implicit contract that determines the course of treatment.

In every first session, every patient will throw out to us the implicit contract, although it may be as an aside. Our patients will tell us in an inadvertent way when we are most distracted, when we are most hooked into their content, or most impressed with their psychological mindedness, their motivation, or their great empathy. We learned to do this as children.

Junior breaks mother's favorite vase. He is afraid to tell mother, cleans it up, and throws it in the garbage can, thinking mother is not going to find out. He feels guilty, however. After three days, he can't stand it any longer as he fears, "She knows. She knows." So Junior waits until mother is on the phone talking to a friend and, in the middle of a conversation, he tugs on her apron and says, "Mommy, I smashed your vase." Mother says, "Yes, I know, Junior. Go watch television." Mother never heard him. Junior says, "Whew, I told her. Now I don't have to feel guilty anymore."

Let's take the example of a middle-aged spinster who looks up and makes an appointment with a handsome young male psychologist. In the course of the first session she says, "I'm glad you have a comfortable office because I'm going to be here a long time." It is said as an aside to the barrage of her explicit contract: she has a terrible principal who doesn't understand her or back up the classroom teachers, and her terrible students slash teachers' tires when they flunk. When the therapist is concentrating on this poor woman's life and the ten more years of torture before she can retire, she slips in the remark about the comfortable office. By not responding to this, the therapist has made a contract for long-term therapy. The patient will conclude, "Well, I told him. Everything's okay. We all know why I'm here." The therapist has agreed not only to long-term therapy, but also to be nontherapeutic during this time. This young man didn't realize until a year and a half later that he was her weekly date in her otherwise dateless life. Nothing happens therapeutically because the patient is trying to get gratification rather than gain understanding or effect change in her life. The saddest part is that the therapist is not dealing with the real pain this woman has.

Suppose you elicit an implicit contract that you know is not therapeutic and cannot be accomplished. With most patients, the best approach is to out rightly discuss it with the patient. For example, a man may come in and say, "I want to save my marriage. I've been very bad. I've not been fair to my wife. I've been having an affair for the last three years. I want to save my marriage. I know it's my fault. I don't need couples' therapy because it's all me. My wife is wonderful." About halfway through the session, he sighs and says, "I'm afraid, no matter what I do, we'll probably end up in divorce."

He just threw out the implicit contract. It is appropriate to ask him, "You know, I don't hear something right. If you've already decided to divorce your wife, why are you seeing me?" In the course of discussion, it turns out the operational diagnosis is that, after three years of hearing him promise that he would leave his wife, his mistress will not take it any longer and has given him an ultimatum, "You either leave your wife or you can't see me anymore." His unconscious fantasy is, "I will come into therapy. My mistress will be impressed. I will say to her, 'How can you rush me. Wait until I work this out in therapy.' If I can get into long-term therapy, I can have my wife and my mistress for another three years." Missing this, you have just made a contract to be nontherapeutic.

More succinctly stated, his implicit contract was, "Let me appease my mistress and my guilt so I can have both my wife and mistress as long as possible before getting a divorce." Unconsciously, he planned to use therapy to hold off his mistress for another three years. But, at some point, he would have to leave his wife to go with the mistress. Then he would want to be able to say to his family and friends, "I did everything in the world to save my marriage, including going into psychotherapy." This must be discussed with him. "This is not a legitimate way to go. You have to make up your mind. Now if you want to come in to save your marriage, that's a legitimate thing to work on. If you want to come in to stall your mistress for three years, I'm sorry. I have too many patients who want to see me so I don't have time to play that game with you." Now, with this kind of man, an intellectually honest kind of person, nothing sociopathic about him, even though he is being manipulative, it will take hold. Unless we are dealing with the garlic patient, the implicit contract is just below the patient's awareness and he grabs it when it is presented. The more you can use the words the patient uses to talk to himself, the more effective it will be.

He responded, "My god, my god. You're right. I don't know what to do."

The therapist responded, "I don't know what you're going to do either, but I want you to take a week and think about it, and come back next week and tell me what you want to come here for. This time I want you to really reach down into your kishkas and come up with the reason. I don't want any of this B.S."

He came in the next week and said, "I've wrestled all week where I want to be, and I've really decided that I want to stay with my wife and children. I want help in extricating from my mistress."

With other patients, the approach is to go with the resistance and bring it around, as in the case described earlier of the woman supporting a man who wouldn't work. With this kind of woman, if you sat down and discussed with her, "You're not able to leave this man right now because of your low self-esteem or poor interpersonal skills," the therapy would not have progressed as efficiently as if you just went with the resistance. She would have agreed, and after spending many weeks in skills training and raising her self-esteem by various means, she still would not have been able to leave her partner.

With more reasonable, open people who can learn from verbal insight, discussing the implicit contract with them might be the best way to go. With garlic patients, discussion is ineffective because they are in denial. They will look you right in the face and say, "No, Doctor. That isn't it at all." The woman in this case was a garlic enabler, and it was most effective to raise her self-esteem by allowing her to experience the futility of her implicit contract.

Resistance is real, but often it is not the main determiner of unduly protracting therapy. Very often, the therapist, having accepted the explicit contract at face value, is working toward a different goal than the patient. The patient always strives toward the implicit contract. There ensues a wrestling match between therapist and patient that unnecessarily prolongs psychotherapy.

How? The Therapeutic Contract and Homework

The operational diagnosis and the implicit contract guide the therapist in formulating the therapeutic contract. In its pure form, the contract says:

> I will never abandon you as long as you need me, and I will never ask you to do anything until you're ready. In return for this, you'll be joining me in a partnership to make me obsolete as soon as possible.

The therapist must operationalize this agreement into a treatment plan with specific objectives and homework assignments to help the patient realize these objectives. Giving homework makes the patient realize that he/she is expected to be responsible for his/her own therapy. These assignments must be meaningful in light of the patient's motivations. They must also be designed to redirect rather than oppose the resistance.

Homework is at the heart of targeted, focused psychotherapy. It is the critical feature that convinces patients that they are truly partners in their own treatment. It should be given at every session, and never in a perfunctory or dispirited manner. Too often, overworked psychotherapists assign homework in a manner that telegraphs to the patient that the therapist does not really regard it as important. The therapist is seduced by the fascinating content of the patient's disclosures, forgetting that understanding is not measured by what the patient says, but by demonstrable changes in behavior and attitudes. Homework is intended to be the first line of behavioral change, opening the door to increasingly greater changes.

Homework must be inspired in its construction and assignment. It must fit the immediate therapeutic needs of the patient. No matter how cleverly contrived, if it does not respond to the moment in this individual patient, it will be of only limited value. Therefore, there is no cookbook of homework from which the therapist can choose items to assign. Homework must always be individually tailored.

The exercises usually found in self-help books are only generally useful. They have demonstrated value in psychoeducational groups, and even in some group therapies, but in individual psychotherapy the homework must reflect the therapist's understanding of the individual patient. As such, homework requires attention to several critical rules.

The homework must not violate the therapist's contract with the patient that he/she will not be asked to do something until able to do so. If the assignment is too hard, it will hinder the therapy. The patient will either feel hopeless or will resent the therapist's betrayal of the therapeutic promise. On the other hand, if the homework is too easy, the patient will lack a sense of accomplishment and will feel either unworthy or, again, hopeless.

The therapist cannot assign homework until both the implicit contract and the operational diagnosis have been determined. To do otherwise will most likely result in the assigned homework being in direct, but undetected, confrontation with the resistance. Accordingly, it will fail along with the therapy. The homework must go in the direction of the resistance, while at the same time having the propensity to diffuse it.

Some brief cases may help illustrate the foregoing principles of homework. The first (discussed in more detail on pages 36–37) is a patient for whom the homework was a paradoxical intention, designed not to strong-arm her resistance, but to address her implicit contract that her lover could be changed. Previously presented to illustrate "psychojudo," it is discussed here to demonstrate how this technique may be incorporated into homework.

Case Illustration: Paula's ver Stunken

This case is a condensed repetition, according the opportunity to present the legend. It is also a prime example of how well-chosen homework can alter behavior in very few sessions.

Paula, a restaurant server in her twenties, asked for help in leaving her abusive live-in male lover who had not worked in two years, and whom we shall call ver Stunken. To have accepted this explicit contract, would have violated her implicit contract, which the therapist skillfully discerned. Paula was looking for ways to change the lover. The operational diagnosis (why is she coming in now?) was the lover's sudden interest in another woman. The therapist assigned the homework that the patient do three things she had never done before that would cause her boyfriend to love her. When the following week she described what she had done to no avail, the therapist reassigned the same homework, stating: "I am still not convinced you have done everything possible to make him love you." This, of course, is what the patient unconsciously was saying to herself. After three weeks of this assignment, the patient came in and reported she had left ver Stunken, stating for the first time that there was nothing that was going to cause him to change, as he would remain worthless. To her surprise, within 36 hours he moved in with another woman. The patient discovered that there is a shortage of ver Stunkens, as there are so many unfortunate women with low self-esteem ready to be victimized.

LEGEND

Psychological mechanism	Displacement
Diagnosis	Hysterical personality
Operational diagnosis	I fear he is getting ready to leave me
Implicit contract	Help me change him through my love
Personality type	Onion
Homework	Love him even more
Therapeutic technique	Paradoxical intention

In the next case example, the operational diagnosis and the implicit contract together expected that the therapist would somehow return the spouse and children without the patient having to change. By verbalizing the patient's implicit demands as if to have made these his own, the therapist forces the patient into the position of taking the therapist's role.

Case Illustration: Leonard the Lush

Leonard, at 43, asked for help in quitting drinking. He had been an alcoholic for many years. His wife had taken the children and left him (operational diagnosis). In keeping with the fact that no addict really wants to quit, Leonard's implicit contract was, "Help me cut down enough to get my wife back. Also, take me back to the halcyon days when I could control my drinking." The therapist challenged the patient's motivation indirectly by suggesting he need not become abstinent. "You've been conning your wife for 15 years. What do you need to do to con her for another 15 years?" If done well, this challenge externalizes the patient's implicit contract, placing the patient in the unlikely role of speaking as the doctor: "No, I must quit. My health and my marriage are both in jeopardy. I can't just con her and myself anymore." This sets up the patient for the first homework, which is to prove to a skeptical therapist that he really wants to quit drinking. In Leonard's case, it was decided that seven days "cold turkey" would convince the therapist of his determination, and earn the patient a second appointment. The length of the period of abstinence must fit the rule of being something the patient can accomplish without its being too easy. Learning from the patient the length of his spontaneous abstinences, as all alcoholics occasionally put themselves "on the wagon," reveals the length of time for the homework. With some patients it can be two weeks, for others two days, and at times only half a day.

LEGEND

Psychological mechanism	Denial
Diagnosis	Alcohol addiction
Operational diagnosis	Wife has left me
Implicit contract	Help me get my wife back by just cutting down on drinking
Personality type	Garlic
Homework	Abstinence
Therapeutic technique	Deny treatment

In addressing the implicit contract, it is important in assigning homework that the therapist always bear in mind the therapeutic contract, which states, "I will never ask you to do something until you are able . . ." In the following example, the therapist skillfully tailored the homework to that which the patient could realistically accomplish, and then enforced it.

Case Illustration: Thelma's Therapist

Thelma was transferred from another therapist. A 28-year-old patient with a borderline personality, Thelma had been indulged by her therapist and allowed unlimited "emergency" phone calls. Her abuse of this ploy clearly had to be limited, and this would be her homework. But Thelma could not go from unlimited phone calls to none. A careful scrutiny with the patient of her phone calls revealed an average of three critical calls in a two-week period. Thelma, therefore, was limited to three calls per two weeks as part of her homework. She could save up unused allowable calls, giving her further incentive to wean herself away from the manipulative overdependence. Thelma used up her first three phone calls in the first week, and discovered that, in keeping with their agreement, the therapist did not respond to the next call.

LEGEND	
Psychological mechanism	Projective identification, splitting
Diagnosis	Borderline personality disorder
Operational diagnosis	Abandoned by previous therapist
Implicit contract	I shall continue to demand unlimited attention
Personality type	Garlic
Homework	Limit emergencies
Therapeutic technique	Set limits (boundaries)

Prescribing the symptom is often useful when the patient has converted anger into a psychophysiological symptom. In the following case of Arlo, he was manifesting his anger at his wife by denying her sexual satisfaction through his impotence. His operational diagnosis had to do with his realization that he was as deprived of satisfaction as was his spouse. His implicit contract had to do with wanting to continue punishing his wife while exempting himself from the deprivation. Many men resolve this dual need through premature ejaculation: the man has an orgasm immediately on entering, leaving the woman frustrated. The therapist sought to prevent the substitution of premature ejaculation for total lack of erection by a homework that mobilized the defiance toward the therapist and away from the spouse.

Case Illustration: Arlo and His Rhino

Arlo had suffered from performance anxiety all of his life, but at 38 he was now impotent every time he attempted sexual intimacy. Arlo's case, like the cases of most such patients, was reminiscent of the story of how to make gold out of dog feces. One places the dog feces in an old fashioned nut grinder. As one turns the crank, if one does not think of the word "rhinoceros" the feces will come out gold. In Arlo's case, the word "rhinoceros" was the phrase, "Will I get an erection this time?"

Of course the fearful thought would prevent the successful performance. Arlo was instructed to have sex without an erection, with the therapist stating that it was important that the patient find ways to be sexually intimate without an erection. He was strongly instructed that, should an erection occur, he must suppress it. After several weeks of the symptom being prescribed, the patient found himself in defiance of the therapist's instructions, the therapist all the while decrying the noncompliance. It is imperative that a paradox of this type be maintained until the patient is ready to give up the symptom. To relax the instructions prematurely will result in the return of the symptom in even more entrenched form. In Arlo's case, this readiness occurred when the patient, himself, revealed the nature of the paradox. "I now know why you did this and I thank you."

LEGEND

Psychological mechanism	Intellectualization, doing and undoing
Diagnosis	Obsessive personality
Operational diagnosis	Impotence
Implicit contract	Help me be defiant without suffering
Personality type	Onion
Homework	Be impotent
Therapeutic technique	Prescribe the symptom

In other cases, the therapy can be concluded without the patient and therapist articulating the nature of the paradoxical intention. This is not unusual in treatment with an adolescent who focuses on the action resulting from the homework and ignores the ideation. Such was the outcome with Jacob.

Case Illustration: Bringing Up Jacob's Parents

Jacob was an adolescent dragged in by his parents who complained he never performed his chores. In an individual session with Jacob, the patient insisted that his parents did not care about him, for when he did one chore it was not acknowledged. They continued to forbid his use of the family car and withheld other privileges. The therapist expressed interest in determining how far "out to lunch" his parents were. He suggested Jacob perform two chores the next week and see whether his parents noticed.

Jacob, of course, reported in the next session that his three (not two) performed chores were completely ignored by the parents. Increasingly over the next several weeks resulted in Jacob's doing all of the expected chores. The patient was smug in his parents' not acknowledging them, while at the same time the parents confided in the therapist that Jacob was a changed boy, but they were afraid to mention it because he might revert to his former obstinacy. Jacob's smugness included the fact that his out-to-lunch parents were now allowing his privileges, including liberal use of the family car.

LEGEND	
Psychological mechanism	Denial
Diagnosis	Adolescent rebellion
Operational diagnosis	They took away the car
Implicit contract	Prove my parents are jerks
Personality type	Garlic
Homework	Do chores as parent trap
Therapeutic technique	Humor the resistance

From the illustrations, and from the more comprehensive case histories presented in this volume, it is apparent that appropriate homework facilitates the therapeutic process. If it is presented cleverly, it will be incorporated by the patient as compatible. Yet, there are times when homework in certain overly obstinate patients must be enforced. Such was the case of Roland (Chapter 7) where confronting his mother was a prerequisite to therapeutic breakthrough, and that of Grace (Chapter 4) in whom there had to be a curtailing of an infantilization of such proportions that therapy was at a standstill.

Enforcing homework is also essential in treating the special circumstances presented with anorexics, who are among the most argumentative of our patients, and with bulimics, who are the most deceitful. Both of these eating disorders pose a threat to life: in anorexics from complications of near starvation, and in bulimics from possible cancer stemming from the constant regurgitation of stomach acids through the esophagus. Both are subject to severe metabolic distress, including electrolyte imbalances. There has been considerable professional and public hysteria regarding the death rate of these cases, with one set of irresponsible statistics estimating that, in 1992, about 50,000 women died of anorexia. The Centers for Disease Control and Prevention asserts that, for that year, there were 17 known cases of mortality. So, even though the danger is considerably less than previously believed, therapeutic caution is still indicated in these life-threatening cases, and homework must be strictly enforced.

The case of Melanie, an anorexic, illustrates the importance of not losing sight of possible life-threatening consequences in enforcing homework. The failure to do her homework, which was the intake of one 1,000 calorie meal per day, would not lead to denying treatment, for that might well accelerate weight loss, but rather to hospitalization, which would result in forced feeding and thus save her life.

Case Illustration: Melanie—Anything but Hospitalization

The patient had been a high school cheerleader and a very pretty and popular adolescent until age 17 when she became anorexic. Her weight had dropped in a few months from 114 pounds to 76 pounds, and her parents and the family's physician were alarmed. Hospitalization was contemplated, and Melanie agreed to come to see the psychologist as a last and desperate attempt to avoid hospitalization. The patient manifested the perfectionism, argumentativeness, and distorted body image that are typical in anorexia. She was meticulously and fashionably dressed and coiffured. Although emaciated, she complained that the fat hung from her arms and wrists and that she had to lose more weight.

The therapist used the leverage of hospitalization to assign the homework, all under a barrage of arguments from the patient. Finally, an agreement was reached. The patient would have one 1,000 calorie meal per day, and her mother, who had been given materials sufficient to assess compliance, would record and document the amount of food intake. Failure to eat a 1,000 calorie meal each day would result in Melanie being hospitalized. The agreement, along with the nutritional charts and other materials given to the mother, was signed and initialed on each page as is recommended with these argumentative patients. Also, a therapeutic plan that included individual therapy, group therapy for eating disorders, and family therapy was signed and initialed on each page. Protesting and arguing each step of the way, Melanie gained weight and emerged from the physiologic danger zone. Menstruation, which had stopped, resumed when she crossed the 100-pound mark.

LEGEND

Psychological mechanism	Displacement, dissociation
Diagnosis	Anorexia nervosa
Operational diagnosis	They want to hospitalize me
Implicit contract	Help me avoid hospitalization
Personality type	Garlic covering onion
Homework	1,000 calorie meal per day
Therapeutic technique	Enforce the homework

It is possible at times to assign homework that cleverly blocks the patient's implicit contract. In bulimia, the implicit contract is usually the requirement that therapy enables the patient to continue denying that she is purging. The denial has been jeopardized by health problems resulting from purging: severe electrolyte imbalances or the appearance of precancerous tissue in the esophagus because of the repeated passage of stomach acid. The homework assigned to Brenda was successful in attacking her denial.

Case Illustration: Bulimic Brenda

Brenda, a fashion model at age 18, kept her fashionable, required figure by purging. She would eat enormous amounts of food, and would induce vomiting or use laxatives, or both. She came to treatment because she had made herself physically ill. She was forced to forfeit several work assignments, and her modeling career was in jeopardy. She was accompanied by her mother, who had been aware for some time of Brenda's bulimic behavior, but had been convinced several times that she had stopped her purging, only to discover that Brenda had lied again. The bulimic patient herself is so into denial that she believes her own lies. As part of this denial, the bulimic will vomit in the toilet or sink with her eyes closed, and then quickly flush or wash the vomit so as not to have to confront it.

The therapist appropriately ascertained that Brenda was not yet ready to stop purging, so he made it clear she could continue to purge, but that she would have to vomit each time into a plastic bag. She was then to freeze the bag and its contents, and bring all the frozen bags to the next session. The patient was shocked and filled with revulsion, but was told that failure to comply would result in termination of her sick leave and a possible end of her modeling career. It was the signed sick leave that was protecting her contract. Of importance here is also the therapist's own revulsion, an understandable countertransference.

Brenda's purging stopped with one incident with the plastic bag. She could no longer maintain her denial as she froze and brought the bag and its contents to therapy. She could not face bringing the bag upstairs to the office, and she and the psychologist went to the parking lot where Brenda opened the car trunk and with intense emotion revealed the bag. Her mother, who was waiting in the car, shared her daughter's revulsion which, secretly, was rivaled by that of the therapist. Brenda never purged again. It has been found that this is a very successful technique, with the purging behavior abruptly abandoned with the first bagging, although some patients go to a second bagging.

LEGEND

Psychological mechanism	Denial of addiction to food
Diagnosis	Bulimia

LEGEND ... *continued*	
Operational diagnosis	Behavior making her physically ill
Implicit contract	Restore ability to purge
Personality type	Garlic
Homework	Purge into bag and save it
Therapeutic techniques	Prescribe the symptom, enforce the homework

Now that our armamentarium has been extended to include onion/garlic, the operational diagnosis, and the implicit contract, as well as homework, it would be useful to review the cases presented in Chapter 4 accordingly.

Amazing Grace, who was diagnosed as a schizophrenic alcoholic, heavily employed withdrawal and denial as her psychological mechanisms, making her a garlic patient. The operational diagnosis was that her first therapist abandoned her, and her implicit contract was that she would continue to run her own therapy. Her homework was no urination in treatment, and no drinking just before treatment. Therapeutic techniques included doing something unexpected (novel), preventing regression to infantile behavior, and encouraging (rewarding) abstinence.

Patricia, the over-protective co-therapist. Her psychological mechanisms were over-identification (with son) and perfectionism. Her diagnosis was postpartum psychosis in remission, and the operational diagnosis (why now?) was, "Okay, I'll see your boss and I will make the same demands." Her implicit contract is obvious in this case: my treatment plan or none. She was overwhelmingly garlic, and prescribing the resistance was very effective as in the homework for her to be the therapist's co-therapist for Billy.

Mona—Lay that Pistol Down. Definitely diagnosed a borderline personality disorder who was using the psychological mechanisms of projective identification and splitting, Mona was obviously garlic. The operational diagnosis was her unrequited love for the therapist, with the implicit contract, "If I can't have her, I'll kill her." The therapeutic technique employed was humoring the resistance by giving her the homework to pretend to be a patient so she could join the scam.

Elaine—Death by Drowning. Here is definitely an onion with the diagnosis of hysterical personality disorder. Her operational diagnosis (why now?) was that the Welfare Department denied her housing request, and her implicit contract was the demand that the therapist perpetuate the dependence. Her homework was to obtain enough Valium to eventuate the therapeutic technique of mobilizing her rage and prescribing the symptom (suicidal intent) through paradoxical intention.

Linda, the Infatuated. She was also an onion with the diagnosis of depressed hysteric who was employing the mechanisms of repression and introjection. The operational diagnosis was that "You have rejected me," making the implicit contract, "Help me by loving me." The therapeutic technique was the mobilization of rage with the homework to destroy the therapist's career.

Glenda's Grandmother. As a narcissistic personality disorder, this garlic patient employed the psychological mechanisms of denial, splitting, and projective identification. The operational diagnosis was that her grandmother was about to stop her allowance, so her implicit contract was for the therapist to join her in fooling grandmother. Her homework was three-fold: abstinence, resume school, and accept a reduced allowance from grandmother. The therapeutic technique was to otherwise deny treatment.

Sam—LSD for the City Reservoir. This paranoid schizophrenic was manifesting the psychological mechanisms of withdrawal, delusion, and projection. His operational diagnosis was the decompensation of his thought disorder, with the implicit contract saying, "I am not crazy or impotent." His contemplated attack certainly makes him a garlic personality, but the therapist used the technique of humoring the resistance and entering the delusion. This was augmented by the homework to teach the therapist the codes.

Dennis, the CIA's Menace. Here was another paranoid schizophrenic manifesting the psychological mechanisms of withdrawal, delusions, and projection. But, in contrast, he is onion in that he wanted to save society, not attack it. What brought him in (operational diagnosis) was the decompensation of his thought disorder, with the implicit contract, "Prove I am not crazy." The homework was to keep a careful log of the spies, while the therapist joined the delusion.

Beth—Death by Neurodermatitis. This very major rage depression was not only using the psychological mechanism of introjection of the object of her rage, but its intensity was way over the top in her determination to kill him by killing herself. The operational diagnosis was simply, "I'll see you for my son's sake," but (implicit contract) "You will fail to prevent my death." Her extreme onion behavior was an incredible suffering. This is a very extreme case in which the therapist used the not recommended homework of giving a definitely suicidal patient the paradoxical homework to kill herself. The therapist did succeed in overwhelming the resistance, but at tremendous risk.

Marlene and her "Schizophrenogenic" Family. This young woman was an onion who was suffering from a schizo-affective psychosis that seemed to involve the entire family's psychopathology. Consequently, the therapist employed the therapeutic technique of psychojudo with the entire family. As a result, the homework involved the family and was novel enough to disarm the family's mythology. The operational diagnosis was the empty nest syndrome, and the family's implicit contract reflected the family need to keep Marlene the identified patient.

6
ONION/GARLIC PSYCHODYNAMICS

Onion that is Analyzable

Of all the facets of the Biodyne Model, the one that seems to universally resonate is the onion-versus-garlic conceptualization. As we all know, if one has onions for lunch and then returns to the office, the aftertaste will annoy the one who ate the onions for at least two or three hours. On the other hand, if one has garlic for lunch, it does not bother the one who ate it, but it is annoying to all who may have to interact with the garlic eater. Thus, we conceptualize that onion patients are those who suffer, while garlic patients make others suffer. In Biodyne training all over the world, we have not encountered a society where this fails to resonate. In recent extensive training in a series of universities and hospitals in China, the onion–garlic concept, even through a translator, invariably invoked the smiles and laughter of acceptance and instant comprehension.

This conceptualization is not just fanciful, but of profound importance. Psychotherapists are trained to treat all patients in the same manner they treat onion patients. This all but assures failure with Axis II patients who are overwhelming the mental health system, using it for other than therapeutic services, manipulating their way in and out of services at will, and crowding out the needy and psychotic patients who could otherwise benefit. Psychologists, counselors, and social workers are trained to be helpers who are kind and accepting and never "judgmental." This literally cripples their ability to be discerning if this requires them to be critical. They set themselves up to be easy prey for facile sociopaths, borderline personality disorders, and even narcissistic personality disorders, all of whom play on the therapist heartstrings with plausible, engaging manipulations. In our invited evaluations of many mental health centers throughout the United States, we have found their systems bogged down with predominantly a population of Axis II (garlic) patients who are in and out year after year, misusing the system as a band aid, to get out of trouble, or just manipulate the environment to their own ends.

After 40 years of experience in large-scale delivery systems, we can say unequivocally: learning to treat garlic and onion differentially and appropriately will reduce therapeutic failures by 90 percent. Onion patients are capable of treatment inasmuch as they can change through insight and understanding. Garlic patients can only be managed and, through adroit management, they begin to see more successful ways of conducting their lives. Onion patients are capable of empathy, while garlic patients are capable only of being self-centered. This is not judgmental, it is discerning. There was a time not long ago when one would never admit that a loved one or a friend suffered from cancer because it was believed that cancer was not so much a disease as it was punishment for not living a "clean life." Unfortunately, well-meaning political correctness has created the kind of so-called "non-judgmental" atmosphere that has permeated psychotherapy and thus cripples our ability to diagnose in accordance with effectiveness, rather than political correctness.

Whereas DSM or ICD diagnoses are required for insurance reimbursement and other administrative procedures, the diagnostic scheme presented in onion and garlic psychodynamics is designed solely to assist the therapist in fulfilling the clinical mission of relieving the patient of pain, anxiety, and depression in the shortest time possible and with the least intrusive intervention. In contrast to the descriptive symptomatology of the DSMs, this schema differentiates diagnoses according to psychodynamics (cause and effect) and treatment implications for psychotherapy, not medication. The collection of symptoms into arbitrary syndromes may facilitate the prescribing of psychotropic meds inasmuch as it lends itself to the principle that "for every syndrome there is a medication." It does not facilitate psychotherapy, and may even hamper it. An example of this is bereavement, which in the DSMs is a form of depression that requires medication, while in the onion and garlic schema it is a natural healing condition that is subject to facilitation by bereavement counseling, with the further realization that antidepressants will interfere with this natural process by hampering and prolonging it.

The refocused psychotherapist maintains two diagnoses. One is for reimbursement and statistical recording purposes and for interface with a medicalized system when such is appropriate or required. The other is a diagnostic system designed to steer the therapist toward the efficient, effective psychotherapeutic intervention the patient needs.

The onion–garlic chart is presented on the following page (from Cummings & Sayama, 1995). This schema differentiates patients on two dimensions: onion–garlic and analyzable–non-analyzable. These two dimensions result in a four-fold chart in which about 90 percent of the cases can be classified according to 14 diagnostic categories. Although the schizophrenic and bipolar diagnoses are included, absent are the neurological conditions such as Alzheimer's syndrome, Pick's disease, and so forth.

Each diagnostic category can be described in terms of the predominant defense mechanism with which the patient approaches life, and each has an entry point

	Onion (Repression)	Garlic (Repression)
Analyzable	Anxiety Phobias Depression Hysteria/conversion Obsessive-compulsive personality	Addictions Personality styles Personality disorders Impulse neuroses Hypomania Narcissistic personality
		Borderline personality
	Onion (Withdrawal)	**Garlic (Withdrawal)**
Non-analyzable	Schizophrenias controlled by individual suffering	Schizophrenias controlled by attacking the environment Impulse Schizophrenia

FIGURE 1 The Onion–Garlic Chart

that will focus and facilitate treatment. All of the analyzable onion people show a generalized defense mechanism called repression, of which there are different types. Garlic patients always show the mechanism of denial. On the chart, patients below the line show the mechanism of withdrawal from reality because of the existence of a thought disorder.

Defense Mechanisms

Defense mechanisms are defined as unconsciously occurring behaviors that are ongoing and intended to bind anxiety. They are not seen by the patient as defenses, and once they are operative the patient is unaware of their existence. They are conversion, denial, displacement, dissociation, intellectualization, introjection, isolation, perfectionism, projection, projective identification, regression, repression, somatization, splitting, and withdrawal. In the treatment plan, it is always important to know the defense mechanism involved. It is important to note that some conditions may involve more than one defense mechanism.

Analyzable Onion

We begin with the less difficult types of patients, those that are both onion and analyzable. But even with these patients, their treatment can be rendered more effective and efficient using psychojudo, as the rest of this chapter will reveal. All patients, whether onion or garlic, will manifest resistance, and each diagnostic entity will employ its own particular array of psychodynamics. Mastering these brings the practitioner one step closer to fulfilling the patient's bill of rights and becoming a master psychotherapist.

Anxiety Disorders

Dynamics

Anxiety neurosis is distinguished by its lack of defense mechanisms. Without any defense mechanism to transform or defeat the anxiety, the person feels naked anxiety and may shake 24 hours a day.

Entry

All anxiety states on presentation are overwhelming and cry out only for immediate relief. The tension, apprehension, inability to concentrate, and tremulousness add up to the patient feeling that he/she is about to jump out of his/her skin. Under these circumstances, attempts to engage the patient in psychotherapy are futile and even cruel. The necessary entry point is anxiolytic medication to calm this patient sufficiently so that he/she can tolerate psychotherapy. It is how that medication is dispensed that makes the difference in treatment. Unfortunately, in an age when non-psychiatric physicians freely prescribe all kinds of tranquilizers, sedatives, and anxiolytics, too often these patients get medication and nothing else. Psychotherapy to develop relaxation skills and insight into their anxiety is definitely needed.

One word of caution should be interjected here. People with personality disorders, when they are in great difficulty with the police, with authorities, with the boss, or with their spouse, tend to develop situational anxiety not over what they have done or any unconscious material, but because they are now being made uncomfortable or are being deprived of something they want. Lowering the anxiety in someone with a personality disorder who is in trouble will merely make him/her comfortable enough to leave therapy. Instead, raising the anxiety in a personality disorder is the entry point to treatment. The psychotherapist must make the differential diagnosis between a neurotic free-floating anxiety or panic and the discomfort of a personality disorder that has gotten into trouble.

Anxiety states require different treatment approaches in accordance with whether the basic, underlying personality is onion or garlic. Unless the therapist is cognizant of this, psychotherapy may never really get underway. The cases below illustrate this important difference.

Case Illustration: Ethan and Donald

Ethan, age 48, was a civil servant working in a sewage treatment plant. He had been married for 24 years and had two grown children when his spouse informed him that she wanted a divorce. A conscientious, methodical man who had always put his family first, he quickly decompensated into an anxiety state. Change had always been difficult for Ethan, and disruption was impossible. He pleaded with his spouse to tell him what he had done wrong. Factually, she had no complaints other than his being just plain dull. She confessed that married life the past several years had been tolerable only because of her secret extramarital affair. It was only a matter of time when both children were out of the home that she would leave Ethan for the other man. These disclosures were devastating to Ethan, and his anxiety was so great he could neither eat nor sleep.

The anxiety grew worse and soon the patient was not able to work. Before that had happened, his co-workers urged Ethan to see a doctor for a tranquilizer. He refused on religious grounds. Early in the marriage, and in response to his spouse's prodding, Ethan had espoused the Christian Science faith. Some time ago, the spouse drifted away from the church, but Ethan continued to be a devout member. To see a physician was a violation of his religion. Instead, he was seeing a Christian Science practitioner daily with no relief from his symptoms. Finally, he accepted the advice of friends that seeing a psychologist in an attempt to save his marriage was not a violation of the prohibition against receiving medical treatment.

At the time Ethan was first seen by the psychologist, he had been in this state for almost two weeks. He paced about the office constantly, pleading "Please help me." He was seen early in the morning and again in the early afternoon. The first two sessions were spent in listening and trying to help Ethan accept medication. Initially, he staunchly refused, but eventually he agreed to a prescription in exchange for the psychologist's asking the spouse to postpone filing for divorce for two months while Ethan continued in treatment.

With the anxiolytic medication and the postponement of the divorce, the anxiety diminished rapidly and Ethan returned to his usual methodical self. He entered psychotherapy, as would be predicted from his basic onion personality, and although the divorce proceeded to conclusion, Ethan was able to adjust to the loss. Several months after psychotherapy was concluded, he came in for two sessions in which he discussed his new love for a woman in the church who had admired him secretly for several years. It was only after Ethan's divorce that she let her feelings be known.

Donald was 47 when his third wife announced she could no longer forgive his marital infidelity and was filing for divorce. She was 15 years younger than Donald, and the marriage was only six years in duration at the time of the separation. Although Donald had two children with each of his two previous wives, all four children either were or had been living with their respective mothers. His present spouse had been married once before, but only briefly, and she had no children.

When Donald first received the news from his spouse, he threw a temper tantrum of such magnitude that the police were summoned. Finding himself blocked in his aggressive acting out, Donald lapsed into a severe anxiety state that, nonetheless, did not curtail his eloquent and manipulative pleas of contrition. In fact, his wife recanted and agreed to postpone the divorce if he sought treatment for his womanizing.

In the first session, Donald manifested the vulnerability of the narcissistic personality disorder. His anxiety, which was intense, revealed the fear that he would not be able to manage without his spouse. He further exemplified the narcissistic wound that such a personality disorder experiences when he is the one who is rejected. He paced about the office, making no attempt to hide his tremulousness and apprehension. He had tried medicating himself with alcohol, but his spouse put her foot down and threatened to leave immediately if he continued to drink.

Arrangements were made through his primary care physician for Donald to receive a 48-hour supply of anxiolytic medication. This would carry him to the second psychotherapy appointment. His family medical practitioner had experienced Donald's manipulativeness several times, and he was eager to work with the psychologist. Despite these precautions, Donald manipulated a seven-day supply of medication from the nurse in a manner that has never been entirely clear. Feeling much better and with the divorce on hold, Donald missed his second appointment. Within five days, Donald was pleading to return. He was out of medication, having taken more than the prescribed dosage, and his spouse had learned that he had failed to keep his second appointment with the psychologist. She was furious and was threatening once again to reinstate the divorce proceedings.

When Donald returned, he was seen with his spouse and limits were set and agreed upon. The patient would keep semiweekly appointments, and only enough medication would be provided to carry him between appointments. Unbeknownst to the patient, the dosage was purposely kept low so that it cut the edge off the anxiety, but did not completely eliminate it. Any attempts at self-medication would terminate therapy. Both patient and spouse agreed that she would be kept informed, and any breach of the rules would require her to proceed with the divorce.

To the extent that someone with a personality disorder was able, Donald settled into psychotherapy. It was his idea to quit his job as a traveling salesman, stating it provided too many temptations and opportunities for philandering. He obtained a position selling automobiles at a local dealership and was home every night.

His sales talents and manipulative ability served him well on the new job, and the couple prospered as Donald became the star salesperson at the dealership. One might say one needs garlic to do the job of garlic. The medication had been discontinued as unnecessary for some time, but the spouse, with the insistence of the psychologist, kept up the heat. Ironically, Donald's marriage was saved whereas Ethan's marriage could not be saved.

LEGEND

Ethan

Psychological mechanism	None
Diagnosis	Anxiety state
Operational diagnosis	Wife's divorce
Implicit contract	Get my wife back
Personality type	Onion
Homework	Re-examine religious prohibition
Therapeutic techniques	Anxiolytic medication and insight therapy

Donald

Psychological mechanism	None
Diagnosis	Anxiety state
Operational diagnosis	Wife's divorce
Implicit contract	Get my wife back
Personality type	Garlic
Homework	No self-medication
Therapeutic techniques	Partial anxiolytic therapy, turn up the heat

Phobic Disorders

Dynamics

The defense mechanism in phobias is displacement. Thoughts or feelings that are unacceptable are displaced onto an event, or a situation, or a geographical location. The unacceptable thought or feeling reflects an ambivalence the patient has regarding a significant person in his/her life. The ambivalence usually started in childhood with a parent or a sibling. It has continued in adult relationships either with that same person or with a love object.

Three things are needed to develop a phobia:

1. This was the first successful response to trauma as a child.
2. The ambivalent relationship continues now into adulthood in a different form, usually with a spouse or lover. The patient wants to leave that person, but is terrified of doing so.
3. In a situation where one's mind is in neutral gear, the unacceptable thought or feeling pops up and then is displaced.

For instance, the most common phobia in America is freeways. So many hours are spent on the freeway in traffic when things slow down. Imagine being a pre-phobic person sitting in a traffic jam. His/her mind is in neutral gear, and suddenly the thought "I want to leave my spouse" jumps out and is displaced onto the freeway. The traffic is stopped. The person can see the exit a quarter of a mile up, but cannot leave, and feels trapped. The phobia replicates the trapped feeling in the ambivalent relationship. It is a reflection of the feeling of being trapped in life with some significant person. The phobia allows the individual to escape the terror of facing his/her ambivalence. "It isn't my spouse, it's the freeway I'm afraid of."

Next, while in a bank line waiting to cash a check, one's mind is in neutral gear, and the thought flashes again. Now the fear is displaced onto banks, next to supermarkets, then to the post office. It never occurs to him/her that the real fear is leaving his/her spouse, or lover, or parent. With each phobia, the world shrinks and eventually one is a full-fledged agoraphobic who cannot leave the house.

Such debilitating phobias must not be confused with normal phobias. Everyone has a phobia acquired around the age of 3. A successful normal phobia is one that does not restrict your life. A phobia of leopards, for example, is a very successful phobia because the chances of encountering it in the course of daily life is virtually nil. A healthy phobia bounds certain very strong feelings in your childhood. For example:

I (Nick) discovered my phobia on a mission in World War II that required evacuation by submarine. Those who have never been aboard a World War II submarine have no idea how small and confining it is. When submerged, it becomes hot, stuffy, and smelly. I had jumped out of airplanes; it never scared me. Even in combat, I wasn't as terrified. In those three days I was aboard this submarine, I thought I was going to die. On a scale of 10 my anxiety was at 9 or 10 for those three days and nights. I didn't sleep a wink. I had a phobia. In my analysis, I found out where my phobia started. My mother used to punish me by locking me in a closet. It was dark, but I was a pretty clever kid and had stashed away a flashlight and reading material in the closet. She always picked one special closet because it was the darkest. I'd sit there with my flashlight, reading by the hour. She could never understand why I wasn't crying, but apparently it had its impact on me.

When I suddenly realized that they didn't expect us to get back, it replicated the hours I must have spent in that closet thinking how cruel and rejecting my mother is for doing this to me. Now the army suddenly became my mother, and my feelings from childhood crystallized in a phobia about submarines. It has been a successful phobia, because I've lived my life very successfully for the past 50 years without going near a submarine.

Entry

The entry point in treating phobias is to train the patient to retreat before desensitization. It is imperative that the therapist remain cognizant that the entry point for phobias is to remember the concept of retreat before desensitization, with desensitization being the ultimate goal of treating the phobia or multiple phobias that most of our patients come in with. The case of Doris, a severely housebound agoraphobic, is an excellent example of how the retreat/desensitization sequence is continued throughout the treatment and becomes part of the patient's way of life after treatment.

Case Illustration: House Call to Doris

Doris had been housebound for three years, the last six months of this in bed. She complained of 29 distinct phobias, ranging from television newscasts to the dark. She had not been out of bed for six months without the presence of her husband, upon whom she had become totally dependent. She was a full-blown, housebound agoraphobic.

As stated earlier, the entry point for treating phobics is *retreat* before desensitization, with desensitization being the ultimate goal. This approach becomes clear in the first session with Doris, which, of course, had to be a house call because she was housebound. The therapist, on a pre-arranged appointment, was ushered by the husband into the bedroom where Doris greeted him with an ultimatum: "If you are here to get me out of the house, you can leave now." She was assured that not only would the therapist not attempt to get her out of the house, but if she, herself, attempted to do so, he would leave. In fact, he was not even going to help her leave the room, as he was there just to assess the extent of her disability. The patient's response signaled her skepticism as she pulled the bed covers tightly under her chin.

As Doris and the therapist talked about her condition and its duration, the therapist wondered if she could remove her right leg from under the covers. The patient, who was modestly dressed in pajamas, said she could, but as she did so she hastily asserted, "but I'm not getting out of the house." She was again assured that no attempt would be made to even get her out of the room, and she was asked to quickly put her right leg back under the covers. This is known as "retreat before desensitization." After she had relaxed, the therapist wondered if she could do the same with the left leg. When she did, she was asked quickly to put her left leg under the covers. This procedure with one leg and then the other was repeated several times to the point of boredom. The patient was now desensitized to removing each leg from under the covers. The therapist explained his requests on the basis that, after so many months in bed, it was important to determine whether she had developed any muscle weakness.

The therapist then wondered if the patient could remove both legs from under the covers. When she complied, the same procedure of retreat and eventual desensitization to the point of boredom was followed with that behavior. Each time she was reassured that no attempt would be made to get her out of the house and if for some foolish reason she attempted it herself, the therapist would leave.

Following the same tedious sequence, she successfully draped both legs over the bed without touching the floor, and then, with desensitization, touching the floor. There followed a long series of retreats and desensitizations where she was asked to stand on the right side and then on the left side of the bed. Eventually, she was walking around the room, and with each brief foray retreating back to the bed. She was doing all of this for the first time in three years without the presence of her husband. The house call took slightly over one hour.

On the second house call two days later, the same retreat and desensitization was applied to getting her to every room in the house. The retreat was always back to the bedroom. During these retreat-and-desensitization house calls, it was learned how Doris, who had been housebound for two and a half years but was comfortable in her kitchen, lost the ability to sit in that room. She was given some books on phobias that she began to read in the kitchen. She was overcome with extreme panic, retreated to her bed, and there she remained the six months just preceding the first house call. Her multiple phobias included any suggestion of violence, so Doris had been reduced to watching only game shows on television. Her husband faithfully taped these programs so she could rewatch them at a time when no game shows were being broadcast.

Again meticulously following the procedures of retreat and desensitization to the point of boredom, the third house call succeeded in getting Doris out of the house and eventually to the nearest corner on her block. The fourth session was in the therapist's office.

The phobic displacement in Doris's case was her wanting to leave her husband. In every case of phobias, the therapist must look for the ambivalent relationship. It will usually be found with someone on whom the phobic person is dependent: parent, spouse, lover, close friend, employer. This person will usually have some dominant behavior toward the phobic patient, heightening the anger. But even without this, no one can accept dependency without anger toward the person on whom one is dependent. The dependency/hostility is resolved by the phobia, which makes it impossible to leave the relationship. This is why, if one does not add sufficient psychodynamic treatment along with the desensitization, the recovered phobic patient will regress back to the incapacitated phobic state when subsequently the ambivalent relationship is exacerbated by life events.

Doris had begun her adult life as a very attractive fashion model, a career that was interrupted when she married and dutifully followed her husband to his next job assignment. She had always somewhat resented her subordinate role, but this was continuously exacerbated through the years as she was asked to move 22 times, each move representing a career advancement for her husband. And each time she was asked to acquire a new home and decorate it in a manner befitting a rising corporate executive. In all these moves, her husband was so insensitive that he had not an inkling that each was a trauma for his covertly angry, but overtly dutiful, wife. The desire to leave him seemed to double with each of the 22 moves, until finally the desire was so overwhelming as to threaten to break through her own denial. A new phobia would occupy her thoughts and bolster the denial. Doris's phobias grew over the years until finally, in her late fifties, she manifested 29 distinct phobias and eventually was housebound and even bedridden. The tables were reversed, as now her husband was her devoted nurse.

The final outcome in this case was not only the desensitization of Doris's 29 phobias, but the complete sensitization of her husband. Beneath the neglecting behavior of a rising corporate star too busy to attend to his wife's needs was a potentially warm and loving man. With a few counseling sessions for him, he became a very attentive, caring man with whom Doris fell in love all over again.

After the first several individual sessions, Doris was treated in an agoraphobia group program, which included regular field trips and pairing with a "buddy" for practice on her own. The first three or four phobias took longer to disappear than the last two dozen, as there is an accelerated rate in recovery. Doris had expected that her worst fear, that of the dark, which had forced her most of her married life to sleep with a bright light, would be tenacious. She was pleasantly surprised when she noticed inadvertently that it was gone. Her recovery has remained stable because the ambivalent relationship, the significant dynamic in her life, had been resolved.

This case further demonstrates the melding of behavioral and dynamic forms of therapy into one treatment approach. It was important not only to desensitize Doris to her multiple phobias, but also to resolve her ambivalent relationship to her spouse. Desensitization would have proceeded without the latter, but without the resolution of the ambivalence a future relapse would be very likely.

<table>
<tr><td colspan="2">LEGEND</td></tr>
<tr><td>Psychological mechanism</td><td>Displacement, perfectionism</td></tr>
<tr><td>Diagnosis</td><td>Agoraphobia (multiple phobias)</td></tr>
<tr><td>Operational diagnosis</td><td>Housebound and now bedridden</td></tr>
<tr><td>Implicit contract</td><td>I do not want to leave my husband</td></tr>
<tr><td>Personality type</td><td>Onion</td></tr>
<tr><td>Homework</td><td>Desensitization practice</td></tr>
<tr><td>Therapeutic techniques</td><td>House call, desensitization insight, special agoraphobia program</td></tr>
</table>

Depression

After a diagnosis of depression is made, a further differentiation must be made between endogenous depression and reactive depression. Endogenous depression may be influenced by external events, but is primarily determined by biological factors. The depression in bipolar disorder is endogenous; bipolar disorder is an inherited condition, with a higher incidence among people of Eastern European Jewish origins. The disorder is best managed with a combination of medication and psychotherapy. Depression diagnosed as dysthymia or major depression must also be carefully assessed to determine whether it is fundamentally endogenous or reactive.

Reactive depression is exogenous, which means it is determined by events outside the body. Reactive depression may be masked or associated with bereavement, but the fundamental dynamic is anger directed toward the self. Patients suffering depression are onion, but depression can also typify a personality disorder. A depressive character is a garlic person who uses his/her depression as a weapon. Their "woe is me" is all over the place, and they must be treated as garlic.

The withdrawn schizophrenic and the depressed patient can present similarly and will both say, "I feel depressed." To make the differential diagnosis between schizophrenia and depression, ask the patient, "Does your mind feel like you're trying to walk in molasses up to your neck, like you're swimming in molasses. Or are your thoughts racing so fast that you can't keep up with them?" If they say, "It's like molasses," they are depressed. If they say, "My thoughts race so fast I can't keep up with them. I'm speeding," it is schizophrenia.

Dynamics

The defense mechanism in reactive depression is introjection. The goal in therapy, in dynamic terms, is to expel the introject. A reactive depression is intrapunitive. The patient is angry at someone else, but either circumstances or his/her psychological make-up preclude this feeling. For example, he/she may imagine that getting angry at his/her boss or spouse will result in dire consequences, or anger may have been equated with irrational violence in his/her childhood and thus must be avoided at all costs. Thus, the only way this anger can find expression is for the patient to psychologically swallow or introject the other, and then punish the other by causing himself/herself to suffer. We miss the mark if we try to comfort depressive patients by assuaging their guilt or shoring up their self-esteem. The real issue is their anger toward the introjected person.

Entry

The entry point with reactive depression is to expel the introject. There are two ways to do this: one is to become like the person who has been internalized and the other is to articulate to the patient what he/she is saying to himself/herself. The next two cases respectively illustrate these techniques.

Case Illustration: John—Still Angry at His Father

John was a young man who dropped out of college when his father died of a heart attack. He was very depressed. This was not bereavement; this was depression. He was furious with his father. As I began to understand where he was coming from, I found out that this young man and his father had never gotten along. He had just begun working through his father–son struggle when his father dropped dead of a heart attack. This totally aborted the father–son relationship, and the son internalized the hostility and became very depressed. I learned that his sister had been the apple of his father's eye. His sister could do no wrong; he could do no right. When he graduated from high school, he was told that his father was on a business trip. He didn't find out till several years later that his father was playing golf across town. He didn't want to cancel the golf date to go to his son's graduation.

His father never had time for him. His father had time for everything else, especially golf and his sister. This all came out in bits and pieces. He didn't sit down and tell me he hated his father. This was my surmise.

In this case, the operational diagnosis was "I got cheated! My father died before I could fix him, before I could tell him off." The implicit contract was "I'm not going to let my father get away with it!" And the only way this man had of not having let his father get away with it was to internalize his father and then beat up on himself. So, you have to understand that this man is going to resist any efforts to make him nondepressed because this is the way he's beating up his father.

I had the advantage of knowing enough about his father to intervene by acting like the father. I never take phone calls when I see a patient, but I instructed the patient coordinator to call me 15 minutes into the hour. I picked up the phone and said, "Oh, yeah. Yeah, what do you mean you can't play golf tomorrow morning? Of course we're going to play golf tomorrow morning." I stayed on the phone for 10 minutes talking about golf, this at a time when John was absolutely spilling his emotions over the floor, telling me how terrible he is, and how he doesn't care about anybody.

I got up, went over to the window, and started staring out the window. He said, "What are you doing?"

I said, "Oh, I'm wondering if it's ever going to clear up, because I want to play golf later."

He complained, "You didn't hear anything I said."

I responded, "Oh, what were you saying?" Even though I had heard everything, I would systematically make comments that told John I hadn't heard anything he'd said. He would tell me something, and then five minutes later I'd say, "You know, I've always wondered about such and such," and he'd look at me and say, "I just told you about that, five minutes ago."

One day, I constructed a fake chart. I made sure that a woman's name was very prominently on the chart. In the middle of this session, I reached into my desk, pulled out this chart, and started going through it. Finally, after about 10 minutes, he said, "What are you doing?"

I said, "Oh, this woman's a very difficult case. I'm really concerned about her." I was replicating John's relationship to his sister. John increasingly got angrier and angrier and angrier. I did this for several weeks.

If you use this intervention, don't stop it until the anger's all out. John had a great deal of anger. He started saying, "You know, you're the worst psychologist in the world. How in the world did you ever get to where you are? You know, I'm going to call up the ethics committee and report you. You're outrageous." He started accusing me of all the things that he'd accused his father of: "You care more about your women patients than you do about men. You care more about golf than you care about me. You don't give a damn about me."

After several weeks, he was talking about how he wasn't ever going to go back to college and building up in a crescendo to climax. He shouted at the top of his lungs, "Why should I ever go back to college, if I should ever be lucky enough to graduate, you'd play golf instead of coming to my goddamn graduation!"

At which point, I yelled back at him, "I'm not your goddamn father!"

He sank back in his chair and said, "My God, that's what this is all about, isn't it?" Then we started very effective and rapid treatment. John did not quit therapy prematurely despite his anger because, when you connect with the patient's problem, your unconscious connects with your patient's unconscious. Patients know something important is happening. They're building up their rage and won't quit. Let me give you an example.

On my ranch, we've always had collies as sheepdogs. Collies have very long snouts. In the summertime in California when all the grass is dry, there are foxtails. Foxtails look like the top of oats, and they go only one way. If they get up the snout of a dog, they will eventually puncture through the sinus and get into the brain, causing an infection that will kill the dog. I noticed one of our collies must have had a foxtail because I saw some bleeding. She sat for almost an hour while, with my wife's tweezers from a cosmetic kit, I reached way up the snout and, piece by piece, pulled out this foxtail. It was very difficult because it won't go backward. This dog was whimpering with pain, but she never once tried to leave. She knew I was doing something healing for her. And it occurred to me while I was doing this, "If our dogs know, our patients must know." Our patients surely know when we're doing something for our egos. They also know when we're doing it for them. After the fact, John was able to comfortably verbalize how the therapist emulating his father was what put him in touch with the anger he had been determined to deny.

LEGEND

Psychological mechanism	Introjection
Diagnosis	Reactive depression
Operational diagnosis	My father died before I could get even
Implicit contract	Help me fix my father without continuing to hurt me
Personality type	Onion
Homework	Continue to hate yourself
Therapeutic technique	Expel introject by mobilization of anger in the interest of health

In the case of Lenore, rather than play the role of the introject, the therapist verbalized what the patient was saying to herself. By so doing, the therapist is already beginning somewhat to expel the introject by externalizing the internalized thoughts. It is almost an unconscious ritual with some reactive depressives to counteract any attempt to break through the resistance by repeating the internalized guilt thoughts silently and often without consciousness. By siding with the patient's guilt/punishment resistance, the therapist can have a profound effect where direct attempts at guilt reduction fail.

Case Illustration: Lenore—Guilty as Charged

Lenore was a 52-year-old woman who 15 years ago left her husband. He did everything to get her back, including threatening suicide. She refused to take him back. Three months after the separation, he killed himself with a bullet to the head. Almost immediately thereafter, Lenore began experiencing severe, intractable headaches. One might speculate that, had her husband shot himself through the heart, she might well have begun experiencing "heart trouble" instead of headaches. In the 15 years afterward, she visited every physician in her community many times and received every evaluation and pain reliever known to modern medicine; however, the headaches not only persisted but grew worse. She also saw every psychologist and psychiatrist in her community, as well as visiting two chronic pain centers. And when psychotherapy did not bring relief, she received several courses of biofeedback training.

Lenore was a very gentle woman whom everyone liked intensely. All those who attempted to help her were too kind. Repeatedly, she was told that her husband's suicide was not her fault. For 15 years, Lenore would nod in agreement, but it was apparent that she was not accepting the good-intentioned attempts to help her. Her headaches became so severe that she could not work, and she was on total disability. In fact, the pain was of such intensity 24 hours a day that Lenore did little else but several times a day visit physicians and psychotherapists. Now that she was on welfare, the state was paying for her ineffective treatments.

Finally, after 15 years, Lenore came to our center because this was a new service available for the first time in her community. She was desperate to get relief and her therapist, as had all of the therapists before him, misinterpreted her desperation for motivation to get well. He treated her in the same kind way, repeating that her husband's death was not her fault. She continued to get worse, and her psychologist came to the senior author for a consultation. The advice, after hearing the facts in the case, was that she should be told that she was guilty of murder and that her sentence was to suffer headaches for the rest of her life.

This intervention was chosen because Lenore, at least on an unconscious level, was saying this to herself. It is important to externalize the life sentence. In analytic terminology, its purpose was to expel the introject. The psychologist, a very kind man, found this intervention to be repugnant. But he was asked whether he wanted to help the patient or whether he just wanted to be nice. He agreed to the intervention, but he had to write it down, and he role played it with another staff member for the several days before Lenore's next appointment.

The psychologist went ahead with the intervention, and Lenore lapsed into silence. It was stated to her several times. The following week she returned for her appointment in a state of subdued anger. She protested that the therapist did not understand the sufficient reasons for leaving her husband, and she criticized her husband for the first time since his death. She told the therapist that her husband had ongoing affairs and brought these women into her own marital bed. When she protested, he beat her unmercifully. It was noted that her headaches had subsided in intensity, and she had two days when she was actually symptom free. The psychologist made a grievous error. He returned to his usual kind demeanor and pointed out that if anyone had the right to leave her husband, she did. Lenore welcomed the statement, but when she returned the following week her headaches were worse than ever.

Now, in his own desperation, the psychologist telephoned for another consultation. It was pointed out that he had accepted prematurely the patient's protests that her husband was no good; at the next session, he should state that he had thought it over and she was still guilty of murder. However, since there were extenuating circumstances as evidenced by her husband's infidelity and beatings, she was guilty of only second-degree murder. She did not need to have the headaches for life. The question now was whether she should have them for 5 or 10 more years.

This time, the psychologist stuck with the strategy, and over several weeks Lenore persisted in relating a long litany of abuses and saying that she had no alternative but to leave him, all the while becoming increasingly and overtly angry at the therapist for insisting on the sentence of second-degree murder. Week after week, Lenore's headaches dramatically decreased, and after she was totally free of them for several weeks she decided to discontinue the appointments because the therapist simply did not understand. But this psychologist had succeeded where all other therapists had failed. This is another reason why brief therapy is hard work. It is the long-term patient who heaps gratitude and gifts on us. In brief therapy, the reward often is only in the patient's recovery.

LEGEND	
Psychological mechanism	Introjection, denial (rage)
Diagnosis	Reactive depression
Operational diagnosis	Welfare required visit to new counseling center
Implicit contract	I am guilty and will not be helped
Personality type	Onion with interspersed garlic
Homework	Determine sentence for murder
Therapeutic techniques	Expel introject, mobilization of rage in the interest of health

The case of John illustrates how the introject is expelled through anger mobilized against the therapist in the transference. The therapist becomes the person who has been internalized and thus enables the patient to externalize the hostility turned inward. In the case of Lenore, the therapist articulated what the patient was saying to herself unconsciously. The first way was to become the introject. Either way, the internalization is externalized where the patient can start directing anger outward at the therapist. Despite eliciting psychic blood, the patient hangs in there because he/she knows intuitively there's something real going on. When this anger has been purged, the process itself can be discussed and resolved.

These interventions must be done within the context of the therapist's own style. Even when assuming the patient's context, the therapist must formulate and deliver the intervention in a manner befitting his/her own style.

Chronic Depression

Sometimes the loss and rage can occur so early in life that they become immutable. These are people who go through life depressed. They present as low-energy people and may be misdiagnosed as schizoid because they have impaired social relationships. They have a lifestyle of depression, but come in when something happens in their life to make the depression worse. When they get over that, they go back to being their old depressive selves. Very often, the therapist does not realize that such a person now has gotten the maximum benefit. This person is never going to change; their lack of energy has become a way of life. These people often cope with their depression with drugs or alcohol. Some become daredevils because cheating death is the only way they can feel alive.

A woman may become this kind of person as a result of having been sexually molested by her father at an early age. A man cannot sexually molest his daughter and still be her father. That little girl's father dies at that moment. So, if this molestation happened when this girl was 5, 6, 7, 8, she may suffer from anhedonic, nonclinical depression throughout her life. Molestation by another adult is traumatic enough, but molestation by one's father is devastating. To protect themselves from overwhelming feelings, these women have reduced their energy so stimuli cannot penetrate them, and they hibernate through life.

Cognitive-behavioral approaches are appropriate with these people, but the therapeutic goals are limited. In Carmel, there is a tree on Cypress Point that is the most photographed tree in the world. It is a gnarled, wind-blown, wave-swept cypress growing on a rock protruding into the ocean. No tree surgeon on earth could ever straighten that tree out. These chronic depressives are like that tree. They cannot be straightened out, but that tree is beautiful, and they need to realize the beauty of their own struggle against the trying circumstances of their lives.

There are instances of chronic depression happening in adulthood, but these are treatable. They may occur when children die before parents. Nature has no provision for the death of a child before the parent. It may also occur when the person has suffered severe trauma, as in the case below. Many survivors of the Holocaust manifest this almost intractable form of chronic depression.

Case Illustration: Rachel, the Chicken Lady

There existed in San Francisco in the 1950s and 1960s a condition affectionately labeled by the psychotherapists involved as the "Petaluma Syndrome." Petaluma is a city about 50 miles north of San Francisco that, at that time, was the chicken farm center of California. Oddly enough, a sizeable number of Holocaust survivors had taken their reparations money and bought chicken farms. This behavior was paradoxical for a group of Polish Jews who had never before seen an unplucked chicken. Once a week, the women survivors boarded a chartered bus to San Francisco where each saw her respective therapist. Then they had lunch together and did a bit of shopping. Thereafter, they reboarded the bus back to Petaluma, only to repeat the trip the following week and each week thereafter. A group of therapists who were individually seeing these women considered it their obligation to render supportive therapy to these victims of the Holocaust. This had been going on for about a decade when the senior author was asked by a leader in the San Francisco Jewish community to replace a psychiatrist who had died.

Rachel came to her new psychologist after 10 years with her now deceased psychiatrist. She questioned his non-Jewish status, but felt satisfied when she learned her new therapist had fought in World War II and had a hand in liberating the Buchenwald concentration camp. The psychiatrist continued the supportive therapy he was told was appropriate, although this kind of treatment was not natural to him. Rachel came in week after week with the same litany. She regularly whined, "Oh, the chickens have caught cold and are not laying enough eggs. Oh, the price of feed has gone up and I'm losing money. And Sammy don't love me no more." This kvetch was recited as if it were a script. The psychologist was properly supportive but felt nothing rewarding was taking place. After all, this survivor had earned the right to complain.

Within six months, the psychologist begged the community leader who had assigned him the case to be excused. The result was the heaping upon him of centuries of Judeo-Christian guilt, under which the psychologist buckled and agreed to continue to be therapeutically supportive of Rachel. But he could not get rid of the nagging feeling he should do more for her. Within another two months, the constantly repeated phrase, "And Sammy don't love me no more," came crashing on him.

In response to this insight, he asked Rachel a number of questions and learned that Rachel and Sam were married in September, 1939 and were on their honeymoon in Poland when Hitler's forces invaded the country. They fled for the Soviet border, having been separated when volunteers interceded to help. Sam went with a group of men, got to the Soviet Union, then to Sweden, and finally to the United States. Rachel fled with a group of women and was captured. She spent the next five years in a Nazi concentration camp. At the end of the war, Sam went to Poland and searched until he found the emaciated survivor who was his wife. This is a heart-rending story, and one that would have to be put aside if Rachel were to be helped to get on with her life.

The psychologist asked gently, "Rachel, have you ever resented that Sammy escaped while you spent five years in hell?" The flash in her eyes revealed her hidden feelings. The therapist was then emboldened to ask abruptly, "Rachel, is Petaluma Sammy's concentration camp?" The patient sat quietly for about two minutes and then she smiled, "You're pretty smart for a guy."

The therapist then wondered out loud why the 10 years she had the chicken ranch did not punish Sammy enough to compensate for the five years she was in the concentration camp. She replied, "Ah, but how many years of Rachel are necessary to make one year of the Gestapo?" The therapist immediately recognized this as Rachel's implicit contract, and a treatment plan complete with homework was constructed accordingly. He advised Rachel that her job would be to ascertain how many more years Sammy must remain incarcerated on the Petaluma chicken farm.

Rachel was beside herself with fury. Week after week, she would refuse to do her homework. The therapist remained unrelenting in the demand she do the homework. She would yell and call him, *Goyishe Kopf*, and he would yell back *Yiddishe Kopf*. She accused him of being insensitive to the plight of the Jews. He accused her of being ungrateful since he had helped liberate the Jews. This was tough love, indeed.

Overlooked in embarking on supportive therapy with this chronically depressed Holocaust survivor is that, as in all depression, the appropriate treatment is to help the patient expel the introject (Sammy) and externalize the tremendous hostility she harbors. In her depression, she was hurting herself more than her husband, who had adjusted fairly well to the unwelcome role of chicken farmer.

Finally, Rachel began to make estimates of how long Sammy should be incarcerated. Her first estimate of three years of Rachel for every year of the Gestapo was promptly rejected by the therapist who extolled that Rachel was really a cream puff and proffered a ratio of five to one. This would mean 15 more years in Petaluma. Within a couple of weeks, Rachel began arguing that Sammy had suffered enough. She feared she might be almost as bad as the Nazis. The therapist exploded! After all, he had fought the Nazis, and a ratio of two to one was unacceptable. Rachel said little in the next four sessions. She seemed preoccupied but not sullen. Then she came in and said, "To a housewarming you should be coming."

Rachel had sold the chicken farm and prevailed upon her fellow survivors to do the same. And they all had bought condominiums in the same upscale building in San Francisco. The psychologist eagerly attended the housewarming, where he met all the "girls," as Rachel called her fellow survivors. It was apparent that Rachel was the group's leader, both in the Nazi camp and in Petaluma. Her fellow survivors had followed her into chicken farming. Then the psychologist was surprised to learn that he was the only guest. He had been invited so Rachel's friends could meet him. The "girls" all affectionately embraced him. "Two concentration camps you liberated, one in Poland and one in Petaluma."

The deep-rooted introject had, indeed, finally been expelled. Although her hate for her Gestapo captors still and always will remain partially introjected, remanding her to the scars of a lifelong depression, at least Rachel was finally freed to rebuild her life rather than to continue the incarceration. On a final note, this case demonstrates that, in spite of all the hostility that is expressed toward the therapist when the anger is being externalized, there is an unconscious recognition that some very real and important healing is going on. Depressives do not quit therapy at such times.

LEGEND

Psychological mechanism	Introjection and denial
Diagnosis	Chronic rage, depression, post-traumatic stress syndrome
Operational diagnosis	My previous therapist died
Implicit contract	Don't tamper with my solution
Personality type	Onion and garlic mixed
Homework	Determine husband's sentence
Therapeutic techniques	Mobilization of rage, paradoxical intention

Anniversary Depression

Both mourning and depression can be postponed to a day of reckoning. Sometimes, this can be for many years. Typical would be the man who never mourned his father's fatal heart attack, but when he reaches the age his father was at his death, the man becomes convinced of an impending heart attack. Or, a woman who never resolved her feelings toward her deceased mother may experience an anniversary depression every year on the date her mother died. Many forms exist, and although they are treated as chronic depression, additionally some detective work may be involved.

In 90 percent of cases in which the depression is triggered by the anniversary of the death of a parent, it is the death of the same-sex parent that elicits conflicted feelings. In most American families, fathers are patsies for their daughters, mothers are patsies for their sons, and the frustrating parent is the parent of the same sex. To resolve this conflict, the child identifies primarily with the frustrating parent. Thus, in cases where the process of bereavement has gone awry, an anniversary depression can be triggered by the guilt the child feels over his/her hostility toward the parent he/she has identified with. The patient postpones a reactive depression and then, a number of years later on, experiences the depression. Thus, Ernest Hemingway put a gun to his head and killed himself at the exact age that Hemingway's father had put a gun to his head and killed himself. Other significant losses can also serve as the basis for an anniversary depression. Whatever the etiology, the treatment is simple: connect the present situation to the postponed situation. Generally, people who can postpone something for long periods are resilient and respond well. Below are two cases of anniversary depression. The first of these on the "due date" resulted in physical crippling; the second was about to cause death.

Case Illustration: Cheryl and the Witch's Curse

At the age of 50, Cheryl came down with gnarled, crippling arthritis within 60 days. Her physician who had referred her was absolutely astounded by the speed with which such severe crippling arthritis had gnarled her extremities. He was baffled, but he didn't refer her for her arthritis; he sent her because she was such a difficult, demanding, impossible woman.

As I worked with her, I realized that Cheryl had an anniversary depression. She hated her mother. They had fought incessantly. When her mother was dying, Cheryl said to her mother, "I'm glad you're going, you witch." Whereupon, her mother said, "I'm going to damn you. At 50 years old you're going to have crippling arthritis and you're going to become a witch just like me." Cheryl forgot the whole blasted conversation. When she reached 50, Cheryl developed crippling arthritis just like her mother, who had always used this condition as an excuse to not be a mother and to not be there for her daughter. At 50, Cheryl not only got the fastest crippling arthritis her PCP had ever seen, she became a witch like her mother. This woman was awful!

Cheryl was assigned to go up to Boise where her mother was buried and redo the final conversation. Cheryl resisted and resisted, but I told her that it was a condition of treatment. I wasn't going to fool around with her any more. She had to go to Boise or end therapy. Finally, she decided to go up, mainly to please me.

When she came back, she told the following story. She flew in and landed about 11:00 a.m., rented a car at the airport, drove out to the cemetery, went to the office, and found the plot. She had a 3:30 p.m. flight back to San Francisco. She intended to stay for a few minutes at the cemetery. As she approached her mother's gravestone, she noticed that it was the only gravestone that the pigeons had left droppings on, and she started laughing. She said, "Even the pigeons don't like my mother." She sat down in front of the mother's grave and started talking. She said, "I kept talking and talking, and when I came to again, it was dark. It had rained. My clothes were soaking wet. I don't remember when it rained. I don't remember how long I was there. I got back to the car, looked at my watch, and it was after 9:00 at night. I told my mother everything I had wanted to say in my entire life." And that's where her arthritis was reversed.

The PCP called up and said, "I can't believe it. I never saw anything like that come and go so fast in my life."

It had been an anniversary depression. Her mother had damned her from her deathbed. Cheryl had forgotten the incident, but it wasn't enough to just connect the arthritis with the damnation. The lifelong history of conflict with her mother had to be resolved, and it finally was by the graveside in Boise.

LEGEND

Psychological mechanism	Introjection, displacement (somatization)
Diagnosis	Anniversary (delayed) depression
Operational diagnosis	Payment is now due
Implicit contract	Help me escape payment
Personality type	Onion
Homework	Talk to mother's grave
Therapeutic techniques	Expel the introject, mobilization of rage

---

Case Illustration: Dan's Date with Death

Dan was 21 when he came for death and dying counseling. He was suffering from lymphoma and had come to this distant city to be treated at University Hospital by one of the nation's leading experts. When first seen, he had lost all of his hair from radiation and chemotherapy. He did not respond favorably to treatment and he had been told to get his affairs in order.

The patient had moved into an apartment built on a hill, as is common in San Francisco. In the basement was an unfinished room, which the landlord planned to have excavated and made into a storeroom. Dan decided to help. Every morning on his way out, he would fill a small paper bag full of dirt and then deposit it in the nearest public trash can. The patient was practicing a kind of magical behavior typical of those who know they are dying. At the rate of one paper bag a day, the large mound of dirt guaranteed that Dan would live a long life. The denial, of course, is that he cannot die until the task is completed.

Death and dying counseling was abruptly interrupted when something Dan said alerted the therapist. Almost as an aside, Dan tossed out the statement, "I feel as if I've made a pact with the Devil." He was unable to account for this statement and, under questioning, dismissed it as his pessimism in the face of death.

Dan had lost both parents at age 8 in a tragic freeway auto disaster. Dan and his 3-year-old sister were staying with grandparents, where the family gathered upon hearing the tragic news. He was awakened in the middle of the night by the crying and wailing of the family members. One by one, his four grandparents came to Dan's bedside and expressed the wish that God had taken them instead of his parents. Each stated, "I've had most of my life. Their death, on the other hand, leaves two orphans." This is all Dan remembers.

There followed a series of intense questions in which the therapist unrelentingly insisted that the patient recall whatever it was he was hiding. Dan reacted with increased violent behavior, often writhing on the floor, screaming there was nothing more. This behavior only convinced the psychologist there had to be more. Eventually, in a particularly intense session during which Dan kicked a chair across the room, he remembered.

On each of the occasions when his grandparents expressed a wish that they had been taken instead of Dan's parents, the patient recalled with much emotion how he thought to himself that he was glad he was not taken. He also recalled thinking that his parents, whom Dan now recalled as quite cold and rejecting, really deserved to die. Then one night, either in a nightmare or in a childhood hallucination, he was awakened by the Devil who came to claim the life of this ungrateful son. Dan recalled crying and pleading with the Devil, "I'm only a little kid. Let me live until I'm 21 and I'll go willingly." The Devil agreed to what seemed a lifetime of reprieve to an 8-year-old. But shortly after his 21st birthday, Dan was diagnosed as suffering from lymphatic cancer. The day of reckoning had arrived.

On learning of these powerful events, the therapist made no promises, but stated that the therapy could well question a contract to die made by a distraught child. The next several months were spent in examining his hostility toward his parents. Dan's mother was a self-centered woman. He could be doing his homework, and when she drove up, she would honk. He would have to come out to open the garage door so she wouldn't have to get out of the car and open the door herself. There was incident after incident like this in which nobody else's time mattered but hers. His father was "out to lunch" and never around either physically or psychologically.

Often, as Dan externalized his anger, the therapist was the recipient of stormy, hostile emotions. At other times, to facilitate expelling of the introjects, the therapist mimicked what he learned had been typical parental behaviors. The stormier the therapy sessions, the stronger Dan became physically. Eventually, the patient, who had been declared terminal, was found by his physicians to be in remission.

His oncologist was skeptical and insisted Dan see him weekly. Dan resisted, but the therapist pointed out that the skeptical oncologist was his best friend: "If there is even one cancer cell in your body, he will find it." Finally, it became obvious to his oncologist that the patient was in full remission. Oncological treatment was terminated. Therapy was also interrupted, with the admonition that if he ever felt a swollen node to call immediately for an appointment.

Dan called three years later. He had since been married and had a daughter. His wife was in the process of divorcing him, and in his distraught state Dan noticed a swollen node. He came in for more therapy, during which time he was helped to separate from his wife and to reconcile himself to the visiting privileges he would have with his daughter. His cancer did not recur.

Over two decades passed before he was seen again. He had read a profile of his therapist in the newspaper and became aware for the first time of the psychologist's advanced age. He came in saying, "I hope you live many more years. But I did not have the opportunity to say goodbye to my father, and I want to make certain I say goodbye to you." He then went on to tell the psychologist about his successful second marriage, his children by that union, and the fact that his first daughter had elected to live with them instead of with her mother. He then went on to tell of his successful and innovative career. He confided that he had followed from afar his therapist's lifelong innovations and he confessed how proud he, himself, was to have innovated in a totally different occupation. It was striking that Dan did not seem to be talking to his therapist, but to his father.

LEGEND

Psychological mechanism	Introjection
Diagnosis	Anniversary (delayed) depression
Operational diagnosis	Help me die peacefully
Implicit contract	You can't change the inevitable
Personality type	Onion
Homework	Renegotiate death contract
Therapeutic techniques	Mobilization of rage, expel the introject

---

Anniversary depressions are so pervasive that on the "due date" the person's life is at stake. The abreaction that Cheryl experienced at the gravesite and Dan upon recalling his pact with the Devil are important, but they mark the beginnings of therapy. There must follow often stormy and always painful sessions in which the aborted relationship with all its postponed hate is understood and resolved. But without the patient's often sudden realization of the anniversary reaction, therapy remains blind, undirected, and usually unsuccessful. The ultimate entry point is the acceptance of the postponed day of reckoning.

Hysteria and Conversion Neurosis

Dynamics

The main defense mechanism in hysteria is pure repression. The hysteric operates on the level of a 3-year-old child caught taking a cookie when told not to. The child can innocently say, "Mommy, I didn't take the cookie. My hand did it." Hysterical symptoms can appear as childish and ludicrous, but hysterics believe their symptoms and are not conning you. The therapist must resist the temptation to even hint at an, "Oh, come on now!" reaction. To do so is to drive the patient away. The failure to keep sexual conflict repressed, along with the fear of intimacy, is at the roots of the anxiety experienced by the hysteric. The failure of heretofore successful repression has been triggered by recent life experiences or circumstances.

In hysteria with a conversion reaction, the primary mechanism of repression is complicated by the displacement of anxiety or hostility onto a body organ. Well-educated people, especially in the health field, can replicate just about any neurological disease. Doctors and nurses can do it to a fine detail because they know the neuromatomy of the body. Unsophisticated people can get anesthesias that are impossible because the configuration of the nerve paths do not follow the commonsensical view.

Entry

The entry point in psychotherapy with hysterics is to reinstate the repression and to reframe the problem as not one of intimacy or sexuality, thus allowing the hysteric to save face. Strong-arming the resistance by forcing the hysteric to confront the content of his/her repression will lead to greater resistance and perhaps increased symptoms as the hysteric fights to preserve his/her self-image.

The case of Melody illustrates to what extent the therapist must go to avoid implying that the problem might be sexual. This involves joining the resistance. When equilibrium is established, the patient signals this as Melody did, indicating to the therapist she was ready for the next step.

Case Illustration: Melody, the Honeymooner

Melody was referred by the emergency room staff following a thorough neurological workup, the results of which were negative. She had gone to the emergency room with her husband with the complaint that she had awakened in the middle of the night to discover she was suddenly unable to read. After several hours of exploration, the emergency room staff's provisional diagnosis was hysteria. Wife and husband arrived at the psychologist's office as a couple, expecting to be seen together.

When an appointment is made for an individual, if that person arrives as a couple or a family, it is important to interview that person first. Otherwise, the therapist is committing prematurely and without foundation to couples therapy or family therapy. It is always imperative to ascertain the operational diagnosis and the implicit contract before agreeing to a treatment plan. The therapist advised Melody's husband that he wanted to meet with the wife first. Should it be indicated, he might very well wish to meet with the husband later. He offered no resistance.

Once in the office, Melody gave the following story. They arrived at their honeymoon destination four days ago very late at night and much too exhausted to consummate the marriage, so they decided to wait until morning. At 2:00 a.m., she awakened momentarily, looked at the hotel information card on the bedside table, and panicked when she realized she could not read it.

In fear, she jumped from the bed and attempted to read other materials to no avail. She then awakened her husband, who tried all kinds of reading material with her, but again with no success. She simply and inexplicably was unable to read a single word.

The therapist handed her a clipboard with a pad on it and asked her to write her name, address, telephone number, and date of birth. She complied, but when asked if she could read what she had written, she said, "No." The therapist interjected, "This is very interesting. You can write but you cannot read." She agreed this was, indeed, interesting.

One is tempted to convey a feeling, "Oh, come on, you don't really believe this. You must be pulling my leg." The other temptation is to make the obvious connection between her symptoms and her fear of sex. Even though the baffling symptom had effectively prevented any kind of sex, to point this out would be to strong-arm the resistance. She was complimented on her very understanding husband, who had the sensitivity not to attempt to make love to her when she was so distraught. She beamed as she began the bonding process with the therapist.

The subject of sex was avoided as the therapist purposely talked with her about her wedding, saying, "You must have planned it for months." She said, "I planned it for over a year." There were 350 guests invited for a sit-down dinner at this large and expensive wedding. She agreed with the psychologist that this was a wonderful but exhausting experience.

Near the end of the session, the therapist shared his suspicion that she could be suffering from some kind of exhaustion syndrome. He also confided that he did not fully understand this, but until they could together get to the bottom of this exhaustion syndrome, he wanted her not to exacerbate the exhaustion. He called in the husband and enlisted his cooperation in helping Melody refrain from three things. The first request was that she discontinue her daily habit of jogging as this was potentially too tiring under her present condition. She was also to refrain from alcohol, inasmuch as that beverage can complicate many neurological problems. And, finally, she was to refrain from sex. The latter was the critical feature; the first two were thrown in to make certain the patient did not think the psychologist was anticipating a sexual problem.

The husband, who was virtually as hysterical as his wife, practically saluted the therapist in his eagerness to be of help. The couple left determined to abide by the prescribed regimen.

When they returned the following week, they assured the psychologist that they had followed the prescription to the letter. The therapist complimented both of them and added that Melody was fortunate to have such an understanding husband.

During the second session, the diagnosis of hysteria was confirmed along with both the operational diagnosis and the implicit contract. Melody had a limit to the intimacy she could tolerate. She could engage in sex before they were married because there was not the commitment of marriage. Once she was married, the commitment was so unconsciously overwhelming that something had to give. So it was either sex without marriage or marriage without sex. To have both together constituted the breaking point of too much intimacy. Despite the so-called sexual revolution where premarital sex is usual, this is far more prevalent a syndrome than many therapists appreciate. Melody was able to present all of this in the characteristic fashion of hysterics who can talk about sex as long as the therapist does not.

At the end of the second session, the therapist confessed, "You know, we still haven't gotten to the bottom of this. So again next week no jogging, no alcohol, and no sex." Once again, the eager husband's cooperation was solicited, and they left with Melody still unable to read. But the operational diagnosis was clearly the inability to have sex, which was created by the honeymoon. The implicit contract was that the therapist would help her avoid sex. To not strong-arm the resistance required that the therapist help her do just that. And it had to be presented in a plausible, face-saving manner.

On the third session, Melody reported there were two periods, one for about 15 minutes and another for only 10 minutes, during which she could read. The therapist admonished that, although this was encouraging, the prescribed regimen should be maintained. Too many therapists make the mistake of prematurely accelerating a treatment plan, only to find the patient has regressed as a result. She was not yet ready to confront her real problem.

By the fourth session, Melody's reading ability had amazingly and suddenly returned. The abandonment of the symptom is the sign to the therapist that the patient is now ready, ever so gently, to begin talking about the real problem. She was now far enough removed from the terror of the wedding and she was with a therapist/parent figure she trusted, so she could talk about it. But the therapist steered her to the subject of intimacy and postponed the terror of sex until a later session.

In not strong-arming the resistance and by offering a rationalization of exhaustion, therapy was effective. Brief therapy most emphatically does not mean using a battering ram. This woman improved very rapidly and by the sixth and seventh sessions she was talking openly about the terror of intimacy in her original family.

In summary, the entry point with hysteria is to help reinstate the failed repression. As in this case, the symptom was reframed so as to allow her to save face and to bond with the therapist. Ultimately, the therapy allowed her to regroup and adjust the new level of intimacy the marriage entailed. But it must be pointed out that her overall identity was still that of a hysteric, albeit a more successful one.

LEGEND

Psychological mechanism	Repression, displacement (conversion)
Diagnosis	Conversion hysteria
Operational diagnosis	New marriage
Implicit contract	Help me avoid sex and deny fear of sex
Personality type	Onion
Homework	No jogging, alcohol, or sex
Therapeutic technique.	Join the resistance (symptom)

It is quite common in practice today to be confronted by an angry, resistive person with conversion hysteria whose exasperated physician has told her, "It's all in your head; go see a shrink." This usually occurs after many months in which the physician has exhausted all laboratory and other procedures looking for a physical explanation of the symptom. The therapist now has the added problem of counteracting the damage done by the physician, because it is still important at the entry point to join the patient's resistance. It is not fruitful in this kind of situation to join the patient in scapegoating the well-meaning, but exasperated, physician. The therapist needs to exercise special skills and inventiveness to repair the therapeutic damage, as in the case of Nancy.

Case Illustration: Nancy's Paralysis

When a patient is told by a physician that her condition is all in her head and she should see a psychologist, she naturally comes in feeling angry, betrayed, and defensive. Such was the case with Nancy, a 27-year-old woman married for two years. She was in a wheelchair, but her neurologist had told her in exasperation that the "paralysis" of her legs did not fit any neurological condition. She interpreted this as meaning she must be crazy. In this kind of case, it is particularly important not to strong-arm the resistance and to give the patient the opportunity to save face.

The husband brought his wife in her wheelchair and did not protest when the psychologist indicated he wished to see Nancy alone. Inasmuch as an individual session was scheduled, to see the patient as a couple would prematurely commit to a treatment modality. As it developed, Nancy would have been unable to say much of what she said with her husband present.

Nancy's entire posturing suggested she did not wish to see the psychologist, but was complying with the physician's referral. Much later, it was elicited that one implicit contract was that she would return to the physician with the complaint that psychology was not helpful. She would by that time also have found a physician who had established the physical cause of her paralysis. Before bonding could occur, this patient's hurt would have to be overcome.

Early in the session, the therapist joined her in a lament that neurology was still a relatively inexact science. She agreed to enter counseling to help her adjust to her paralysis. Hastily, as if to anticipate any questions, she insisted that her marriage was a very happy one. She and her husband loved each other, and he was very sympathetic and patient. But she worried that her inability to have sex because of this paralysis might eventually pose a threat to the marriage. For these issues, she agreed counseling could be helpful.

Near the end of the first session, the therapist set the stage for saving face. But first it was important to go with the resistance and emphasize that, even though a lack of sex could pose a problem in their marriage, it was important to her physical well-being that she for the time being dismiss all such considerations from her mind. Then he launched into an elaborate and seemingly unrelated explanation that baffling neurological conditions can have unexpected remissions. The psychologist used multiple sclerosis as an example of a condition in which the paralysis can come and go inexplicably. The foundation was laid without further comment, while she agreed she would not only not attempt sex, but also not worry about the lack of it.

At the second session, she began to talk about the cramping in her legs during sexual intercourse and several weeks before the onset of the paralysis. She wondered if these cramps might be the precursors to her paralysis. The psychologist agreed that these could well have been prodromal signs and complimented her on her astute analysis. She ended the session with confirming that counseling was, indeed, helpful and she felt much better emotionally after each session.

At the third session, she reported that she had been able to get out of the wheelchair as much as a half hour at a time on three different days during the preceding week. On each instance, she returned to the wheelchair when she experienced the beginnings of cramps in her leg. She thanked the therapist for telling her about this prodromal sign, seemingly forgetting that the idea was first hers. The psychologist expressed pleasure at her improvement, but strongly cautioned her against attempting too much too soon. Even if she felt up to it, she should limit her time out of the wheelchair. He further reminded her of her promise to refrain from sexual activity, pointing out that this would be far too strenuous. She reiterated her agreement.

In the fifth session, she came without the wheelchair, saying she had not needed it for the past six days. Occasionally, she would experience slight cramping of her legs and she would sit down until it subsided. She was grateful to the psychologist for her improvement, and attributed it to therapy's helping her relax enough to permit the spontaneous remission. At the psychologist's insistence, she agreed to continue abstinence from sex until the baffling neurological condition was better understood.

During the next several sessions, the patient was able to face the feelings that had accompanied the initial cramps, which had first manifested themselves during sexual intercourse. She admitted that she did not enjoy sex, but felt guilty and hid this feeling from her husband. He enjoyed sex tremendously, and soon her guilt feelings turned to resentment toward her husband and his pleasure. She eventually recalled that she began to experience the fantasy during the sex act that she would raise her leg abruptly and kick her husband in the scrotum. It was not long before the fantasy advanced to a strong temptation, which disappeared from consciousness when the cramps appeared. The cramps were a struggle to keep from kicking her husband in the groin and the paralysis was the resolution of that conflict. Not only was she unable to kick her husband, but the paralysis put an end to their sexual life. Her husband was too concerned and sympathetic to even entertain the thought of sex.

With the disclosures, the patient was able to address her fear of intimacy and her fear of letting go in the sex act. Treatment was now fully underway. Her homework, which up to this time had been to refrain from sex, now became a series of small excursions into trusting herself and her partner. As she allowed sexual pleasure to happen, she also permitted herself the luxury of a letter to her neurologist in which she pointed out that his bedside manner had all the professionalism of a runaway bus. This case illustrates how, by abandoning the presenting symptom, the patient signals her readiness to explore her underlying problems.

Obsessive-compulsive Personality Disorders

Dynamics

At the opposite end of the neurotic spectrum from the hysteric is the obsessive-compulsive. The defense mechanism for obsessive-compulsive neurosis is isolation, isolation of affect from thought or from events. Emotions have to be expressed, but the obsessive-compulsive will express emotion when it has nothing to do with the event or the thought.

One obsessive-compulsive patient had a little daughter who almost died. She was in the hospital with an incredible fever for several days, teetering on the verge of dying. This man never shed a tear or showed a bit of anxiety through the whole ordeal. After his daughter was recovering, and recovering very rapidly, he was watching "Lassie" on television one day. Timmy and Lassie are separated and running all over trying to find each other. The patient dissolved in tears for an hour. Obsessive-compulsives have to protect themselves because they can't handle feelings, so they amputate themselves at the neck.

An obsession or compulsion is a distraction. It distracts you from what is bothering you. It allows you to isolate your affects. We all experience an obsession at times like a tune that reverberates through our heads. The more you try to get rid of it consciously, the more the tune stays in your head. Instead, you should ask yourself honestly, "What am I trying to avoid facing right this moment by having this tune reverberate through my head?" If you are courageous enough to answer that question, the tune is gone.

Entry

To break up the isolation of the obsessive-compulsive, the entry point is the magical system by which they isolate their affect. If patients report washing their hands

50 times a day, don't strong-arm the resistance by attacking that symptom. You must identify the magical system that is empowered by other ritualistic behaviors. A very common one is getting out of bed in such a way that both feet touch the ground at the same time. If one foot touches the ground before the other, the obsessive-compulsive has to get back into bed and get out the other side of the bed, making sure that both feet touch the ground at the same time. If again he fails to do that, he must get back in bed and try a third time on the other side of the bed, and keep going until he gets it right. Other obsessive-compulsives have to have the right foot touch before the left foot. The conflict underlying the ritual is so layered and long lost in the patient's isolation that it may not be possible to discover. In the case below, the patient illustrates this ritualistic behavior.

Forbidding the ritualistic behavior is not strong-arming the resistance; the resistance is in the repetitive behavior, as in the case of the hand washing. For example, in the following case, Walter has been wearing white socks since he was about 5 years old and this was not connected to the symptom. It was a successful way of life, a defense mechanism that successfully isolated this man's affect. The symptom that bears the resistance is the hand washing, or the repetitive behavior. The identified symptom, which has become ego dystonic and brings the obsessive-compulsive in, should not be the focus of therapy. Rather, the magical behavior, which is ego syntonic and a part of the way of life, offers a more potent, undefended entry point into undermining the patient's isolation and facilitating the integration of affect into the personality.

The magical system employed by the patient to keep affect and thought separated is usually so seemingly insignificant that it is almost overlooked by the therapist. Yet, this trivial behavior is the keystone to treating the obsessive-compulsive patient. This is keenly apparent in the case of Walter, whose white socks were the bulwark of his defenses.

Case Illustration: Walter, the Cathodic Engineer

Walter, 42 years old, came to therapy because his indecisiveness was becoming too much of a problem. He always had trouble making up his mind, but it seemed as he got older that it was more and more difficult to choose. He gave as an example the fact that he had been going to the same restaurant for lunch for almost two years. He knew the menu by heart and was tired of the same old food. He would look longingly across the street to another restaurant and determine he would go there for lunch tomorrow. But the next day he would begin to obsess, "What if it is worse than the one I am going to?" In the end, he would return each day to the same old restaurant.

Walter was approaching a midlife crisis, which he avoided by his interminable array of obsessions. He was a cathodic engineer for an oil company and he would walk the several blocks that separated his office from the commuter train station. He lived in the suburbs where his wife cared for their three children and was deeply involved with church work. On his walk to or from his office, he had elaborately constructed in his mind that it was permissible to cross against a red light at some intersections, but not at others. The system made sense to him: on small alleys, with little traffic, it was all right to ignore the stop light, while on larger thoroughfares it was not. What irked Walter was that other pedestrians did not abide by his rule and he would find himself getting inwardly furious with them. However, unbeknownst to Walter, the degree of his fury had nothing to do with the number of pedestrians who violated his rule, but rather with the number of times this mild-mannered man had suppressed his anger with his colleagues that work day. Or, if this was in the morning walk to the office, his annoyance with the pedestrians was directly proportional to his unrecognized anger at his wife. Walter was an obsessional neurotic. This was only one of scores of obsessional systems.

Walter was unaware that he was angry with his wife, but he could discuss difficulties with her without much feeling. He told the story of the time his wife was freezing peaches. She had run out of aluminum foil and asked him to drive quickly to the store and buy some before the peeled fresh peaches turned brown. Walter dutifully drove to the supermarket where he discovered there were two kinds, one quilted and the other not. His wife had not told him which one she wanted, and after 40 minutes of vacillation during which he made several aborted trips to the checkout stand, Walter returned empty-handed. By this time, the peaches were spoiled and his wife blew up with exasperation. Neither was aware, however, how passively hostile Walter's indecision had been. Walter was genuinely disturbed that he had upset his wife, but he was isolated from his feelings of anger.

In fee-for-service practice, obsessional neurotics are bread-and-butter patients. They never express anger at the therapist, they do not call after hours, they keep their appointments, and they pay their bills on time. These advantages do not pertain to capitated practice, where their intractableness and interminability are disadvantages. Yet, the therapist's best intentions to move the case along are seldom successful. Even Freud, who was comfortable in long-term therapy, told an obsessional patient in his tenth year that, whatever the outcome, they would terminate in three more years!

The defense mechanism by which the obsessional neurotic avoids the anxiety that would result in facing the real problem is called "isolation of affect." The patient can talk about the actual problems in his life, but since feeling is absent, no change or real understanding occurs. Feelings are isolated and discharged later. Just as Walter discharged anger at the pedestrians on his walk, he discharged affection by crying during mushy television programs. In fact, Walter could overlook his cold, detached manner toward his family by recalling how sensitive, warm, and tender he would be watching a movie. In treatment of the obsessional neurotic or the compulsive neurotic, the therapy must create a situation where the event and the feeling are simultaneously present.

Strong-arming the resistance by forbidding the obsession is a frustrating experience for both therapist and patient. The therapist is foiled, while the patient experiences an increasingly broader obsession. The entry point for the obsessional is through the magical system that enables the neurosis to exist. Every obsessional has at least one magical behavior, and usually two or three. The therapist will not learn what these are without probing.

Walter was well dressed in a dark suit and dark tie, but his white socks were startling in this context. On the second session, he was dressed the same way, suggesting this was not a one-time aberration. When asked, Walter responded that he wore white socks only. He would not feel comfortable with colored socks. Suspecting the "foot magic" often found in many obsessionals, the therapist asked if Walter had a certain way he would get out of bed each morning. Indeed he did. Both feet would have to touch the floor at the same time. If one foot touched first, the patient would get back under the covers and emerge from the opposite side of the bed, making certain this time that both feet touched the floor simultaneously.

The therapist waited two more sessions until the patient had bonded with him. Then he advised Walter that it was important to his therapy that he wear black or dark blue socks and that he get up in the morning with either foot touching the floor first. Under no circumstances should both feet touch first. If inadvertently they did, he should get under the covers and emerge from the other side of the bed, this time making certain only one foot touched the floor.

Walter was silent and noticeably uncomfortable for over 10 minutes. He eventually broke the silence himself, asking why he was being asked to do this. The therapist replied, "This is one of those times in therapy when the why is not important, but the what is." The patient was silent for another 10 minutes, and then wondered whether or not he could do this. "It would be like getting started all wrong every morning. And I can't explain it, but the white socks make me feel protected." The therapist interjected, "Would insulated be a more accurate word?" Walter nodded, "Yes, that's the right word." The therapist insisted and the patient agreed, but thought it would be "very hard" to do. The therapist countered that if the patient found it too difficult, he should telephone for an appointment earlier than the one scheduled the following week.

Walter called two days before his scheduled session and was seen that day. He was very anxious, but had kept his promise on both counts. He had been too tense to sleep and had trouble concentrating at work. "I'm a nervous wreck." It was in sharp contrast to the emotionless man who had come in the previous sessions, insisting his only problem was indecisiveness. His obsessional systems had disintegrated. Now, when he talked about his problems, both the event and the affect were present.

He did not know what to do, as he felt he was constantly on the verge of blowing up at his co-workers. In fact, to his chagrin, he had exploded with anger on two occasions, and it seemed he was perpetually angry at his wife. He was clearly anxious and was sweating profusely. The therapist interjected, "Walter, this is the way you have been feeling for a long time, but you've covered it up with stoplights and aluminum foil. Let's talk about what has been really bothering you."

The following sessions continued to be filled with anxiety and emotion. His previously dormant midlife crisis was now overwhelming him. He hated his job, he was bored with his wife, and, above all, he was tired of having been "proper" all of his life. He was able to admit for the first time that he had fantasized how it might be with another woman. He had even focused upon one of the women at work who had noticed that, whenever she was near him, Walter would become red-faced and uncomfortable. Finally, she asked him to stop as he was making her self-conscious. In exasperation, she had said, "Either ask me out on a date or quit acting like a sick calf." Walter was mortified and would make sure he was never near her again.

Little by little, Walter learned to express himself appropriately. As a result, he became more comfortable with both his anger and his lust, and learned that neither was inevitable or fatal. Throughout, he kept his promise to wear colored socks and to abstain from his morning ritual. His indecision all but disappeared and he became assertive and happy with his wife and a real father to his children. He thanked the therapist for getting him through the midlife crisis and particularly thanked him for "getting me over my lifelong obsequiousness."

LEGEND

Psychological mechanism	Isolation of affect, intellectualization
Diagnosis	Obsessive-compulsive personality
Operational diagnosis	Entering midlife crisis
Implicit contract	I am not angry
Personality type	Onion
Homework	Wear dark socks, refrain from morning ritual
Therapeutic techniques	Forbid the enabling magic, turn up the heat (anxiety)

7

ONION/GARLIC PSYCHODYNAMICS

Garlic that is Analyzable

For the garlic patients that are analyzable, even though they may be Axis II individuals, they are still able to change through appropriate understanding. Their difference from analyzable onion patients is that their improvement follows experience rather than insight. It will be noted on the onion and garlic chart that the narcissistic personality disorder is still within the analyzable sector, while the borderline personality disorder is over the line and borders the non-analyzable garlic sector. This will become clearer as these types of cases are discussed.

Addictions

Dynamics

The main defense mechanism in addictions is denial. The denial is pervasive, and addicts are likely to come to treatment only because there is external pressure on them or because they seek to recapture the halcyon days when the addiction worked, and not because they are motivated to achieve abstinence.

Their implicit contract is likely to be, "Turn me into a social user." There is no such thing because addiction results in physiological tissue change and drug tolerance. The more you take of a drug, the more you need in order to get the kick, and the more cells in your body are committed to neutralizing that drug. The body turns addictive substance into a food or a necessity. To express it as an axiom: the highest level of a chemical needed to bring about the high becomes the minimum daily requirement for life. It may take an alcoholic 20 years to build up to a quart of whiskey a day. That alcoholic can be dry for 10 years. If he starts drinking again, within days or a couple of weeks, he will be back to a quart of whiskey a day.

Addiction is not merely popping something into one's body, but a constellation of behaviors that constitute a way of life. An addict can be likened to an unfinished house that has only an attic and a basement. Addicts understand this metaphor exactly because they know only two moods: elation and depression. They do not experience the limited, normal mood swings common to other persons because, as they start to fall out of the attic, they run quickly to the bottle, the pill, the needle, anything to prevent falling clear down to the basement. The first thing we have to teach them is how to build a floor in that house, because you cannot live just in elation or depression. As one philosopher put it, "Those who are chronically depressed are damned to pursue pleasure constantly."

Addicts are damned to this fate because insight is soluble in alcohol, in calories, in cocaine, in amphetamines, or in whatever addiction the addict uses to escape anxiety and depression. Patients may be addicted not only to drugs, but to food, gambling, sex, or work. Additionally, the orgiastic nature of an addiction allows the addict to stay in perpetual denial by relieving the anxiety and depression that might otherwise force him/her to change.

Entry

The entry point in psychotherapy with addicts is to refuse treatment, thus avoiding conflict with the patient's denial and engaging the addict's own characteristic obstinacy to challenge. In this technique, the therapist skillfully verbalizes the patient's own denial, while at the same time withholding treatment as something not worthwhile for that particular addict. For example: "You can beat this yourself." "You have been conning your wife for over 10 years and with a little effort you could con her into taking you back." "Your boss is a softy and we can figure out a way to get him to hire you back." Hearing his covert beliefs expressed by the therapist, the patient begins to talk like the therapist. For example: "I can't continue to fool myself." "My wife (or boss) deserves better." The person who came in determined not to continue is likely to demand to be seen. More details of treatment, including the need for skilled triage along a continuum of care and the games addicts play, can be found in *The First Session with Substance Abusers* (Cummings, 2000).

The technique of reducing the impenetrable denial found in chemical dependency must be modified in addictions other than alcohol and drugs. Yet, the overall approach is also useful with food addicts, defined as persons who eat when depressed, anxious, or lonely. This modification is illustrated in the case of Mary.

Case Illustration: Mary, The Foodaholic

Mary was a 25-year-old, 347-pound single woman who was first seen with her even more obese identical twin. She was not seen again for several months, when the operational diagnosis was that her sister had just died of the complications of morbid obesity. This event had a profound effect in motivating Mary to lose weight, but not nearly as much as another unexpected event that occurred early in her therapy.

The patient had failed in a number of food addiction programs and her implicit contract was that she would change her eating habits just slightly enough to avoid dying like her sister. She was not prepared for the abstinence approach of this program.

All addictions are garlic and must be treated as such. No addict can recover as long as the denial is fueled by the addiction. Abstinence is the pathway into the program, and continued abstinence is required for continued participation. But where alcoholics and drug addicts can be asked to completely abstain, the foodaholic still has to eat. Therefore, the approach to abstinence needs to be modified. As a prerequisite to entering the program, foodaholics must lose a modest amount of weight, continue to lose more weight each week, and refrain from eating their nemesis foods. The latter are defined as those foods that the person will binge on if he/she eats just a little of it. These foods differ from individual to individual, and every foodaholic knows his/her own nemesis foods. Any pounds lost above the weekly requirement go into a bank, to be drawn upon at times when no loss occurs. Failure to maintain the prescribed regimen results in varying degrees of exclusion from participation.

Without going into great detail, suffice it to say that Mary succeeded through one 20-week addictive group program in which she lost 55 pounds, and was granted a second 20-week program in which she lost an even greater amount of weight. But midway into the first program, Mary began to falter, and it appeared she would fail the program. Then the unexpected happened.

Mary arrived for her group session in a state of agitation. A small, wiry young man began talking with her at the bus stop and within five minutes proposed marriage. He got on the bus with her and in the 35-minute ride to the therapist's office he proposed marriage a half dozen more times. Once off the bus, he followed her into the waiting room, where he continued to plead with her to marry him. Mary was noticeably upset. She had met her first "chubby-chaser," men who have an irresistible compulsion to be with very obese women.

The psychologist ordered him out of the building, but he waited outside for her. He began to appear everywhere in her life. Complaints to the police were of little avail as the chubby-chaser ignored orders to stay away. Mary, who was just about to fail the program, declared she would lose weight so as to get this man and any others like him out of her life. She made good her promise, and when she dropped below the critical level that triggered this man's perverted eroticism, he disappeared as suddenly as he had appeared.

Mary eventually stabilized her weight between 170 and 180 pounds, and maintained that level for years. She always joked that she was driven to fitness by a chubby-chaser.

LEGEND	
Psychological mechanism	Denial
Diagnosis	Food addiction
Operational diagnosis	Sister died of morbid obesity
Implicit contract	Reduce weight only enough not to die
Personality type	Garlic
Homework	Lose modest weight, avoid nemesis foods
Therapeutic techniques	Humor the resistance, special addictive program

There is controversy as to whether what has been termed by many psychotherapists as "sex and love addiction" is actually an addiction. On the one hand, the behavior fits many of the characteristics of addiction: a high followed by a low (crash), with the urgency to repeat the behavior. Abstinence reveals an underlying depression. The behavior, like alcohol and drugs, "protects" against intimacy and rejection. Despite these shared characteristics, others say that calling such behavior an addiction has led to the label being attached to such varied and far-fetched activities as "compulsive shopping" and "compulsive Nintendo playing." In the authors' view, such nonchemical highs such as those derived from compulsive sex and compulsive gambling create biochemical conditions in the body that resemble, to some extent, those induced by excessive alcohol, drugs, food. Yet, without coming down on either side of the controversy, a case of so-called sex and love addition is given here because of its frequency in our society and the extent to which psychotherapists tend to treat it as if it were onion rather than garlic.

Ted's search for the perfect woman was appropriately treated as garlic, in spite of the fact that beneath the exterior there was hidden a frightened little boy terrified of being rejected by women.

Case Illustration: Ted, in Search of the Perfect Woman

Ted was a 29-year-old single lawyer working for the government, who came in complaining of a "bathroom problem." Upon explanation, this was a symptom that had developed over the past year in which Ted would experience sudden abdominal cramps and diarrhea. This would occur at the most inopportune times, and he would have to interrupt whatever he was doing to rush to the restroom.

In fact, this occurred twice during the first session. This was very obviously a symptom of anxiety.

The patient was referred by a young female psychologist whom he had seen several times. She believed he had an erotic transference with which he did not wish to deal openly, so she recommended he be transferred to the care of a male. The patient agreed, but denied any romantic interest in her and stated flatly, "She was not that good looking." The psychologist remembered the woman therapist to be exceptionally attractive and asked the patient why he did not think so. He responded emphatically, "She's too skinny." As if to justify his conclusion, he went on to state that he had spent the past 10 years studying the perfect female form and was thus an authority.

Eventually, Ted brought in an extensive collection of charts, beginning with the foot. He had constructed the "golden mean" of how a woman's foot should look, so that the size was proportionate to her height. There was a "golden mean" for each height, by half-inch increments, from 5 feet to 6 feet. He did not regard a woman under 5 feet or over 6 feet as attractive, so for the range he chose there were 24 drawings of perfectly proportioned feet. As if this were not complicated enough, he had had drawn by an artist 24 specifications, according to height, for the ankle, knee, thigh, hips, buttocks, waist, bust, shoulders, and neck. In order to display the "golden mean" for a woman, 240 drawings were thus necessary. He could never bring all of these in at one time, but to demonstrate the process he brought in for a woman of 5 feet 6 inches the 10 drawings for the perfect foot, ankle, knee, thigh, hips, buttocks, waist, bust, shoulders, and neck. Realizing he had overlooked the arm, he was in the process of constructing drawings for both the forearm and upper arm. This would add 48 drawings.

Ted confided that once he found the woman who had all of the golden means, he would marry her. Unfortunately, he had found only near-perfect women so far. "Even the best of them will be imperfect in just one part." Then he added that the perfect woman would also have to have a big "bush." Although this was not on the drawings, it was the last criterion of perfection, and one that would have to be ascertained by going to bed with the woman.

In his search for the perfect woman, Ted was always "on the make," because only in total nudity could he fully assess how perfect or imperfect the woman's form was. He meticulously kept an annual diary of all the women he slept with for the sake of his quest. He would record each woman's name, proportions, and other pertinent data. Two years ago, he had his best year, having slept with 93 different women during that 12-month period.

Beneath all of these rituals, Ted was a sex addict. In time, it was also learned he was a pornography addict. Each weekend, he would rent 15 to 20 pornographic videos to copy. Being impatient with any activity other than the orgiastic sequences, he would fast forward the tapes until he had reduced 15 to 20 videos to 2 hours of concentrated visual orgasms. He bragged that years of such effort had resulted in the finest and wildest library of pornography in the world. The psychologist named him the Duncan Hines of pornography. Ted relished the appellation.

All of this did not come out at once. Rather, this information was revealed in small pieces over a number of sessions. Eventually, it was also discovered that Ted was a compulsive masturbator. His greatest pleasure was obtained through onanism, and even his sex with women was both pornographic and masturbatory. His thrill was to watch a woman perform oral sex on him. At the critical moment, he would pull away and masturbate in her face. Ted's thinly disguised embarrassment was not hidden by his bragging that he was the heir to the crown left by Don Juan, Casanova, and Errol Flynn.

Ted's presenting symptom, his "bathroom problem," began when he decided to study for the state bar examination. During that year, he developed so much anxiety that studying was futile. He wanted the psychologist's permission to not take the bar examination. After all, he did not need it as a government lawyer and he planned to remain in government service. He could not make the decision on his own, as his father was urging him to become a member of the bar. Within the first 10 sessions, he had formed a strong transference and accepted the therapist's permission as a substitute for his father's disapproval. Almost immediately, Ted's "bathroom problem" disappeared, only to return a few months later, bringing him back to treatment.

When he returned, he stated that the reappearance of his "bathroom problem" was interfering with his ability to seduce women, as it would disrupt his activity at the critical moment. It was also apparent that the patient liked the psychologist and enjoyed the closeness he had never experienced with his father. He wanted to continue therapy.

The patient acknowledged that he was a sex-pornographic-masturbatory addict, but he seemed to want the therapist's stamp of approval for his behavior. He attempted in many ways to manipulate the therapist into seeing his sexual activity as positive. Failing to get it, he decided he would achieve a compromise wherein he would be in charge of his addiction, rather than his addiction driving him. He announced that he was going to be the first patient to "beat the addiction without abstinence." His "bathroom problem" grew worse.

Ted staunchly denied that his search for the perfect woman was a rationalization for his fear of intimacy with women. Since he would never find the ideal, he could avoid forever his fear of an ongoing relationship. As if to prove the therapist wrong, he announced at his appointment that he had all but found the perfect woman. A date at the beach revealed a bathing suit-clad figure that was perfect. All that remained was to determine if she also had the required thick pubic hair. He threatened the therapist, "If she has a big bush, you'll see how wrong you are. I'll propose to her."

The following week, Ted came to his session dejected. The woman in question did have a profusion of pubic hair, but she had no navel. It seems that when her umbilical cord was removed, the infant developed an infection which resulted in deep and extensive scarring. At age 3, her pediatric surgeon covered the area in plastic surgery. Ted dramatically displayed anger, crying, "I finally found the perfect woman and she has no belly button!" The therapist had difficulty stifling a laugh. The patient hesitated and then also laughed.

To attempt to prevail upon Ted to abandon his seduction of women or his use of pornography would be to strong-arm the resistance. The entry point in his treatment would be forbidding the gratification derived in masturbation, either alone or with a partner. After considerable argument, Ted agreed. It was also agreed that if he broke his abstinence, he would come in for his appointment, briefly tell the therapist how it happened, and then forfeit the session. With the blocking of this gratification, some surprising changes began occurring. But even more surprising was that Ted had to forfeit only one session over the next several months.

Ted found himself in a three-month relationship with a woman, a period that was like a lifetime for this man who specialized in one-night stands. At the end of three months, she broke off the relationship. Ted was devastated. His "bathroom problem," which had abated with abstinence from masturbation, returned with a vengeance. The patient berated the therapist, for it was he who got the patient into this. Then, Ted developed a severe neurodermatitis, which persisted for several weeks. He continued to blame the psychologist.

During this time, Ted began to have important insights. His father was in the Vietnam War when Ted was 2 to 3 years old and his mother, grandmother, and several aunts doted on him as "the man of the house." The day came when his father was coming home. Ted was dressed in a specially tailored and authentic little soldier suit as he and his mother met the father's troop ship. His excitement turned to disappointment over the ensuing several days and into the following weeks. Mother and father became absorbed with each other, ignoring him. He could have tolerated losing his status as the "man of the house," but his father was incapable of truly relating to Ted or his two brothers, who were born when he was 4 and 5. He had lost his mother without gaining a father.

As he grew older, he became an excellent athlete in an attempt to gain his father's approval. Not only did his father continue to ignore him, but with puberty when all his fellow athletes began growing tall, Ted remained short. His athletic career was over. Ashamed, Ted discovered elevator shoes and pornography. The first made him feel tall, the second made him feel strong. No longer did he have to trust a woman who would betray him as did his mother. With pornography, he was in charge of his gratification and his self-esteem. When he became sexually active with young women, he continued his masturbatory attitude, remaining romantically aloof as he was successfully seductive. So angry was Ted at his mother (and subsequently all women) that he did not attend her funeral.

As these insights unfolded, Ted volunteered that he had destroyed all of his pornography tapes. "What good are they if I can't masturbate?" A few weeks later, he realized he also had to destroy his cherished diaries. "I never wanted to admit it, but those diaries were supposed to make me feel adequate in my old age and after I'm impotent. I don't want to end up being that lonely old man."

Ted has now been in a relationship with a woman for almost two years. When he is being honest with himself, he admits he loves Laura. But most of the time he complains that she fits none of his criteria for the perfect woman. He has not masturbated for over two years, but he continues kicking and screaming as he drags himself deeper and deeper into intimacy.

LEGEND

Psychological mechanism	Denial
Diagnosis	Pornography addiction
Operational diagnosis	Sudden anxiety diarrhea
Implicit contract	Don't touch my pornography and compulsive masturbation
Personality type	Garlic
Homework	Abstinence
Therapeutic techniques	Block gratification, special addictive program, humor the resistance

---

Personality Styles and Disorders

Dynamics

In personality disorders, impairment has occurred early in life, thus coloring the personality generally. The earlier the impairment, the more garlic a personality is likely to develop. Personality disorders can be of any neurotic type. For example, there are depressive personality disorders. In contrast to a depressive neurotic to whom one might offer encouragement to be assertive, a depressive personality disorder would be flattening everybody in the family. Again, the axiom of garlic before onion applies.

In clinical practice, it is useful to distinguish a level of impairment resulting in a distorted style of personality but which may not meet the DSM-IV criteria for a personality disorder. Although the impairment is more severe with the personality disorder, in both the patient denies the effect of his/her personality in interpersonal interactions and his/her responsibility for consequences. The entry to treatment is also the same.

Entry

The entry with personality styles and disorders is to turn up the heat. The anxiety that motivates the patient to seek treatment must be maintained to sustain the therapeutic leverage for change. This must be done without narcissistic blows to the patient's ego, an approach that requires considerable sensitivity.

Roland has been chosen as an example because most therapists would treat him as onion, noting that treatment is necessarily protracted because the condition of a schizoid lifestyle is intractable. It is our contention that this is therapist error, and that personality lifestyles are amenable to change if the interventions take into account that the lifestyle is denial, and thus garlic.

Case Illustration: Roland, the Pretender

Some personality disorders seem to be suffering so much on presentation that it is often difficult for the therapist to keep in mind the fact that the patient is garlic. This can be especially so if the personality disorder is at the moment displaying the anxiety that often accrues from the consequences of one's own garlic behavior. Such a patient was Roland, a schizoid 35-year-old man who, in spite of being married, was very isolated from people and generally insulated from life. It never would have occurred to him to seek psychological help were it not for his wife's preparing to leave. This impending change in his life had generated considerable anxiety in a man whose usual demeanor was one of distance and aloofness.

Roland had constructed his life in accordance with his schizoid isolation. His home was built in two wings, one in which he lived, and the other housing his wife and two children. Whenever he wished, he could enter the family wing, but his wife and children were forbidden to enter his wing without his express permission. In fact, the door into his wing was kept locked and only he had the key.

His occupation also reflected his isolation from people. As a telephone installer, he could harbor the illusion that he was interacting with people, where actually the brief encounter with no subsequent contact with the customer suited Roland's aloofness.

The wife complained that at no time had Roland ever kissed or embraced his children. Sex with her was mechanical, conversation was shallow, and any semblance of warmth was completely absent. Originally a naive farm girl whom Roland had brought to the city, in the following years of marriage, this woman had grown up and wanted more than this cold man could offer.

Clearly, the patient was here now (operational diagnosis) because his wife was about to leave him. The implicit contract was: keep my wife from leaving me without my having to change. His resistances were all toward preventing closeness at all costs. The wife sincerely believed Roland to be so fragile that, without help, he would collapse when she left. So she decided to remain in the marriage until he was able to rely on his therapist. Thus, Roland's implicit contract was initially fulfilled and he cooperated in treatment on that basis.

Roland was not pleased at being assigned to group therapy, but he went along with it. This treatment plan reflected the patient's need for socialization, but, as painful as the group process was to him, it was preferable to the potential terror of having to relate to a therapist in individual treatment. As a schizoid, Roland was more likely to respond to a diluted group transference, while he would have distanced himself from any possible individual transference. Accordingly, when the group assigned homework within the framework of that which was doable, Roland would wince, but comply.

Responding to the fact Roland had never kissed either of his children, the group assigned the homework of kissing each child on top of the head when he arose from the breakfast table each morning to go to work. His protests turned to surprise when he reported within two weeks that he was also kissing the children each evening when he returned home. He had not been asked by the group to do this, and he grudgingly confessed that he enjoyed the children's positive response. With a multitude of such small steps, Roland was finally displaying more and more affection to his wife and children, and was even relating slightly to co-workers. His wife was seriously reconsidering her decision to divorce him. All was going well until Roland's life myth, which enabled his isolation, was revealed in the group.

Roland was born in a small Midwestern town and never knew his father. He was aware he was born out of wedlock. While he hated his mother for it, he sustained an elaborate fantasy from his early childhood. He believed his father was either the president of the Chase Manhattan Bank or the United States ambassador to the United Nations. This startlingly specific fantasy further stated that this father, on his deathbed, would recall this bastard son and send for him. Upon seeing Roland, he would be so overcome with guilt and remorse for having abandoned him that he would change his will, leaving Roland the bulk of his multimillion-dollar estate. While awaiting the fulfillment of this prophecy, Roland would not have to succeed at anything: occupationally, socially, or domestically. All would be given him at the appointed time. This fantasy was the core of his personality disorder, and it both justified and enabled his aloofness.

The group assigned the homework that Roland would visit his mother and ascertain from her exactly who his father was. The patient resisted the idea for weeks. Finally, the group, at the suggestion of the therapist, made it a condition of continued treatment. It is therapeutic to do so in limited and well-thought-through instances where treatment would be stymied if it were not insisted that the patient take that step. Roland went to the Midwest and confronted his mother.

At the next group session, Roland was a stunned, anxious man. He was floundering, as his well-constructed schizoid personality with its cold aloofness had fallen apart. His denial (garlic) was shattered. He was pleading for help.

He had learned his father was a musician who had come through town on a one-night stand.

Subsequently, Roland entered individual therapy, established for the first time a deep emotional attachment in the transference, and succeeded in making a number of remarkable changes.

LEGEND

Psychological mechanism	Withdrawal
Diagnosis	Schizoid personality disorder
Operational diagnosis	Wife is divorcing me
Implicit contract	Prevent divorce without changing me
Personality type	Garlic
Homework	Pretend to love children, confront mother
Therapeutic techniques	Group therapy, prescribe the resistance (i.e., verify famous father)

Impulse Neuroses

Dynamics

Impulse neuroses, which include such varying conditions as peeping toms, exhibitionists, and compulsive gamblers, are often called compulsive disorders because the individual builds over time to an anxiety level that is relieved only by acting on the impulse. Because of this confusion of terminology, it is important for the psychotherapist to be reminded that, whereas obsessive-compulsive disorder is onion, impulse neurosis is garlic. It becomes even more imperative since the impulse neurotics are almost never seen unless they are in trouble. The situational anxiety will be so intense on presentation that patients will appear to be onion. The psychotherapist must be mindful that successful therapy with such cases requires ignoring the situational stress and treating the garlic. This is not easy, as the patient will manifest a great deal of obvious distress. Reducing this stress results in the patient's feeling better and concluding that treatment is unnecessary. Garlic is denial, and impulse neurotics, as with all personality disorders, do not regard themselves as abnormal.

Entry

The successful treatment of such patients involves the often difficult triad of:

1. raising the patient's anxiety by raising the "heat";
2. blocking the gratification usually experienced by acting on the impulse; and
3. taking advantage of the profound increase in emotional distress created by the first two.

This approach can be demonstrated in the case of Oscar.

Voyeurism as an impulse neurosis is so prevalent and the recidivism so complete that society feels helpless to reduce its incidence. Most authorities regard it as a nuisance, for with our jails clogged with violent criminals, our criminal justice system metes out probationary period after probationary period. Psychotherapists have been of little help, as our usual therapeutic interventions are unsuccessful. The key to treating voyeurism and all impulse neuroses is to:

1. see it for the garlic it is; and
2. turn up the heat by forbidding the primary gratification.

In voyeurism, the primary gratification is compulsive masturbation, an activity that the usual forms of turning up the heat (jail, probation, fines, loss of job or reputation) do not touch. Consider, for example, a prison system that attempts to forbid masturbation, surely an inappropriate restriction for all but the impulse neurotic. On the other hand, a skillful therapist can use the threat of the justice system, coupled with denying treatment, as motivation to impose abstinence from masturbation. As shown in the case of Oscar, this is really turning up the heat.

Case Illustration: Oscar, the Voyeuristic Optometrist

The patient was a 31-year-old married optometrist with two children. He had been arrested while on business away from home. Oscar had actively been a peeping tom since early adolescence. He had been apprehended a number of times, but regarded by an overworked police force as a nuisance rather than a threat, charges would be dropped or probation with the requirement of treatment would be ordered by an equally overworked court. Follow-up had been sloppy, and Oscar never continued therapy beyond the first few sessions. Before seeing his new therapist, he had gone for treatment four different times, only to discontinue once the "heat" was off. This time, the charges were serious, and Oscar was worried and upset.

While on a business trip in another part of the same state, Oscar positioned himself on the hotel fire escape and witnessed two women in a lesbian act. He denied at first that he masturbated while peeping, but it was soon established that masturbation accompanied all of his voyeuristic acts. The women discovered Oscar, who in his excitement had thrown caution to the wind, and he was apprehended by the hotel's security force and turned over to the police. Similar discovery had occurred on other occasions and Oscar expected to be only inconvenienced. He had not anticipated the militancy of the two women he had victimized. They demanded Oscar be prosecuted and they sued the hotel for damages due to their neglecting to protect its guests. There was considerable publicity and the trial promised to be a major media event in that city.

Following his lawyer's recommendation that Oscar should avoid a highly publicized trial, he pleaded no contest. He was awaiting sentencing, and a hearing with the state's Board of Optometry had already been scheduled. It was rumored that the judge would "throw the book" at the defendant and Oscar could well have his optometric license revoked. He needed and sought a prominent practitioner who would vouch that Oscar was in successful psychotherapy and well on his way to being cured.

In the first session, Oscar put his best foot forward. He described his successful practice and his devoted wife who was sticking by him, and he downplayed the extent and duration of his peeping tom behavior. The psychologist was direct and straightforward. He pointed out to Oscar that not only was his story full of inconsistencies, his description of his behavior did not fit the syndrome. He had the privilege of consulting another therapist, but if he were going to work with this one, he would have to come clean. Oscar hesitated for a few minutes, then told the entire story. As a child, he found ways of spying on his mother when she was undressing, and after puberty he became the neighborhood peeping tom. He was involved in several skirmishes in which irate husbands almost caught him, but he escaped detection until adulthood. He was arrested several times and always managed to get through the ordeals with a minimum of damage to himself and his practice. He described how a steady build-up of anxiety would eventually drive him to seek the only relief possible, and he boldly asked the psychologist to testify to the court the helpless nature of his behavior, his sincerity in seeking treatment, and the assurance he would never do this again.

The psychologist countered that the best he could do was to ask the court to delay final sentencing for 90 days while treatment proceeded. During those 90 days, the patient would keep semiweekly appointments, refrain from both voyeuristic and all masturbatory behavior, and diligently apply himself to his therapy. The restriction was so stringent that he could not even look at female underwear or bathing suit advertisements, and masturbation was forbidden even without voyeurism inasmuch as the patient was adept at conjuring vivid mental images. Violation of these conditions would result, at the conclusion of the 90 days, in the termination of further treatment and the rendering to the court of a report indicating Oscar was a poor rehabilitation risk. The patient was very upset, but realized he had no choice.

Over the course of the next several weeks, Oscar's anxiety grew at times to almost intolerable proportions, but he abided by the rules of treatment. He began to learn alternative ways of discharging anxiety, the first of which was a clumsy heaping of anger on the therapist. Later, he learned to refine his anger. He also learned that turning to his wife in a needful attitude invoked in her a caring that was very helpful. He also began to enjoy his two children in a more meaningful way. But treatment was turbulent, and Oscar was never totally without his denial. One manifestation of his resistance when an interpretation was made or an insight was looming was for this optometrist to remove his glasses, and then declare, "I just don't see that." Therapists often overlook the magical fulfillment in such symbolic denial and fail to forbid the behavior. Doing so in Oscar's case both curtailed the denial and facilitated understanding. Whenever he would begin to remove his glasses, he would stop, laugh at himself, and say, "There I go trying not to see something again."

At the end of the 90 days, the therapist and Oscar agreed that therapy should continue. The court placed him on two years probation, and his license was placed by the board on three years probation. Recidivism is high among impulse neurotics, but Oscar never again engaged in voyeuristic behavior. He had learned other means of handling his anxiety before it reached volcanic proportions. This did not mean he was not tempted, and he considered himself not "cured," but in recovery. During periods of unusual stress in his life when Oscar was strongly tempted, he would make an appointment to see his therapist. The key to his recovery is his continued abstinence from any masturbatory behavior.

LEGEND

Psychological mechanism	Denial
Diagnosis	Impulse neurosis
Operational diagnosis	Fear of incarceration
Implicit contract	Get me out of trouble without changing me
Personality type	Garlic
Homework	No voyeurism and masturbation
Therapeutic techniques	Turn up the heat, block gratification

Hypomania

Dynamics

Hypomania is always garlic and exhausting to treat. Hypomanics are very, very emotional and infectious people. They are ebullient, happy, and self-confident, and people love them. But, in reality, they are very depressed people. Hypomania is depression turned upside down, and treating it successfully is likely to plunge the patient into a profound depression.

Entry

The treatment of choice for bipolar disorder is lithium carbonate, which effectively controls most cases. However, the need for psychotherapy for these patients is not necessarily counterindicated. Bipolars can feel their subdued elation and depression cycles behind their medication, and some, welcoming the elation, temporarily stop taking the lithium. They enjoy the initial hypomania, but as the condition progresses they desperately overdose on lithium. When seen, the patient is not only manic, but also suffering from lithium toxicity. Other patients stop their lithium for 10 to 12 months so as to have a baby without risking the possible and severe cardiovascular side effects on the fetus. During this time, they must be supported by psychotherapy. Still other patients suffer kidney failure or other physical complications and must discontinue their lithium.

Psychologically, the entry with patients suffering from hypomania is to assign an enormous task appealing to their narcissism. In this way, they are kept occupied until arrangements can be made for hospitalization, as in the following case.

Case Illustration: Eleanor Flying High

Eleanor was a 39-year-old bipolar patient whose lithium was effective as long as she took it. On three occasions, however, being mildly aware of her elevated mood that was being kept under control, she decided to allow herself that "wonderful feeling." She stopped her lithium ostensibly for a couple of days, but as she became more hypomanic, she was enjoying the experience too much to resume taking her medication. Interestingly, her husband did not see the warning signs even though she had done this on three previous occasions and with devastating results. One morning, she awakened feeling very high and, after her husband had left for work, she went to a travel agent and bought a first-class airplane trip around the world. She charged this on credit cards and was gone when her husband arrived home from work that evening. She had left him a note saying she would see him in three weeks.

Four days later, Eleanor was remanded by the airline to the authorities in Hong Kong. She had not slept for many days and her behavior on the flight from Honolulu was so outrageous that the pilot had called the Hong Kong police by radio. They were waiting for her when the airplane landed. The husband was contacted, and he made arrangements for his wife to be returned under heavy sedation and in the care of an accompanying nurse.

Once back home, the effects of the sedatives wore off and Eleanor was once again in a manic state. She resumed her lithium, but in very heavy doses, and she convinced her husband she had her medication and would be all right. She did not wish to go to the hospital. He unfortunately agreed, and by the next three days Eleanor was not only still manic, but also toxic. He called the psychologist who had treated the patient several years earlier, as he was the only one Eleanor would agree to see. She threatened to run away if the husband attempted to take her to the hospital or to another practitioner. She was brought to the office.

Anyone who has not seen a manic turn from an elated state to an abusive, belligerent state cannot appreciate the extent to which the manic person can be hateful and physical. They can destroy every object around them, attack others, and require several people to restrain them. The husband, who had seen his wife in such a state, knew better than to attempt to force her to go somewhere she did not wish to go.

As a psychologist, the therapist could not prescribe medication or treat her lithium toxicity. He also had the goal of getting her to the hospital without her running away or becoming abusive and uncontrollable. In the meantime, she was everywhere in the suite of offices, talking volubly, and disrupting all activity. The therapist sat her down in a vacant office and asked her to write her autobiography, with particular emphasis on all of her talents and successes. She was to think of this as the manuscript for a book that could be entitled *Eleanor, a Very Remarkable Woman*. The receptionist would keep her supplied with paper.

The next two hours, while arrangements for hospitalization were completed, Eleanor had written on two full reams of typing paper. She thanked the psychologist for helping her get in touch with the special person that she was, and she went willingly, but noisily, to the hospital.

LEGEND

Psychological mechanism	Denial
Diagnosis	Mania
Operational diagnosis	Failure to take lithium
Implicit contract	Help me stay high
Personality type	Garlic
Homework	Write autobiography
Therapeutic technique	Increase compliance with lithium regimen

Narcissistic Personality Disorder

Dynamics

The narcissistic personality strongly resembles the borderline personality, but with one important difference that renders the patient more accessible to treatment. Both manifest the mechanism of splitting and projective identification. Like the borderline personality, the narcissistic personality is self-centered, susceptible to a variety of addictive behaviors, and given to sexual aberrations and perversions. Neither is capable of bonding and the transference is always tenuous. Both have been denied loving parenting and do not expect to find it in either life or psychotherapy.

However, where the borderline personality was abused, the narcissistic personality was indulged in childhood. This indulgence was a substitute for real parenting, but the patient became dependent upon it. This dependency is repeated in adulthood with persons who can supply the patient's narcissistic needs, but the attachment to such an individual is entirely egocentric and is based on "what he/she can do for me." Failure to meet the patient's expectations triggers the same kind of berating and derogating of the person that is found in the borderline. This is the projective identification: the person becomes the projected "bad part" of the patient. However, in contrast to the borderline personality, the narcissist is highly vulnerable to losing the person who is meeting his/her needs. This mitigates the immediate rejection that is characteristic of the borderline personalities, since the narcissistic personality desperately clings to the needed person in a panicky attempt to continue the narcissistic supplies. This feature renders the narcissistic personality more accessible to understanding his/her own behavior and adjusting it so as not to lose the object. Consequently, where the borderline personality must learn almost solely from painful experience, the narcissistic personality, though still mainly dependent on experience, is capable of some insight and anticipation.

The narcissistic personality shares with the borderline personality the lack of bonding, the self-centeredness, the propensity to addiction and sexual perversion, the hysterical acting out, the inability to tolerate stress, and the tendency to go in and out of psychotic-like states. But, in contrast to the borderline, the narcissist has an extreme vulnerability. Whenever there is the threat of losing the therapist, the narcissist will become compliant and even pleading.

Entry

The patient with narcissistic personality disorder is extremely dependent on the therapist for narcissistic gratification, and the therapist must use this to set limits and consequences for the patient.

The treatment of Neil was complicated by a previous therapist who, for 11 years, acceded to the patient's every demand. This is not unusual, as many bright, gifted narcissistic personalities are witty, affable, and successful. They are admired by many of their acquaintances, who aspire to emulate their success. When their vulnerability does show because of a rejection or a setback, they can be ingratiating and receive the attention and help they desperately need. Many are able to hide for long periods the contempt for others that is a part of their self-centeredness. When they are vulnerable, they appear as onion, but actually the appropriate treatment is to regard them consistently as garlic. All of this is illustrated by Neil, who unfortunately typifies to many the dashing, successful, affable, and handsome American male.

Case Illustration: Neil's Life in the Fast Lane

Neil came to the West Coast from the Midwest when the cable television industry saw him as a rising star. He had been in charge of advertising sales for a small television station. With his new job came a six-figure salary, a large expense account, and the "big time."

A 38-year-old single man, he was referred by his therapist who had been seeing him for 11 years. He did not make contact until he had been on the new job for several weeks and had encountered his first difficulty. Neil epitomized the stereotypical man of the 1980s: successful, egotistical, self-indulgent, and greedy. On his first appointment, he asserted that his only interests were fast money, fast women, and fast cars, in that order. He pushed the envelope to the edge and when he ran out of energy, there was cocaine to provide the necessary boost. He lived hard, worked hard, and cared only for himself.

The patient had people he admired, but the admiration was based on their usefulness to him. He liked knowing celebrities and flaunting his acquaintance with them. However, his tenuous admiration was dramatically illustrated by his mildly contemptuous description of the therapist he had relied upon for 11 years: "I was his life's work. He was always available, any time of the day or night. I wonder what he's doing without me."

To describe the patient as demanding would be an understatement. He wore his self-esteem on his sleeve, and if a woman he hit on rejected him, he would be so devastated he would call the psychologist in the middle of the night from a bar for a psychological Band-Aid. He liked to be the one who left the woman, and he took pride in how many lovers he had "trashed."

After ignoring the referral for several weeks, he called in a state of extreme agitation. He had demanded that the car the company provided him be replaced by a Jaguar. When his boss refused, he yelled at him and, after a one-hour battle, the boss fired him. Neil saw himself as blameless and was bewildered with the boss's refusal to give him the Jaguar. "Please do this for me," was a legitimate demand to Neil. He asked the psychologist to contact the boss on the patient's behalf and was angry when the therapist explained why he could not do so. After all, Neil's previous therapist "did these things for me all the time." On his own, the boss reconsidered, rehired Neil, and bought a Jaguar for him. But Neil expressed his contempt for his boss by having sex late one night with the boss's secretary on the boss's desk.

Neil was a "menopausal" baby and was doted on by his older parents. For 11 years, he had a doting psychologist and now he had found a doting boss. The reality check in his life would have to be his therapist, who informed the patient of this in terms he would understand and remember. Pulling open his suit jacket, the therapist said, "See, I have no tits." This became the shorthand between patient and therapist. Whenever the patient made vociferous and unreasonable demands, without saying a word the therapist would pull his suit jacket open. Usually, the patient would resign himself to the reality. The few times that Neil would continue his demands, the therapist would remind the patient of their agreement and invite him to get another therapist.

Limits were set for the patient consistent with the structure of therapy: the treatment would help the patient anticipate the consequences of his reckless narcissism, but if he ignored the warnings and got into trouble, it would be his sole responsibility to extricate himself. This simple therapeutic contract was subjected to every possible test by the patient each time he got into trouble.

Despite his outrageous personal behavior, Neil was very good at his work, which was selling advertising on the cable network. This is not unusual for narcissistic personality-disordered persons if they are in jobs where their affability, good looks, extraversion, breezy self-confidence, and ingratiating manner are assets. Throughout all the turmoil of Neil's therapy, his employers were pleased by his sales record and amused by his playfulness.

There were innumerable instances where Neil tested the limits, of which the following was illustrative. The patient was driving away from the trendy bar in which he was known as the "mayor" when he had an automobile accident. The police, who regularly patrol that fashionable part of the city as the trendy bars are closing, were there instantly. Neil had been drinking and he had done a line of cocaine as he was leaving the bar. He was also in the company of the wife of a member of the city council. Neil called the psychologist in a panic at 2:30 a.m. on his car phone, but in keeping with the therapeutic contract the psychologist refused to take the call. He learned the details at Neil's next appointment. By that time, the entire matter had been hushed up, ostensibly because the city councilman's wife also had cocaine and alcohol in her bloodstream. The matter did not escape the attention of the news media, however.

The councilman and his wife were in a messy divorce a few weeks later. Neil was dragged through the media spotlight and, although he appeared confident and likeable on television, he responded with his usual inability to tolerate stress. He was refused his whining requests for a sedative, which persisted for several weeks. In accordance with the therapeutic contract, had Neil obtained sedatives or tranquilizers elsewhere, his therapy would have been terminated. Also in accordance with the therapeutic contract, Neil forfeited the two sessions following the one in which he reported the incident. This was for having used cocaine, as all illegal substances were forbidden in his therapeutic contract. Neil protested loudly that at the time he needed the therapist the most, "Your dumb rules forbid me to see you."

Neil continued to cling to the therapist as his lifeline and, with each test, he seemed to become a bit more responsible. Neil is still a narcissistic personality, flashy, self-possessed, and affable. But he is considerably more responsible. He no longer sells television advertising, having become a station manager. On his new job, extraversion remains an asset, but the distinguished look of a senior broadcaster is required. He is playing his role of a responsible community leader well. So well, in fact, that Neil no longer gets into any kind trouble. He sees the psychologist infrequently, and *before* he gets into difficulty.

To the idealistic therapist, this may seem insufficient. In response, attention can be called to years and years in analysis expended to change basic personality. The patients are happier and more successful, and this is commendable. But so is Neil. No one can make a redwood tree out of a magnolia. The best we can do is eliminate the aphids in the magnolia.

LEGEND

Psychological mechanism	Denial, projective identification
Diagnosis	Narcissistic personality disorder
Operational diagnosis	Replace my doting previous therapist
Implicit contract	Fulfill my narcissistic needs
Personality type	Garlic
Homework	Abstinence
Therapeutic techniques	Set limits, take advantage of vulnerability

Borderline Personality Disorder

Dynamics

Every borderline is a 5-year-old who has managed to terrify his/her parents and is enjoying every minute of it, but underneath has the terror of feeling, "My gosh, what if I need somebody? Who's going to be there for me, because I'm stronger than my own parents?" The borderline relishes the fantasy and the victory of being stronger than you and vanquishing you, but the moment they do vanquish you, they hate you because they also harbor the hope that you will be strong enough to be the parent they never had. The borderline needs your strong ego.

Borderlines are the product of dysfunctional families, are increasing geometrically, and may come to dominate caseloads in the future. Parents of borderlines are likely to have been drug dependent, and as a child the borderline has experienced neglect and/or abuse from birth. Thus, the borderline never learned to bond and cannot develop healthy interpersonal relationships. Their defenses are characterized by projective identification and splitting. In order to survive their abusive childhood, they learned to be manipulative and destructively hostile, and rejecting. In therapy, they project this "bad" self onto the therapist and test the therapist's strength and honesty. In their social environment, they alternately seduce or infuriate people, thereby splitting groups and pitting members against each other.

People with borderline personalities do not have schizophrenic overlaps. The greatest event that can befall a borderline is to be diagnosed as schizophrenic, which then gives him/her a pass to all the wanted hospitalization. Borderlines dive into psychosis like one dives into a pool and comes out at the other end. A schizophrenic does not come out the other end. The borderline jumps into primary process and comes out at will. The schizophrenic cannot come out at will. Borderlines want hospitalization when it is going to suit their purpose. Once they have accomplished their purpose, there is no reason to keep hearing the voices, so they stop all of this primary process. One question that can differentiate between the borderline personality and the schizophrenic is, "Are the voices inside your head or outside your head?" The schizophrenic will look at you and say, "Huh?" The borderline will say, "Oh gosh, I've got to get the right answer." To the schizophrenic, there is not a right or wrong answer. The voices just are. The borderline will try to outguess the examination. Borderlines are so named because they are on the borderline of suffering a thought disorder, but their etiology of their impairment is psychosocial and not physiological as in the thought disorder of the schizophrenic.

Borderlines are survivors. Borderlines do not do themselves in. Borderline patients are remarkable human beings. They survived dysfunctional families that would have flattened all of us. Borderlines kill themselves only in despair, if they no longer can play the game. A borderline remanded to the back ward of a state hospital will kill themselves because they can no longer engage the world in their game.

Entry

Rapid changes can occur with borderline patients when they are properly treated. They should not be allowed to muck around in their childhood, but instead should be corralled in the here and now with structure and props that will make them less and less like leaves in the wind. They are best treated in groups, and a protocol for doing this is found in Appendix II of *Focused Psychotherapy* (Cummings & Sayama, 1995).

With borderline patients, you can be as outrageous as they are, but not one iota more and certainly not less. When you have outwitted a borderline, you will see something very interesting: a little flicker of a grin, just a little bit on the edge of the mouth, or a glint in the eye. If you want to become successful, use the same outrageousness they use. But when they are being absolutely impossible, you say, "You're really obnoxious today. What the heck is this all about? Why are you so obnoxious today? You are really trying to drive me up the wall? What's going on?"

They'll love you for it. They'll think, "This person is not a hypocrite. Every therapist I've had was so busy being nonjudgmental that they would tell me I was good when I was terrible." You can be very, very straightforward with borderlines as long as you are not angry with them. The moment you get angry with a borderline, you have disqualified yourself as a therapist. Borderlines set out to make you angry. They set out to prove you are no better than their parents were. They are out to disqualify you as a therapist. As they get angrier and angrier with borderlines, most therapists think that they do not have a right to be angry with the patient, and so they suppress it. In suppressing it, they respond to the borderline with more and more kindness. That is when the borderline absolutely destroys you with your hypocrisy. Ultimately, what the borderline is searching for is honesty. They will try to knock your honesty down, because they do not believe that there is any such thing as an honest human being. After all, their parents were not, and you cannot be any better than their parents. But they need you to be there for them. The key to treating borderlines, especially, and all character disorders is not to get angry at them, but to be very straightforward instead.

Borderlines are particularly adept at becoming whatever they discern is of interest to the therapist. And because so many therapists are intrigued by multiple personalities, survivors of incest or other sexual abuse, and so-called victimization in general, the borderline personality disorders will emulate these conditions. This does not mean that multiple personality disorder or victimization does not exist, but the conditions do not need the well-meaning, inept therapist to proliferate iatrogenic simulations. Preventing a borderline from acquiring a syndrome is illustrated in the case of Sandra.

Case Illustration: Sandra et al.—a Case of Multiple Personality

When the nation's first psychotherapy benefit was implemented at Kaiser Permanente in San Francisco during the late 1950s and early 1960s, the psychotherapists were startled by the high percentage of multiple personality disorders in their female patients. Before psychotherapy was included as an insurance benefit, it was largely the penchant of the upper middle class, which was both highly educated and able to pay out of pocket. It was hypothesized that in the less educated general population for whom psychotherapy was now available dissociative disorders were far more prevalent. This did not prove to be the case, for as the glamour of multiple personality disorder wore off, the syndrome all but disappeared.

The implementation of the nation's first comprehensive psychotherapy benefit had coincided with the movie, *The Three Faces of Eve*, after which Joanne Woodward received the Academy Award for her portrayal of Eve and subsequently married Paul Newman. These events popularized and glamorized multiple personality disorder, which, as all fads must do, faded in time. In recent years, glamorization of the disorder has been revived by a series of books and made-for-television movies, but particularly by psychotherapists who seem to encourage its emergence. There are findings that suggest that although real multiple personality disorder exists, it is rare, and most instances are iatrogenic. Borderline personalities are particularly adept at mimicking any fad disorder. When agoraphobia was the glamour condition in the 1980s, borderline patients became housebound and were admitted to agoraphobic group programs, which they disrupted. Whereas agoraphobics are the epitome of onion, the borderline is unrelentingly garlic. Many a psychotherapist learned the hard way that buying into a borderline patient's pretense at being agoraphobic spelled failure for the group program.

With these concepts in mind, it would be useful to review the case of a rapidly emerging multiple personality disorder. Sandra was 23 when first seen by a therapist who specialized in that condition. Within two sessions, a second personality emerged, and by the time the therapist was promoted and transferred to another state, she had four personalities. All of this had occurred within three months, and within 11 sessions. The therapist who inherited the case was suspicious that Sandra was really a borderline personality who had taken her cues for dissociation from her previous therapist. She prevailed upon the senior author to see the patient on his upcoming visit. The patient seized the opportunity when she was told of the visiting psychologist's reputation, and she confirmed the exhibitionism expected of a borderline personality. She knew the entire staff would be watching through a one-way mirror.

Once in the office with the visiting psychologist, the patient plunged into her abused past as a child. Everything she described was consistent with the background expected of a borderline personality. It was also consistently embellished and highly dramatized. The psychologist seemed markedly disinterested, at which point the patient became flirtatious and seductive. In response to the question, "And who are you?" she replied, "I'm Terry." The psychologist then asked, "How did you get in here?" Sandra, now as "Terry," tossed her head back and defiantly stated, "I come out whenever I want. Nobody tells me what to do." The psychologist then looked the patient intently in the eye and stated emphatically. "Psychotherapy is a confidential relationship between the doctor and the patient. No third person is allowed to intrude. If you do not leave now, the session is terminated." The patient, still in the role of "Terry," seemed stunned, but she remained—whereupon the therapist stood up, announced the session was over, and began to leave the room. Suddenly the patient, as Sandra again, pleaded, "Don't leave. It's only the two of us here."

The patient and therapist spent the remainder of the session talking about the patient's so-called multiple personalities. It was clear that Sandra was aware of the other three personalities, something that she had not revealed to her previous therapist. The psychologist took the position that all of these personalities were no more than aspects of Sandra, and Sandra was aware and responsible for all of them. The correct diagnosis now having been established, Sandra agreed to enter the borderline group.

LEGEND

Psychological mechanism	Projective identification, dissociation
Diagnosis	Borderline personality disorder
Operational diagnosis	Perform/impress visiting supervisor
Implicit contract	I'll convince you I'm a multiple personality
Personality type	Garlic
Homework	Keep therapy one on one
Therapeutic techniques	Limit setting and confrontation, special borderline program

---

Extreme borderline patients are intent upon proving that the world is just as unworthy as their parents. They will grab control and maintain it by threats of suicide, malpractice suits, or whatever will intimidate a therapist or a clinic. The longer they are successful, the longer will be the time required to create that psychological structure they so desperately need. Such an extreme case was Peggy.

Case Illustration: Peggy, the Borderline Center Director

When the senior author arrived at one of the busy staff model centers in the South for its annual clinical audit, he found that the entire staff was eagerly awaiting his help with a patient who had literally exhausted, one by one, each of the psychotherapists except one. The one who survived her onslaught was the one therapist she refused to see again.

Peggy was a woman in her early thirties who was very obviously manifesting a severe borderline personality disorder, but knowing the diagnosis did not shield the staff from her incessant demands. To complicate matters, she was married to a master's level licensed counselor who supported her in all her acting out and constantly challenged the treatment and diagnosis accorded his wife. Peggy attained health plan eligibility in February. By early July, she had succeeded in all but paralyzing both the health plan and its mental health contractor. In those five months, she was hospitalized 6 times, treated in the emergency room 23 times, usually late at night and sometimes twice the same night, and given 17 emergency, daytime drop-in sessions. She was also scheduled for semiweekly regular appointments, of which she kept only two. Whenever a staff member tried to set limits, she responded with either suicidal threats or gestures. Her counselor husband was always by her side to challenge the therapist's behavior as colleague-to-colleague, adding each time a not-so-subtle threat of lawsuit. Together, they had filed over a dozen formal complaints to the health plan, and the person in charge of patient relations spent most of her time attempting to mollify this one couple.

The center director took the liberty of scheduling Peggy as a therapy demonstration patient, an opportunity Peggy seized. As the staff and patient filed into the conference room, Peggy immediately took the center director's chair and presided over the meeting as if she were queen rather than patient. The center director, on the other hand, unwittingly found herself in the chair that had been designated for the patient. Peggy's current therapist, the most recent of a succession of therapists, began the session by asking Peggy to describe for Dr. Cummings the problems that brought her to treatment. The patient launched into an articulate history of the abused childhood, embellishing every detail as she wallowed in her self-pity. Clearly, Peggy relished every moment of an exercise that was not only unproductive, but deleterious. The more a borderline is allowed to wallow in self-pity, the more likely he/she is to regress.

The senior author gently but insistently brought her back to the present until finally she defiantly refused to talk about anything but the past. She was unable to ignore the reasonable request that it was important to understand her situation today, so as a last resort she lapsed into determined silence and began rocking in her chair. Apropos of all Peggy's acting out, it was pointed out to her that she had initial control of this rocking behavior, but if she continued beyond a certain point she would be unable to stop. She was asked whether she preferred to be in control of herself or to punish Dr. Cummings for not allowing her to dwell deliciously on her abused childhood. Momentarily, she stopped, but then made the decision to be defiant. She resumed her rocking motion and soon she was in a trance-like state. From then on, nothing got through to her. At the end of the time allotted for the case conference, she refused to leave and Dr. Cummings announced adjournment. All but Peggy left the conference room.

Once alone, Peggy did three things. She sat on the floor and wedged the full force of her 6-foot, 2-inch frame and 240-pound weight against the door. Then she began banging her head against the door in perfect cadence. Then, while continuing the first two, she telephoned her husband, who appeared within an hour, and notified the office of patient complaints at the health plan, which called the center director telling the staff Peggy was in the process of slashing her wrists in their own conference room at that very moment.

Peggy was definitely in control of the situation. The center staff, on the other hand, was near panic. Attempts were made to push the conference door open and rescue the patient before she ostensibly bled to death. But Peggy dug her heels into the carpet and pushed her back against the door with all her might. It became apparent that to attempt by sheer numbers of staff to push the door open could cause Peggy serious bodily harm. The staff looked to Dr. Cummings for a solution. The question was put as follows: "If you had a 4-year-old throwing a temper tantrum, what is the best response?" Everyone agreed that the 4-year-old should be ignored, but this was easier said than done since the staff—who were by now clearly the real patients—sought for ways to rescue Peggy. Again, this was true of all but the one aforementioned staff member.

All but one of the psychotherapists at this center, including the center director, were women whom Peggy had manipulated by getting them to believe she was truly dangerous to herself. The one male therapist had not been taken in by the manipulation, even when he saw her for the first time late one night in the emergency room. This male psychologist happened to be on call, but he knew a great deal about Peggy, as she had been the subject of almost every clinical case conference since her first contact with the center. He refused to hospitalize her since his clinical findings counterindicated inpatient treatment. She angrily left the hospital and called at 4:00 a.m. Still on call, the same psychologist responded. Peggy described how, since leaving the hospital, for hours she had been wandering in the middle of the streets in a trance. She was awakened from her trance by an automobile horn from a car that in the dark almost ran over her.

The psychologist asked in a calm voice what kind of car it was, and then responded, "That's a very expensive car, Peggy. You are such a big woman you could have done great damage to it if he had hit you." Peggy hesitated for a few seconds, then slammed the phone down in a rage. But the important thing is that from then on, before going to the emergency room, she would first telephone the center to ascertain who was on call that night. If this particular psychologist was on call, Peggy would postpone her "emergency" until his time on night duty was completed. She steadfastly refused appointments with him when the center director, having now recognized that this psychologist was the one whom she should see, tried to transfer her to his care.

This case thus far demonstrates that when a borderline personality disorder seems most out of control, within the chaos created the patient is really running the show. Furthermore, research has shown that the stature of the therapist diminishes each time he/she is successfully manipulated. While the patient seems to delight in dethroning the therapist to the same rubble to which the parents are assigned, deep inside is a frightened child who is begging to be stopped. The terror stems from an inner realization, "If I can defeat everyone, who will be there for me?"

After about an hour of refusing to come out of the conference room, Peggy heard her husband outside and dashed into the waiting room where she grabbed him and they hastily departed. It was soon to be learned that they reported to the emergency room to have her "slashed" wrists stitched. She had left behind several slightly blood-stained pieces of tissue.

Much of the time during which Peggy was closeted, both the center director and Dr. Cummings were on the phone with an extremely critical patient complaints clerk. It had become apparent during these conversations that this clerk was, herself, a borderline and for the past five months had unwittingly been enabling the patient's acting out. Fortunately, the medical director was a competent, thoughtful man who agreed with Dr. Cummings' strategy for managing the patient. He had examined the superficiality of the cuts on the wrists and concurred with both the diagnosis and the treatment plan. Peggy was told she had no choice but to return to the center. If she refused to cooperate, she would be dropped from the health plan rolls.

There ensued two hours of negotiations on the telephone between the center, on one side, and Peggy and her husband on the other. Ostensibly, Peggy had her lawyer on another line, insisted on quoting him profusely, but no one else actually talked with him if, indeed, he existed. Finally, Peggy agreed to come in with her husband after the center backed away from insisting that they be seen separately. Peggy even voiced the fear, "I won't give you the chance to win him over." By agreement, and seeing them as a couple, would be her most recent therapist and Dr. Cummings.

Before they arrived, her therapist and Dr. Cummings had agreed on a strategy and the need to maintain firmness. Peggy was presented with a treatment plan that involved semiweekly regular appointments that must be kept. Also, since she was fearful she could not be seen in case of an emergency, she would be permitted five emergency sessions during the next 30 days. This figure was arrived at by a careful examination of her pattern of presenting herself in "emergency" conditions. It was apparent that about one emergency per week was actually legitimate. So, on the basis of not asking a patient to do more than she can, one emergency each week was acceptable, with an additional one thrown in for good measure, to five for the month. She could use all or none, immediately or spaced, but once they were used up she would be eligible for no more mental health services until the 30 days had passed. Peggy accepted the conditions with a defiant smirk, then promptly used all five of the emergency visits allotted for the month within the following three days. She then embarked on a series of so-called suicide attempts, appeals to the health plan, telephone calls from a lawyer and several community leaders, and the involvement of the police. Peggy had mobilized and was manipulating the entire community.

This time, her therapist remained steadfast. At the end of the 30 days, it was Peggy and not the psychologist who was exhausted. She returned to the center and, for the first time, entered treatment. Her admiration for her newfound strong, firm, and reliable "parent" was the basis for a new and productive therapeutic relationship. This did not mean that Peggy did not occasionally test her therapist to reassure herself that the therapist was strong enough to be there for her. But the therapist consistently met the tests and Peggy continued to settle down and make use of the treatment, which now disregarded her very abused childhood, but concentrated on helping her meet the problems of daily living without regressing to a helpless, temper tantrum-driven, terrorized little girl. And the designated center director resumed her rightful role as the real head of the center.

LEGEND

Psychological mechanism	Denial, splitting, projective identification
Diagnosis	Borderline personality disorder
Operational diagnosis	The boss is coming to town
Implicit contract	I shall continue to run the center
Personality type	Garlic
Homework	Get self expelled from treatment
Therapeutic techniques	Paradoxical intention, set limits

It cannot be reiterated too often that borderline personalities are such because they actually were abused. Their stories are so heart-rending that therapists fall prey to emotions of sympathy, throwing therapeutic effectiveness to the winds. It cannot be overemphasized that feeling sorry for a borderline is antitherapeutic. It is in the worst interest of the patient and may help to eventually destroy him/her. Being caring people, psychotherapists are easy prey to what are most often spigot tears that are turned on and off. To help a borderline, the therapist must have a mental image of a huge neon sign that flashes GARLIC whenever the borderline begins to cry. Andrea is typical of thousands of borderline patients who receive more sympathy than help, and eventually are rejected by an exhausted therapist who is totally unaware of his/her own anger toward this frustrating patient that "I gave so much to."

Case Illustration: Andrea and the Abuse Excuse

After 11 years of therapy, Andrea's therapist left the state to accept an impressive professional position. The social worker, a very dedicated and caring woman, wanted to make certain Andrea was left in expert hands. She hounded the new therapist until he agreed to accept the patient in an already overburdened schedule. When he met the patient and became aware of the tremendous demands she had been making on her former therapist, the psychologist could not help but wonder if this ostensible promotion might have been her way of extricating herself from an ever engulfing vortex.

Andrea was an intelligent borderline personality whose manipulative ability was enhanced by years of training in well-meaning psychotherapy. She was the only child of affluent parents who were more interested in their successful business than in their daughter. Unable to give her love, they showered her with gifts, which fell short of Andrea's expectations. She became the epitome of the love-starved "spoiled brat." The family lived in Southern California's wealthiest community, and although they were well-to-do, their income was in the low range for the residents. Consequently, they could not afford to give Andrea the car and the Rodeo Drive clothes that her friends took for granted. As a teenager, Andrea became very adept at shoplifting whatever she wanted, getting caught only once in her high school years. This was hushed up in the manner typical of upscale residents who can afford expensive lawyers.

Now age 31, Andrea was estranged from her parents, who had all but disowned her. Spectacularly beautiful, she was always able to make a good living in marginal executive positions where attractiveness, charm, and manipulativeness were the key ingredients. At the same time, and at three different periods of her life, she also supplemented her income by being "kept" by wealthy men. Nonetheless, no income could satisfy Andrea's ravenous appetite for expensive clothes and jewelry. Her other career was shoplifting.

Early in the 11 years of therapy, Andrea and her therapist, through hypnosis, uncovered repressed memories of sexual abuse by both parents during her childhood. And six times during those same 11 years, the therapist testified in court on behalf of Andrea when she had been arrested for shoplifting. In all six cases, the defense was the same: Andrea was the victim of incest. The transcriptions of the court cases, all meticulously preserved by her previous therapist, were instructive. The therapist was eloquent and persuasive. The defendant (patient) was better than a trained seal. At just the right moments and in just the right amounts, there were tears, contrition, and victimization. A judicial system, already overburdened with shoplifting cases, and with jails overcrowded with violent offenders, found it easy to grant probation and order more therapy all six times!

The court transcripts were revealing on another dimension. The incest had grown in 11 years of therapy from a simple case of a father sneaking into the daughter's room and the mother refusing to believe it, to rape with a broom handle by the father as the mother held the child down, to the parents sexually sharing their daughter with their adult friends, and finally to Satanic rituals. It seemed that the elaboration of the original alleged incest over 11 years more closely approximated newspaper and television headlines than any uncovering of repressed memories. The new therapist could not help but be reminded of daytime television shows in which a group of borderline personalities tell their stories of abuse, which, by the end of the hour, have been elaborated to include details from all the guests' stories.

It was important to set limits early. The previous therapist had been available to Andrea without limit, a potentially destructive approach in an adult "spoiled brat" syndrome. For example, a cocaine-spiked spat with her boyfriend at 1:00 a.m. warranted a two-hour telephone therapy session. An agreed-upon system of when and how the therapist would be available was formulated and put in writing. The shoplifting was put in abeyance, waiting for the moment the patient would bring it up. The therapist did not have to wait long.

On the fourth weekly session, Andrea sought assurance that if she were caught shoplifting the therapist would come to her aid. She feared that arrest was probable and acknowledged that for every time she had been caught she had shoplifted 50 times or more, but she couldn't help it. The therapist made it very clear he did not regard the patient as a kleptomaniac (kleptomaniacs are persons whose compulsion typically drives them to steal things they cannot use). He recounted the example of one of his patients who could not stop stealing bobbie pins even after she had stolen over 100,000 of them. Persons who steal very expensive clothes and jewelry are thieves, not kleptomaniacs, and he would say that in court. The patient first attempted to inundate the therapist with her history of childhood sexual abuse. When that failed, she quickly agreed to take responsibility for her shoplifting rather than have her overly elaborated history of abuse called into question. The stage was set for a showdown and the curtain went up early.

Three days later, Andrea was arrested for attempting to steal an $18,000 fur coat. She screamed at the psychologist, "See how wrong you are. I am a kleptomaniac. As an animal rights activist, I would never wear a fur coat." Some garlic is truly of gourmet quality!

The therapist remained faithful to the agreement, and Andrea went to the county jail for 90 days. She was placed back on continued probation and remanded to the psychologist for psychotherapy. The court order had enough leverage to make therapy possible and the psychologist was very open with the patient about how he intended to use it therapeutically. Falling off the wagon (shoplifting) would mean increasing jail terms. Not atypical of borderline personalities, Andrea seemed relieved and began to engage in her therapy. She was placed in the special borderline group program where, through therapy and advancing age when borderline personalities run out of steam anyway, she learned to control many of her impulses, including shoplifting. Interestingly, there came a time when she repudiated all of her so-called repressed memories and reconciled with her now aging parents.

LEGEND

Psychological mechanism	Projective identification, splitting
Diagnosis	Borderline personality disorder
Operational diagnosis	Therapist leaving
Implicit contract	My incest/abuse history justifies all
Personality type	Garlic
Homework	No shoplifting
Therapeutic technique	Set limits with consequences for antisocial behavior

8

ONION/GARLIC PSYCHODYNAMICS

Onion that is Non-analyzable

In the onion and garlic chart, schizophrenia is divided into schizophrenias controlled by individual suffering (onion) and those controlled by attacking the environment (garlic). The discussion in this chapter pertains to both categories.

As has been noted in previous sections, in the current era of medicalized behavioral care, the diagnosis of schizophrenia invokes the immediate prescribing of antipsychotic medication. But the diagnosis is incumbent upon the presence of delusions and hallucinations, whereas in the Biodyne Model schizophrenia is a thought disorder that exists, often for years, without regression into an active psychosis (i.e., delusions and hallucinations). Experience during the past three decades has made apparent that something exists in the schizophrenic before the active psychosis. But since the DSMs have rejected, or at least omitted the concept of a thought disorder that is not necessarily an active psychosis, there are under consideration various names embodying the idea that some people may be susceptible to psychotic episodes. As this concept takes hold, it can well be expected that, in short order, there will be medications ascribed to treating this pre-psychotic schizophrenic condition.

On the other hand, the psychosocial model that has regarded schizophrenia as the end of a continuum of severity of emotional distress is also without credence. A schizophrenic is qualitatively different from a neurotic because the thought disorder interferes when the primary processes of right-brain thinking are to be mediated by the logic and reason of left-brain thinking. Schizophrenia is a dysfunction of the brain that may be heritable and is certainly susceptible to certain environmental factors that are yet far from being understood. The psychiatric exuberance that resulted from the serotonin and dopamine theories of the past couple of decades has not been sustainable, leading to questions as to their validity, and even disappointment at the lack of answers (Carlat, 2010; Kirsch, 2010; Whitaker, 2010).

In the Biodyne Model, schizophrenia is a thought disorder that is usually pre-psychotic and effects as many as 5 percent of Americans (Fromm-Reichmann, 1929/1950) but only a minority will ever manifest a psychosis (delusions and hallucinations) and be hospitalized. In society, these people may be thought of as odd or peculiar, but not crazy. They may be unduly stubborn and suspicious as the paranoid personality, given to far-out ideologies or cults. They can be particularly susceptible to the many conspiracy theories that abound. For example, there are intelligent people who still believe the landing on the moon was staged in a Hollywood movie set, and many more that are convinced space aliens actually landed in New Mexico some years ago and the government is hiding the facts. In the mid-1980s, a psychiatrist was treating patients who ostensibly had been abducted by space aliens, taken to outer space, and later released. Harry Stack Sullivan (1927, 1940), who derived much of his knowledge from his own schizophrenic thought disorder about which he was quite candid, called this form of thinking parataxia. Carl Whitaker over coffee one night described to the senior author how he became aware of his schizophrenia in his late teens, and he further described the various techniques he used to keep his thought disorder in check. We have had a number of prominent, successful colleagues who were, by their own thought disorder and their candidness, able to increase our understanding of the process.

In the Biodyne Model, in contrast to the current medication model, which sees delusions and hallucinations as pathology, these are known as restitutional symptoms. It is the attempt of the crumbling ego to account for what is happening. For example, if suicidal ideation begins to intrude, and the person may fear an inability to prevent suicide, the fear may manifest itself as the belief that "someone is trying to kill me." Distortion, yes, but it assures the person will not commit suicide, at least as long as the delusion holds.

We can discern three levels of intensity of the thought disorder, as increasing failure in its functioning necessitates escalated levels of parataxic thinking that precede the ultimate breakdown in the attempt to understand. These precede the rise of delusions and/or hallucinations as a last resort to comprehend what is happening. We have labelled the three levels (i.e., attempts to restore the ego) as *latent*, *patent*, and *blatant*. Consider the following example.

A man who all of his life felt misunderstood and unappreciated at work, and attributed his not having been promoted not to the fact that he was withdrawn, suspicious of his co-workers, and avoidant of his boss, but to the belief his co-workers had it in for him. He was a lonely, schizoid man who at this stage was in the *latent* stage. As his unhappiness and dissatisfaction steadily increased, he began thinking that perhaps his co-workers were actively withholding information that, if he had it, he would surely use to pass them up in performance. He found excuses to work late, and while alone in the office he would invade his co-workers' computers looking for this information. He had now escalated to the *patent* level, all in an effort to forestall losing control. Where the latent-level response had the effect of relieving him of his own feelings of inferiority and unworthiness, the patent stage did not have such a secondary compensation, and he soon escalated to the *blatant* level in which he imagined his co-workers were plotting against him, stealing his work products, and distorting them into gibberish where actually his confused thinking was producing garbage. He went over his boss's head to the Human Resources department, where he filed a long, rambling report that on investigation had no basis in fact, and he was as a consequence dismissed from his job. At this point, he became totally delusional, physically attacked a co-worker, and was hospitalized. If there had been a psychotherapeutic intervention in the patent stage, the blatant stage might have been prevented.

When those with a thought disorder begin decompensating into psychosis, joining a cult can often indefinitely forestall the breakdown. The message is that we are the chosen few who know the truth, which proves "I am not crazy." Also, becoming a leader and getting someone to believe in your delusions also prevents decompensation into full-blown psychosis. Consider the case of James Jones and his followers who set up a colony of the faithful and their children in South America. Their beliefs were outrageous to outsiders, which gave them the solace of having found a safe haven away from civilization while they alone pursued the truth. The problem came when their leader decompensated and ordered all to drink poisoned Kool-Aid, after which he took his own life the same way. Ever since, in the vernacular, so-called "true believers" are referred to as Kool-Aid drinkers.

Schizophrenic Over-sensitivity

Only about 1 percent of the estimated 4 percent or 5 percent of the population that has a thought disorder will ever manifest a schizophrenic psychosis or be hospitalized (Rosenhan and Seligman, 1984). It depends how life treats them, how heredity endowed them, what kind of family they grew up in, and how lucky they are in life.

The people most overly sensitive to rejection are schizophrenics. They are 100 times more sensitive to rejection than people of low self-esteem. This is only to be expected, however, since schizophrenics have been rejected all their lives. As children, they've been seen as strange. The other kids pick on them. They are called FLKs in school, "Funny Looking Kids." If they get nervous, they walk funny. There is something going through their minds that is making them very nervous. Repetitive movements, athetoid movements, repetitive speech, all of these hit the poor schizophrenic when he/she is nervous. If they are nervous about the first day of school, or starting a new year in a brand new school where they do not know anyone, with the last school having been a disaster, schizo-phrenic children are terribly nervous. When the teacher goes around the room and asks the children to say their names, the schizophrenic child just falls apart and starts doing repetitive movement. "My name is Tom. My name is Tom. My name is Tom." All the kids laugh, and it is downhill from then on. A life filled with such humiliation and rejection naturally results in the extreme sensitivity of the schizophrenic. For example:

I was driving with a patient across a bridge with a toll booth only on one end so that the fee is collected only once for a round trip. We got on the bridge and were driving on when the patient said, "You didn't pay the toll." I said, "This is the free direction." He said, "You must pay the toll!" I said, "No, no. This is the free direction."

He got repetitive and said, "You must pay the toll. You must pay the toll. You must pay the toll. You must pay the toll." And he is screaming by this time, and I am getting desperate.

I start doing foolish things. I am being logical. I reach in my pocket, get a bunch of change, open the window, throw it onto the bridge, and say, "There, I paid the toll."

He said, "You did not pay the toll. You did not pay the toll. You did not pay the toll," and continued to decompensate.

I am struggling, and think, "This has nothing to do with the damn bridge. What does the toll have to do with his feeling rejected?" When a schizophrenic patient gets like this, 99 times out of 100 they feel rejected. I look over and on his lap he had a novel that he had been reading. The title of the book is *Love is a Bridge*. I turned to him and said, "Do you have the feeling that if I don't pay the toll on this bridge, I don't love you?"

He looked at me and said, "It's not true?"

I said, "No. It has nothing to do with if I love you."

He sank back in the car seat and said, "Thank you."

Treating the Pre-psychotic Schizophrenic

With the advent of psychotropic medication, the importance of delineating and understanding the *pre-psychotic* schizophrenic thought disorder that affects many persons has been forgotten or neglected. Our approach, with its emphasis upon reducing therapeutic failures, has extended the onion–garlic chart to include the pre-psychotic schizophrenic who decompensates into full-blown psychosis when subjected to uncovering (analyzing) psychotherapy.

Recognizing this thought disorder is particularly important because the non-psychotic schizophrenic, being very close to primary process thinking, presents a richness of pathological material that is tantalizing and seemingly begging for analysis. As the layers are peeled off, the therapist feels rewarded by an ever-increasing gold mine of pathology. Then suddenly the patient is overwhelmed and engulfed in psychosis and requires hospitalization.

Persons with a schizophrenic, but non-psychotic, thought disorder come into psychotherapy because adverse circumstances are eroding the boundaries that contain the potentially psychotic thinking, and the patient feels vulnerable and threatened. The treatment of choice for these patients is a type of covering therapy, or a restoration of controls before the patient is overwhelmed. This requires special skills that concentrate on the here and now, helping the patient restore equilibrium by coping with the adverse events. Of considerable importance is the strength of the therapist, for as the patient's ego weakens, he/she can rely on the therapist's ego strength.

In addition to the decompensation that can be precipitated by uncovering therapy, a patient suffering from a non-psychotic schizophrenic thought disorder can suffer an equally adverse effect from certain anxiolytic and antidepressive medications. Typically, psychotherapists do not concern themselves with medication issues, but this is an area in which a competent diagnostician can be of immeasurable services to the patient and of help to the prescribing physician. Very few psychiatric and non-psychiatric physicians are trained to recognize this thought disorder, which is so recognizable to psychologists on Rorschach testing. Such patients with this thought disorder may become anxious or depressed as they struggle with circumstances that are threatening their stability, and they are often given otherwise appropriate medications. With these patients, such medications disrupt emotional stability and often accelerate decompensation to the point where psychotherapy is difficult or impossible, and hospitalization is necessary. The medications with the greatest deleterious potential are the benzodiazepines and their more recent pharmaceutical second cousins.

The nonmedical practitioner, in discussing with physicians the potential deleterious effects of certain medications on his/her patients, should be particularly sensitive to the physician's authority and pre-eminence in psychopharmacology, which must be unquestioned. The role of the psychotherapist is to alert the physician to psychological problems that would not have come to the physician's attention. When the interprofessional relationship is a comfortable one, the physician is eager to have the benefit of the psychotherapist's intense contact with the patient.

Although all schizophrenics are non-analyzable, some can be considered onion and others garlic. The latter are the more difficult to treat because, in addition to having a thought disorder, they are also antisocial. As will be seen, for some garlic schizophrenics such as serial killers, there currently exists no viable intervention other than a type of quarantine called incarceration.

Treating Psychotic Schizophrenia

Remembering that delusions are restitutional symptoms, in refocused psychotherapy we do not try to eliminate them by medication or otherwise, but rather join the patient's delusion to help the patient in his/her struggle to restore a malfunctioning ego. In other words, we augment and increase the patient's efforts to understand and master the conflicts and struggles that fostered the decompensation in the first place. To state it succinctly, the delusion is the therapist's ally, and the therapist's entry point.

Joining the delusion takes skill, as it has to be done without the patient feeling he/she is being mocked or lied to. In the case of Dennis, the CIA Menace, the therapist found ways to be credible without lying by saying "yes" when asked, "Do you believe me?" Once begun, joining the delusion must be constant and unwavering, for digressing one iota will betray the patient. The technique of joining the delusion can be used with onion schizophrenics as with Dennis, as well as with garlic schizophrenics such as Sam, who was going to poison the reservoir with LSD. However, the approach varies somewhat as addressing onion versus garlic always does.

The success rate with this kind of intervention is very high if the patient has not been previously medicated, especially for a long period of time. Prescribing antipsychotics seems to have the propensity of initially curtailing the patient's delusions, but because they seem to permanently alter the patients serotonin levels, their long-term use is made necessary to prevent relapse (Carlat, 2010; Greenberg, 2010; Kirsch, 2010; Whitaker, 2010). To employ this technique, the patient must be medication free and experiencing the delusion. Even after a period of medication, if once medication free and the delusion returns, the psychotherapist must make an educated decision of whether joining the delusion would be efficacious with this particular patient. Such a therapy judgment can only come after considerable experience with the technique.

The restitutive nature of delusions was well illustrated in the cases of Dennis and Sam in the preceding section on joining the delusion in Chapter 4. The totally decompensated schizophrenic in the back ward of a state hospital is a vegetable without delusions, without hallucinations, and with an overwhelmingly apparent thought disorder.

Functioning in schizophrenia varies according to the degree of severity of the disorder. When schizophrenia is latent, the individual is able to contain his/her anxiety and hostility in a viable delusion that enables him/her to function in society. Schizophrenics often present as neurotics until the process of psychotherapy or increasing stressors undermine their defenses and the thought disorder emerges. For example, after five or six sessions, an obsessional character who has a compulsion to brush his teeth may say, "I have to brush my teeth 25 times a day because I can't use the toilet brush to brush my teeth in the morning." Or a hysterical woman may say, "The reason why I can't have an orgasm is because at the moment the next door neighbor sends radio waves through our bedroom."

Another form of latent schizophrenia is the pseudoneurotic schizophrenic who looks like a neurotic but whose neurosis and personality traits keep changing. The pseudoneurotic schizophrenic may present as the perfect hysteric, but then looks like the perfect obsessive-compulsive and then perhaps the perfect phobic. Because of this liability, pseudoneurotics are often misdiagnosed as borderlines.

Many latent or patent schizophrenics have harmless propensities that would be inconsequential if it were not that the missing of their diagnosis often renders them victims of iatrogenic exacerbation of a mild condition. This is illustrated by the case of Olga, whose mother and next door neighbor desperately sought the psychologist's help.

Case Illustration: Anastasia, Czarina of Russia

Olga was a 16-year-old who had refused to get out of bed for almost all of the past year. Originally, she agreed to see the psychologist, but on the day she was to come to the office she characteristically refused to get out of bed. Her mother, who had been bringing meals on trays to her bed, and in all other respects had been waiting on her, was at her wits end. The mother was an apparently passive woman who had difficulty expressing herself. A neighbor had taken the initiative and pushed the reluctant mother, who feared her daughter would be found to be "crazy," to make the appointment with the psychologist. Seeing their desperation, the psychologist agreed to see them even though the appointment had been made for Olga. A determined woman, the neighbor did most of the talking while the mother sat wringing her hands.

Olga was born in the United States, but her parents were born in Harbin, China. She was the youngest generation of a large group of émigrés who fled to China following the Bolshevik Revolution in 1917, remained there for a few decades, and eventually entered the United States. She was part of a group of people who lived in fantasy and in the past. Setting aside their menial occupations, at the community functions they revelled in the glory of obsolete titles and elegantly tailored costumes. If one's grandfather had been a count or a general, one affected that position on the frequent Russian holidays that were occasions for these adults to "dress-up," pathetically childish as this may have appeared to outsiders. A fry cook by day, a man would don a general's uniform at night and receive all the deference accorded his grandfather in Czarist Russia. Olga grew up in this atmosphere, ostensibly the granddaughter of an ambassador. Her father, who simulated that role until he deserted the family, had not been seen since Olga was age 10.

Seeing no other effective way to engage Olga, the psychologist arranged for a house call. The home was modest, as were most homes in the district the Russian émigrés had settled, but Olga herself was elegantly dressed as she sat propped up in bed among satin pillows and sheets. She extended her hand, splendidly jewelled with the fortunes of her grandmother's generation. The psychologist felt as if he were in the presence of royalty.

Olga spoke in a deep throaty voice and with a decidedly Russian accent. It was difficult to keep in mind that she had, indeed, been born and reared in the United States. She also had a number of repetitive and manneristic motions that were schizophrenic rather than affected royalty. Initially, Olga was very skeptical of the psychologist, but spoke with him politely, if not haughtily. She explained that she had decided to be waited on in a manner befitting her position and she berated her mother for not insisting on the deference she deserved from her surroundings. She even hinted that her mother was actually a woman to whose care she had been entrusted. Instant rapport was established when the psychologist bent down and whispered in her ear, "Are you Princess Anastasia?"

Students of history as well as devotees of Ingrid Bergman movies will recall the legend that the Czar's daughter was smuggled out of Russia as a very young child. Not only was she the heir apparent to the Czarist throne, but she also was the rightful owner of the Romanoff fortune that had also been smuggled out of Russia. There have been many pretenders to that position, none of whom had been authenticated. In her own mind, Olga was the latest pretender, no matter that the real princess, if she did exist, would be an old woman by now.

She began addressing the psychologist as Czar Nicholas, playing off his real first name and ignoring the fact the real Czar had been dead for more than half a century. Seizing the windfall rapport, the psychologist extended an invitation that she visit him in his office. She did so and never became bedridden again. In the privacy of her individual sessions, the psychologist addressed her as Anastasia, and she reluctantly agreed to address him with a simple Nicholas rather than the full title she believed was his. The initial sessions with her addressed practical issues, but putting them in the context of her having to live without the luxury of being on the throne. Until the Czarist Empire was restored and restitution was made, she would have to finish school and then get a job. She agreed. After all, as she pointed out, even Czar Nicholas was working as a psychologist. She graduated from high school, attended a business school, and obtained a job as a secretary. She was seen infrequently and at her request, usually two or three times a year.

During the sessions, the psychologist would review her intervening activities since the last session, and helped her sort out inappropriate behavior. Olga could be very inappropriate. At one session, she asked immediately upon entering the office if she could have a drink. The psychologist went to the water cooler in the waiting room and when he returned to the office with a paper cup of water, Olga had taken a bottle of red wine and a crystal wine glass from her purse and was sipping an expensive vintage. When it was explained that this was inappropriate behavior for a doctor's office, she complied but responded that exceptions should be made for a princess.

In her late twenties, Olga married a contemporary she had known all of her life but paid no attention to until she saw him on leave and in his army uniform. At the same time, he was both her handsome "soldier boy" and a general. The bubble burst when he returned from the Vietnam War and donned civilian clothes. She became extremely anxious and would not allow him to touch her. She called for an appointment, but the psychologist was out of the country. In the emergency room that night, she was given a benzodiazapine by the psychiatrist on call. Three days later, Olga was hallucinating, created a scene in a large downtown bank as she demanded Anastasia's wealth, and was taken to the psychiatric ward of the county hospital.

Schizophrenics respond negatively to benzodiazepines, as well as to most antidepressive and anxiolytics. However, in an era where schizophrenia is not seen as a thought disorder and the condition is reserved for the blatant schizophrenic with obvious delusions and troublesome hallucinations, the latent and patent schizophrenics are misdiagnosed in accordance with the presenting symptoms. Schizophrenics can become very anxious on occasions, but their behavior is qualitatively different if one observes the thought disorder that is just beneath the anxiety. A nonphysician therapist experiences considerable difficulty questioning a prescribing psychiatrist's choice of medication. It is seen as an inappropriate response by a nonphysician. But it is not the physician's unquestioned authority to prescribe that is being challenged, but the inability to diagnose schizophrenia that is latent or patent. Once the medication has pushed the patient into blatant schizophrenia, there is no longer any question whatsoever as to the correct diagnosis.

Olga divorced her husband and continues to work. She calls for an appointment when she feels she needs one, sometimes going more than a year without contact. But she has had four hospitalizations, each following the prescription of any anxiety-reducing medication. In these instances, the psychologist was not available and she saw an emergency room physician. The problem has been eliminated by giving her a prescription for antipsychotic medication that she takes infrequently and around episodes of what she calls being "very nervous." She relies upon this appropriately and has not been hospitalized again. Her greatest crisis came at the time of "glasnost" in the Soviet Union. Olga, who had patiently waited all these years, became agitated as she thought the time to ascend the throne had arrived. She and her therapist worked through the crisis. She is quietly living her life, and although she still believes she is Anastasia, she also believes she will never be acknowledged as such. In a sense, she has given up the throne.

LEGEND

Psychological mechanism	Withdrawal (patent delusion)
Diagnosis	Adolescent schizophrenia
Operational diagnosis	Mother will no longer care for me
Implicit contract	Accept my imperial royalty
Personality type	Onion
Homework	Behave as royalty
Therapeutic technique	Join the delusion

When a schizophrenic patient decompensates, the treatment plan must focus on shoring up the defenses and covering up the thought disorder. Otherwise, interventions will precipitate a psychotic episode.

In blatant schizophrenia, there are prominent psychotic symptoms. Blatant schizophrenia most frequently emerges between the ages 18 and 25 and thus was once known as dementia praecox or the dementia of youth. The inability to make a transition from adolescence to adulthood results in a breakdown of coping, and the schizophrenic's thought disorder overwhelms him/her.

Schizophrenias Controlled by Individual Suffering

Dynamics

Schizophrenics who control their anxiety and anger by individual suffering sacrifice a portion of their functioning in order to achieve a reality they can cope with. When logic is sacrificed, as in paranoid schizophrenia, delusions of various kinds are prominent. There are several common types: somatic, world-reconstructionist, grandiosity, and persecution, to name a few.

When emotion is sacrificed, as in hebephrenic schizophrenia, the person avoids life by jumbling the emotional response. Informed of his/her mother's death, a hebephrenic will laugh uproariously. Informed of winning a lottery, he/she will cry for hours. Hebephrenics blunt a world that they cannot handle by giving up appropriate feelings.

When intellect is sacrificed, the simple schizophrenic presents as mentally retarded. The movie *Rain Man* paints a beautiful portrait of a simple schizophrenic. This type of schizophrenic can add seven-digit numbers virtually instantaneously, but would not be able to calculate the change if he/she bought a loaf of bread for a dollar and a candy bar for a quarter and gave the clerk a five dollar bill. The difference is that the first situation is abstract; the other is living. They withdraw the intellect from living. By giving up their intellect, simple schizophrenics control their anxieties and their anger but will score in the mentally retarded range on simple IQ tests. Unfortunately, the diagnosis of mental retardation precludes effective treatment.

When motility is sacrificed, the result is catatonic stupor. In one way, this is the most successful schizophrenic mechanism of all because it literally immobilizes the schizophrenic from acting on his/her desire to kill out of rage, but it is also the most devastating if the mechanism breaks down. The most dangerous schizophrenics are not the paranoids, but the catatonics whose loss of control over motility ends in mania rather than stupor. These are the people who would walk into a McDonald's or a schoolyard and kill all the people there because their immobility is no longer extant. Before demonstrating blatant symptoms, an emerging catatonic will display frozen positions or repetitive movement or verbal expressions. Diagnosing a catatonic at this stage can preclude the serious deterioration.

Entry

In working with schizophrenics, do not challenge the delusion. Do not do uncovering. Stay with the here and now. In the blatant schizophrenic, join the delusion as an ally, as in the example of Dennis, the CIA menace in the section on psychojudo. This case illustrates an axiom: a delusion occupies psychological space for which there is room for only one person. If you can get into the patient's delusional space, if the patient lets you in, the patient has to leave it. He/she can leave it, however, because he/she has identified with your ego. You cannot communicate with schizophrenics until they let you in. Schizophrenics cannot bond, but once they let you into their psychological space, it is like glue more than any bonding you will ever experience. They absolutely cling to your every word. You become their eyes, their ears, their brains. But every once in a while, because you do not think like they do, you will do something that leads them to conclude you are rejecting them.

Somaticized responses, usually among latent or patent schizophrenics, often follow fads. There are alleged "syndromes" that can suddenly appear, become epidemic among a sub-group, and then disappear almost as dramatically as they appeared. Such is the case of so-called yeast infections, a concept prevalent 30 years ago to explain all kinds of seemingly emotional difficulties. This "syndrome" has all but disappeared, but it has been replaced by multiple chemical sensitivity (MCS), which has prompted some communities (e.g., Marin County in California) to ban perfumes and other common chemicals from public meetings. The unproven theory is that a small chemical exposure can "sensitize" certain individuals to not only that chemical, but also a huge number of other chemicals and products found throughout the environment. Examination of the histories of these patients suggests that almost anything can trigger the sensitivity.

As in all epidemics that occur and then subside suddenly, it is important that the therapist bear in mind that any actual syndrome can be mimicked by a person in emotional distress. We have seen how borderline personalities simulate multiple personality syndrome. Similarly, latent or patent schizophrenics can "acquire" MCS, making it virtually impossible for the therapist to differentiate this from the medical condition. For such a patient, MCS fulfils all of the requirements of somatization where all interpersonal difficulties, social isolation, and fear of the world are explained by an ostensible physical condition. Yet, the psychotherapist can treat a patient with MCS without having to either establish the medical criteria or challenge the belief, as the case of Samantha illustrates.

Case Illustration: Samantha: Please, No Perfume

Typical was the case of Samantha, a divorced woman, age 32, who was referred for psychological evaluation by her physicians. They had concluded an exhaustive examination following her complaint that she could not work in an office where her co-workers wore perfume. She had demanded that the employer ban perfume and, upon the refusal of the company to do so, she filed a disability claim, which put into motion weeks of medical investigation. All the results were negative and her claim was denied.

Samantha kept weekly appointments with the psychologist only because to not do so would have jeopardized the appeal of her denied claim for disability. Her behavior, however, was anything but cooperative. She harangued the therapist with "proof" that all of her symptoms were physical and not psychological. The therapist was careful not to reveal a belief one way or the other. He conveyed an open mind and confessed that he was not an expert on MCS. This is all Samantha needed. She deluged the psychologist with books, reprints, newspaper clippings, and other materials intended to prove the theory of MCS. Over the course of four appointments, she grew steadily worse. When her appeal was denied, her sensitivities so worsened that she went to a "safe house" in Texas for several weeks.

The patient returned to therapy when her appeal was reopened and psychotherapy was made a condition for reconsideration. Fresh from Texas, Samantha was feeling much better and she was armed with a diagnostic work-up that indicated she was sensitive to no less than 80 common chemicals, and possibly more than 100. Sensitivity to perfumes was at the top of this list. She triumphantly presented these findings to the psychologist who, without challenge, accepted them in amazement. She resented having to see the psychologist, but apologized for her previous antagonism and seemed open to some kind of coexistence.

From the previous session, the psychologist had noted that Samantha's difficulties long preceded her MCS symptoms. She had manifested severe social problems throughout her life. In high school, she was very much the social isolate and particularly resented a clique of girls from well-to-do families who flaunted their clothes and other manifestations of affluence. Without ever connecting it to the present, Samantha once uttered, "I could smell them coming a mile away from their expensive perfume, and I would do anything to keep from seeing the haughty smirk on their faces."

Samantha had a series of brief, tumultuous relationships with men, which always ended with her breaking off the affair. Following each break-up, she would experience a period of several months where she sought isolation. She did not have any close female friends, either. When asked about this, she replied, "All the women I like wear perfume, so I can never really get to know them." It was very apparent, however, that Samantha's current severe symptoms began with her relationship with Harry, a dentist with three children from a previous marriage. Samantha and Harry had been sleeping together for two years and he wanted to marry her. She resented the occasions when she was required to play mother to Harry's children, and accused her lover of wanting to marry her so his children would have a mother. The more Samantha became attached to Harry, and the more he pressured her to marry him, the worse the MCS had become. However, the psychologist was meticulous in not making this connection. Rather, the psychologist took his cue from Samantha's desire to coexist in a situation she did not want. He said, "Samantha, let's let the doctors fight over your chemical sensitivities while we stay out of that here. Why don't we do something they don't expect. We can take advantage of the situation and spend our time exploring your relationship with Harry. We know that has nothing to do with MCS and it is something I as a psychologist just might be able to help you with." She wondered if our exploration might reveal that she should leave Harry. The therapist pointed out, "If that is to be, better to know it early on." She agreed and plunged into the task with enthusiasm.

All of Samantha's life, except for the chemical sensitivities, became the subject of her therapy. Over the next several weeks, she slowly came out of her social isolation; as she improved, so did her MCS. Neither patient nor therapist made this connection. However, Samantha found she could tolerate the chemicals in the office when, at her request, her employer transferred her to a desk a short distance from her co-workers. She got the courage to approach a co-worker she liked and invited her to have dinner. She asked this woman whether she would mind not wearing perfume and received a positive response. In time, she was friendly with several women, all of whom volunteered for the sake of their newfound friend not to wear perfume.

Harry and Samantha were married in a small, private ceremony. The patient quit her job and is enjoying being a full-time homemaker. She meticulously maintains a chemical-free home, but she has an ever-expanding circle of friends. She is amazed that she can even tolerate perfume on the many social occasions she and Harry happily attend. For the first time in her life, Samantha is not a social isolate. The therapy was concluded with the connection between her symptoms and her interpersonal problems never having been made.

LEGEND

Psychological mechanism	Withdrawal (delusion)
Diagnosis	Somaticizing schizophrenic: MCS
Operational diagnosis	Denial of disability claim
Implicit contract	Prove my condition is physical and not emotional
Personality type	Garlic covering onion
Homework	Keep MCS out of therapy
Therapeutic technique	Accept the resistance

Whereas MCS can engender a great deal of sympathy from society and even interest from physicians, a blatantly paranoid somatization is rejected by both society and the medical profession. Yet, the interventions follow the same therapeutic principles employed in other delusional formations. This is illustrated by the case of Ken.

Case Illustration: Stinky Ken

Somatization can be baffling to a physician who must order more and more tests in an effort to find the physical disease. When somatization reaches psychotic proportions, however, the physician quickly recognizes the mental illness. In this way, Ken was referred to the psychologist.

An 18-year-old freshman in college, Ken was referred by the emergency room physician when he appeared there complaining that one of his abdominal organs was rotting. He was not certain which one, but he knew this was so from the odor it gave off. This is a form of paranoid schizophrenia, sometimes called "organ psychosis," and the complaint is a delusion in every sense, and should be treated as such (see case of Dennis in Chapter 4). Having been alerted on the telephone by the referring physician, the psychologist prepared himself.

After Ken was ushered into the office and he and the therapist had exchanged greetings, the psychologist got up from his chair, saying, "Excuse me a minute." He then took a can of air freshener and extensively sprayed the room. The patient asked, "How bad is it?" The therapist replied, "Nothing I can't live with. How long has this been going on?" He responded that it began with a mild aroma about five months ago.

It is important to note that, although the therapist joined the delusion, at no time did he specifically state that he smelled the odor. This is an important distinction in that behavior is more reassuring than words, and the therapist has not said anything he is not able to say with conviction. The paranoid is extremely sensitive to even the slightest hint of insincerity.

Ken was an overly protected son who lived in a devoutly religious home. Most of his contacts had taken place with his church group, and he had attended Christian day schools all of his academic life. His family had hoped to send him to a distant Christian college, but the father's untimely death and a series of financial reverses made that impossible. His mother was a proud woman who did not want to accept charity. So Ken went to the state university where he had obtained a scholarship. This was his first experience living away from home.

The real world was both intriguing and frightening to Ken. His new friends teased him about his religious fundamentalism and embarked on a well-meaning campaign to get him to "loosen up." Ken tried alcohol and pot for the first time, and had his first sexual experience. Ken became more and more like the other men in the dormitory, until one day, as if he had rediscovered his religious convictions, he abruptly returned to his previously strict religious behavior. His former friends lost interest in him. Seeing him as boring and even embarrassing, they avoided him. Soon, Ken began experiencing difficulty concentrating and he responded by skipping classes. He became increasingly withdrawn and isolated, but he recalled only that five months ago he developed a mild odor that was generating from his abdomen. The odor grew steadily worse until he realized one of his internal organs was rotting.

This delusion, as are all delusions, was restitutive. It accounted for his friends avoiding him and it spared him the turmoil of questioning his rigid upbringing. It also punished him for his brief period of alcohol and drug intake. Ken was certain that either alcohol or pot had damaged him physically, or that God was punishing him for transgressing. All of this was, of course, not directly discussed with Ken until after he had given up his delusion.

In the beginning, Ken agreed to use air freshener in his dormitory room so people would not be discouraged from visiting him. Also, he had to make every attempt to keep up with his classes. While in class, he would try to sit near an open window or away from the main group. Then, Ken was asked whether the rotting was physical damage or punishment from God. Ken thought it was probably the latter. The therapist agreed inasmuch as the rotting of the internal organ had not caused him to become seriously and systemically ill. The patient was asked to construct an elaborate penance, accompanied by prayers for forgiveness. Until he was forgiven, he was to use lots of air freshener and deodorant.

Each time Ken came in to the therapist, the latter sprayed the office with air freshener. And on each visit, Ken reported on his religious recompensation. Each time, they both learned a little more about Ken's problems. But the therapist was careful not to delve into them. In the fourth session, the patient announced that the therapist did not need to spray the office. Ken had given up his delusion, and this was a signal that he was ready to discuss the issues of an overly protected son who needed to grow up.

LEGEND

Psychological mechanism	Psychotic (delusional) somatization, projection
Diagnosis	Schizophrenia, paranoid
Operational diagnosis	Leaving home to go to college
Implicit contract	I am not crazy
Personality type	Onion
Homework	Use air freshener
Therapeutic techniques	Humor the resistance, enter the delusion

As is stated in the section on obsessive-compulsive neurosis, an elaborate obsessional system can often hide and mitigate an underlying thought disorder. The persons are potentially obsessional schizophrenics; as long as the obsessional system works and remains intact, the thought disorder is never manifest. Acquaintances and co-workers do find such a person a bit "peculiar" and "rigid," but an underlying potential psychosis is never suspected. If all continues in this vein, none will ever become manifest. However, often in such obsessionally defended individuals, there may occur events that cause the defense to decompensate. A latent schizophrenic may become patent, or even blatant. This is illustrated by the case of James, who was always regarded as a bit peculiar, but certainly okay by his fellow state employees. Then, one day, all this began to change.

Case Illustration: James to the Rescue

An obsessional schizophrenic can for many years contain the thought disorder with an elaborate obsessional system that is plausible enough to escape being identified as psychotic. Such a system can be a world reconstruction fantasy, a psychological representation of the patient's attempt to reconstruct a fragile ego to keep it from crumbling.

James, for over 10 years, had worked for the state highway department as a surveyor. He had barely graduated from college with minimally passing grades in engineering and never attempted to obtain a job as an engineer. He was satisfied to work as a surveyor, a skill he learned in his engineering curriculum. He had settled for the security of a civil service job, and no one suspected how troubled he was with his self-image as an underachiever. He was regarded by everyone who came in contact with him as a fussy, meticulous man who had a slavish devotion to orderliness. He drove everyone to exasperation with his orderliness, so people just stayed out of his way. No one suspected that beneath all of this he was psychotic.

In his job as a surveyor in the highway system, James had witnessed the aftermath of many automobile accidents, some of them fatal. It was only natural he would be obsessed with highway safety. His solution to the problem raised a few eyebrows, but it was seen as well-meaning and, though unworkable, harmless enough. James had devised an elaborate system of stripes for the highways that would be color-coded to signify different speed limits for each lane. Each speed would have its own color, and a thin electrical wire imbedded in the paint had the capacity to change the color of the stripe from a central control panel. The colors of the stripes could be varied in accordance with traffic conditions. Speed limits would be decreased during congestion or bad weather, and increased when traffic conditions warranted it. James was convinced his system would prevent accidents and save lives. He would discuss his system with anyone who would listen, and he always had handy his briefcase with engineering drawings for the scheme. To everyone, James was a "pleasant nut" to be politely avoided. It is not surprising that at age 36, James was still living alone.

Suddenly, James became more of a nuisance when he insisted that the traffic situation was soon to be out of control. To prevent the ensuing carnage, the state highway department had better implement his system before it was too late. He imposed himself on his superiors, and when they put him off, he went behind their backs to the highway department director. Soon he was sending urgent faxes to the state legislators and to the governor. James was no longer a "pleasant nut." His immediate supervisor was told to control him. James's world reconstruction fantasy had now become a world destruction fantasy, signaling the decompensation of his obsessional system and the crumbling of his ego. When James disobeyed his supervisor and even accelerated the number of faxes to important persons, he was suspended from his job.

James retreated to his apartment for several days, and on Sunday, when the road crews were not working, he went to the highway department yard and stole a truck loaded with highway barriers. He was closing off the third freeway entrance when arrested. When apprehended, he was severely agitated and incessantly screamed that the end of the freeway system was at hand. He was remanded to the psychiatric ward of the local hospital by the police. It was there that James, now in full-blown psychosis, was seen for the first time since his underlying, long-term schizophrenia had previously been contained by his obsessional system.

The precipitating event was an involvement with a woman that James met inadvertently in spite of his own shyness. It was she who took control and got them together over a period of weeks. When eventually they went to bed, James was impotent, experienced a heterosexual panic, and bolted. At home that night, he began having homosexual fears, which soon translated into his awareness that the end of the freeway system was at hand. James was treated in the hospital and released two weeks later. He entered outpatient therapy and began working back from his color-coded highway lane stripes to his real fears and concerns that had impaired his intellectual functioning and kept him isolated all of his life.

LEGEND	
Psychological mechanism	Psychotic (delusional)
Diagnosis	Schizophrenia (patent to blatant)
Operational diagnosis	Sexual affair for first time, with sexual panic
Implicit contract	I am not crazy
Personality type	Onion
Homework	Refrain from sex
Therapeutic technique	Enter the delusion (highway codes)

Because in the current psychiatric nomenclature only blatant schizophrenia is recognized, psychotherapy can miss the early signs of decompensation and thereby also miss the opportunity for early intervention. The case of Sherrill is provided to alert therapists to early signs of catatonia in patients who, like Sherrill, would never ordinarily be regarded as a fast-approaching psychosis.

Case Illustration: Sherrill, the Catatonic Nurse

Because the stuporous symptoms of catatonia respond so well to antipsychotic medication, most psychotherapists today have never seen a case of catatonic schizophrenia. Coupled with the fact that the catatonic's thought disorder is the least in evidence of all the schizophrenias, psychotherapists are very likely to miss a case of early catatonia. This is exactly what had happened with Sherrill, a 26-year-old registered nurse.

Sherrill's psychotherapist was baffled by the patient's complaints, which included a failed sexual relationship with a male physician and the threat of seduction by an ardent lesbian nurse, both of whom were on the same hospital staff with her. Yet, Sherrill was really not very attached to the physician, although she talked a great deal about the brief, torrid affair. And even as she complained of the advances from the other nurse, she was distant, and even detached, from the so-called threat. Because Sherrill manifested no discerned thought disorder, schizophrenia was not considered a diagnosis, and her flat affect was misdiagnosed as major depression. The psychotherapist, an astute and experienced psychologist, was not comfortable with the provisional diagnosis of major depression and requested that she interview the patient behind the one-way mirror with the entire staff present on the other side. This was arranged, and the senior author happened to be present on a routine visit to the center.

The staff concentrated so much on what Sherrill was saying that they missed the cardinal symptom. They struggled to understand her interpersonal difficulties, her inability to adequately do her nursing job, and her desire to be alone most of the time. They did not question the misdiagnosis of her flat affect as major depression, and they did not even notice her catatonic posturing. For the entire 45-minute session, Sherrill's right foot was frozen six inches off the floor. A person has great difficulty maintaining such a position for more than one minute. Yet, Sherrill's right foot remained suspended in mid-air for the entire session and no one even noticed. So much for nonverbal cues!

When the senior author mentioned this in the follow-up session, the staff was skeptical. Fortunately, the session had been videotaped, and a fast forwarding of the tape confirmed the prolonged catatonic posturing. The staff was stunned with its own nonperceptivity. Sherrill's diagnosis was changed to that of catatonic schizophrenia, she was started on antipsychotic medication, and the meaning of her symptom was addressed in therapy. In time, it was understood that Sherrill was giving up her motility so as not to physically attack the married physician who used her and then dumped her. Had she not been treated properly, in all likelihood the patient might have acted out her rage (catatonic mania) or, more likely, she would have denied the rage by regressing into catatonic stupor. Sherrill was an onion catatonic and was unlikely to attack. A third possibility would have been a sudden, seemingly senseless running away. This, too, would have been an onion response.

LEGEND

Psychological mechanism	Withdrawal, give up motility
Diagnosis	Early catatonic schizophrenia
Operational diagnosis	Trouble at work
Implicit contract	I am not angry
Personality type	Onion
Homework	Don't see your physician ex-lover
Therapeutic techniques	Antipsychotic medication, insight into sexual affair

---

It is not infrequent that an early schizophrenic is misdiagnosed as a depressive and prescribed an antidepressant rather than an antipsychotic. A withdrawn early schizophrenic can resemble a slowed-down depressive. When asked, "Are you depressed?" a patient may erroneously report yes because he/she does not know the difference. The tragedy is more than the patient's being deprived of the appropriate treatment, for treatment with benzodiazepines and antidepressants can often propel an early schizophrenia into full-blown psychosis. An example of such mishandling is the case of Randall, whose father's diagnosis was more accurate than that of his doctors.

Case Illustration: Randall, the Jumper

Randall, a 28-year-old unemployed single man living at home with his widowed father, was presented to the senior author because the patient seemed to be decompensating on the antidepressant regimen he had been on for the past three months. Since the patient was regarded as suicidal, the psychologist was reluctant to question the medication, but he asked for help in understanding this case.

The psychologist and the senior author interviewed the patient and his father together. From the onset of the interview, it was apparent that the identified patient's immobility and slow response were not manifestations of a retarded depression. His immobility was accompanied by repetitive, stereotyped, and highly manneristic movements when he did speak. Through most of the session, his left arm was suspended above his head. His speech, though infrequent, was circumstantial and manneristic.

Inquiry into the alleged suicide attempt was revealing. Randall had been hospitalized with the diagnosis of psychotic depression. Early on his second day of hospitalization, he became increasingly more agitated until about 4:00 in the afternoon when he jumped out of the hospital's third-floor window. He landed on both feet and broke both ankles. In spite of this, Randall proceeded to walk over three miles. He recalled that there was absolutely no pain. He was apprehended when he attacked without provocation and with his fists three policemen who were guarding a visiting dignitary. The patient manifested a tethering of a feared garlic reaction. His jumping out the window was a substitute for attacking the hospital staff and his attacking the police was an expression of his rage in a way that would really not hurt anyone else.

Somewhat belatedly, the current diagnosis of catatonic schizophrenia was made. The antidepressants, which were causing decompensation, where discontinued in favor of antipsychotic medication. In therapy, Randall was treated as a schizophrenic and he rapidly improved.

Interestingly, the father had been aware of his son's schizophrenia for over a decade. He was comfortable with caring for his son, an activity that filled a void caused by his wife's untimely death 12 years ago. This father could not help but note his son's mental aberrations, and he read and informed himself as to better care for Randall. His entreaties to his son's psychiatrists that Randall was a schizophrenic were cavalierly ignored until now.

LEGEND

Psychological mechanism	Withdrawal, give up motility
Diagnosis	Catatonic schizophrenia
Operational diagnosis	Father's concern
Implicit contract	I am not angry
Personality type	Onion suppressing garlic
Homework	Let father help you
Therapeutic techniques	Discontinue antidepressant in favor of antipsychotic, help father care for schizophrenic son

9

ONION/GARLIC PSYCHODYNAMICS

Garlic that is Non-analyzable

Schizophrenias Controlled by Attacking the Environment

In schizophrenias controlled by attacking the environment, defenses against acting out hostility have been overwhelmed. Catatonic mania occurs when the loss of control of motility leads not to stupor, but to destructiveness, as in the following case of Alvin. Attacking paranoia occurs when delusions and personality types coalesce to make acts of destruction not only logical, but necessary for salvation, as in the case of Ernesto below.

Entry

The potential of destructive violence must be carefully considered in attacking schizophrenia. The intensity of psychosis must be reduced by medication and the patient stabilized before psychotherapy is possible. Then, treatment should be focused on solving specific problems in daily living. A biopsychosocial plan of rehabilitation and access to the full continuum of care may be necessary.

Fortunately for those around him, Alvin turned his original attacking schizophrenia back onto himself. Although the result was grossly to his own detriment, the extent of the rage manifested could have produced drastic consequences had he attacked the environment. That the catatonic hears and sees while in a stupor is also dramatically illustrated by the case of Alvin. Therapy, patiently and painstakingly applied, can even have positive results with a person in a catatonic stupor.

Case Illustration: Old MacDonald Had a Son

Alvin, a 17-year-old adolescent who lived on a farm with his father and stepmother, was first seen after he had amputated both of his legs above the knees. He was also mute and in a total catatonic stupor. Had not the hired man found him lying in the barn shortly after the self-amputations, applied tourniquets, and summoned help, Alvin surely would have bled to death. The surgeon who stitched up the stumps marveled at how skillfully the patient had amputated his own limbs. Examination of Alvin's blood revealed no alcohol or drugs of any kind that might have lessened what had to be excruciating pain. Many weeks later, after he came out of his stupor, Alvin stated that he absolutely felt nothing as he sawed both of his legs with an ordinary carpenter's saw. He was only acutely aware of the annoying, cutting sound and that the bleeding got in the way.

The patient was, of course, unresponsive to verbal psychotherapy, and his antipsychotic medication was force-fed, as was also his nutrition. The psychologist decided on a treatment plan in which he would visit Alvin daily during the lunch hour and conduct a one-sided conversation for about 15 minutes. The monologue each time was similar: "Hello, Alvin, I'm Dr. Cummings. This is your sixth day in the hospital and it's April 9th. It rained last night and this morning. You don't have to talk, but when you're ready, I'm here to listen." The remainder of the 15 minutes would be filled with news and other events of the last 24 hours. Then, the psychologist would conclude, "Goodbye, Alvin, I'll see you at noon tomorrow." If it were Friday, the goodbye would be modified to state the psychologist would see the patient on Monday following the weekend. All communications were brief, simple, but very precise.

For weeks, Alvin remained unresponsive, staring into nothingness as he ignored the psychologist. Then, one day, his lips moved almost imperceptibly, but what he said was inaudible. Attempts to get him to repeat what he had said were unsuccessful and were promptly dropped so as not to risk increasing the patient's negativism. Another week went by before Alvin spoke, this time quite audibly: "I'll get well if you don't send me home." Then he lapsed back into his mute, immobile state.

The psychologist now altered the content of the daily monologue to report progress in arranging transfer to a halfway house when Alvin was ready to leave the hospital. In due time, the psychologist reported that all the arrangements had been made and all that remained was Alvin's ability to leave the hospital. The patient remained unresponsive for several days. Then, one day when the psychologist came to visit, Alvin was in a wheelchair, transporting himself all over the fifth floor of the hospital, and talking with staff and fellow patients.

Psychotherapy now began in a more formal sense as Alvin was also fitted for and taught to use artificial limbs. It was then that the full story came to light. Alvin's mother died when he was age 14. The father was distraught, lonely, and depressed. The burden of seeing that all the farm chores were done fell on Alvin, as his father was too depressed to attend to what was necessary. Also, the father moved Alvin into his bed where he remained for two-and-a-half years. The father would have bad dreams and often embrace Alvin in his sleep, thinking he was the deceased wife. Just before Alvin's 17th birthday, the father met a woman, fell in love, came out of his depression, and married.

Alvin was returned to his former bedroom where every night he could hear the giggles and the lovemaking. The stepmother resented Alvin, and the father was too engrossed in his new life to pay the boy much attention. After several months, Alvin began experiencing, in the middle of the night, an uncontrollable urge to go into the adjacent room and murder his stepmother. One night, the urge was so strong that Alvin got dressed, went to his high school, broke in, and did thousands of dollars worth of damage as he smashed everything in sight with a sledge hammer. He was awaiting determination of his case by juvenile authorities when the uncontrollable urge to kill his stepmother occurred again. This time, instead of a garlic (attack) reaction, Alvin chose the penultimate onion reaction and amputated his own legs.

As is typical of catatonic stupor, Alvin was aware of and remembered everything he saw and heard during the more than two months he was in that state. He recalled all the details of the 15-minute conversations and described in the subsequent therapy his mute and motionless inner struggle as to whether he should trust the psychologist. During the stupor, the mind of the catatonic is very clear, and insensitive remarks are remembered and resented.

LEGEND

Psychological mechanism	Withdrawal, give up motility
Diagnosis	Catatonic schizophrenia
Operational diagnosis	Father's remarriage
Implicit contract	I'll stay in my stupor
Personality type	Garlic retreating into onion
Homework	Remain in stupor
Therapeutic techniques	Accept patient's stupor, arrange halfway house

---

A case of paranoid schizophrenia, which was misdiagnosed and mishandled by professionals over a number of years, had a tragic ending that attracted much media attention and generated a great deal of hindsight. It is important that we as psychotherapists learn from a case as tragically mishandled as Ernesto.

Case Illustration: Ernesto the Constant Cuckold

Predicting violent behavior on the part of the paranoid schizophrenic is difficult, if not improbable. Yet, observing the history of the paranoid behavior to determine whether it is onion (suffering) or garlic (attacking) can be extremely helpful. It should be assumed that all garlic paranoids have the potential to attack, and appropriate precautions should be initiated and kept in place. Had this taken place with Ernesto, three small children and their mother might be alive today. With the visual acuity that accompanies hindsight, it might be helpful to assess how therapeutic ineptitude did nothing to avert a tragedy.

Ernesto, a man of 33, was seen for evaluation after a quadruple murder and attempted suicide. He had shot and killed his wife and three small children, and then critically wounded himself. His bungled suicide enabled the piecing together of a garlic paranoia that was abetted by therapy in its eventual deadly attack.

From the first day of his eight-year marriage, Ernesto was insanely jealous of his wife, Louisa. On the first night of their honeymoon, he beat her for allowing too many male guests to kiss her on the cheek as they went through the wedding reception line. Inevitably, whenever they were out in public, he would accuse Louisa of making amorous eye contact with a total stranger.

About every three to four months, matters would come to a boil. Ernesto would "discern" that Louisa was having a sexual affair with someone they both knew, and he would slap her, badger her, and torment her for hours until she broke down begging his forgiveness. Whereupon Ernesto would tenderly wipe her tears, embrace her, and magnanimously forgive her. They would pray on their knees to God for another two hours, asking also for divine forgiveness for Louisa. These episodes were repeated three to four times a year. They were always preceded by two to three weeks during which Ernesto would secretly follow her and otherwise spy on her. His job as automobile insurance claims adjuster gave him considerable leeway to leave his job during the day to spy on her. Invariably, once the torment session was over with the granting of divine forgiveness, Ernesto would go through a 10-day to two-week period of insatiable sexual appetite in which he made love to Louisa three times a day.

In his early twenties, before he married Louisa, Ernesto had experienced a religious conversion in which he left the Catholic Church and joined a Pentecostal sect. He sincerely believed that a devil would possess Louisa, a naturally loving and chaste woman, and cause her to perform unspeakable acts with other men. He further believed that God's providence had instructed him to cast out this devil.

Ernesto and Louisa sought psychological help for their marital difficulties on at least two dozen occasions during their eight years of marriage. Sometimes the children's nightmares, enuresis, and other problems were the excuse to seek this help. Unfortunately, the mental health service of the HMO to which they belonged provided only crisis intervention. This was also true for the community mental health center to which they presented themselves or their distraught children on a number of occasions.

The crisis workers concentrated on helping the couple in their marriage. Ernesto's behavior was attributed to a combination of cultural factors (Filipino), religious fervor, and deep personal insecurities and low self-esteem as a man. If medication was prescribed, it would be antidepressants. Only once was Ernesto given an antipsychotic. In his paranoia, Ernesto distrusted any medication and never took it as prescribed. No one followed up to see if he had complied. In all of this, no one listened or probed enough to discover that Ernesto had an elaborate, well-systematized delusion that sought constant corroboration. This delusion was on a collision course with tragedy.

The delusion was named Breckenridge. Although the first name was James, Ernesto thought and spoke of him only as Breckenridge. In the patient's mind, Breckenridge was a combination of James Bond, the Red Baron, and the Count of Monte Cristo. He was dashing, urbane, fabulously wealthy, and exceptionally virile. He had seduced Louisa when she was only 16, and she had been in love with him ever since. But God had informed Ernesto that Breckenridge was really the Devil in human form. He had the ability to possess Louisa because of her persistent love for him. It was God's plan for Ernesto to cast out this devil. If he failed, he would have to kill her and also the children since they, too, would be possessed. The ability to cast out the devil from Louisa was the key to the future. In the meantime, Louisa's infidelities, driven by Breckenridge, would be God's way of testing Ernesto's faith. None of this delusion was ever revealed to the various mental health professionals who had been seen; not surprisingly, they were not looking and probing for psychosis.

After years of struggling with Ernesto's periodic torments, Louisa announced she was leaving him. If she carried out her threat, how, then, could Ernesto continue his work of purifying Louisa? Within hours, Ernesto received his answer and instructions from God. He should kill Louisa and the three children, as well as himself. Then all five of their souls would be transported to Heaven where there is no sin and no divorce. The family would be intact through eternity and free of Breckenridge at last! Ernesto thanked God in his prayers for this deliverance, and set out to accomplish his divine mission.

In eight years of mental health crisis contacts, Ernesto had never been properly diagnosed. The establishing of the diagnosis of paranoid schizophrenia would be only the beginning. The paranoid delusion, as well as his overt behavior for eight years, was clearly garlic, indicating the potential to be an attacking paranoid. The elicitation of the delusion would have made clear that the family needed protection and Ernesto needed antipsychotic medication with the follow-up to assure he was complying with the regimen.

LEGEND	
Psychological mechanism	Withdrawal (delusions), attack, projection
Diagnosis	Paranoid schizophrenia

LEGEND . . . *continued*

Operational diagnosis	Wife announced divorce
Implicit contract	I must join my family in Heaven
Personality type	Garlic
Homework	Comply with medication regimen
Therapeutic techniques	Antipsychotic medication, suicidal precautions

Impulse Schizophrenia

Perhaps the most egregious of the schizophrenics are those who combine their thought disorder with sociopathic propensities and behavior. An impulse schizophrenic is one who cannot suppress the impulse to kill, and this impulse is often combined with ritualistic behavior that precedes the homicide. The ritualistic nature of the killing, as with San Francisco's never caught Zodiac Killer who had to kill people in accordance with a certain progression in the zodiac charts, is in actuality a restitutive symptom. It is an attempt to keep from killing wantonly, and perhaps even more frequently than otherwise would take place.

The rituals may range from a proscribed period of stalking, to the need to choose victims who fit certain characteristics, or those governed by events on the calendar. They may be disguised in so-called ideology, such as in the case of an African American named Williams who was steadily killing black youth in Georgia because he saw that his mission was to reduce the African American population by killing boys before they were old enough to father offspring. The presence of the thought disorder was evident in a number of ways, not the least of which was the inability to appreciate the fact that reducing the number of females, not males, is the fastest way to reduce a population. Until they apprehended this serial killer, the authorities felt certain that the killer had to be a vengeful white man.

Diagnosis

It is interesting to note that the debate among psychiatrists is whether these serial killers suffer from bipolar disorder, or whether they are just plain sociopaths who know right from wrong but who respond to their pathological impulses. In refocused psychotherapy, serial killers are seen as impulse schizophrenics in whom a schizophrenic thought disorder is combined with a sociopathic personality, because their behavior far exceeds that of a sociopath. Many are cannibalistic, such as Jeffrey Dahmer who kept body parts of his victims in his freezer and occasionally feasted on them. Most are sadistic, enjoying hurting their victims and mutilating them while they are still alive, and necrophilia is common. Sequestering their victims and revisiting them regularly to perform sexual acts is frequent. Ted Bundy, for example, would spend hours with some of the corpses of his decomposing victims, grooming them and performing sexual acts, long after putrefaction had created an odor that hardly anyone else could have tolerated it. Saving body parts of the victims, such as the head or hands, is also common.

Perhaps more than psychiatry, the Federal Bureau of Investigation (FBI) may understand the most about serial killers. As part of its extensive collection of data of past serial killers, the FBI has developed effective profiling to aid in detection and capture. Additionally, it has at its headquarters in Washington a museum of personal effects of past serial killers, along with their writings, that would point strongly to the existence of a schizophrenic thought disorder in these sociopaths. One of the reasons the thought disorder is not a consideration among psychiatrists is that a pre-psychotic schizophrenic thought disorder is no longer recognized by them.

Though rare, female serial killers also exist. One such was a prostitute who was living in a lesbian relationship with another woman. She would hitch a ride with a prospective male victim, and after collecting money for sex, she would murder him and dump his body on the side of the road. She operated along interstate routes mostly in the Midwest, and she prided herself at removing undesirable males from existence. In spite of the fact that, when found, the corpses revealed signs of recent sexual activity, because of the rarity of female serial killers the authorities for some time continued to look for a male suspect.

Case Illustration: Ted Bundy, Handsome and Charismatic

In the mid-1970s, I haplessly found myself seeing Ted Bundy, ostensibly in a first and only psychotherapy drop-in visit. I was covering the psychotherapy walk-in clinic on that particular morning when the receptionist said there was a most needy, likeable young man who was passing through town and needed desperately to be seen. She had him waiting eagerly just outside my office even though he had filled out only part of the intake form, leaving out the pertinent information as to why he needed to be seen. "He says it is so confidential he must speak to you about it only in person," and then she pleaded, "Please see him." She handed me the form with the name Theodore Robert Bundy, with a Florida address, and with nothing else. This was not like Lorraine, who was generally a stickler for having the intake form properly completed.

She ushered into my office an affable, smiling, and handsome young man who immediately informed me everyone calls him Ted. He charmingly filled the first 10 minutes without giving me even a clue as to why he was here. I advised him that drop-in visits are seen at half-hour intervals, and we needed to get to why he was seeing me. Even with apologies and assurances that he really did need to see me, the rest of the time he continued to be equally baffling, but totally charismatic. I dismissed him at the end of 30 minutes with the conclusion that the receptionist had been charmed by this man and I had been used, but for what purpose I knew not.

Shortly thereafter, the news was filled with the capture of this serial killer, and 10 years after that he finally confessed to 30 plus killings. I speculated after his capture why he had bothered to see me, and concluded that he needed the assurance of being able to fool a prominent psychologist. My reputation in San Francisco was that of the shrink of last resort, seeing everyone's therapeutic failures. If he were able to fool me, he did not need to fear whether he could also fool the police and the FBI. Why else? Although I will never know for sure, years later I was reminded of this when I was seeing another man who presented as possibly the most "normal" patient I had ever seen. My suspicion led me to contact Sergeant Hansen of the San Francisco Police Mental Health Squad. Indeed, it turned out he actually was a wanted and suspected serial killer, so the heads-up is being proffered to be on the alert for the rare possibility that a serial killer may be seeking reassurance he can fool the authorities.

Entry Point

Impulse schizophrenics often have a long history of being seen in the mental health system, but they will not relate this to you. They will come in hoping that by some magic you will be able to fix them, and they generally leave you wondering, "That was such a charming, healthy, normal human being. Why the hell did he come in?" They have looking normal down to a science and are even more clever than sociopaths. They come in hoping that somehow someone by magic can remove the impulse to kill.

There is no treatment for impulse schizophrenia; there is only incarceration to remove the possibility of acting on the impulse. Yet, even when the courts have removed such a person from society, our system of justice often releases the serial killer and the tragedy may be repeated.

Case Illustration: Harry, the Serial Killer

Within the confines of the state hospital, there was a 52-year-old silver-haired, distinguished looking man who had brutally killed eight women. His murders demonstrated the classic signs of both ritual and choice of women who fit certain criteria. Yet, during his past four years in the state hospital, his behavior belied his psychotic brutality. Harry was charming, especially toward women. He had ingratiated himself with nearly everyone, was accorded freedom of the grounds, and had been assigned to the library as patient-assistant. Whenever anyone, staff or patient, needed help, Harry was there. His silver tongue matched his silver hair. Everyone seemed to have forgotten who Harry was and what he had done.

Then, Harry filed a writ to be released from the hospital as cured. The hospital contested the writ and Harry became his own advocate.

The psychologist was asked to administer a battery of psychological tests in anticipation of the court hearing. Harry cooperated fully and yielded a surprisingly healthy profile. The psychologist was uneasy: Harry's responses were too normal. Either he was the healthiest person alive, or there was something odd about the test results. In thinking through the matter, the psychologist was struck by the answer. Harry had access in the hospital library to all of the tests and pertinent books. A highly intelligent and resourceful man, he had memorized both the tests and a set of responses.

A technique known as "testing the limits" was then applied. Harry was asked to respond to a second administration of the Rorschach inkblots without repeating any of his previous responses. Harry complied with an incredibly healthy profile. He had memorized a back-up set of responses! The Rorschach was administered a third time and with the same restriction. Harry finally revealed himself, but only momentarily. He described card III as a wood carving of two men and stated the red was the bleeding from the carving. When asked how wood could bleed real blood as it was being carved, Harry quickly recovered. He knew he had revealed himself, but he laughed it off.

As significant as the psychotic response is to a psychologist, it would not be understood or appreciated by a jury that would be charmed by Harry. When the hearing arrived, Harry was, in fact, so likeable that it was obvious the jury had been won over. The psychologist presented his test findings, which Harry, doing the cross-examination on behalf of himself, cut to shreds. He even had the jury laughing about the alleged significance of the one silly response to an inkblot, especially since the psychologist had to admit all of the other many responses were quite normal.

The jury did not release Harry, but only because the psychologist described with every gory detail how he had tortured and killed eight women. This was repeated annually for the next three years. Harry's writ was denied repeatedly because the jury was filled with revulsion when the murders were described. But Harry was not to be outdone. In putting in his fifth writ, he had already ascertained the psychologist would be out of the country and unable to appear. On that occasion, Harry charmed another jury and, with nothing to counteract the favorable impression, he was released.

Within 72 hours of his release, Harry killed again. This time, he decided he would dispose of the body in such a way as not to be detected. In the murdered woman's home, he began cutting up the body and putting it piece by piece in the garbage disposal. Not being a surgeon, Harry totally underestimated how long it would take to cut up a body, flesh and bone, in pieces small enough to be ground up in the garbage disposal. He had been at it for hours when the utility company meter reader walked past the side window and saw the blood-smeared kitchen. He called police and Harry was apprehended for his ninth murder.

This text describes a number of difficult cases and innovative ways to treat them. Unfortunately, psychotherapy has not acquired the sophistication to offset the risks to society of a serial killer, and the recommended approach to such patients is hospital commitment in a locked ward. There is currently a movement among some psychologists and psychiatrists to treat patients such as Harry in an outpatient setting so as to enhance their self-esteem toward eventually helping them overcome their drive to violence. A caveat here is important. A relapse in a serial killer is not as inconsequential as an alcoholic simply falling off the wagon. The consequences are literally deadly. A psychotherapist's obligation is that any treatment attempted should be in a locked setting. The possibility of enhancing Harry's self-esteem cannot outweigh the probability of another victim.

LEGEND

Psychological mechanism	Denial, attacking, projection
Diagnosis	Impulse schizophrenia
Operational diagnosis	Writ of habeas corpus for release
Implicit contract	Testify I am sane
Personality type	Garlic
Homework	Remain in hospital
Therapeutic technique	None available other than continued locked hospitalization

10

TREATING SUICIDAL PATIENTS

Patients are far more resilient than many therapists realize. The greatest consequences of incompetent therapy are that the patient abruptly quits the therapist or that the treatment process is unnecessarily protracted. Although these outcomes must not be taken lightly, they do not compare in magnitude with mistakes made in therapy with suicidal patients where treatment can be terminated abruptly by death. It is not surprising, therefore, that therapists tend to err on the side of too much caution, often inadvertently increasing suicidality and complicating recovery.

Skillful psychotherapists will differentiate their suicidal patients in terms of onion and garlic, and treat each accordingly. The silent, long-suffering patient (onion) depressive may commit suicide without even telegraphing the intent, while the loud, complaining, depressed patient with a borderline personality disorder (garlic) will learn quickly to use suicidal threats as a form of blackmail to obtain hospitalization when this suits his/her agenda. Overly cautious therapy may very well miss the lethality of the first example, while escalating the non-lethal suicidal activity of the latter. It is as important, therefore, to differentiate onion and garlic suicidal patients as it is with all other categories of patients.

This is also true with regard to a patient's being analyzable versus non-analyzable. Reactive depressions require skillful uncovering psychotherapy leading to the expulsion of the introject. Depressed borderline and other personality disorders require that uncovering be eschewed in favor of strengthening boundaries in the here and now.

As we have found in therapy with other categories of patients, most psychotherapists are more skillful with onion patients. But, in addition, the depressed garlic patient can present an overlay of suffering onion that will cause the psychotherapist to forget the requirement that garlic is always treated before onion. Therapists' offices are filled with garlic depressives who are exhorted in treatment to "speak up," while their baffled family and friends are being flattened by the patient's verbal and physical hostility.

The differential treatment of onion and garlic depression is critical to effective and efficient treatment, as the following case examples will demonstrate.

Suicide: Taking Responsibility for Another's Life

The suicide of a patient is a devastating experience for a psychotherapist, especially if the patient commits suicide at you. A psychiatrist sought treatment after a woman patient opened her purse in the middle of a session, took out a revolver, put the barrel in her mouth, pulled the trigger, and splattered the wall behind the therapy chair with blood and brains. He could no longer bring himself to see patients. He, of course, could not help but wonder what he had done and what he might have done differently. Many colleagues have been absolutely shattered and could not continue with their careers because of patient suicides.

Suicide follows families to the fourth generation. Even three generations later, people will whisper about grandma or grandpa or other family members killing themselves. The guilt and concern linger because all of us as human beings, some more and some less, have thought of suicide. A very common fantasy in childhood after being punished by mom or dad and sent to one's room is, "I'm dead. I'm sitting up here watching my own funeral and my parents are running around crying, 'Why weren't we nice to our child while still alive?'" Suicide scares us because there is no one who has not flashed on it. Thus, when confronted by depression in a patient, our first inclination is often to be overly kind.

The Suicidology Center at the National Institute of Mental Health (NIMH) studied suicide for over a 20-year period and sponsored hundreds of psychological autopsies on people who committed suicide. In studying these cases, one must come to the conclusion that most suicides are directed at somebody. This leads us to the axiom: never, ever take responsibility for another person's life.

A psychiatric social worker was in an addiction group for his amphetamine addiction. The therapist announced to the group, "I won't be here next week. I'll be away, but we'll still get our requisite number of sessions. We'll just tack it on the end." I usually don't tell my patients why I'm away, because I'm interested in what their fantasies and transferences are. One woman in the group waited outside my office for several hours, convinced that I was seeing all of my patients but her. Finally, in the middle of the afternoon, she realized nobody was going in and out of my office, and that I really was away.

This social worker, however, had read in one of our professional newspapers that I was going to NIMH to receive an award. This angered him. He thought, "Nick's going away on this frivolity while I need him."

On the day that I was receiving the award, he went to the end of the pier at Aquatic Park just below the Golden Gate Bridge, wrote a six-page suicide note in which my name was on every other line, took off his shoes, weighted the note down with his shoes, and then lowered himself from the end of the pier into the water. The water in San Francisco Bay, winter or summer, is around 50 degrees. As he is lowering himself in, he imagines the banner headlines in the San Francisco Chronicle, "PATIENT DROWNS SELF WHILE PSYCHOLOGIST RECEIVES AWARD." As he got up to his armpits in this ice cold water, he heard my voice say, "You dumb jackass."

He pulled himself out of the water, tore up the suicide note, threw it in the trashcan, put his shoes back on, and, being too embarrassed to catch the bus home because he was soaking wet, walked home. It was in the middle of January. He came in to the next session with this terrible cold and said to us, "If I thought for one moment I could ruin Nick's career by killing myself, I would be dead now."

A psychotherapist must not take responsibility for another human life. In reality, you cannot; in practice, if you do, you set yourself up to stand for the significant person in the patient's life he/she wants to commit suicide at. This does not mean the therapist lacks empathy. However, misdirected empathy must not be allowed to encourage lethality. For the social worker, I stood for the father who was never there when he needed him. I had the audacity to be like his father when he was having a hard time staying clean. In his mind, I had the audacity to go to Washington, DC to get an undeserved award. The fury is disproportional to the event, but it was fueled by the years of fury at his own father.

Only the patient can make the decision to live. It is the therapist's responsibility to ignite in the patient the will to live. Without this, the therapist is really helpless. Hospitalization must at some point end, as must a nonsuicidal therapeutic contract (see the case of Linda in Chapter 4). The therapist, no matter how empathic and vigilant, cannot "police" the suicidal patient around the clock and into perpetuity. The significant number of suicides in psychiatric hospitals demonstrates our helplessness in the face of a determined patient. The therapist's responsibility, to reiterate, is to so hone his/her skills as to be able to help the patient's decision to live. This is often difficult, because our inclinations are to overly empathize and identify with someone suffering so much that he/she wishes to die. Successful interventions might require tough love, or what we term the spilling of some "psychic blood."

The threat of suicidality varies in seriousness and style according to diagnostic categories. Selected categories are discussed below, along with suicidality among adolescents and the elderly.

Suicide Among Hysterics

Hysteric patients very frequently, vocally, and histrionically threaten suicide. Hysterics are not of themselves lethal, but hysterics are the stumblebums of psychotherapy. They frequently miscalculate and kill themselves even when they do not intend to.

In one case, a man came in distraught because his wife had just committed suicide. They had been married for four years, and three or four times a year they would play the following game: they would argue. She would run to the bathroom, lock the door, and swallow a bottle of pills. He would break the door down, scoop her up, and drive her to the emergency room, where they would pump her stomach. Three or four times a year they would play this game. On this particular occasion, they were at a New Year's Eve party. They argued all the way home. They got home, and while he was putting the car in the garage, she ran into the house, locked herself in the bathroom, and swallowed a bottle of pills. He came into the house and passed out on the couch because he had had too much to drink. When he came to, she was dead.

Even though hysterics are most likely to be gesturing, their threats must be taken seriously because they can and do miscalculate. But this does not mean that it should be taken so seriously that unnecessary hospitalization is seen as the answer. Expedient hospitalization can further exacerbate the suicidal risk. Hysterics will conclude, "My God, they really think I'm crazy," and in their hysteria be more prone to attempt to kill themselves.

Techniques that can be utilized in helping hysterics strengthen the part of them that is determined to live are illustrated in earlier case illustrations (Elaine, Linda). In both of these cases, misguided empathy would have been interpreted as pity and would have fueled the suicidality. Two caveats are indicated: the therapist must take the time to know and understand the patient, and the therapist must have honed his/her skills sufficiently so that the intervention is believable. This is why some of these interventions are not for the unskilled or the faint-hearted (e.g., the case illustration of Lenore).

Suicide Among Borderline Personalities

Borderline personalities are less lethal than hysterics because they do not miscalculate. The borderlines are survivors. In one case in Orlando, a woman borderline demanded hospitalization, and her therapist appropriately refused. She called him at 11:00 that night and said, "I'm giving you your last chance to hospitalize me. If you don't, I'm going to shoot myself." He refused, and the next thing he heard was "BAM!" He then heard the phone drop to the floor and a body fall. The therapist kept his cool, got to another line, left that line open, called 911, and the call was traced. The paramedics picked her up and took her to the hospital.

The therapist followed her into the hospital. The emergency room surgeon came out and said, "You know, she shot herself in the chest. But probably what you don't know is that this is the third time in two years she has shot herself in the chest and has never hit a vital organ. I as a surgeon knowing anatomy could not do that."

No one knows how they do it, but they do. In Phoenix, a borderline patient threatened the therapist when she was not hospitalized. She said, "I will leave here and kill myself by running my car into a telephone pole." She got in her car, hit the first telephone pole, knocked the telephone pole down, totaled her car, and didn't have a scratch on her. But 20,000 people in Phoenix were without power for several hours. Surviving their dysfunctional families must make everything else in life seem like a picnic to a borderline.

Borderlines will kill themselves in despair. When everyone has given up on them and they are locked on the back ward of a state hospital, they will kill themselves because they no longer can act out. As long as they can strut, can continue their projective identification, raise an uproar in the community, they stay alive. The acting out is the lifeblood of the borderline personality.

When one is working with borderline patients, maneuvers that will result in the flicker of a smile or the mischievous blink of an eye are effective. For example, one maneuver the senior author has used is to say, "You know, in 60 years of practice I've never had a successful suicide, and if you want to kill yourself, you could be Nick Cummings' first suicide. I have some feelings about this because I've had so many colleagues who have had patients who have suicided and I may retire very soon without ever experiencing how it feels to have a patient commit suicide. I'm going to ask you a favor. If you're going to be my one and only suicide in my entire career, make it worthy. Come up with a suicide that will at least make the headlines. Go home and think about it, come back next week, and tell me what you've decided."

They may say, "Well, I've decided to jump off the Golden Gate Bridge."

I would respond, "Jump off the Golden Gate Bridge!? There's been over a thousand people who have done that. No big deal. Go on. Is that the best you can do? Kill yourself any way you want to, but you're not worthy of being my first suicide. The hell with you."

You'll see that flicker of a smile.

If borderlines see that you're strong enough not to be conned, they love you. They start to think, "Maybe this is the person that will be able to stop me." Then they try you again, and every time you pass a test the respect goes up a thousand points. Until, finally, the testings grow further and further apart. But in the beginning they'll test you every five minutes. Your disaster comes when they write you off as a wimp. When they cannot feel secure that you're there for them, they will act out to punish you.

Janet Cummings, who can now challenge a hysteric or a borderline personality patient to be her first successful suicide in 25 years of practice, often uses a paradox she calls "spitting in the soup." This is especially effective in patients who would suicide at someone. The therapist can muse that the object of the wrath can now have the house, or the car, or the inheritance, or raise the children without your interference, or whatever would make the vengeful suicidal patient pause.

Paranoid Schizophrenia

Paranoid patients are lethal. Many successful suicides and notes have a paranoid flavor. You cannot make a suicide pact with a paranoid. It will have no effect because paranoids do not kill themselves. They go on to a higher plane of existence. A paranoid will kill his wife, children, and then shoot himself to keep his family intact. There is no divorce in Heaven, so they all go to Heaven where they live for eternity as a family. Paranoids believe that! Paranoids who are threatening suicide need to be in the hospital on antipsychotic medication. After they are stabilized, then psychotherapy is possible, but medication management must be a critical part of treatment. Paranoids are not only lethal to themselves, but, because their defense mechanism is projection, they can be lethal to others as in the following (see also the case of Ernesto in Chapter 9).

This is a case the senior author encountered as chair of the APA Insurance Trust. One of our psychologists was sued for malpractice. The wife called in wanting to see this psychologist although he practiced some 100 miles away from their home. Her father-in-law had done so well with him and had recommended the psychologist highly. She said that her husband was suicidal.

It was sometime between Christmas and New Year, when all psychotherapists are busy up to their elbows, so the psychologist scheduled them as his last appointment. At 6:00 p.m., the psychologist went into the waiting room and saw a couple out of the 1960s and 1970s. He was in bell-bottomed trousers with a 1970s hairdo. She had long, ironed out, perfectly flat hair and wore a flowing, busy little flowered peasant skirt. The therapist suspected they were on drugs but then determined that they were not. During the session, the wife said that she had decided to leave him and her husband was threatening suicide. The therapist noticed that he kept attending to his tennis shoes and asked, "Why are you staring at your tennis shoes?"

The husband said, "Well, that's how they're conveying the messages."

"What messages?"

"Well, they're going to kill my wife."

After talking to them as a couple, the therapist saw the wife alone for an hour. The wife explained that she had been trying to leave this man for several years, that she kept backing off because he threatened suicide, but that she was determined to leave this time. She wanted to get him into therapy because she was afraid he was suicidal. After finishing with the wife, the therapist spoke with the husband. Four times during the interview, the husband said, "They're killing my wife in the waiting room." The therapist had to go outside the office, go downstairs to the waiting room and show him that his wife was safe. Four times. At the end of this, he called them both back in and asked to see the husband the next day. The husband could not come in the next day or the day after, so they made an appointment three days later.

The couple left. By that time, it was quite late at night. They drove the 100 miles home. Somewhere between 2:00 a.m. and 3:00 a.m., the therapist was awakened by the emergency room in their town reporting, "We understand that these two people are your patients. He shot her, then shot himself, and miraculously they're both still alive." They recovered and they sued the psychologist.

The defense attorney took the position that a therapist cannot know everything about a patient in one contact. The consultant said, "You'd better settle this one for what you can, because he should have known this." Because the defense mechanism in paranoia is projection, "They're going to kill her," means "I'm going to kill her." If they say, "They are going to kill me," it means, "I am going to kill me."

The Undetected Lethal Patient

The undetected lethal patient is the one who has been depressed over some time and does not respond to any therapeutic intervention. Just as you are getting very discouraged, the patient tells you, "Gee, doctor, I'm feeling better. Pressure's been lifted." Before you congratulate yourself, you must make sure that this patient's depression has not lifted because he/she has made the unverbalized determination to commit suicide and therefore no longer has to struggle.

If patients have made such a decision, they have decided when and how, and then have become amnesic to it. This is autohypnosis with a posthypnotic suggestion when and how to kill themselves, and the patients are no longer aware of the sequence. They go on autopilot because they do not have the courage to face the decision they have made, but even so they will always give the therapist a clue. Even after they have decided to kill themselves and are relieved that they will no longer have to struggle, the will to live in human beings is so strong that they will give the therapist one last chance to save them. But this last chance is most often missed by the therapist. Several examples follow.

A man was in treatment for depression, but there was no improvement for months. One day, the patient came in and said, "I'm feeling great. Thank you. You've finally helped me. My depression is lifted." During the course of the session, he said, "When I leave here, I'm going to the escrow office where I'm concluding the sale of our mountain cabin. I'm putting the money in a money market fund." The therapist knew that the man was an outdoorsman who loved hunting and fishing, and his wife was a city woman who hated the outdoors. She had been after him for years to sell that mountain cabin and invest it in a money market fund for retirement. He'd say, "No, I don't want to do that because when I retire I'm going to spend most of my time in that mountain cabin, hunting and fishing."

He is now going to sell the cabin because he's not going to be around to retire and use it. He left the therapist's office and bought 25 feet of garden hose on the way home. As he pulled into his driveway, his next door neighbor was trimming the hedge. He joked with his neighbor, opened up the trunk, pulled out the garden hose, and said, "You know, I don't know what the heck I bought this hose for. I must have 400 feet of garden hose around this place." He drove the car into the garage, closed the door, attached the new garden hose to the tail pipe, put the other end through the partially opened car window, sat in the front seat, and turned on the engine. When his wife came home, he was dead of carbon monoxide poisoning.

Another patient suffering from an illness that left him disabled and in a wheelchair was despairing that after three previous debilitating episodes, this time he would not have a remission. The therapist was not grappling with the issue successfully. After dropping out of therapy twice, the patient said in a session, "Last week I saw Dr. (name deleted). I thought he could help me because he was a student of (name deleted). This was my last hope. He referred me back to you." Yet, in spite of his stating that the other therapist had been his "last hope," the patient is happy as a clam. He is no longer depressed about his condition. The therapist missed the significance. The patient went home. His wife said that in the next two days she had never seen her husband happier. He called up all his old friends and chatted with them. About 8:00 at night on the second day, he told his wife, "Well, it's finished. That was the last one." He wheeled himself into the bedroom, took the gun out of the bedside table, and killed himself. He was saying goodbye to all his friends. He had decided to kill himself and told the therapist, "Dr. (name deleted) was my last hope." The therapist had missed the incongruity between his affect and his statement.

A depressed woman was in treatment for weeks with nothing happening. She always talked about her wedding ring, which had belonged to her great grandmother. It had been passed down through the generations when her grandmother, mother, and she were married. Her dream was to give the ring to her daughter, who at that time was 11 years old. One day, she came to therapy feeling much better and said during the session, "I gave my wedding ring to my daughter." She did this because she wasn't going to be around for the wedding. She wanted her daughter to have it now. The woman went home and poisoned herself.

The clue is there, but we are swept away by the sudden improvement. In the absence of any psychological reason for an elevation in mood, be suspicious. If you suspect that your patient is on automatic pilot, confront it in the most forceful way you know, "When and how did you decide to kill yourself?" You've got to get him/her out of automatic pilot. Two times out of three, you'll have a false positive. The patient will say, "Huh? I didn't decide to kill myself." Then you can apologize, "I picked up certain signs. I'd rather be safe than sorry. I'm sorry. I don't mean to alarm you." But that one time out of three, the patient will look at you and say, "Oh my God, it was the day before yesterday when I was sitting in my office. I decided, and here's how I'm going to do it." The next hour must be spent going over and over the plan in every detail, over and over again, to make sure the patient comes out of automatic pilot and will not be able to go back in.

Interrupting the Autopilot

Such patients as the preceding are said to be on a psychological autopilot. They have finally made the decision to end it all, and at the same time have also chosen the method for the suicide. Then the entire decision is repressed, and the patient goes about putting into effect the method and unconsciously choosing the time and place. During this time, the patient is suddenly remarkably improved, to the relief and delight of the psychotherapist who may have been struggling with the patient for weeks or even months, but with no avail.

Of importance is that the therapist state (more than ask) the question forcefully, almost screaming, "WHEN AND HOW DID YOU DECIDE TO KILL YOURSELF?" While the patient is seemingly caught off guard, this should be repeated just as loudly and as many as three times if necessary. The lethal patient will suddenly be plummeted out of automatic pilot and be very surprised as he/she begins to describe the when and how. The patient's reaction will be such as to portray the fact that the suicide has definitely now been interrupted. There will be an obvious sense of relief and gratitude. Yes, the many patients who were not on automatic pilot when this technique was employed will be initially startled by the therapist's seeming accusation, but when the reason is explained, we have never had a patient who remained offended.

Do not be timid or shy. Yell! Do it with the knowledge that you may be saving a life. And then some day you, too, will be able to say that, "In 25 years of treating severely depressed patients, I have never had a suicide."

Suicide Among Adolescents

Jay Haley said, "Adolescence is not a time of life, it's a disease, that only age will cure" (Haley, 1976). In some ways, every adolescent is pathological, depressed, hysterical, acting out, and counterphobic. It is the time of major transition, of differentiating from our parents, and of establishing our own identities. The incidence of adolescent suicide has risen dramatically, however, because of drugs and cult rock music.

So many groups glorify suicide. The songs are constructed so adult ears do not hear it. The kids hear it. This does not mean ostensibly subliminal messages, but rather the cult rock music that blares out the naked glorification of suicide. They tell kids to kill themselves. If they are depressed and on drugs, suicide sounds like a great idea to adolescents. If a group is getting stoned and listening to cult music, one particularly disturbed adolescent can lead a mass suicide.

If therapists and parents are not inquiring about their adolescents' drug habits and their music habits, they are out of touch with the reality of the adolescent. If an adolescent tells you, the therapist, about a rock group that you know nothing about, say, "Burn me a CD" or "Send me a Spotify or YouTube link," and listen to it until the words become understandable. If it is a cult and heavy metal kind of group that pushes suicide, forbid it. If they are also taking drugs, forbid this as a condition of treatment. If you do not, you are flirting with adolescent suicide. Because adolescents do not want to come in anyway, you might tell them, "It's up to you, but unless you come in here, your parents won't let you use the car. Your parents aren't going to trust you for this and that. Let's you and I work something out. In return for this, let's agree that we will see each other three times, for three weeks. Now you mean to tell me that you can't give up this damn music and these drugs for three weeks. You can't, can you? I can just see it in your face." This will often elicit the adolescent's oppositional compliance.

If it were not for cult rock music and drugs, the suicide rate among adolescents would probably be half what it is. There are other factors, but there have always been depressed adolescents. There have always been adolescents whose families are so achievement-oriented that if kids get a B+ instead of an A, they want to kill themselves. This is not what caused the epidemic. Drugs, depression, and cult music are a lethal combination.

Suicide Among the Elderly

An elderly man who has lost his sexual function, as often happens after prostate surgery, can get depressed to the point of being suicidal because male identity is so tied into sexuality, much more so than with women. This is the nature of the situation. A woman can fake interest in sex, but a man cannot. Many elderly men commit suicide because they would rather be dead than impotent.

The elderly person with a terminal illness who requests that he/she be taken off life support represents a special case. In such cases, it is important to have a bedside consultation with the person and make it very clear that it is not a philosophical issue that opposes suicide and that you are not there to reverse the patient's decision. One can appreciate how a person who has lived in dignity wants to die in dignity instead of in excruciating pain with triple the dosage of painkillers, and life support systems that allow for no quality of life. After the therapist has bonded, which can be accomplished in about an hour alone, by the bedside, then say to the person: "I have three questions I want to ask you: (1) Have you done everything that you need to do before you die? (2) Have you said everything to your loved ones that you want to say before you die? (3) If the answers to the first two are yes, would you be willing to have all of your family assembled by your bed? And I mean all. I don't care how far away they are. They should fly in to celebrate not your dying, but your life. Would you be willing to do that? I want you to think about these three things and I'll come back the day after tomorrow and we'll talk some more."

Invariably, the person will tell me, "No, I haven't done everything I need to do before I die. And I haven't said everything to my loved ones that I want to say before I die." My response" is, "Well, let's get about it. And then we'll have the celebration of your life. And I want to be involved in that."

Every time this was done, the outcome was always the same. The person so reconnects with all of his/her loved ones and there is such an outpouring of love that the person comes alive and wants to hang onto the last few months of life to participate in this outpouring. The assembly of the family around the bedside, not to talk about death but to celebrate this person's life, is an incredible experience. The dying persons have told me this overshadowed everything—their wedding day, their graduation, the birth of their children. It was like all of this rolled up into one. It leaves them with such a glow that the last few weeks or months of life become not a drudgery, but a joy. Serendipitously, when the person finally goes, he/she goes in a tremendous spirit of love and the family is left with a very joyous feeling. There is no unfinished business.

Finally, the recently widowed patient may be so depressed that he/she is determined to join the deceased (see the case of Arthur in Chapter 5). It is usually depression, not bereavement, that may trigger suicide in the surviving spouse. In the former, it is imperative to treat the introjection. In the latter, it is important to encourage mourning; crying, loneliness with yet the desire to be alone, giving in to missing the deceased.

The Changing Elderly Population

The elderly who lived through the Great Depression and World War II who Tom Brokow named "the greatest generation" has reached the age in which it is dying at the rate of one thousand a day. It is still adding to the ranks of centenarians, and although it has the greatest longevity in our history, the end is in sight. On the other hand, the early Baby Boomers are reaching their mid-sixties and retiring, but they have not demonstrated the resiliency and potential for longevity as their predecessors. Primary care physicians are noting early serious diseases with the speculation they are not as healthy as their parents, and there is the added speculation they may be the first generation in our history in which longevity declines.

For our treatment purposes, it must be noted that these are the "Haight-Ashbury-kids" who indulged early on in drugs and have now aged. The new elders are the fastest growing users of street drugs in society today. It is as if they are saying, "We are retiring and we can go back to enjoying pot (or other drugs)." Additionally, with the aches and pains of aging, and with the advent of the newer, more potent, and highly addictive pain medications that, unfortunately, are over-prescribed, a note of caution is indicated. Just because the patient sitting in your office resembles the sweet Grandma Moses or the likable old grandpa, be alert to the possibility that the mental confusion or other troublesome behavior they are presenting may have at its basis the deleterious effect of prescription drugs or even their having returned to street drugs, and especially marijuana. In their misdirected effort to recapture the halcyon days of Woodstock, they are unaware that the cannabis of today is much more potent than that of bygone years, and that there is bound to be a differential effect due to their own aging process. No, Ponce de Leon, there is no Fountain of Youth, even with botox.

Psychotropic Medications and Suicidality

Virtually all antidepressants have the potential to precipitate suicidal ideation and even suicide itself. In the late 1950s, when antipsychotic meds began to be extensively prescribed, there was a sudden rash of suicides in state mental hospitals that was alarming. Instead of attributing the suicides to the medications, psychiatry concluded that previously vegetating schizophrenics had now had their spirits suddenly lifted so they had the strength and the determination to end it all. As was previously discussed in early chapters, it is the propensity of intuitive medicine to blame the condition or disease, not the treatment. So when in bloodletting the patient died, the death was attributed to the disease, not the loss of blood. In the late 1950s, psychiatry was very much intuitive medicine, even as it still is. When your sole armamentarium (having abandoned psychotherapy) is a medication, the profession blames the patient and the patient's condition, not the medication.

Furthermore, all anxiolytics, because they are depressants, can precipitate suicidal ideation as well as suicide. This should not be surprising, for in its attempts to reduce anxiety these medications also may inadvertently depress one's spirits. In the past, the psychiatric literature typically blamed the patient's condition, not the psychotropic medications. But there has been a plethora of lawsuits establishing the propensity of these meds, and suicidal ideation as well as suicidal behavior are recognized side effects.

The psychotherapist who is treating patients on these medications must be alert to signs of suicidal side effects and immediately confer with the prescribing psychiatrist or other physician. Bear in mind that in the United States today 80 percent to 85 percent of psychotropic meds are prescribed by non-psychiatric physicians who may not be as well versed in behavioral manifestations as you are.

11

CO-LOCATED INTEGRATED BEHAVIORAL/PRIMARY CARE

The Hallway Handoff

A history and description of co-located integrated behavioral/primary care is extensively delineated in *Behavioral Integrative Care* (O'Donohue, Byrd, Cummings, & Henderson, 2005). Forty-six years passed from the first co-located demonstration project conducted by the senior author in 1963 and the adoption of the concept by the American Psychological Association (APA) in 2009. After resisting and even disdaining co-located care for those decades, the adoption by the APA was largely due to the effort of the then APA president James Bray (Bray, 2011), even though it had been unsuccessfully embraced a few years earlier by APA president Ronald Levant. Once adopted, the scurrying to get on board has led to a spate of deficient and even counterfeit projects, threatening to discredit the concept. Amazingly, many who suddenly jumped on board were the very colleagues who earlier rejected the model, and now even have the audacity to claim having invented it. On the other hand, the Biodyne Model of integrated care has 46 years of proven research and successful practice.

This section addresses the mainstay of co-located care, the hallway handoff, with appropriate examples illustrating its extensiveness. We prefer that the title of the integrated practitioner be that of behavioral care practitioner (BCP), as the initials are euphonic with those of the primary care physician, or PCP. However, each integrated care system may, for various reasons, prefer its own title, a matter that should not be argued. It is anticipated that, in due course, the abbreviations of BCP and PCP will become standard.

There are a number of principles that must be headed, as the BCP that violates these or over-steps his/her authority will breed animosity and even rejection of the concept of integrated care.

- Co-located behavioral/primary care, though integrated, is still taking place in the "house of medicine." The physician is the acknowledged head of this house, and must be respected as such. American Biodyne historically was the only national health system that established a "psychological house" in which the psychologist was the head of the house.

• Respect is not the result of the title doctor of behavioral health, or any other such doctorate or title. Respect is earned by demonstrated competence over a sufficient period of time.

• As you need to be trained, physicians must also be trained in the best use of integrated care. Since formal training may usually not exist, it is incumbent upon you to subtly train the physician over time on the value of your services.

• Clinics, hospitals, or group practices in which you are working are as much a business as any other small business. Many decisions are made on the basis of economics and finances, dictated by the many exigencies of reimburse-ment, government regulation, and just plain business sense. Instead of resenting these, your appropriate training in economics, management, and entrepreneurship will render your suggestions and contributions welcomed.

• The current clinical psychology doctorate does not prepare one to serve as a BCP in a co-located behavioral/primary care setting. One must be conversant with medical terminology, have an appreciation of how the health system operates, and even though the BCP may not be issuing script (i.e., prescribing), a knowledge of psychopharmacology is imperative. The doctor of behavioral health program described in Appendix I is the first doctoral program designed to fully prepare the practitioner to be a full-fledged BCP.

The Hallway Handoff Has a Range of Activity

Historically, the term "hallway handoff" derived from the procedure in which the physician, once discerning the patient had a psychological problem, would walk him/her to the co-located office of the BCP. In time, however, it came to stand for any exchange regarding a patient between the PCP and the BCP, even if it were just asking for the BCP's advice or recommendation without the BCP even having seen the patient. A not infrequent example is that of an estranged husband or ex-boyfriend demanding that he be allowed to accompany the patient to the examination room. The answer is, "No, but I would be willing to see him while you are examining her." The following case is illustrative.

Case Illustration: Maria the Martyr

A Hispanic woman in her late twenties was seeking medical attention for a series of injuries she sustained ostensibly falling down the stairs at home. She was accompanied by her husband who demanded he accompany her to the examination room, and although she did not say so, it was apparent Maria did not want him there and was afraid to openly say so. As the patient did not appear in immediate physical danger from her wounds, the PCP made a hallway handoff to one of two BCPs available. She chose the BCP who was of Hispanic descent and who spoke fluent Spanish.

Having seen many battered women in her career, the BCP made an early diagnosis, even while the patient denied any physical abuse. The husband was firmly refused admission to the session, and the clinic's security personnel were there to enforce this if necessary. Through her fluent Spanish, the BCP succeeded in establishing successive degrees of rapport and trust until the patient, in tears, finally blurted out a several-year history of violence toward her by her husband. The BCP described in sympathetic terms the battered women's shelter that was available, assured her of the safe haven there, and in time obtained the patient's assent and cooperation to go there by convalescent car, all without her husband's knowledge of the admission and her whereabouts.

Maria had presented herself to clinics and emergency rooms on numerous occasions, never disclosing her husband's brutality. Complicating the picture was her illegal immigrant status, making it difficult for her to file charges against the husband lest in the process she would be deported. That she and the BCP were both Mexican nationals provided the trust needed to finally put an end to this senseless brutality. Without this hallway handoff, Maria could have spent many more years in emergency rooms without any relief in sight. The shelter aided and protected Maria in not only a permanent separation, but eventually a divorce.

Seeking Solutions versus Addressing Symptoms

Much of what passes as intervention in the hallway handoff in many integrated settings is merely symptom reduction, symptom relief, or symptom management. This is the usual approach of the behaviorist-oriented practitioner. Just because the BCP has only 15 or 20 minutes is no reason not to strive to understand and solve the problem. This would seem to reflect what has happened in mental health generally, a kind of behavioral aping of the same unfortunate emphasis found in medication treatment (e.g., the symptoms of depression or anxiety are lessened and there is no concern as to the cause of the symptoms).

This is even reflected in the psychotherapy parlance of today. Once upon a time, our patients had problems. Now our clients have issues. Problems require (lead to) solutions; issues require (lead to) being addressed. This does not mean that the BCP can solve the problem in the 15 to 20 minutes allotted, or even half an hour in the occasional extended hallway handoff. But the problem can be discerned and a pathway to its solution delineated.

Recently we attended an all-day seminar conducted by a highly skilled colleague who refers to his extensive experience as that of a "behavioral health consultant." He is the author of a well-regarded book that describes his approach (Hunter, 2010). There is no question that what he does, he does well, and there is no attempt here to demean what he demonstrated in the all-day seminar. Rather, it is for purposes of contrasting the behaviorist approach from the hallway handoff that employs the Biodyne Model. The contrast is reflected in the two videos he presented, each with a real patient.

The first was what appeared to be a 30-ish man whose complaint was that tension led him to be argumentative and to eventually "blow up" in an uncalled-for and inappropriate manner. He did this at home with his wife as well as with his co-workers. He had been on medication for a couple of years, which relaxed him so that he could refrain from being argumentative, but it was no longer working effectively. In the interview, he was highly compliant and even deferent, readily agreeing and buying into what the psychologist was saying as he led the young man to a behavioral conclusion. He was to continue the medication, along with behavioral techniques through which the psychologist took him step by step. There was no question in our minds as we viewed this video that the patient would be highly compliant with the regimen. The psychologist regarded this as a highly successful handoff, and commented that it was perhaps too easy.

Our concern is that this man was remanded to more years of medication and stopgap behaviorist techniques while the cause of his tension was unaddressed. In our model, we would look for cause and effect; that is, what pushes him to the untoward behavior that needs constant medicating along with perpetual relaxation techniques. How long would it be before these, too, would no longer work? Only the symptoms of the problem had been addressed.

Because the interview did not go in the directions we would have taken it, we have no idea what the problem was, although the symptoms are obvious. Had we conducted the interview, we would be running in our minds hypotheses that his responses to our questions would suggest, and these hypotheses would be pursued or rejected in accordance with the patient's further responses. One such hypothesis was suggested by the patient's spontaneous reference to his being argumentative with his wife at home. Is this man suffering from marital discord that he is taking with him to the office? Very quickly, this could have been verified or rejected as a hypothesis. Since it was not followed, and the interview went in other directions, no further speculation can be entertained.

The second case, which the psychologist described as very, very difficult, was totally transparent to anyone trained in differentiating garlic from onion. He was a man in his fifties who had been suffering from what he described as severe back pain that, in 18 years, no doctor had been able to help. He had also been grossly overweight all those same years, admittedly resulting from a totally sedentary lifestyle. He was overly smiling throughout the interview, but his body language was one of absolute defiance. While his words were polite, his perpetual smile would become more of a smirk whenever the psychologist tried to lead him through the prescribed steps of his method. When a constructive suggestion was made, he would seemingly writhe in pain. Valiantly, the psychologist persisted in trying to lead him into buying into losing some weight while the patient scoffed, "I've been this same weight for 18 years." With a dismissive smirk, he seemed to be telling the psychologist that if you don't cure my back pain first I won't lose weight. Near the end of the interview, the patient pretended to comply with the idea of losing some weight, but it was apparently a sham, as he never followed through and he was never seen again.

Rather than approaching this man as if he was onion, within a few minutes of the interview it was apparent he should be approached as garlic. He stated spontaneously that, in 18 years, the only time he was free of the severe pain was recently when with a group of bikers he rode his motorcycle several hundred miles over several days to Maine. Both of the authors rode motorcycles for a number of years and can attest to the fact it is no activity for one with severe back pain. Without speculating how factitious this man might be, it is apparent he was proud of the fact he had stymied for 18 years all attempts to treat him. This defiance is a reflection of his garlic personality and he should be approached accordingly.

One such approach would be to go in the direction of his defiance, shamefully throwing in the towel, so to speak, by admitting defeat before the patient can defeat you. "I'm ashamed to admit it, but I don't know what to do for you. You've seen a lot of doctors in 18 years, most of whom are smarter and have more experience than I have. I'm hoping you can give me something I can put in your chart so I won't look like an utter fool to my superiors." With persistence in this approach, often the patient will take the bait, disdainfully taking charge of the interview and even begin offering suggestion. In this reversal of roles, the BCP will reject each, pointing why this one or that one will not work. There are other such approaches, but the point is that this patient should be met with psychojudo, not straightforward attempts to help him in the face of his defiance. Done adroitly, the Axis II patient can be led from defiance to cooperation, as described in previous chapters.

The repeated assertion of this behaviorist in these two demonstrations that diagnosis is not important is not warranted. Imperative is a psychotherapeutic working diagnosis, not a DSM diagnosis, if we are to fully understand the patient so that we can then understand the problem and arrive at solutions, not merely address issues.

The hallway handoff can employ the same kind of unique interventions, as have been seen in preceding chapters. This also applies to schizophrenics, who quite often are candidates for the hallway handoff.

Case Illustration: Talkative Thomas

Thomas was a 53-year-old schizophrenic who was being treated for diabetes. On this occasion, he failed to show up for his appointment with the PCP, and it was later discovered that on his way to the physician's office he was detained by the police, who held him overnight so that he could be examined by a psychiatrist. When he finally got to the medical offices two days later, he confided that he had been thus detained a number of times, examined, and then released as psychotic but harmless. In the hallway handoff that followed, the BCP discovered that Thomas was a chronic, but harmless schizophrenic who not only heard voices, but also carried on loud, often boisterous conversations with these voices and in public places. He had been on antipsychotic medication for years, and although this made these voices benign, it seemed also to generate long, animated conversations with the patient gesticulating, sometimes yelling, but generally in attention-getting animated "conversations."

Needless to say, this often alarmed bystanders who then called 911 to report a dangerous "crazy" person. The BCP quickly assessed the situation as troublesome, but not dangerous. Furthermore, since the antipsychotic medication did not eliminate this behavior, but rather seemed to exaggerate it, he arrived at the following solution. When he would be carrying on these animated conversations with the imaginary voices, he was to hold a cellphone up to his ear so that bystanders would assume he was talking on the telephone. The cellphone need not be turned on or connected with anyone, but those around him would not realize this. He presented the plan to the patient as if it were some kind of game that would fool bystanders and prevent complaints that would lead to his frequent detention. The patient agreed this game of fooling his surroundings would be fun, and immediately instituted the plan. It worked, and he was never again detained, while he always arrived on time for his medical appointments.

One morning, when I (Janet) was serving as a BCP, a woman brought her younger brother to the clinic. He was a rather disheveled young man in his early twenties who was loudly complaining of "raw, jangled nerves" that were driving him to distraction. The physicians were all very busy, with even more patients waiting to be seen ahead of him, so I decided to see him immediately and prior to his seeing a physician. Once in my office, he continued to complain of raw, jangled nerves for which he could not get help because every psychiatrist and physician he saw thought he was crazy and prescribed "crazy medicine," which was his term for antipsychotics.

It was obvious that the patient was schizophrenic, but rather than try to talk him into accepting antipsychotic medication, I empathized with his plight. At that point, the receptionist came into the room to announce that the physician could now see him. Knowing the sequence that was about to follow, I invited him to see me again after finishing with the psychiatrist. It turned out this was not necessary, as the psychiatrist did a hallway handoff back to me because the patient was upset with his having been prescribed an antipsychotic and was threatening not to take it. Once back in my office, I asked to see the prescription. I then exclaimed with delight that we were in luck, as this particular drug had been found to be very effective with raw, jangled nerves. We discussed this at some length while the patient arrived at the decision to take the medication as prescribed, but for raw, jangled nerves, and never let on to the psychiatrist that he was doing so, thus ensuring that if it worked his script would continue to be renewed.

A month later, the patient came in to have his prescription renewed, and afterward he came by my office waving it and laughing, "The doctor has no idea I am taking this for raw, jangled nerves instead. It is our little secret." Thereafter, he continued to come by my office whenever his prescription was refilled, smiling as he exclaimed, "I still have the doctor fooled and I don't have raw, jangled nerves anymore." Even in the hallway handoff, there are opportunities to enter the patient's psychotic world by adroitly joining the delusion.

Of concern in behavioral care is that the vast majority of successful suicides kill themselves without ever having discussed the idea of suicide with anyone, much less with a professional. The borderline or the hysteric patient who loudly telegraphs suicidal thoughts and/or intent is far less likely to commit suicide than the depressed patient who has never revealed suicidal thoughts or behavior, whose depression has suddenly improved for no apparent reason, and then surprises everyone by committing suicide without the slightest warning. As if this hazard were not troublesome enough, we now have the suicide that occurs as a function in a certain percentage of patients, and particularly adolescent patients, who are taking antidepressants. These patients are on what has been described as automatic pilot. Interestingly, however, even in the face of the determination to do away with oneself, the will to live gives us one last chance to intervene, but it is always done in a disguised manner that almost invariably is missed by the untrained practitioner. Since many, if not most of these individuals are not in psychotherapy, the primary care setting is very often the place in which this last chance, but disguised warning, is conveyed.

Case Illustration: Happy Hannah

A 43-year-old divorced woman whose two children were both off to college had become increasingly depressed over the last two months. Her PCP had prescribed an antidepressant that seemed to help at first, but then in spite of the medication she began to slide back into depression. The PCP in the usual practice setting probably would have just tried another antidepressant, or would have added another medication. But having a BCP available, she handed off the patient, mainly asking his advice on what might be a better medication course for such a patient.

Appropriately, the BCP probed beyond the reason for referral, and during the course of this gentle prodding the patient mentioned as an aside the fact that her mother had committed suicide on a certain month and day of the week. An alarm bell was suddenly sounded in the BCP's head, as the anniversary of her mother's suicide was just three days away. Anniversary depression is the kind of reactive depression that occurs around the anniversary of the death of a parent or other significant figure. Anniversary depressions are always reflective of a resolution or bereavement that involved postponement—usually, the anger at the parent (or whomever) for committing suicide when the survivor, usually a child, very much needed the parent or other important figure. This anger turned inward surfaces at a very predictable time. Ernest Hemingway, for example, killed himself at the same age and on the anniversary date of his father's suicide, and in the same manner.

The BCP paused, and then in a loud voice, asked, "Hannah, when and how have you decided to commit suicide?!!!" This was forcefully repeated three more times while the patient was stunned and was visibly shaken. As if recalling this decision for the first time, Hannah slowly and painfully described how she had been squirreling away barbiturates for years, and had enough to kill at least three people. Then, with a sudden sense of relief, she said she had decided to take these the day after tomorrow. The BCP had adroitly discerned the patient's automatic pilot, and her life was saved. The patient began psychotherapy that same week as she successfully began to expel the interject that otherwise would have resulted in her killing herself to destroy her angrily interjected mother.

Panic Attacks Frequent the ER

Patients who suffer frequent panic attacks usually present themselves to the emergency room believing they are suffering a heart attack. These patients need to believe this because to them the alternative would be, "I must be losing my mind," or "I'm going crazy." The prescribing of a relaxant or a sedative is usually the treatment, and this "medical" response only reinforces in the patient's mind the belief: "I must be having a heart attack because I'm not going crazy." The usual treatment is anti-anxiety medication, which may take the edge off, but sooner rather than later the patient will be back with another "heart attack." Each successive appearance in the ER, rather than yielding a practice effect (i.e., reassurance because I've been here before), only increases the panic inasmuch as the patient says to oneself, "This time for sure they will find a real heart attack, or they will find me crazy and lock me up." The hallway handoff interrupts this perpetual cycle and most often embarks the patient on the appropriate path to recovery.

Case Illustration: Morgan—I Wish I Could Go to College

Twenty-year-old Morgan had been accepted by a prestigious college away from home, but for two years had to write to the school and have her acceptance postponed because of severe panic attacks, which she had misrepresented in her letters to be severe heart attacks. The women's college was very sympathetic and three times her acceptance was postponed to the following year. The panic attacks began at age 17, almost to the day she received her college acceptance. At first, they occurred once every six or seven weeks, but in recent months they became more frequent, so that now they occurred every 10 days or so. Because she was somewhat ashamed, she rotated her ER visits among four different hospital emergency rooms and two emergency clinics.

On this particular occasion, she presented to the ER of a hospital that had recently incorporated an integrated behavioral/primary care format. Morgan was rapidly handed off to the BCP by the ER physician on duty. The BCP made an incisive diagnosis of agoraphobia as she revealed a history of ever-enlarging parts of the environment that provoked her panic attacks. Beginning shortly after her college acceptance was the terror she experienced if she traveled more than 50 miles from home (the boarding college was roughly 100 miles away). But over the two years, this narrowed in successive steps to where she was unable to leave the house.

The BCP followed up with a house call the very next day and not only established rapport, but succeeded in desensitizing Morgan sufficiently so that the two of them could walk around the block from her home. In the desensitization process, she was assured she could retreat at any time. She also motivated her to join the agoraphobia program in which the ambivalent home situation that was trapping her came to light and was resolved. In this more complicated case, the ambivalent relationship was a triangle instead of the usual duo. Morgan's divorced mother favored her two years younger brother, and it was only on the occasions in which Morgan complained loudly did the mother offer her any attention, and then it was only perfunctory. Morgan believed within her own mind that if she left for college her mother would become totally engrossed with her brother and forget her daughter entirely. As she gained insight and emotional strength, Morgan was able to directly and poignantly confront her mother, who soon acknowledged her bias and embraced her daughter as she had wanted her own rejecting mother to embrace her. Several months later, free of panic attacks, Morgan eagerly entered college.

The Hallway Handoff when the Child is the Identified Patient

Integrated behavioral/primary care has made excellent strides in many pediatric clinics; in fact, pediatric medicine has embraced the presence of a BCP even more than adult primary care. The pediatric setting is ideal for observing the interaction between parent and child, and lends itself to intervention by the BCP. Pediatricians welcome the hallway handoff with unruly or frightened children and with an uncooperative parent, usually an overprotective or competitive mother. Both were present in the following case.

Case Illustration: Non-attentive Andy

A mother brought her hyperactive and non-attentive 8-year-old to the pediatrician, but for a common cold that was particularly severe. When examined, Andy refused to sit still and was uncooperative with the pediatrician's requests. He darted out of the examining room twice and had to be retrieved by the mother.

Andy was diagnosed with ADHD and was prescribed Adderall, which is essentially a combination of Ritalin and another stimulant. The mother was a registered nurse who had interrupted her career to raise her three children, and was very troubled by the idea of subjecting her son to continuous stimulants at such an early age. She and the pediatrician clashed, and she became almost hysterical as the pediatrician was insistent and even made a referral to a psychiatrist to confirm the diagnosis and reaffirm the medication. In fact, the mother was so shaken that the pediatrician handed her off to the BCP.

This registered-nurse mother was not a naive patient, and she was acquainted with the literature that suggests:

a.   that ADHD is overly diagnosed; and
b.   that children receiving stimulants because of such a diagnosis result in a high percentage of drug addiction in adulthood.

The BCP very sympathetically and methodically went over the entire range of alternatives available, one of which is psychotherapy and other psychosocial interventions that are drug free. The mother settled down, cooperated with the BCP, and then accepted a referral to a psychologist who specialized in psychotherapy with ADHD children, or children who might be misdiagnosed. As it turned out, Andy's distracted, unruly behavior was a response to the teasing and bullying he was receiving from his classmates. His fellow third-graders were picking on him because of his exceptionally short stature, and Andy was respond-ing thus. In a combination of the psychotherapist's helping Andy cope with and respond to this teasing, along with a sudden growth spurt, the boy settled down while he no longer resembled a case of ADHD. He was still the shortest boy in the class, but not unduly so. In later years, when the mother returned to nursing, she was an avid advocate of integrated behavioral/primary care.

Axis II Patients and the Hallway Handoff

Borderline and sociopathic patients characteristically move in and out of the mental health system, as it might suit their purposes at the moment. Actual psychotherapy is usually not the motive. Rather, there is a difficult event in their lives with potentially negative consequences that they wish to manipulate in their favor. The range of difficulties is infinite and may be domestic, employment, legal, criminal, or any other issues in which the sympathetic intervention of the healthcare system may stay the usual consequences.

More and more frequently, borderline patients may present bearing a previous diagnosis of bipolar disorder or even schizophrenia. For a personality disordered patient, such a diagnosis is manna from heaven, making it possible to escape all kinds of consequences. Axis II patients who have been misdiagnosed as schizo-phrenics feign symptoms and threaten suicide in order to get psychiatrically hospitalized as a way of avoiding a jail sentence. Do not be misled by a false diagnosis. If you "smell" garlic behavior, respond accordingly.

In another note of caution, in their quest to be misdiagnosed as part of their manipulative behavior, Axis II patients have learned how to fake the usual depression and other scales to suit their admission or discharge from the hospital. The scales routinely used by psychotherapists such as the Beck Depression Inventory (BDI) or the PHQ-9 are known as "face valid tests." This merely means that what the question asks is what the question is getting at, as opposed to a test such as the MMPI, in which it is more difficult to discern the intent of a question. Consider, for example, a question on the Likert Scale, "How sad or hopeless do you feel?" Patients who want to be hospitalized to avoid jail can fake the test so as to appear not only severely depressed, but even suicidal. After a brief hospitalization during which charges are dropped, a fake retaking of the test shows unequivocally that the patient is recovered enough to leave the hospital. Face valid tests are valid only with honest patients who are answering the questions honestly.

In a final note of caution, it should be noted that older borderline patients who can no longer endure the effects of their wild acting out will resort to factitious behavior to create sympathy and achieve the desired end. Factitious disorder is the faking of illness, severe pain, and even disability to get what they want. People feel so sorry for them that they put themselves out for this ostensibly suffering person. Factitious disorder differs from both the somatizing patient and Munchausen's syndrome. In somatoform disorder, the patient is unconsciously translating emotional problems into physical symptoms. They are a severe drain on the health system in that physicians persist in their quest to diagnose the elusive disease, but these patients are not faking. They really feel pain, discomfort, palpitations, insomnia—in other words, all the symptoms of actual disease. Munchausen patients actually have an illness or condition that they actually and deliberately cause. A variation of this is Munchausen's by proxy, in which the parent (almost always the mother) deliberately makes her child sick.

Case Presentation: Lonnie's "Voices"

Lonnie was a 43-year-old twice-divorced woman who had a long history of writing bad checks, and when apprehended she would suffer an escalation of her severely bipolar behavior in which she had to be hospitalized. She was brought to the clinic from the county jail by the police for an evaluation. Her case folder revealed several instances in which Lonnie was diagnosed a bipolar who passed bad checks while in ostensibly manic phase shopping sprees, during which she bought expensive clothes and jewelry. She was living with a man slightly older than she who was a hard-working plumber and who worked very long hours while she kept the books for his business. While living with Arnie for the past two years, she had amassed a startling number of bad checks that finally caught up with her whereabouts. Threatened with criminal charges, Lonnie paid off all the bad checks by depleting Arnie's business bank account. This all came to light when Arnie's checks to suppliers began to bounce. Now discovered, Lonnie fled, after which Arnie filed charges. It did not take long for her to be apprehended, as she continued to pass bad checks for her living expenses.

The PCP found no physical illness and handed her off to the BCP who within 10 minutes of their interview discerned severe garlic and proceeded accordingly. Frustrated that her ruse was not working, Lonnie asked in the perfect "barking" of a "trained seal," "Aren't you going to give me a depression test?" The BCP ignored the question, whereupon Lonnie began to describe the very scary voices she claimed she was hearing. Calmly, the BCP asked whether the voices were inside her head or outside her head. Stumped, Lonnie hesitated interminably until the BCP repeated the question. With hesitation, as well as obvious concern, and with a half questioning voice, Lonnie haltingly replied, "Outside?" Seeing the therapist look up at the ceiling with apparent disdain, she quickly interjected, "No, I mean inside!" Lonnie did not know the right answer, and when she knew she was caught changing tactics, she began trying to gain the BCP's sympathy, to no avail.

The BCP patiently and professionally explained to Lonnie that her report would not find her suffering from bipolar disorder. She further explained her role as a psychotherapist and invited the patient back after she served her term, if that were to be the outcome. Indeed, Lonnie was sentenced to three years in prison. She never returned to this clinic, and her life after prison is unknown. What is clear is that without this BCP's having discerned the misdiagnosis in this garlic patient, she would likely have "beat the rap" a fifth time, once again encumbering the mental health system with undue costs.

Case Illustration: A Severe "Emergency"

A well-dressed 38-year-old man staggered into the emergency room gagging as he spit out gobs of blood. The ER crew went into emergency action as it appeared on the surface that this man was hemorrhaging badly either from his lungs or from his digestive system. On examination, an astute physician was immediately struck with the extensive scars from prior chest and abdomen surgery. He immediately suspected Munchausen's syndrome, but was baffled as to the origin of the profuse blood. Close inspection of his mouth, along with imaging of his esophagus and trachea revealed no lesions. He patiently allowed the blood to be totally disgorged, mildly sedated the patient, and asked the BCP to make a visit to the ER.

On interview, the patient was amazingly calm in the wake of what had transpired, but cooperated with the interview until once again he began to spew up gobs of blood. The ER physician immediately stepped in, and while moving the patient to surgery, the BCP informed the physician that a few minutes prior to the severe bleeding, and while he was looking again at the patient's chart, he witnessed out of the corner of his eye the patient thrust his finger high up on the inside of his left cheek and then seemingly physically traumatize it. A more precise and thorough examination of that area revealed that the patient was maintaining a hidden, open lesion that could be caused to bleed profusely at any moment. This, of course, confirmed the diagnosis of Munchausen's syndrome. A wrap-up session with the BCP before discharge from the ER was on the surface cooperative and attentive. However, the patient was never seen again, as he probably moved to another city where he could continue his ruse.

The Career of the BCP

When contemplating practice as a behavioral care practitioner, there is usually hesitation and even skepticism. It is as far away as can be from the dream of a comfortable individual practice in a private office, with a Mercedes Benz or a BMW parked in the parking lot, and a paying clientele of intelligent, middle class patients who have often been described in healthcare as "the worried well." Increasingly, this has become an unrealistic fantasy as we struggle with decreased reimbursement schedules, diminishing referrals for psychotherapy in favor of medication, burn out from boredom, and increasing overhead. The life of a BCP embodies Michael Balint's prescient exhortation that physicians need to become more like psychologists, while psychologists need to become more like physicians (Balint, 1957).

A career as a BCP is exciting and rewarding, but it is not for everyone. Astute, innovative, and energetic doctorate-trained potential BCPs are usually hesitant at first, but very shortly with experience they espouse that career as exciting, rewarding, and prestigious. Within a few short months of working together, PCPs and BCPs develop a mutual respect for each other's abilities, congenially rely on each other, and the BCP acquires a level of regard and acceptance between physician and non-physician not found anywhere else in healthcare.

Most states now permit practice partnerships between physicians and psychologists. This was not always so, as the medical practice statutes expressly forbade a physician to partner with a non-physician. The repeal of this archaic rule has its beginning with Dr. Herbert Dorken, Nick's co-principal investigator in the Hawaii Medicaid Project. Herb is both a psychologist and a registered lobbyist who has authored and had enacted 49 federal and state healthcare laws. Along with this beginning, there came the U.S. Supreme Court decision in the 1980s that healthcare was subject to antitrust and restraint of trade laws. When the existing archaic healthcare laws are challenged, as did American Biodyne when it hired psychiatrists who worked under the direction of psychologists, when it acquired hospital and ER privileges, or when the ApA attempted to enforce outdated statutes, Biodyne prevailed.

At the present time, there are a number of private practices throughout the United States in which PCPs and BCPs are partners, and with indications that their numbers will grow. Not surprisingly, physicians have expressed a preference to work and partner with psychologists over psychiatrists. There is also reverse behavioral/primary care integration in which a physician or physicians work within an otherwise essentially psychotherapy practice. Here, with the hallway handoff, rather than as physician to behavioral practitioner, the BCP hands off to the PCP to ascertain or rule out physical disease. Healthcare is changing and evolving, and its future in part lies in the hands of well-trained, but innovative, readers of this book.

12

EXTREME THERAPY

The term "extreme therapy" was originally intended as an invective by critics of the Biodyne Model who regarded any behavioral interventions outside the sanctity of the therapy office to be extreme and unwarranted. In going in the direction of the resistance, the authors affectionately adopted the title, which very much pertains to co-located behavioral/primary care and many other approaches, but does not apply to the case of Lenore and the cyanide capsule. We reiterate: that is definitely out of bounds and was presented to demonstrate beyond any doubt the potential power of psychotherapy incisively applied.

Restricting our psychotherapy and other behavioral interventions to the office or even to the extended medical setting will result in our inability to treat far more potential patients than the short-sighted psychotherapist realizes. A remarkable extreme therapy is illustrated by a literally 10-second intervention that saved countless lives in World War II.

Jump Door Fever

My (Nick's) earliest acquaintance with psychotherapy was long before I had ever taken a psychology course. It was while I was a combat officer with the celebrated 82nd Airborne Division, our army's very first paratrooper unit that saw extensive combat during World War II on D-Day in Normandy, and in Italy, Yugoslavia, Greece, and across France and Germany until the Allied Forces reached Berlin. About 40 percent of the casualties were attributable to what came to be known as jump door fever. Jumping in very fast military parachutes into enemy lines and behind enemy lines was far more than just a difficult experience, but it was aided by a superstition among troopers that resulted from their not understanding the law of averages. The average life of the paratrooper was three combat jumps, with the fourth jump resulting in death, wounding, or capture. It was two and three, respectively, for an officer. This of course means someone might be killed on the first jump, while someone may even survive a sixth or seventh jump. But the misunderstanding aided the trooper on the first three combat jumps with the false assurance, "It is not my time to die." But then there came the anticipated fatal fourth jump and often the trooper would freeze at the jump door.

When jumping in combat, a certain cadence has to be maintained. Jumping too soon would subject the troopers to possible entanglement in mid-air, while jumping too slowly would cause the unit to overshoot its target. The sergeant at the jump door would count to 10 while loudly and repeatedly ordering the distraught trooper to jump, and if he had not done so by the count of 10, he would put his boot in the small of the trooper's back and push him out. Invariably the trooper would go into a number 10 panic, forget all of his training, and would become a ready target for the enemy. Hence, the 40 percent casualty rate of jump door fever. Something had to be done.

William (Will) Menninger, brother of Karl and co-founder of the later world-famous Menninger Clinic in Topeka, Kansas, was the chief military psychiatrist during World War II, holding the rank of general. Among his many innovations, he created the School of Military Neuropsychiatry in Long Island, New York where master's level psychologists and social workers were trained to be mental health interventionists at the battalion aid station level at the front lines. World-famous psychoanalyst Dr. Frieda Fromm-Reichmann was brought in to train a select group of paratroop officers on how to deal with jump door fever. I was one in a handful of participants who was flown from combat in Europe to attend a most remarkable two-week course.

Fromm-Reichmann taught us that although love is the strongest human emotion, it is slow and unpredictable, while rage is immediate and compelling. She taught us in just two weeks how to talk the trooper out the door within 10 seconds by so enraging him that he jumped willingly in defiant rage, circumventing panic and thus saving his life. Her training was rigorous, compelling, and incisive, and I never lost another trooper to jump fever after she taught me how to save his life in 10 seconds. As I look back on my 60 years as a psychologist, it is the briefest therapy I have ever done. It also convinced me that if psychology can do that, I wanted to be a psychologist.

My training was soon to be put to a test, as on our next combat jump a young trooper from Brooklyn of Italian descent froze at the jump door. Yes, it was the so-called "fatal fourth." He had been in my unit for several weeks, so I knew him well and respected him as a really fine soldier, but now I had to grossly insult him in a way that is anathema to me. In World War II, the Italian army disgraced itself, having to be rescued by the German army repeatedly. The only country it defeated was the then very primitive Ethiopia, hardly a great military conquest. As we approached the count of eight, I yelled in his ear (as the rush of air at the jump door is incredibly loud), "Andriotti, are American Wops as yellow-bellied as Italian Wops?" He turned to me in rage and yelled, "Fuck you, Captain," and jumped out the door. Later when I found him after our successful military engagement I put my hand on his shoulder, but before I could say anything he said, "Thank you, Captain. I know why you did that." Not only was Andy's life saved, but he survived the rest of the war.

Our "Office" on the Freeway and in the Subway

In refreshing our knowledge of phobic behavior, we are reminded that the ambivalent relationship to a loved one upon whom the phobic is dependent (spouse, parent, lover, employer, etc.) results in living restrictions whose meaning is, "How can I leave him/her when I can't even leave the house, drive a car, get on the subway?" and so on. Geographic phobias (freeways, bridges, tunnels, the post office, retail stores) begin when there is some kind of delay, a waiting period, a long line, stopped freeway traffic, or other such behavioral restriction in which the mind wanders, threatening to relate the trapped feeling to the feeling of being trapped in a life situation. The ambivalence is expressed unconsciously thus: "How can I leave my spouse when I can't even drive (shop, leave the house alone, etc.)?" In the Biodyne Model, such agoraphobias are treated in specially designed phobia programs in which the ambivalent relationship is understood and resolved, and in the "field" where the patient is desensitized to the phobia. This involves baby steps in which the dreaded situation is approached, then the patient retreats from it until the series of approaches/retreats has resulted in a complete desensitization. Where there are multiple phobias, desensitizing the major one results in the rapid desensitization of the subsequent ones. This approach/retreat sequence was well illustrated in the previous presentation of housebound Doris.

Case Illustration: Francine—"I'll Never Drive Again"

Francine was a 29-year-old woman who was married for six years to a control-freak husband whom she increasingly disliked through the years. He was, however, a very successful man with a very large income, and he indulged her fondness of expensive clothes and jewelry, and he tolerated her being a spendthrift. She was very reluctant to relinquish her role as a high-maintenance wife, but she resented his domineering attitude and his reducing her to the role of a marital bauble. More and more, she began to fantasize leaving him, but her fantasies always concluded with her ending up as a single waitress in some honky-tonk, and she would quickly dismiss the notion of leaving him. Often the fantasy she would abort occurred when she was driving the interstate highway to their lavish suburban home. She would pretend she would drive beyond her exit, and on to freedom, but to her dismay she always took the right exit.

One afternoon, she was giggling while driving home because she had just bought in defiance an expensive diamond bracelet that her husband had asked her not to purchase, when suddenly there was a severe pile-up of several cars ahead. Traffic was at a standstill, and it was 40 minutes before it was moving again. Being an impatient woman, she felt increasingly trapped, and as her mind wandered, she thought of how she was trapped in her marriage. Unable to tolerate the fantasy of leaving her husband, she actively tried to dismiss the fantasy. Finally, the traffic began to move again, but when she got to her exit it was blocked with wreckage and she was instructed to drive to the next exit and return home via surface streets. Many times she had fantasized driving past her exit, then driving on and on into freedom. By the time she got home, she was shaking. The next day, she found to her dismay that she broke into a sweat when she tried to drive. The more she tried, the more she panicked.

After several sessions in the agoraphobia group program in which she had discussed her relationship with her husband with increased understanding each time, Francine agreed to accompany the therapist in his car. He drove one block away from her house, then retreated back to her driveway. This was repeated until she not only felt totally comfortable driving two blocks from home, but began to find it boring. This, of course, is the sign the therapist can move on. She was given the wheel, with the therapist sitting beside her in the passenger seat, but she was able to drive only one (rather than two) blocks before she was urged to turn around and head for home (i.e., retreat). Little by little, Francine increased the distance until she could drive freely, but only on surface streets. On a subsequent session, she was desensitized in this same advance/retreat fashion to driving on the freeway.

In her group therapy, Francine learned to alter for the better her marital relationship, and in the field she was desensitized to her driving phobia. Often we have desensitized two or three patients at a time in one car. This works very well, as the patients seem to feed off each other's successes at each baby step. Similarly, several patients at a time can be desensitized to subway phobias, starting out with first just walking down to the train level and then immediately upstairs again, several times until they are bored and ready to board the train. The first such boarding is to a very nearby stop, and then back again, increasing it to two stops, then three, and so forth as the patients respond with boredom to each increased baby step.

House Calls

House calls by physicians were regularly conducted until after World War II in which they were replaced by the provision of convalescent cars or a prepaid taxi service that would bring the patient to the doctor, rather than the doctor to the patient. They were never a regular part of mental healthcare, and there has been no apparent discussion as to when they might be necessary. Yet, there are situations in which they are imperative, such as housebound and bed-ridden Doris whose case was discussed previously. That no one other than the Biodyne Model has addressed the matter of treating the housebound agoraphobic at home suggests why such patients are absent in almost all psychology settings, resulting to the erroneous conclusion that such agoraphobics are non-existent. These patients would rather suffer than make the terrifying trip to our offices, clinics, or treatment centers. When they are seen, it is usually in the ER where they present as suffering from possible heart failure, are diagnosed with suffering from a panic attack, given medication, and sent home, only for them to show up again a few weeks later.

But there are other incidences that might require a house call. Erik Erikson treated many children, and when he received a referral for child therapy he first had himself invited to a family dinner. He stated he could learn more about the family system and interaction in that one family dinner than he could in six to eight sessions with the family in his office. Now, under our well-meaning but knit-picking ethics codes, this might even be regarded as unethical, as it violates rigid and often unnecessary boundaries.

There are cultural groups that are sensitive and even guarded regarding possible mental health issues in members of the family, and will often designate someone in the family to care for the afflicted member. Such was the case in the very large Chinese population of the generation preceding the current one, and our staff often made a confidential house call as the initial contact. Such has been true of the older generation among the Filipinos in Daly City, just south of San Francisco, which comprises the largest such population outside the Philippines.

Case Illustration: Pilar, the Family Pillar

Pilar, the 92-year-old venerated matriarch of a large Filipino family, had for almost two years demonstrated understandable cognitive deficits along with difficulties in caring for herself. Family members secretly cared for her, made excuses why she was unable to attend cultural events, and largely guarded her mental deficit. Unquestionably, Pilar was a very proud woman with a highly respected reputation in the community, and her family, especially the generation just younger than she, took very seriously its role to protect that reputation. Pitted against this protectiveness was the need to have Pilar declared mentally incompetent and disabled, as she would then be eligible for much needed nursing care under Medicare. To bring Pilar to the clinic for appropriate evaluation placed her in danger of being seen by other Filipinos who would surely also be in the physicians' waiting rooms. Nick offered to make a house call, as he had often done in similar situations.

When he arrived at the house, he found to his surprise that 43 family members had gathered, all of whom insisted on watching the examination. No big deal, thought this psychologist, as they watched in respectful silence. In fact, their presence facilitated the examination, as Pilar was comfortable being surrounded by her loved ones. The problem arose at the conclusion of the examination. All 43 members of the family had brought an ethnic dish and they insisted on thanking the psychologist by treating him to a lavish, several-hour banquet. I was due back at my office, but to have declined would have been a devastating insult to this proud family. I called the office and cancelled the rest of the day. (By the way, in the rare instances in which I unavoidably have to cancel a patient appointment, the patient's next session is conducted free of charge.) Word spread, and quickly I became the psychologist of choice in the Filipino community of Daly City.

Outreaching the High Utilizers of Healthcare

There probably does not exist a more effective cost-saving intervention than the outreach program for high utilizers of medicine and surgery. Including it in our armamentarium is a value added, as it must be remembered that payers (government, insurance, managed care) are far more concerned with medical/ surgical costs than they are about mental health. At the same time, patients who are translating psychological problems and emotional distress into physical symptoms (called "somatization") will finally receive the appropriate treatment through behavioral services. Widely known for over 40 years, somatization is the subject of over 300 published studies and is definitely explicated in an edited volume by Cummings et al. (2002).

Beginning as early as the mid-1960s, it was shown (Follette & Cummings, 1967; Cummings & Follette, 1968) that:

a.   60 percent to 70 percent of patients seen in primary care are either somatizing or have psychological issues that are impeding the healing of an actual physical disease; and
b.   outreaching these patients, who comprise 15 percent of the highest utilizers of medicine and surgery, and providing appropriate behavioral services reduces overall health costs (after deducting the cost of the behavioral care) by a total of as much as 40 percent.

So impressed was the National Institute of Mental Health (NIMH) that it named the methodology medical cost offset. The outreach is performed by a psycho- therapist specially trained so as not to challenge the patient's belief that all his/her symptoms are physical. In other words, care is taken not to label the patient a somatizer. A simple message that invites the patient to come in on the basis that "someone who is having so many medical issues as you are having must surely be upset about it" is sufficient to bring in 11 percent to 12 percent of this 15 percent—enough to result in the substantial medical cost offset. Other techniques have been developed to gain the cooperation of most of the remaining 3 percent to 4 percent.

Medical utilization is a straightforward tabulation of physician and physician ancillary visits, laboratory and imaging tests, emergency room or drop-in clinic visits, hospital days, and each issued prescription. The creation of a weighted system for the various services did not in any way improve the accuracy of the findings, and was abandoned as too cumbersome. The reason usually given why this method is not universally deployed is that, in all but a few health systems, the medical and psychiatric databases are not compatible and the appropriate tracking of behavioral interventions on medicine and surgery is not possible.

Outpatient Therapy in the Hospital Emergency Room: A Paradox that Works

The practice of performing outpatient therapy in the ER seems like a paradox, but by this simple method, American Biodyne was able to reduce psychiatric hospitalization by 90 percent (Cummings et al., 1997). The simple concept that if a patient responds to outpatient treatment, he/she does not need hospitalization seems logical, yet it is almost universally doubted as attested by the usual ER procedure with potential psychiatric patients.

Emotionally distressed patients often find themselves in the ER late at night, usually brought there by family or referred there by evening drop-in care. The sequence of events usually follows a pattern: a psychiatrist is called, and over the telephone the patient is admitted to a mental care ward overnight; the psychiatrist arrives to evaluate the patient the following morning. By that time, the patient has spent the night in a "crazy place" and decides, "I must be crazier than I thought," and reflects that conclusion. So invariably the patient is admitted to the psychiatric unit or hospital as a psychiatric patient. Psychiatric hospitalization is costly, upward of thousands of dollars a day. But beyond cost, it is of benefit to a patient to prevent psychiatric hospitalization unless it is absolutely necessary.

In the Biodyne Model, a specially trained psychologist or social worker who is on call is dispatched immediately in the middle of the night, and begins outpatient treatment immediately upon arrival to the ER. If the patient responds to the outpatient intervention, the same as he/she might have done in a psychotherapy outpatient office during the day, the patient is sent home with family and seen in the outpatient behavioral care service the next morning, and for several consecutive mornings if this is deemed appropriate. All of this costs only a fraction of what would be the cost of even one day in a psychiatric hospital.

Case Illustration: Machete Mel and His Terrified Parents

Melvin, or "Mel" as he hated to be called, was a 23-year-old schizophrenic man who lived at home with his parents, who had learned invariably how to quiet him down in his somewhat frequent and unpredictable outbursts. On this particular occasion, the new housekeeper of only two days, while turning down his bed, made the mistake of calling him Mel instead of Melvin. He flew into a rage, which terrified the unsuspecting middle-aged housekeeper. Immediately, the parents stepped in, explaining that she was new and did not know better, a subdued approach which would have sufficed had they not added the reasoned,

"Almost everybody refers to anyone named Melvin as Mel, and there is nothing wrong with that." That kind of reasoning threw their son into an uncontrollable rage beyond anything they had ever seen. He threatened to kill his parents with a machete, and they were so terrified they called 911.

The psychologist saw Melvin, and interviewed his parents shortly after midnight. By this time, the patient had calmed down, and although he insisted his parents were stupid in saying the nickname "Mel" was okay, he did not seem to pose a threat. Nonetheless, his parents were still terrified and demanded he be hospitalized. The psychologist quickly calmed them down by asking if there was a machete in the home. Surprised at first by the question, they replied there was not. The psychologist explained to them that Melvin did not really want to hurt them, and even through his seemingly out-of-control schizophrenia he had made it impossible by deliberately choosing a non-existent weapon.

Melvin was sent home with his parents who realized that the therapist he had been seeing was very much over his head in treating a young schizophrenic. They helped their son transfer to a colleague of the psychologist who had seen him in the ER, and who also knew how to treat him by joining his delusional system.

The Immediate Group as Illustrative of the Three Es

Providing coverage 9:00 a.m. to 5:00 p.m. so that patients in crisis can be seen immediately is a costly and inefficient procedure that is regarded by almost all treatment centers as inevitable. Some clinics have one person covering the entire day, while others rotate therapists so that a different one is present from hour to hour. The inefficiency occurs when an hour or more passes without anyone needing to be seen, with rarely a complaint from psychotherapists who are delighted to have a free hour. An effective and efficient response is to tell all patients who call wanting to be seen immediately to come in at 3:00 p.m., called the "immediate group," avoiding critical labels such as "crisis group." Patients need not be labeled in advance as being in crisis, thus fostering a self-fulfilling prophecy. The patients are not told in advance they will be seen in a group, but this is implied in the statement, "Three in the afternoon is when we see all patients who need to be seen today." This is repeated when the group assembles.

The characteristics of the immediate group are that:

a.   one professional sees all the patients in a group session;
b.   by meeting from 3:00 p.m. to 5:00 p.m., there is still time to hospitalize a patient who might need it; and
c.   attendees are encouraged to return the next day should they wish to.

Thus, along with persons who are there initially, the group is composed of those who are returning the second, third, or fourth time. Rarely will there be a fifth time.

Because of its uniqueness, and before the immediate group was made standard procedure, for 12 months patients who called were randomly assigned to the traditional mode or the immediate group. The results showed the superiority of the immediate group over the traditional method in that only 23 percent of those attending the immediate group needed to go on to specialty mental healthcare versus 68 percent for the traditional method. As for the total sessions required (crisis plus follow-up), those in the immediate group averaged 2.8 sessions, while those assigned to the traditional mode averaged 7.4 (crisis plus follow-up). The cost of the immediate group was less than one-third of the traditional approach, and it was made standard procedure at Kaiser Permanente in San Francisco in 1967 (Cummings & Cummings, 2000). Its use in most settings constitutes a decided efficiency reform.

Case Illustration: Typical Immediate Group Composition

On this particular day, there were seven in the group. There was a man in his fifties here for his third day who had just lost his wife in a tragic automobile crash, and just began talking about rebuilding his life. He was able to intercede positively with a 30-ish man there his first day whose wife had left him, by admonishing him he was obviously not losing a loving spouse, and that he might be better off to find this out at an early age. A distraught teenager was there her second day, fearful of attending school because of bullying from the mean girls. She was accompanied by her highly intelligent, educated mother and the two of them began to talk of finishing the last nine weeks in a charter school willing to accept her. Another teenager who had been arrested for shoplifting and who initially denied she was guilty as charged was also there her second day. She was addressed by the psychologist as a garlic patient and by the end of the session admitted culpability and a desire to alter the shoplifting behavior, which had begun several months earlier. For a 40-ish alcoholic man, who was there for his first day, the psychotherapist began to lay the groundwork for the "sobriety challenge" (see Cummings & Cummings, 2000). Finally, in the last 10 minutes of the two-hour session, an effeminate teenage boy who had been beaten up by his classmates gained enough confidence to begin telling his story, and eagerly expressed his desire to return the next day.

Enforced Homework

Psychotherapists are always looking for a way to bridge the treatment hiatus between sessions, and they usually resort to scheduling two and even three sessions a week. With managed care's limitations, this is becoming more and more difficult to do. Ever since Budman and Gurman (1988) showed this could be done effectively by assigning homework after each session, the practice has become somewhat common, although too often sporadic and even haphazard, among psychotherapists. Very frequently, the patient will present alibis as to why the homework was not done, and characteristically in such situations the psychotherapist does not enforce the homework, even in the all-too-frequent occasions in which the alibi is rather lame. Unfortunately, because the homework was not enforced, mental health circles soon erroneously deemed it ineffective and homework was largely abandoned. On the other hand, it has been demonstrated that when the homework is incisively assigned and enforced, it is highly effective. It extends the thrust of therapy throughout the intervening week and into the next session with no demonstrable hiatus. It is as if the patient has been in continuous treatment (Cummings & Cummings, 2000; Cummings & Sayama, 1995).

At the outset, the patient agrees that if the weekly homework is not completed, the patient forfeits that session in which the homework is due. The patient must attend the session, and after admitting the homework was not done, leaves. Care must be taken so that the "explanation" (read, alibi) does not absorb more than the first couple of minutes, as garlic patients can cleverly extend it to engulf a large part of what is to be a forfeited session. This may sound harsh, but seldom does the psychotherapist have to send the patient home more than once, while the positive effect of a session extended throughout the week is rewarding. Through the enforcement of the homework, the patient is convinced beyond a doubt of the veracity of the therapist's word, as well as the therapist's dedication and commitment to a successful outcome. It underscores its seriousness. Many therapists, however, will have to undergo a shift from well-meaning but misguided compassion to one of effectiveness. Stated simply, the psychotherapist must be more like a doctor than a nun.

There is no list or reservoir of homework. It is important that the homework is tailored so that it follows what is pertinent to the treatment, and carries the session into the next week.

Case Illustration: You Are Mean to Poor Audrey

This 28-year-old divorced woman was as garlic as she was beautiful. She used her attractiveness, combined with pouting, to always get her way, especially with men, as most were no match for her wiles. She had attempted on the first visit several weeks earlier to emotionally seduce the psychotherapist. Failing miserably, she decided to be a difficult, demanding patient. Along with that, she embarked on a campaign to give her current, hapless boyfriend a bad time, all the while playing the role of a poor, misunderstood, and lonely little girl. At times, she approached honesty, laughing at the attention she obtained when she feigned hurt. Dabbing her tearful mascara with her handkerchief was especially effective, as gullible men would melt, acceding to her demands.

During the previous session, she had bragged incessantly how she always got her way. Her homework for today's session was to list all the techniques she uses to (a) belittle men and (b) cynically get her way. She arrived distraught, not having done her homework. She ran out of gas on the way to her therapist's office, found to her dismay that her AAA roadside service policy had expired, and walked in the rain the last four blocks to the session. She blamed the therapist for this happenstance, as it was his fault she broke up with her boyfriend before he had refilled her gas tank, as well as to pay for it as usual and as he had been doing for several weeks. Arriving drenched and distraught, she began to relate how she broke up with Ralph before he filled her tank, all of which was the psychologist's fault. She had never learned to pump gas, as gas stations were smelly and dirty.

She was interrupted in mid-complaint, instructed to come in next week with the homework completed, along with the added homework of learning to pump gas. She stormed out of the office, vowing never to return. However, this garlic patient did indeed return, having completed her vamp list, as well as having learned to pump gas. Psychotherapy progressed, with the usual bumps provided by such a determined garlic patient, to its eventual successful conclusion. She was still Axis II, but she had learned with much happiness to go through life with more emotional maturity and greater impulse control.

The Community as Your "Patient"

There are times when a mini epidemic may overload a delivery system and the answer may be outside your office, and even outside the delivery of psychotherapy. Such a problem arose in one prepaid healthcare setting when several dozen women all presented with a variety of vague complaints, ranging from tension headaches to depression. An astute observation by one of the receptionists revealed that all of these mothers had something in common: all had a son in a certain Catholic grammar and junior high school. Following this revelation, targeted inquiries were made by their various psychotherapists; these revealed that all their sons who previously had been good students had lost interest in school and were doing poorly. Further inquiry also revealed that the local Catholic school district had exchanged nuns with a contingent of Irish nuns; the American nuns were spending the year teaching in Ireland while the Irish nuns were doing the same in this community.

It was time to meet with the monsignor, who was the local superintendent of Catholic instruction. Over lunch, he stated he had already incurred dissatisfaction, and he conjectured that the strictness and authoritarian attitude of the nuns from Ireland were not suitable for the American classroom. It was near the end of the first semester and the monsignor arranged to return the Irish nuns to Ireland and the American nuns to their community before the beginning of the second semester of that school year.

Overnight, the "epidemic" of anxious, depressed mothers abated. Had the emphasis remained in the treatment room, undoubtedly the clinic overload would have persisted the entire year. This is only one of many instances in which efficiency requires stepping aside from the traditional role and outside the office of the psychotherapist. Yes, this extreme therapy is far from the 50-minute hour for which we traditionally trained.

The Therapeutic "Shopping Spree"

Chronic schizophrenics can often be helped to make an adjustment to daily living if they can avoid the crises that result in their re-hospitalization. It is through repeated, yet often avoidable, hospitalizations that costs mount in the treatment of this population. A crisis to a schizophrenic is not what most people would think of as a crisis. It can involve buying a pair of socks or ordering something to eat.

In their childhoods, chronic schizophrenics learned to be intimidated by people without knowing why. Their mannerisms, often peculiar speech patterns, and the fact they did not grasp things like most children singled them out for ridicule. They developed a shyness and avoidance pattern that followed them into adulthood and even grew in severity. Confronted now with buying a pair of socks, the chronic schizophrenic is fearful in the bustling department store.

While in line approaching the cashier, he/she feels as if everyone is staring and is about to make fun of him/her. The intimidation grows by the minute, and soon the feeling of fright is producing mannerisms in speech, walk, and general demeanor. Other customers notice this behavior and move farther and farther away from the schizophrenic. Adults do not ridicule as do children; they walk away. They become concerned when odd speech mannerisms commence and often the store security detail is called. Security personnel are not trained to differentiate aberrant behavior as to whether it is dangerous or benign, mis-understandings escalate, and the harmless schizophrenic is whisked off to the hospital, where his/her record of previous hospitalizations result in a speedy re-admission, often in restraints (medicinal or physical).

Programs in daily living, conducted in groups, can teach chronic but otherwise stabilized patients to purchase clothes or a meal, ask directions on public transportation, check out a library book, and the myriad of day-to-day activities that are simple to most people but are terrifying to these patients. The authors and their colleagues have conducted such outings for years, and have found that stores, restaurants, and public transportation systems are remarkably understanding when they are informed in advance and their cooperation solicited. Such outings are usually two to three hours in length, and although this exceeds the traditional 50-minute hour in length, as many as six patients can participate at any one time.

The patients who have already let the psychotherapist into their inner world and trust him/her through techniques previously described are emboldened once they have learned simple everyday behaviors, and the therapist also finds it rewarding. In our experience, chronic schizophrenics are more willing to participate in such field programs than psychotherapists are willing to leave their entrenched offices and conduct them. Yet, the effectiveness of such programs indicate they should become part of behavioral healthcare delivery. They exceed the effectiveness of relying on meds to keep the patient out of the hospital inasmuch as the medicinal side effects cause chronic schizophrenics to stop taking their medications, thus resulting in their re-hospitalization.

Conclusion

Certainly the hallway handoff, joining the patient's delusion, going in the direction of the patient's resistance, and other techniques described in previous chapters would qualify under our affectionately adopted rubric of extreme therapy. All are illustrations of the need for psychotherapy to be responsive to the three Es: efficacy, effectiveness, and efficiency.

13
PSYCHOPHARMACOLOGY FOR BEHAVIORAL CARE PROVIDERS

Practicing in the medical setting renders it imperative that the behavioral care provider (BCP) has a working knowledge of psychopharmacology. This chapter is not intended to qualify the BCP for prescription privileges or to compete with the prescribing physician; rather, the psychotherapist needs to know what medications have been prescribed for the patient being treating, what their side effects might be, and whether they are appropriate for the condition for which you are providing psychotherapy. It will enable you to be alert to any untoward or inappropriate medications, the emergence of side effects, and to cooperate with the physician to provide the best care possible for your patient.

A general knowledge of what is contained in this chapter is imperative, but it is not necessary to memorize it in detail. Rather, use it as a useful reference guide. When you have a patient who has been prescribed a certain medication, look up the drug in this chapter, become acquainted with that drug's appropriate and inappropriate uses, its side effects, its interactions with foods or other drugs that have been prescribed, and ponder whether that drug is appropriate or useful for your psychotherapy patient whom you know better than does the prescribing psychiatrist, and even more often by the prescribing non–psychiatric physician.

Remember, by virtue of their penetrating training, Biodyne-trained psychotherapists are instrumental in taking far more patients off medication than they request be put on medication. But in relating to the prescribing physician, utmost tact is paramount, working toward a relationship of mutual trust and respect that can only be earned by a long-term demonstration of your knowledge, skill, and dedication to the best treatment for your psychotherapy patient.

Finally, this chapter includes drugs of abuse. The sad fact is that as many as 40 percent of patients seen today have drug abuse issues, both street and prescription drugs, and often along with alcohol, that are unbeknown to the psychotherapist. A patient who is abusing drugs does not do well in psychotherapy, and the therapist that does not recognize substance abuse issues is remiss in his/her responsibility. Furthermore, prescribing psychotropic medications to the patient with an undetected and undisclosed substance abuse issue can prove dangerous.

Medication Management

In the Biodyne Model, the behavioral practitioner has recourse to the most effective psychotherapeutic interventions and thus is not limited to today's usual practice, which is predominantly psychotropic treatment. As a result, only a relatively few patients are on meds, as behavioral treatment is the mode. It is not surprising, then, that the skilled psychotherapist confers with the physician more often in regard to taking patients off meds rather than conferring on what medications should be prescribed.

Sustained patient improvement is dependent upon the "art" of medication management, and the more complicated the case, the more "art" is necessary. In approaching the entire subject, as a non-medical practitioner the BCP must possess tact, be able to form a therapeutic alliance, and provide reassurance. In addition, the BCP must manifest perseverance, and be creative in medication strategies. Paramount is the ability to predict, identify, and resolve resistance. All of this requires persuasiveness.

In the Biodyne Model, a patient first sees a behavioral practitioner who, if he/she determines in the course of treatment the patient could benefit from an appropriate medication, would approach the PCP or psychiatrist. This ideal is rarely found today inasmuch as the physician or psychiatrist has already seen the patient and has prescribed. After seeing the patient, if the psychotherapist has determined that the patient would do just as well, if not better, without medication, or worse, if the medication prescribed is inappropriate, the utmost tact is imperative if the psychotherapist is to function in the best interest of the patient. The more complicated the case, the more "art" and tact are required.

In summary, the practice of clinical psychopharmacology by the non-medical psychotherapist requires skill as a diagnostician, skill as a psychotherapist, knowledge of the available drugs, and the ability to plan a psychotherapeutic regimen. The selection and initiation of drug treatment should be based on:

a.   the patient's past history;
b.   the patient's family history;
c.   the patient's current clinical state (medical and psychological); and
d.   the treatment plan.

In all of this, it is necessary to know the purpose or goal of the drug trial, and the length of time the drug needs to be administered to assess its efficacy. One must also know the adverse effects that are likely to occur and how to manage them, including a knowledge of alternative drug strategies should the current one fail. Of importance is the assessment of whether or not long-term maintenance is indicated.

As the patient's compliance is imperative, the treatment plan should be explained to the patient and possibly to other family members, as the patient's reactions to the drug trial, as well as the patient's ideas about the drug trial, will likely impact his/her adherence. If the BCP believes that accommodating the patient's wishes would hinder treatment, this should be explained to the patient.

Appropriate Diagnosis

An issue confronting the psychotherapist today is that diagnostic categories have become too broad. For example, "depression" now includes such things as grief and normal life difficulties. For far too many physicians and psychiatrists, the finding of any depression ipso facto means the automatic prescribing of an antidepressant. This can rob the patient of nature's own indicator that the patient should attend to some aspect of his/her lifestyle.

Appropriate diagnosis requires the understanding of depression as a symptom of any number of conditions, just as headache is a symptom that can reflect anything from simple eye strain to a brain tumor. The BCP does not arrive at a treatment plan until the presenting symptom has been subjected to a cause and effect determination. More often than not, in direct contrast to usual practice today, medication is not indicated.

The Biodyne Protocol for Medication Management

1. Through clinical interview, mental status exam, family history, and psychological symptoms, the clinician defines the nature of the disorder, and answers the question, "Is the disorder medication responsive?"
2. The clinician must be familiar with the classes of psychotropic medications, their appropriate uses, as well as their adverse reactions. One must also know the methods and routes of administration and the dosages ranges.
3. The attitude that the clinician portrays to the patient is important. It should be one of optimism and hope, and totally devoid of pro-drug or anti-drug prejudices.
4. Use non-medical treatments when they are at least as effective as drug treatments. For example, in most cases of phobias, behavior therapy is superior to medication, as is cognitive insight therapy for neurotic depression.
5. Do not deny a patient appropriate medication, but carefully weigh the appropriateness.
6. Choose the drug with the fewest adverse reactions and greatest potential clinical effects.

7. Administer the lowest effective dose of medication for the shortest period of time.
8. Prescribe the simplest drug regimen to increase compliance. For example, a single bedtime dose of an antidepressant might be the simplest regimen.
9. Whenever possible, avoid polypharmacy. Combinations of drugs are rarely more effective than a single agent, and in most cases it is best to stay at a dosage range that does not require a second medication to treat side effects. If polypharmacy cannot be avoided, use "rational polypharmacy," which entails the following:

   a. use the least number of medications needed to achieve optimal improvement; and
   b. combine medications if necessary to treat two or more distinct symptoms (i.e., symptoms not attributable to one underlying cause).

10. Exercise special care in medicating children, the elderly, and the medically ill.
11. Administer each drug trial for an appropriate length of time.
12. "Taking the edge off" is of more value to the patient than over-medication.
13. If medication is likely to cause unpleasant side effects, start with a small dose.
14. Consider the patient's prior experience with this and other medications, his/her attitude toward medications, his/her family's attitude toward experiences with medications, and their PCP's attitude toward psychotropic medications.
15. It is not uncommon that patients who want or demand medications do not need them, whereas patients who do need medication are often resistant to taking it.
16. Psychotropic medications work best when combined with appropriate psychotherapy. Psychotropics are not used alone, but only in conjunction with psychotherapy.
17. If a patient is clearly unwilling to use medication, it is usually best to respect that patient's wishes. The exception may be the patients who are incapable of making good, informed decisions for themselves.

It is important to keep in mind that many, if not the majority of physicians and psychiatrists would disagree with most, if not all, aspects of this protocol. Utmost tact, therefore, is imperative. Over time, as the clinician demonstrates knowledge, competence, and especially success in the treatment of patients, trust will follow.

Common Medical Abbreviations on Prescriptions

If it is determined that the clinician cannot read a prescription, he/she will be deemed incompetent to recommend or participate in determining a medication regimen. The following are the most common medical abbreviations for prescriptions.

It is important that the BCP be able to read prescriptions as a prerequisite to assessing the nature of the medication treatment. There follows a list of commonly used abbreviations for constant reference, until they become part of your vocabulary.

Rx = prescription/by prescription
OTC = over the counter
h.s. = hora somni = hour of sleep = bedtime
a.c. = ante cibum = before meals
p.c. = post cibum = after meals
b.i.d. = bis in die = twice a day
t.i.d. = ter in die = three times a day
q.i.d. = quater in die = four times a day
q.o.d. = every other day

q = every
qhr = every hour (e.g., q12 = every 12 hours)

c = cum = with
s = sine = without

prn = pro re nata = as needed

O.D. = oculo dextro = right eye
O.S. = oculo sinistro = left eye
O.U. = oculo uta = both eyes

gtt = gutta = drop

mg% = milligrams/100 cc fluid
ml = milliliters (= cc)
mEq/L = milliequivalents/liter of fluid
mg = milligram
µg = microgram
G or g = gram
mg/kg = milligrams per kilogram
IU or U = international unit (measure of biological activity, not mass)

The Metric System
100 µg = 0.1 mg
1000 mg = 1 gram

PO = per os = by mouth
IM = intramuscular injection
IV = intravenous injection or drip
SQ = subcutaneous injection
SL = sublingual = under the tongue

Potential Problems with Abbreviations:

What is Written	*Misinterpretation*
qhs (at bedtime)	qhr (every hour)
qd or q.d. (every day)	qid (four times a day)
qod or q.o.d. (every other day)	qd (daily)
IU or U (international unit)	IV (intravenous)
μg (MICROGRAMS)	mg (milligrams)
IU (international unit)	1U (1 unit)

Antipsychotics

Traditional Antipsychotic Medications

Medications prescribed for psychoses, principally schizophrenia, are also known as neuroleptics or major tranquilizers. Their anticholinergic side effects are blurred vision, constipation, dry mouth as well as dry nasal passages and eyes, esophageal reflux, and urinary retention. Acute dystonia is an extrapyramidal side effect: spasm of the tongue, face, neck and back, which occasionally resemble seizures. With long-term use, there can be pseudo-Parkinsonism, which resembles Parkinson's disease but may not be permanent if the medication is withdrawn in time. Usually seen after months or years of treatment are perioral tremors, which resemble rabbit-like motions of the mouth.

Usually seen from days 5 to 60 of treatment may be akathesia, characterized by motor restlessness (usually pacing), which is too often misdiagnosed as agitation, with the wrong treatment of more antipsychotic given to reduce the agitation. The opposite, akathisia, may develop. The apathy, indifference in initiating activities, a paucity of movement, and the lack of speech initiation can be misdiagnosed as depression or residual schizophrenia.

Tardive dyskinesia (oral-facial dyskinesia, muscle twitching of the trunk, and shuffling gait) are seen in 14 percent of patients on these meds for over three years, and they are most common in elderly women. There may be slow, gradual improvement if caught early, but this becomes permanent if not caught early. The symptoms may be masked by the antipsychotic medication and seen when the medication is withdrawn.

These extrapyramidal side effects respond to various drug treatments, except tardive dyskinesia, which is worsened by the most common drugs used. Examples are the anticholinergics such as benztropine (Cogentin), or antihistamines such as diphenhydramine (Benadryl), and bromocriptine (Pariodel), which is a DA receptor agonist. There is some evidence that vitamin B-6 (400 mg/day) may help reduce the symptoms of tardive dyskinesia.

Traditional antipsychotic medications are classified as potent (use in low doses) or weak (use in high doses, as more drug is needed to bind to the receptor sites). Potent antipsychotics generally have low anticholinergic effects, but high extrapyramidal side effects, while weak antipsychotics generally have high anticholinergic side effects and low extrapyramidal side effects.

Traditional Antipsychotics

Reserpine (Serpasil, Diupres, Hydropres, Ser-Ap-Es, Demi-Regroton, Regroton, Diutensin) is no longer used for psychosis due to sedation, decreased blood pressure, postural hypotension (aka orthostatic hypotension), profuse diarrhea, post-nasal drip, cough, and severe depression. However, it is still used rarely as an anti-hypertensive.

Phenothiazines are comprised of three groups, all of which block DA:

1. Peperidines (weak) are thioridazine (Mellaril, 100–600 mg/day), mesoidazine (Serentil, 100–400 mg/day), and piperacetazine (Quiide, 20–160 mg/day, but not available in the US). These medications are excellent for latent and patent schizophrenia, as physicians are more willing to prescribe them to patients without blatant symptoms because of the lower possibility of extrapyramidal effects.
2. Piperazines (potent) are fluphenazine (Prolixin, Permitil, 5–60 mg/day, injectable, fast-acting, lasts for weeks, but the side effects also last for weeks), trifluoperazine (Stelazine, 5–60 mg/day), perphenazine (Trilafon, 8–64 mg/day), prochlorperazine (Compazine, 10–150 mg/day), which is also a good anti-emetic, butaperazone (Repoise, 30–100 mg/day, but not available in the US), acetophenazine (Tindal, 20–100 mg/day), and carphenazine (Protekazine, 100–400 mg/day, but again not available in the US).
3. Aliphatics (moderately weak, but there are some NE blocking effects in addition to the DA blocking, so they have many side effects), such as chlorpromazine (Thorazine, 100–2,000 mg/day), triflupromazine (Vestrin, 20–150 mg/day), and promazine (Sparine, 40–800 mg/day).

Side effects include postural hypotension, especially so with the aliphatics; impaired thermo-regulation, with possible heat stroke and/or sensitivity to hypothermia; obstructive jaundice (rare); blood dystrasias (i.e., increased susceptibility to infection due to the decreased number of white blood cells); such diverse skin reactions as hives, dermatitis, and photosensitivity; abnormal pigmentation of the skin (blue-gray), especially with Thorazine; weight gain; lowered seizure threshold with grand mal seizures (except Mellaril); increased prolactin (breast enlargement in men and women); menstrual irregularity or cessation in women; inhibition of ejaculation or retrograde ejaculation in men (especially with Mellaril); decreased libido; neuroleptic malignant syndrome, which is rare but fatal in 20 percent of the cases. This syndrome is characterized by altered states of consciousness, dangerously high fever, delirium, Parkinson-like rigidity, increased pulse, profuse sweating, and possible kidney failure. All of these side effects are more common with the potent antipsychotics.

Thioxanthenes are potent and are structurally similar to phenothiazines, with side effects very similar to the phenothiazines. Chloroprothiazine (Taractan, 100–600 mg/day) is very similar to the piperazines.

Butyrophenones are potent and chemically are very similar to the piperazines. The side effects are similar to the phenothiazines, except they produce little or no weight gain. Haloperidol (Haldot, 2–100 mg/day) is available as an injectable—droperidol (Inaspine, Innovar).

The Next Generation of Antipsychotic Medications

Diphenylbutylpipereidines, such as pimozide (Orap, 1–10 mg/day) and clozapine (Ciorazil, 25–500 mg/day), and dibenzoxazpines that are intermediate potency such as loxapine (Loxitane, 30–250 mg/day) and dihydroindoles that are intermediate potency such as molindone (Moban, Lidone, 10–225 mg/day) are referred to as "next generation antipsychotics."

Orap is a very selective DA blocker, which may decrease long-term side effects, but it has cardiotoxicity problems. It is approved by the FDA only for Tourette's syndrome, but it is occasionally prescribed off-label for mania or other psychosis. Clozaril had been used in Europe for 20 years prior to its approval in the US, and it has a low incidence of extrapyramidal side effects, and no side effects on prolactin. It is effective for the residual symptoms of schizophrenia, and patients who do not respond to other antipsychotics may respond to this. However, there is a potential for lethal blood problems (agranulocytosis) in 1 percent to 2 percent of patients, thus requiring costly weekly monitoring of the white blood cells. Along with cardiac effects such as tachycardia, it also causes seizures even more than the phenothiazines. Recent research indicates that severe movement disorders and cholinergic rebound symptoms are possible when it is abruptly discontinued with schizophrenia or schizo-affective disorder. Furthermore, limb and neck dystonias and dyskinesias can last 5 to 14 days after withdrawal, with some patients during that time unable to walk, having a lurching gait, or gagging when eating or drinking. Anticholinergic agents can be used to minimize these withdrawal symptoms.

Moban and Lidone result in little or no weight gain, and do not have a tendency to lower the seizure threshold, but they are less efficacious. Other uses for next generation antipsychotics include as antiemetics (Haldol, Compazine), and the treatment of intractable hiccough, Tourette's syndrome, and Huntington's chorea, which is a heritable movement disorder with dementia that is eventually fatal. They are also used in the initial management of mania, and only occasionally used in the management of agitated depression, as it is not worth the risks. As a last resort, it is used to treat combativeness in mental retardation, AIDS dementia, Alzheimer's, and intoxication.

Drug Interactions

- Antacids decrease absorption (especially the phenothiazines).
- There is a potentiation of nervous system depression by depressants (e.g., benzodiazapines, alcohol).
- There is a potentiation of opioid effects (respiratory depression, mental clouding).
- The beta blocker propranolol (Inderal) can increase Mellaril levels three- to five-fold because Mellaril is not broken down.
- There is a mutual potentiation of anticholinergic effects with anticholinergic medications. Therefore, do not use weak antipsychotics with anti-cholinergic antidepressants. The exception is the decreased absorption of Thorazine by co-administered anticholinergics (anti-Parkinson's drugs).

Caution: Withdraw antipsychotics *slowly* when possible to avoid withdrawal symptoms of aches, chills, sleep disturbance, and withdrawal emergent dyskinesias.

Patients dislike taking antipsychotics because of their side effects and the decreased responsiveness to the environment. Furthermore, psychotic patients may harbor delusions about the purpose of medications.

Atypical Antipsychotics

There are atypical antipsychotic medications that may selectively block mesocorticolimbic DA receptors. Risperidone (Risperdall, 16 mg/day, with 4–8 mg/day being typical) has an increased compliance if the dose starts low, with increases of 0.5–2.0 mg/day toward a goal of a maintenance dose in six to seven days. It mimics Clozaril in that it shows few motor side effects and without the risk of agranulocytosis, cardiac effects, and seizures. It also has fewer side effects than either traditional or next generation antipsychotics, but the reduction in motor side effects may be limited to lower dosage ranges. The literature also suggests this drug may be helpful for obsessive-compulsive disorder, as well as an adjunct treatment for mania. Curiously, both a fast-dissolving sublingual tablet (Risperdal M-TAB) and a long-acting injectable (Risperdal Consta) were approved by the FDA in 2003.

Olanzapine (Zyprexa, beginning dosage 5 mg/day, with the usual dosage 10–15 mg/day) is reported in some of the literature to have fewer side effects than Risperdal, but not all the literature supports this. Early claims that it would reduce withdrawal, isolation, and decreased sociability in schizophrenics have not been adequately demonstrated, as it seems to be no better than other antipsychotics. Although seizures and tachycardia are not major problems, its side effects include headaches, decreased blood pressure, dizziness, constipation, dry mouth, weight gain, drowsiness or agitation, runny nose, tremor, rigidity, and weakness. It was thought that agranulocytosis was not a problem, but some cases have now been reported. The risk is still much less than with Clozaril, probably less than 1 in 10,000, which is much less than the risk of suicide without adequate treatment. The FDA has approved it for mania, either alone or with lithium.

Quetiapine (Seroquel, 150–750 mg/day) is a DA-type 2 and 5-HT-type 2 antagonist with low extrapyramidal and anticholinergic side effects, but there may be fast or slow heartbeat, constipation, drowsiness, dizziness, stomach pain, weight gain, and dry mouth. It is considered to be particularly safe for the elderly, and it may be a better choice for treating aggression than other antipsychotics. It has been used off-label as a sleep medication. There are interactions with L-Dopa, anti-seizure drugs, some high blood pressure, and thyroid replacement meds.

Ziprasidone (Geodon, 40–160 mg/day, with the usual dose 80–160 mg/day) is a DA-type 2 and 5-HT-type 2a antagonist, and a moderate inhibitor of NE and 5-HT reuptake (some antidepressant and anti-anxiety effects). It has low extrapyramidal and anticholinergic side effects, and early research suggests it may be of some help with the negative symptoms and cognition in schizophrenics. This sounds good, but the side effects include sleeplessness/tiredness, weight gain, nausea, constipation, dizziness, restlessness, abnormal muscle movements, diarrhea, rash, and respiratory disorders (cold symptoms and upper respiratory infections). But it gets worse. There is the risk of prolonging the QT interval (the length of time it takes the ventricles to electrically discharge and repolarize), which can cause serious arrhythmias and sudden death. The FDA has banned two other medications (terfenadine, or Seldane, an antihistamine; and cisapride, or Propulsid, a GI stimulant) due to prolonged QT time. Geodon cannot be used with other medications that prolong the QT interval (e.g., Orap and Mellaril, both anti-psychotics; Avelox and Zagam, both antibiotics used to treat urinary infections; and antiarrythmia meds, including Quinidex). Tegretol decreases Geodon's effectiveness, while the antibiotic Nizoral increases its effect and also its side effects.

Lurasidone (Latuda, 40–80 mg/day, with once-daily dosing) was approved by the FDA in 2010 and is the newest atypical antipsychotic. Whether it offers any new mechanism aside from the tried and true D2/5-HT2A antagonism remains to be seen. Experimental dosages of 120 mg/day are more likely to cause akathisia, Parkinsonism, and other adverse events. So far, Latuda seems to have a low incidence of both metabolic and extrapyramidal side effects, and no evidence of changes in ECG QT interval, but time will tell. Latuda must be taken with food due to limitations in absorption. Because it is metabolized by CYP3A4, it should not be taken with strong CYP3A4 inhibitors (such as ketoconazole) or strong CYP3A4 inducers (such as rifampin). The FDA recommends against use of Latuda in treatment resistant schizophrenics or the elderly. The safety and efficacy in patients under the age of 18 have not been established. Other possible side effects include: neuroleptic malignant syndrome, metabolic changes, high cholesterol and increased triglycerides, hyperprolactinemia, agranulocytosis, orthostatic hypotension, dystonia, and heat sensitivity.

General Issues of Atypical Antipsychotics with Antidepressants

An important consideration is that fewer side effects make it easier to get "latent" or "patent" schizophrenics treated. It had been thought that the newer antipsychotics (including Clozaril, Risperdal, Zyprexa, and Seroquel) carried no risk of extrapyramidal side effects, but we now know they do carry some risks, although they are less than the older antipsychotics. It should be noted, however, that the risk increases with higher doses. Therefore, it is recommended that these drugs not be used above the following dosages:

Clozaril: 400 mg usually, and 500 mg if that is ineffective
Zyprexa: 20 mg
Seroquel: 450 mg usually, and 600 mg if that is ineffective
Risperdal: 6 mg

Clozaril is the least likely to cause extrapyramidal side effects, followed in that order by Seroquel, Zyprexa, and Risperdal.

Many clinicians expect patients to have a rapid response to antipsychotics, and when that does not happen they are quick to increase the dosage. Such a higher dose is not likely to bring about any faster improvement, so it is better to start with a lower dose and wait long enough to give it a fair try.

There is mounting evidence that the atypical antipsychotics contribute to disturbances in glucose regulation and type 2 diabetes, with Clozaril and Zyprexa as the worst offenders. In patients with genetic predisposition to diabetes, atypical antipsychotics may hasten its development.

The New Generation of Antipsychotic Medications

Aripiprazole (Abilify, typical dose 15–30 mg/day) was approved by the FDA in 2002, and it is also used for the treatment of mania. It is a partial agonist at DA-type 2 and 5-HT-type 1a, and it is the first in a new class of drugs called "dopamine system stabilizers," or DSSs. Originally these were going to be called "partial dopamine agonists" in contrast to other antipsychotics that are "dopamine agonists," supposedly to strike a balance between too much and too little DA. DA transmission is preserved or enhanced where it is too low, and is reduced where it is too high. The goals are:

a. to reduce hyperactive DA neurons that mediate psychosis (mesolimbic pathway) and negative symptoms of schizophrenia (mesocortical pathway);
b. to preserve physiologic function in DA neurons that regulate motor movement (nigrostriatal pathway); and
c. to preserve physiologic function in DA neurons that regulate hormonal functions such as prolactin release (tuberinfundibular pathway).

Abilify may also modulate the 5-HT system, which contributes to psychosis. Therefore, it is supposed to treat both the positive and negative symptoms of schizophrenia. In early studies, no extrapyramidal side effects or hyperprolactin-emia were seen, but there is now evidence that akathisia (motor restlessness, such as pacing) is a potential side effect. Other side effects are nausea, dizziness, headache, weakness, GI upset, anxiety, insomnia, and weight gain. It may also cause neuroleptic malignant syndrome, which is potentially fatal, but is usually treatable if diagnosed early. Extensive Abilify marketing touts this drug as the solution to treatment-resistant depression when used to augment antidepressant medication.

Asenaphine (Saphria, 5–20 mg/day) was approved by the FDA in 2009 and is in the form of sublingual tablets. Its mechanism of action is thought to be an antagonist for DA-type 2 and 5-HT-type 2a receptors. It has a high affinity for each of numerous receptors, including various 5-HT, adrenergi, DA, and histamine receptors. It may be useful in bipolar disorder. Side effects include neuroleptic malignant syndrome, tardive dyskinesia, high blood sugar, weight gain, severe akathisia, sedation, dizziness, insomnia, and sudden changes in BP.

Hoperidone (Fanapt, 12–24 mg/day) was also approved by the FDA in 2009. It is an antagonist for certain DA, NE, and 5-HT receptor subtypes. Its side effects are extensive: cardiovascular adverse events (including stroke), dizziness, dry mouth, tiredness, weight gain, sleep disturbance, serious drop in BP, tardive dyskinesia, elevated blood sugar (diabetes), increased prolactin levels, priapism, neuroleptic malignant syndrome, agranulocytosis, decreased resistance to infection, QT prolongation, seizures, elevation of core body temperature, aspiration pneumonia, suicide by overdose, and cognitive and motor impairment.

Paliperidone (Invega, 3–12 mg/day) is a DA-type 2 and 5-HT-type 2a antagonist that was first approved in 2006, and received a secondary approval for treatment of schizophrenia in 2009. It is available as an oral once-a-day dosing, or a once-a-month injectable. It can produce extrapyramidal effects such as tardive dyskinesia and restlessness, while other side effects include sexual dysfunction (especially if combined with SSRIs), neuroleptic malignant syndrome, heart rhythm changes, high blood sugar (diabetes), elevated prolactin levels, narrowing of the GI tract, dizziness/fainting, decreased alertness, seizures, and increased sensitivity to heat (dehydration).

Important is the warning that Saphria, Fanapt, and Invega are not approved for use with the elderly with dementia-related psychoses, as they increase the risk of death from stroke and other causes in these patients.

Combination Drugs

Antipsychotic and antidepressant drugs are sometimes combined into one medication. Examples are Triavii/Etrafon (Trilafon plus Elavil) and Symbiax (Zyprexa plus Prozac). These are not commonly used, as it is impossible to change the dosage of one without changing the dosage of the other.

Antipsychotics Under Development

Sertindole (Select, 12–24 mg/day) was released in 1997 and withdrawn in 1998 because, in the Abbott clinical trials, 27 out of 2,194 patients died within six months of use and because 4 percent of patients show alterations in cardiac rhythm. Other side effects included nasal congestion, dry mouth, vaginitis in women, and decreased ejaculatory volume in men.

Amisulpride (Solian) is still under review, but it has a unique pharmacological profile. It selectively blocks DA-2 and DA-3 receptors in the limbic system, but not in the basal ganglia. It does not bind to DA-1, DA-4, or DA-5, and there is no known activity with 5-HT-2 receptors. Furthermore, there are no known anticholinergic, adrenergic or histamine effects. At low doses (50–300 mg/day), it blocks presynaptic DA receptors (increases DA release); therefore, DA activity in the mesolimbic system is increased. This may be why this drug seems to be effective for dysthymia, depression, negative symptoms of schizophrenia, affective psychosis, and chronic fatigue syndrome.

Antidepressants

Antidepressant Medications

In psychiatry, "depression" is seen as a set of symptoms, with the further categorization only on severity, not on etiology This, of course, hampers effective treatment, as symptom-only is not addressing the behavioral root cause. In the Biodyne Model, there are five types of depression:

1. Endogenous depression may be influenced by external events, but primarily it is determined by biological factors. Examples are bipolar depression, depression as a medication side effect, PMS, and depression secondary to hypothyroidism. The treatment of choice is appropriate medication with supportive psychotherapy as an adjunct.
2. Reactive depression, or exogenous depression (i.e., outside the body), is a neurotic depression characterized by internalized rage, with the main defense mechanism being introjection. The treatment of choice is psychotherapy to expel the introject. Antidepressant medication will interfere with the process of expelling the introject (i.e., externalizing the rage).

3. Chronic depression originating in childhood stems from a loss such as the death of a parent at a very early age, or severe and chronic abuse or neglect, factors early and severe enough to have become chronic or characterological. The treatment of choice is a combination of temporary antidepressant medication combined with supportive psychotherapy. The goal is to manage the patient's condition, ideally teaching the patient how to manage the chronic condition.

4. Anniversary depression is a postponed bereavement or reactivated trauma. The treatment of choice is psychotherapy to discover and resolve the anniversary. It is difficult, and even impossible, to discover the anniversary and resolve the depression by initiating much delayed bereavement as long as the patient is taking antidepressant medication.

5. Bereavement in its basic form is not a depression, but nature's healing process in response to a loss. It typically is at its highest for one year as the patient relives past events that were experienced with the lost loved one. Therapy is designed to facilitate the process by encouraging the patient to grieve. The taking of antidepressant medication prolongs the bereavement process, inhibits it, or may even derail it. In cases where bereavement is complicated by reactive depression, the patient is not able to effectively go through the bereavement process, and psychotherapy for the reactive depression must precede mourning.

Note: Recent research into post-traumatic stress syndrome (PTSD) reveals that, as painful as it is, PTSD is nature's way of healing the severe emotional injury, so medication inhibits or unnecessarily prolongs the process, and can even foster suicide.

Tricyclic and Tetracyclic Antidepressants

These antidepressants comprise essentially three groups, as follows:

1. Tertiary amines are sedating, such as amitriptyline (Eiavil, Endep, 50–300 mg/day oral or injection). Other examples are clomipramine (Anafranil, 50–250 mg/day pill or IV); dexepine (Adapin, Sinequan, 5–300 mg/day); imipramine (Tofranil, 50–300 mg/day); trimipramine (Surmontil, 50–300 mg/day).

2. Secondary amines are a stimulating type of tricyclic and include disipramine (Norpramine, Pertofrane, 50–300 mg/day); nortryptyline (Pamelor, Aventyl, 50–150 mg/day); protriptyline (Vivactil, 15–60 mg/day).

3. Tetracyclics, such as amoxapine (Asendin, low sedation, 50–400 mg/day oral or IM injection), which PET scans indicate has mild antipsychotic properties; and maprotiline (Ludiomil, high sedation, 50–300 mg/day).

These drugs block NE reuptake, with some blocking of 5-HT reuptake. The body converts tertiary amines to secondary amines (e.g., imipramine to desipramine and amitriptyline to nortriptyline). There is a "therapeutic window" in that doses above or below the window are ineffective. Therefore, blood monitoring is helpful, especially for patients at high risk of cardiotoxicity. The therapeutic effects require two to three weeks, while treatment continues for three to six months, followed by a gradual cessation in order to ensure the stability of the patient and to minimize a withdrawal symptom of malaise, chills, and muscle aches. The vegetative symptoms improve before the mood does, and there is no euphoria in normals. Since there is no improvement of empathy or interpersonal relationships, the patient must also undergo psychotherapy.

Side effects are of two types. ANS effects are anticholinergic (dry mouth, eyes, and nasal passages; constipation; blurred vision; urinary retention; edema; increased sweating). Most patients develop some degree of tolerance. CNS effects include tremors, insomnia (especially with Vivactil), sedation, dizziness, nausea, dysphoria, rare delusions, decreased seizure threshold (especially with Asendin and Ludiomil), and induction of seizures (with Surmontil above 300 mg/day).

There can be cardiotoxicity: delayed conduction (partial heart block) and increased myocardial contractibility (arrhythmia). Cardiotoxicity is more common in children and the elderly, so these patients should be monitored with EKGs. An overdose stops the heart, and Elavil is particularly at risk, as a 10-day supply can prove lethal.

Other side effects are weight gain, a "switch-over" to mania, suppression of REM sleep, sleep blockage, rare ataxia, orthostatic hypertension, and possibly with Asendin, Parkinsonism and tardive dyskinesia. A sore throat in the first few months may indicate an allergic reaction, and patients manifesting such a sore throat should be referred back to the prescribing physician.

Drug interactions to watch for include: with antihypertensives, there may be a decrease in the effect of the anti-hypertensive. With depressants (such as alcohol, benzodiazepines, and some OTC cold medications), there is an additive sedation and enhanced metabolism of the tricyclic. With sympathomimetics, there can be serious cardiac effects. With anticonvulsants, there is an additive CNS depression (sedation) and a decreased anticonvulsant effect. There is an enhanced effect of any anticholinergic (including antipsychotics). Plasma levels of tricyclic or tetracyclic meds decrease with phenothiazines, aspirin, oral contraceptives, Dilantin (an anticonvulsant), and scopolamine (for motion sickness or irritable bowel syndrome). Note: the long half-life of these medications may cause drug interactions for weeks after termination of therapy.

These drugs have been used to decrease cocaine craving (Desipramine if started within two weeks), to treat obsessive-compulsive disorder (especially Anafranil), and to treat impulse control disorders (especially Anafranil and Tofranil). They have also been used in cases of enuresis and also with chronic pain, neuralgia, and migraine (especially Amitripyline), as well as ADD (especially the residual type), narcolepsy, anorexia/bulimia, and panic disorder.

Second Generation Antidepressants (Novel Structured Antidepressants)

These have years of use and continue to be frequently prescribed medications.

Alprazolam (Xanax, 0.5–6.0 mg/day is the usual dosage range) is a benzodiazepine indicated for unipolar depression with severe anxiety. It must be administered at high levels for the antidepressant effect (4–8 mg/day), and lesser dosage for an anti-anxiety effect (0.75–3.0 mg/day). Its antidepressant action is uncertain, but it probably works on the GABA system. There are no anticholinergic effects, but it does produce drowsiness. Of concern is its strong physical dependence and abuse potential, and it can take up to a year to taper off from a high dose due to withdrawal seizures. Xanax is listed here because it is occasionally used as an antidepressant at very high dosages, but the authors have never advocated this use.

Trazadone (Desyrel, 50–400 mg/day) is a 5-HT and NE reuptake blocker with no anticholinergic side effects. It has some cardiac effects, but it is safer than tricyclics and tetracyclics and it is more difficult to overdose. It produces drowsiness, headache, and GI distress, and it can cause priapism in men. It is thought to be a good sleeping pill, although it does result in morning sedation due to its longer half-life.

Bupropion (Wellbutrin, 75–450 mg/day) is a unicycle antidepressant that may block DA reuptake, but its mechanism is uncertain. It has low anticholinergic activity, little or no weight gain, and few problems with cardiotoxicity, but it does lower the seizure threshold. It can be stimulating and can cause agitation or worsening of pre-existing schizophrenia. Wellbutrin manifests less "switchover" to mania than other antidepressants. A sustained release form was approved by the FDA in 1996, and it is used for smoking cessation as "Zyban" and experimentally for weight loss as "Wellbutrin SR."

Monoamine Oxidase Inhibitors

These are used for depressions that do not respond to other antidepressants, and especially anxious depressions. Examples are pheneizine (Nardil, 30–90 mg/day), isocarboxazid (Marplan, 20–50 mg/day), tranylcypromine (Parnate, 20–60 mg/day), clorgyline (not available in the US), pargyline (Eutonyl, 10–100 mg/day), and selegiline (Endepryl, Deprenyl, 5–10 mg/day). This latter drug is also available in transdermal form in which the therapeutic effects are much faster than the oral medication, which also eliminates toxic interactions with food. It is used more often for Parkinsonism than for depression, although it is very effective for people with both anxiety and depression.

The mechanism of action is to block the enzyme (monoamine oxidase) which breaks down the monoamine neurotransmitters, and thus increases the availability of NE and 5-HT. It is well-absorbed orally, with maximum levels in

5 to 10 days and the therapeutic effects in two to three weeks. It has little or no anticholinergic action, and common side effects are anorgasmia/impotence, orthostatic hypotension, muscle cramps, urinary hesitancy, constipation, dry mouth, and weight gain, with some patients gaining as much as 30 percent of their body weight! Less common side effects are excessive CNS stimulation with tremors and/or insomnia (especially with Parnate), confusion, and hallucinations.

With overdose, there is agitation, hallucinations, hyper-reflexia, high fever, and convulsions, making it a very dangerous drug. Use with tricyclics causes potentiation of therapeutic effects, but there is also a potentiation of the tyramine interaction. The following should not be used in conjunction with MAOIs: local anesthetics containing epinephrine (although Lidocaine and Procaine are safe), many anti-asthmatic meds, many anti-hypertensives, diuretics, L-Dopa, L-Tryptophan, SSRIs, narcotics (especially demerol), sympathomimetics, and OTC cold, allergy and sinus medications (especially those containing Dextro-methorphan, although aspirin, acetamenophen (Tylenol), and menthol lozenges are safe. Antihistamines, disulfiram (Antabuse), and propranolollderal (Inderide) should be used carefully.

MAOIs interact with tyramine (an amino acid found in certain foods) to cause hypertensive crisis (increased BP with possible cerebral hemorrhage). Foods containing high tyramine content are: alcohol (especially beer and wine), fava beans, broad beans, Italian green beans, aged cheese, beef or chicken liver, orange pulp, pickled or smoked fish/poultry/meats, packaged soups, yeast, vitamin supplements, brewer's yeast, meat extracts, and summer (dry) sausage. Foods with moderately high tyramine content are: soy sauce, sour cream, bananas (especially very ripe ones), avocados, eggplant, plums, raisins, spinach, tomatoes and yogurt. As this list is so extensive, a 1996 study that found only the following foods to be of dangerous levels is good news: chicken liver (aged nine days), air-dried meats, and sauerkraut.

It is possible that a more accurate list of problem foods may lead to better compliance with dietary restrictions. And although recent evidence suggests that food interactions are not as problematic as once believed, the effects are cumulative and caution is indicated. However, it is the interaction with other drugs as indicated above that can be very lethal.

Finally, other uses for these drugs have been with narcolepsy and panic disorders (especially Nardil).

Serotonin-specific Reuptake Inhibitors

These are also known as SSRIs and Serotonergics, of which there are several.

Flouxetine (Prozac, Sarafem, 5–80 mg/day) has a half-life of 4 to 6 days, while the active metabolite norfluoxetine has a half-life of 4 to 16 days. The longer half-life may be helpful in poorly compliant patients, and it enabled the development of Prozac Weekly (approved February 2001). A 90 mg dose once a week is equivalent to a 20 mg/day dose of Prozac. In order to be switched from a daily to a weekly dose, the patient must be in a "steady state." There is the added side effect of back pain. Also, diarrhea is more common in the weekly dose, but the enteric coating makes nausea less common than the daily variety.

Sertraline (Zoloft, 50–200 mg/day).

Paroxetine (Paxil, Paxil CR, 10–50 mg/day). This is also approved for GAD.

Fluvoxamine (Luvox, 50–300 mg/day).

Citalopram (Celexa, 20-160 mg/day) has been used in Denmark since 1989, but it was approved in the US 10 years later. Its advantages are that there are no withdrawal or cardiotoxic effects, there are fewer side effects (mainly nausea, dry mouth, sedation, and insomnia), there are fewer drug interactions, and it is well tolerated by the elderly.

Escitalopram (Lexapro, typical dose is 10 mg/day; higher doses are rarely more effective, but the recommendation is 10–40 mg/day). It is similar to Celexa, but with the removal of the active ingredient theoretically responsible for the side effects (half of the molecule, the R-enantiomer). In the clinical trials, the side effects on discontinuation were the same as placebo.

The mechanism of SSRIs is to block reuptake of 5-HT. They are well-absorbed by the GI tract, with peak plasma levels in four to six hours, and therapeutic effects 10 days or even sooner. There are no known effects on the DA system, and there are no (or at least very low) anticholinergic effects, along with minimal sedation, minimal cardiac effects, and a minimal change in the seizure threshold. There is no weight gain (except for Paxil), and some patients even lose 5 to 10 pounds. Most patients have few side effects, but CNS effects may include headache, nervousness, insomnia, drowsiness, dry mouth, anxiety, tremor, and dizziness. GI side effects may include nausea, diarrhea, anorexia, and stomach upset.

It should be noted that there may be induction of mania as well as an exacerbation of schizophrenic symptoms. Rashes may occur, and extrapyramidal effects, which are rare, may include suppression of REM sleep, arrhythmias, palpitations, hypotension, excessive sweating, and easy bruising and bleeding due to slowed clotting time. There may be a dose-dependent, reversible frontal lobe (amotivational syndrome) especially in adolescents and primarily with Prozac and Paxil, which may occur after several months of treatment.

There may be sexual dysfunction (including anorgasmia and delayed orgasm) due to increased levels of serotonin in the spinal cord. Up to 80 percent of patients experience some sexual dysfunction, which may be reduced by the following measures:

a. Augmentation with bupropion (Wellbutrin, about 50 mg/day) can reduce this effect significantly, although studies are limited.

b. Two antiemetics have recently been shown to counter this effect, namely Granisetron Kytril, a drug also used to reduce nausea in chemotherapy (1 mg one hour before sex); and ondansetron (Zofran, 4 mg) might also work.

There is anecdotal evidence only for augmentation with nefazodone (Serzone, 7.5 mg/day) and mirtazapine (Remeron, 25–50 mg/day). Sildenafil (Viagra, 25-50 mg half an hour to 4 hours before sex) is a phosphodiesterase type 5 inhibitor that increases blood flow in the penis and possibly also in women's genitals, and has been shown by two very small studies to be helpful in treating SSRI sexual dysfunction, but more study is indicated. Furthermore, possible interactions are unknown, and it is not known whether Viagra causes birth defects.

Although not proven in controlled studies, the following drugs are reported to decrease sexual dysfunction resulting from SSRIs: yohimbine (Actibine, Yucon, Yohimex), which is used to treat impotence; amantadine (Symmetril), which is an antiviral; cyproheptadine (Periactin), which is an antihistamine; buspirone (BuSpar), which is an anxiolytic; D-Amphetamlne (Adderall), which is a stimulant; and pemoline (Cylert), which is also a stimulant. Of course, there is always the recourse to change to another class of antidepressant.

With overdose, there is the "serotonin syndrome": agitation, restlessness, insomnia, nausea, vomiting, tachycardia, seizures, and possible death, though a lethal overdose is rare unless combined with other medications. Even at low doses, the serotonin syndrome can occur if the SSRI is combined with another serotogenic drug such as: other SSRIs, MAOs, or tricyclic antidepressants; Tryptophan; St. John's Wort; buspirone (BuSpar). The latter is used as an augmentation agent with SSRIs. However, good research (circa 2000) has shown that it can cause serotonin syndrome when combined with an SSRI because it is a partial serotonin reception agonist.

There are interactions to be considered. With alcohol, there is an increase of alcohol effects, and a decrease in the effects of the SSRIs. Foods containing tryptophan or L-tryptophan (poultry, veal, and some health food store protein powders), all increasing the risk of serotonin syndrome. Tricyclic antidepressants, trazadone (Desyrel) or benzodiazepine increase plasma levels of the antidepressant or the benzodiazepine. MAOs increase the risk of serotonin syndrome, as does BuSpar. The OTC stomach acid reducers Tegretol and Tagamet, Warfarin (Coumadin), Digoxin (for cardiac arrhythmias), phenytoin (Dilantin), and theophylline prolong the elimination of these drugs. Propranolol (Inderal) increases the plasma levels of the beta blocker, while lithium levels are altered (except with Zoloft).

Abrupt discontinuance can cause "SSRI withdrawal syndrome," which can last up to 25 days (except Prozac, which is self-titrating due to its long half-life), whose symptoms are irritability, nausea, diarrhea, dizziness, eye movement disturbance, and rebound depressive symptoms. Withdrawal effects have been seen in newborn babies exposed prenatally to SSRIs, with Paxil having been most successfully studied. In addition to the aforementioned withdrawal effects, these babies showed breathing difficulties. More recent research (circa 2009–2011) indicates that SSRIs may cause heart abnormalities in babies exposed prenatally.

Other uses of SSRIs include PMDD (premenstrual dysphoric disorder, or PMS), dysthymia, obesity/anorexia/bulimia, anxiety (although this can be worsened in some cases), impulse control disorders, and obsessive-compulsive disorder (especially Luvox). It is also used to treat mood swings in borderline personality disorders as well as other Axis II disorders. Thus, treated mood swings may decrease over time, but it may take a long time. Furthermore, reducing the mood swings with meds does not eliminate acting out behavior. Thus, these meds are not a substitute for psychotherapy, and especially for the borderline group.

When SSRIs stop working, they can be augmented with any of the following, although the research is limited: pindolol (Visken), a beta blocker which has been the subject of some studies to test the effectiveness of antidepressant augmentation. For first line augmentation, lithium, thyroid hormone, and BuSpar have all been used. For second line augmentation, Desyrel, dopamine agonists, estrogen (for women), testosterone (for men), and benzodiazepines have been used. Additionally, all of the following have been used for augmentation: tricyclics, Wellbutrin (less common because of serotonin syndrome), Tegretol, psycho-stimulants, antipsychotics (especially Abilify), reserpine, steroid inhibitors, and yohimbine.

Does Prozac Cause Self-mutilation, Violent Behavior, or Suicide?

This criticism originally came from the Church of Scientology, not from medical research. However, SSRIs can induce mania in bipolars and exacerbate schizophrenic symptoms, which may cause latent or patent schizophrenics to become blatant. Suicide is more likely when the vegetative symptoms of depression begin to remit, as vegetative symptoms often improve before the mood improves. The warning signs may be overlooked inasmuch as PCPs often prescribe SSRIs without psychotherapy.

The New Generation of Antidepressants

We now know there are at least 14 different subtypes of 5-HT receptors within at least seven types in the brain. When Prozac was approved in the US, only two subtypes were known.

Serotonin Adrenergic Reuptake Inhibitors (aka SNRIs or SNaRIs)

Venlafaxine (Ejjexor, typically 75–375 mg/day, up to 3,000 mg/day experi-mentally) has a number of side effects, which include weakness, sweating, nausea vomiting, constipation, upset stomach, anorexia with weight loss, sleep disturbances, dry mouth, dizziness, blurred vision, increased BP anxiety or nervousness, tremor, sexual dysfunction, impotence, yawning, and chills. It has been shown to increase diastolic BP at high doses (above 300 mg/day). It does not seem to affect BP in patients who had elevated BP prior to administration under 300 mg/day. It has been shown to induce seizures above 1,100 mg/day.

The initial therapeutic response is not always maintained, and withdrawal can be difficult. It is usually necessary to use another antidepressant (such as Zoloft or Lexapro) during the withdrawal process to reduce withdrawal emergent depressive symptoms. It has been shown to be useful with borderline and ADD patients; however, it may require up to 1,500 mg/day to treat ADD. It was approved for the treatment of GAD in 1999.

Duloxatine (Cymbalta, 40–120 mg/day) is a dual action 5-HT/NE reuptake inhibitor similar to tricyclics, but with fewer side effects. It may be helpful with the physical symptoms of depression such as backaches, headaches, and muscle/joint pain. It is also being studied for urinary incontinence. The most common side effects are nausea, dry mouth, and somnolence (extreme drowsiness). Some studies indicate it may raise BP, while other studies say it does not. It does not seem to cause weight gain.

Serotonin and Norepinephrine Reuptake Inhibitors (aka SNeRIs)

Nefazodone (Serzone, 200–600 mg/day) so far is the only drug in this class. It blocks reuptake of 5-HT and NE, and has the advantage of not causing sexual dysfunction in most patients. Its side effect profile is similar to that of the SSRIs, except patients tend to have fewer of the side effects. It works well with pindolol (Viskin), a beta blocker. In 2000, Canada removed Serzone from the market because of at least 20 deaths from liver damage, but the US has only added a black box warning on the packaging.

Noradrenergic and Specific Serotonergic Antidepressants (aka NaSSAs)

Mirtazapine (Remeron, Remeron SolTab, 14–45 mg/day) so far is another drug that is the only one in its class. It stimulates 5-HT and NE release, and blocks the reuptake of 5-HT. SolTab dissolves in the mouth, thus eliminating the need to swallow a pill. The side effects are increased or decreased appetite, weight gain, dizziness, sleepiness or sleeplessness, constipation, headache, blurred vision, and decreased sexual functioning. Most patients experience only very mild side effects, although sedation and weight gain (about eight pounds) are problems with some patients. There is some risk of developing agranulocytosis, a serious condition affecting bloods cells, and whose initial symptoms are fever, chills, sore throat, or other flu-like symptoms.

Noradrenaline Reuptake Inhibitors

There is only one drug so far in this class. Reboxetine (Edronax, Norebox, Prolift, Solvex, Davedex, Vestra) was approved in the UK in 1997 and is currently used in about 50 countries, but not in the US due to its lack of evidence of efficacy. It increases the availability of NE by blocking its reuptake. Side effects are dry mouth, constipation, increased perspiration, insomnia, increased heart rate, and increased BP. (Aipha-1 noradrenergic stimulation can look like anticholinergic side effects.) This drug promises increased energy, improved sexual functioning, and few or no drug interactions. However, there is evidence that certain antibiotics (ketoconozole and erythromycin) inhibit Reboxetine's elimination, thus increasing concentrations of side effects. This drug may help patients who do not respond to SSRIs or tricyclics.

Combinations of Antidepressants

These are used when depression is severe and a single agent is ineffective, although research is limited and what is often seen is no improvement with the combination. The term "rocket fuel" refers to Effexor plus Remeron, or Effexor plus Wellbutrin.

Newer Twists on Older Eli Lilly Drugs

Sarafem is a repackaged flouxetine. R-flouxetine is one of the isomers of flouxetine (Prozac) and is a mirror image of the flouxetine molecule. (Note: an isomer is the same chemical formula, but different chemical and physical properties due to a different arrangement of the atoms in the molecule.) It was hoped that this isomer would have fewer side effects and drug interactions than Prozac, but it is completely ineffective.

Symbyax is olanzapine (Zyprexa) in combination with fluoxatine (Prozac) and it is used to treat depressive episodes associated with bipolar disorder. It was approved in 2004. It is now being tested for treatment-resistant depression, such as for people who are so treatment resistant that they are being remanded to ECT.

Antidepressants Under Development

There are a number of antidepressants in various stages of clinical trials, with some existing antidepressants being tested for new uses.

Flesinoxan is generally well tolerated, with only 2 percent of the test subjects terminating treatment due to intolerance, but it can produce nausea and dizziness.

CP-9, 393 (experimental dose is 0.1 mg/kg/day) may be found to be helpful in major depression and GAD. Side effects are headaches, nausea, and insomnia.

INN 00835 is a new class of small chain peptides (a polypeptide which blocks cholecystokinin receptors in the brain). No other antidepressant works this way. It is administered by daily low-dose injection, with an oral formulation also under development. Its response is likely to be rapid, with virtually no side effects. It is hoped it will be more effective than SSRIs.

In one experiment, 0.5 mg of TRH (thyrotropin-releasing hormone, or Protilelin IV) was injected into the CSF of depressed patients, and although most responded positively, the therapeutic effects were short-lived. Side effects, which can last one to 11 hours, were sweating, shivering, and restlessness. This drug may be subjected to further research in the future.

CRH antagonists (Anta/Armin) may have modulating effects on an overactive hypothalamic-pituitary-adrenal (HPA) axis and decrease the stress response.

Glucocorticoid receptor antagonists: mifepristone (Mifeprex), block glucocorticoid receptors, thereby diminishing the effects of cortisol. This may be helpful for patients with psychotic depression.

Glutamate receptor antagonists include memantine (Namenda), which has been approved for Alzheimer's, and riluzole (Rilutek), which has been approved for amyotrophic lateral sclerosis. Both of these drugs are under investigation as possible antidepressants. Gepirone is a 5-HT-1A agonist of the same class as BuSpar, which may not have some of the side effects generally associated with antidepressants (e.g., sedation, weight gain, and sexual dysfunction).

Phosphodiesterase (POE) inhibitors include Rolipram. This drug was under investigation as an antidepressant, but nausea and liver toxicity became problematic.

Agrepitant (Emend, 300 mg/day in the experimental dose) is under development by Merck. It is a new class of drugs called "substance P antagonists." (Note: substance P is responsible for the pain response as it is released from the spinal cord in response to painful stimuli, and this is also a factor in the stress response.) The drug blocks the neurokinin 1 receptors that are associated with emotion and the perception of pain. It is being tested for depression, anxiety, anxious depression, schizophrenia, and bipolar. It may also be helpful in the treatment of nausea. So far, it seems to be effective against depression and to have anxiolytic effects similar to Paxil.

The hypothesis is as follows: when people have mental problems, they are in emotional pain. Substance P is co-located in areas of the brain that contain NE and 5-HT. If substance P is in hyperdrive there, this would result in mental disorders. Substance P may alter NE and 5-HT in these areas, so by targeting substance P in our treatment, we are getting at the root of the problem rather than attacking an intermediate point in the process. Pfizer is studying a similar substance P antagonist known as compound A.

Reversible inhibitors of monoamine oxidase, type A (RIMAs):

Momoclobemide (MDC, Aurorex, 300–600 mg/day) is being used throughout much of the world but not in the US. It is useful at high dosages for severe depression.

Brofaromine (BRO) is not being studied at this time for reasons unrelated to efficacy or side effects.

Befloxatone (10–20 mg/day) results in hypertensive crisis over 20 mg/day. It is similar to older MAOIs, except that dietary restrictions are not necessary and hypertensive crisis is rare. It is distinguished from the older MAOIs by its selectivity and reversibility.

Clovoxamine is a new SSRI that is under development, but it may never be marketed, as SSRIs are becoming obsolete.

Tianeptine is a new novel antidepressant. It is a novel both structurally (a modified tricyclic) and in terms of its pharmacological profile (so far in rats), which includes that it stimulates reuptake of 5-HT in rat brains, it increases the levels of 5-hydroxyindoleatic acid (S-HIAA) in cerebral tissue and plasma (note: 5-HIAA is a metabolite of 5-HT), it reduces serotonergic induced behavior, and it reduces the hypothalamic pituitary-adrenal response to stress. The relative lack of sedative, anticholinergic, and cardiovascular adverse effects may make it particularly suitable for use in the elderly and in patients following alcohol withdrawal, as these patients have an increased sensitivity to psychotropic drug adverse effects.

Milnacipran (Savella) blocks NE and 5-HT reuptake. It was approved in 2009 for the chronic pain associated with fibromyalgia, and in the future it may obtain secondary approval as an antidepressant.

The selective dopamine reuptake blocker amineprine (Survector) is similar to the tricyclics in structure and it selectively reduces DA reuptake. At higher doses, it also promotes DA release. It also brings about an increase in extra-cellular NED in the frontal cortex and dorsal hippocampus. With longer term treatment, it induces down regulation of DA-2, beta- and alpha-2-adrenergk receptors. It is a mild but pleasant psycho-stimulant and a fast-acting mood brightener. It does not impair cognitive functioning or impair libido (in fact, it may cause spontaneous orgasm), so it is likely to have abuse potential. There were some cases of liver toxicity reported in Europe. It is not marketed in the UK or US, and in Europe it has been driven into the pharmaceutical "gray market." This is because pressure from the FDA led to withdrawal of its product license in 1999, causing substantial problems for both patients and physicians.

The dopamine receptor agonist pramipexole (Mirapex) is used in the treatment of Parkinson's disease, and it is being studied for its possible use as an antidepressant. It is a DA-2 receptor agonist that seems to have some antidepressant effect with 1.0 mg/day, and with maximum benefit at the 5.0 mg/day dosage, which is slightly higher than the 4.0 mg/day dosage for Parkinson's. However, in studies so far, the drop-out rate among test patients has been high. The side effects include nausea, dizziness, trouble sleeping, constipation, unusual weakness, stomach upset and pain, headache, and dry mouth. At higher doses, there are additional side effects: twitching, confusion, fainting, leg/foot swelling, restlessness, chest pain, unusually fast or slow heartbeat, a sudden irresistible urge to sleep, muscle pain, vision problems, fever, and severe muscle stiffness.

Central Nervous System Depressants

Central nervous system depressants include anti-anxiety drugs, sedative-hypnotic drugs, and alcohol. Psychiatrists write fewer than 20 percent of these drugs, with non-psychiatric physicians writing the remainder. They are often given to patients with true somatic disease, and all too often they are inappropriately given for grief, anger, or depression. Considered appropriate uses include initial management of anxiety with panic attacks, for agitated depression, or obsessive-compulsive disorder. They are not useful for depression, with the possible exception of alprazolam (Xanax) for agitated depression.

Anxiety in schizophrenia is often treated with an anti-anxiety drug along with an antipsychotic. But since anti-anxiety medications alone tend to increase schizophrenic symptoms, anxiety should be decreased just enough.

Even though the FDA has stated that behavioral interventions work best for sleep disorders, they are frequently used for short-term sleep disorders. Problems arise in that, in general, benzodiazepines decrease stage 1 sleep, increase stage 2 sleep, decrease stages 3 and 4 sleep, and increase REM sleep. Furthermore, they cause rebound of suppressed stages of sleep upon discontinuation. They may also cause sleep "hangover."

Reactive anxiety rarely requires anxiolytic medication, as most cases can be treated with psychotherapy. If medication is necessary, antidepressants can be used to treat reactive anxiety in most patients. At best anti-anxiety medication is only part of any treatment protocol, and psychotherapy is necessary for the best results.

Benzodiazapines

Benzodiazepines are also known as "minor tranquilizers." They facilitate GABA neurotransmission, resulting in blocking of nervous system stimulation that originates in the brainstem reticular system and diminishing of activity in areas associated with emotion (e.g., amygdala, hippocampus, hypothalamus). Each typically has a half-life, which can be much longer for the elderly and for those with liver disease. The legend for the following listing:

+   No significant active metabolites (shorter half-life, more severe withdrawal syndrome due to rapid decrease in levels).
★   Not active by themselves (pro-drugs that are converted to active chemicals).
Marketed as "hypnotics" (sleep aids).
^   Also an anticonvulsant.

Diazapam (Vallium, Valrelease)
(2–40 mg/day)
Half-life: 20–90 hours (drug), 5–100 hours (metabolites)

Chlordiazepoxide (Librium, Libritabs, Libritrol)
(5–100 mg/day)
Half-life: 5–10 hours (drug), 5–100 hours (metabolites)

Prazapam (Centrax, Vestran) *
(10–60 mg/day)
Half-life: 50–100 hours (metabolites)

Chlorazepate (Tranxene, Azene, Gen-XENE) *
(11–60 mg/day)
Half-life: 50–100 hours (metabolites)

Oxazepam (Serax) +
(45–120 mg/day)
Half-life: 3–21 hours

Lorazepam (Ativan) +
(0.25–5.0 mg/day)
Half-life: 12–18 hours

Temazepam (Restoril) + #
(15–30 mg/day)
Half-life: 8–16 hours

Flurazepam (Dalmane) * #
(15–30 mg/day)
Half-life: about 2 hours (drug), 40–250 hours (metabolites)

Triazolam (Halcion) + #
(0.125–0.5 mg/day)
Half-life: 3–5 hours

Halazepam (Paxipam) *
(20–120 mg/day)
Half-life: 14 hours (drug), 50–100 hours (metabolites)

Midazolam (Vevsed) +
(7.5–4.5 mg/day, injectable only)
Half-life: 1–4 hours

Clonazepam (Klonopin) ^
(0.5–5.0 mg/day)
Half-life: 18–28 hours

Flunitrazepam (Rohypnol, about 3 mg/day = usual therapeutic dose) is marketed legally in Mexico, South America, parts of Europe, and Asia, but it is illegal in the United States where it is sold illegally as roachies, La Roche, rope, rib, rophies, roofies, and riffies. Mixed with alcohol, the individual will be extremely "high" but still show legal alcohol levels. It is very disinhibiting, and is known as "the date rape drug." It is used to enhance low-quality heroin.

Side effects of central nervous system depressants can be impairment of motor skills, muscle weakness, ataxia, drowsiness, headache, occasional increased aggressiveness, occasional nightmares, memory problems, and respiratory depression. As for other problems, there is an increase of psychosis in schizophrenic patients, a worsening of depression in depressed patients, confusion and disorientation in patients with organic problems and the elderly, a disinhibition in Axis II patients, especially in borderlines (Cionazepam), and can also result in "alcohol equivalents."

Dependency can be decreased by dosing schedules, but a shorter half-life means higher abuse potential. A longer half-life sustains levels, thus minimizing the severity of withdrawal, which can include anxiety and sleeplessness. Severe withdrawal can be characterized by depression, paranoia, delirium, and seizures. It is best to taper the drug by 8 percent to 10 percent per day at the most. High dosages can take up to year to taper. This is especially true of Xanax due to the risk of withdrawal seizures. Flumazenil (Romazicon) administered by injection reverses benzodiazepine effects, but the half-life is only one hour. Nevertheless, it is useful in cases of overdose or mixed overdose.

Barbiturates

There are three types:

1. Those of ultra-short duration used as anesthetics such as Thiopental and Thiamytal.
2. Those of medium duration used as sedatives or hypnotics, such as pentobarbital (Nembutal, 30–200 mg/day), pecobarbital (Seconal, 100–300 mg/day), and hexobarbital (Evipal, Sobulex).
3. Long duration used as anticonvulsants, such as Phenobarbital (15–600 mg/day) and Mephobarbital (32–400 mg/day).

Frequent side effects are hangover, paradoxical excitement (irritability and hyperactivity, especially in children), confusion (especially in the elderly), induction of liver enzymes, which causes complications with other drug therapies, and an interference with all stages of sleep, especially in the suppression of REM sleep. It is not effective for long-term treatment of insomnia because tolerance level develops in about two weeks. There is a rebound of REM sleep upon discontinuation. There is a high potential for dependence and cross-dependence to benzodiazepines and alcohol, with a generally high abuse potential. The symptoms of overdose are respiratory depression, hypothermia (which in turn increases the effects of the drug), and decreased cardiac function. In short, it is potentially fatal.

With toxicity, initially there is sedation, nystagmus (flicking of the eyeballs), and ataxia, soon followed by irritability, hyperactivity, and confusion. On withdrawal, there is sweating, fever, psychosis, and seizures, with death a possibility. Furthermore, barbiturates are dangerous in that they potentiate all depressants, while they are potentiated by methylphenidate (Ritalin) and MAOs. Unfortunately, the widespread use of barbiturates is in spite of the serious potential dangers.

Outdated Anti-anxiety/Sedative Medications

Meprobamate (Milltown) was overly prescribed as a safe medication for even minor anxiety in the 1970s, which resulted in widespread abuse. At parties, Milltown and martini, called "M and M," was popular. It is a severely sedating anti-convulsant, with the medicinal dosage ranging from 200 to 1,600 mg/day. At the height of its popularity, its high physical dependency was substantiated, and its use rapidly declined. Withdrawal can cause grand mal seizures and death.

Corisoparadol (Soma) is the precursor compound to meprobamate, and after it is absorbed it is rapidly metabolized to meprobamate.

Chloral hydrare (Noctec, dosage 600–2,000 mg/day) and troclofos sodium have many barbiturate-like effects. Since there is little respiratory depression at hypnotic doses for the first several nights, it is a good short-term (one to three nights) sleep aid. Thereafter, a metabolite accumulates and can cause respiratory depression. Gastro-intestinal upset is a frequent problem, as well.

Glutethimide (Doriden) and methyprylon (Noludar) are barbiturate-like substances, and Doriden may be useful in motion sickness.

Paraldehyde is a barbiturate-like liquid that, with a dosage of 5 ml IM or 5–10 ml PO, was formerly used in alcohol withdrawal. This practice diminished because the patients preferred it to alcohol in spite of its GI irritation and bad breath.

Methaqualone (Quaalude, Sopors) is a barbiturate-like substance that is useful as an anticonvulsant, anesthetic, and antitusive. Because of its very high abuse potential, it is now illegal in the US, but it is sold on the street as "ludes" or "soaps." It is often sought out illegally, and increases sexuality in women, but withdrawal is worse than that of barbiturates, and is characterized by delirium and convulsions, possibly even death.

Other Anti-anxiety/Sedative Medications

Antihistamines such as hydroxamine (Vistaril, Atarax, Marax) and benactamine (Deprol) have anti-anxiety and anti-emetic effects, along with mild anticholinergic side effects. They are useful for treating anxiety when the patient has a history of CNS depressant abuse (e.g., alcohol or benzodiazapines). Other antihistamines such as OTC Benadryl (25–50 mg at bedtime) can be used as sleep aids.

Buspirone (BuSpar, 15–25 mg/day) relieves anxiety, but with fewer side effects. It is not a sedative, so it has low abuse potential, and it also has a mild antidepressant effect. There are few reported side effects or drug interactions, but grapefruit and grapefruit juice significantly increase the amount of the drug that is absorbed, far above the 5 percent that usually reaches systemic circulation. Side effects are headache, nausea, and dizziness. However, it is possible that the drug causes extrapyramidal effects with long-term use. Nonetheless, it is difficult to overdose inasmuch as it would require 160 to 850 times the normal daily dose. It may increase psychosis in schizophrenic and schizo-affective patients. Patients do not find it as effective as benzodiazepines, so it is difficult to switch patients to BuSpar from benzodiazepines. Some patients report a "falling" sensation with BuSpar and need to discontinue the drug.

Beta blockers act on certain cells in the heart and blood vessels known as beta cells, thus slowing heart rate and controlling blood pressure. They are useful for situational anxiety with physiological effects, such as public speaking or performance anxiety. The most commonly used beta blocker for anxiety is oropranolol hydrochloride (Inderal, 10–40 mg dose, up to four times a day). Side effects are excessively slow heart rate, fatigue, depression, insomnia, GI distress, low blood pressure, and exacerbation of asthma symptoms. It interacts with other medications that alter heart rhythm, and other meds that bind to beta-adrenergic receptors (e.g., epinephrine).

Zolpidem (Ambien, 10 mg at bedtime) and eszopicclone (Lunesta, 2 mg at bedtime) are used as a short term (seven to 10 days) for insomnia. Side effects are dizziness, daytime drowsiness, headaches, nausea, vomiting, and hallucinations (especially with Lunesta). These drugs bind to the benzodiazepine 1 receptor (BZ-1, omega) causing sedation, muscle relaxation, and anti-convulsant activity. The half-life for Ambien is about two to six hours, and for Lunesta about six hours, so some people experience next-day sedation. Ambien CR was developed for those who experience middle insomnia or early awakening with Ambien. Generic Ambien is available, but there is no generic for Lunesta.

Zaleplon (Sonata, 5–10 mg at bedtime) is a short-term treatment for insomnia, and with such short-term use, few withdrawal symptoms are seen. Because of its short half-life (one hour) it can be taken as little as five hours before wake-up time without daytime sedation. However, patients who frequently awaken are less likely to be helped by this med. But for the usual patient, it can improve the quality of sleep as well as the duration. The mechanism is similar to Ambien, as it binds to the BZ-1 omega receptor, causing sedation, muscle relaxation, and anti-convulsant activity. In one study, there were no withdrawal symptoms after 28 days of use.

Doxepin (Silenor, 6 mg taken within 30 minutes of bedtime) was approved in 2010 for patients who have trouble staying asleep, but it cannot be taken unless the patient has seven to eight hours to devote to sleep. It must be taken on an empty stomach (no food for three hours prior to administration). In its action, it may block histamine receptors.

Ramelteon (Rozerem, usual dose 8 mg taken 30 minutes before bedtime) is a melatonin receptor agonist approved for treatment of insomnia characterized by difficulty falling asleep. It is considered okay for pilots to take the night before a flight. However, the effects may take one to two weeks, and it is so expensive that it is not covered by most insurance companies.

Alcohols

Ethyl alcohol (grain alcohol, ethanol, ETOH) is in beer, wine, whiskey, gin, vodka, tequila, and cocktails. It is a CNS depressant self-administered to produce disinhibition (drunkenness). Its effects are impairment of judgment and reaction time at 0.05 percent blood level, with increased pepsin and gastric acid secretion in the stomach, with reflex increase in salivation. There is a dilation of the peripheral blood vessels, especially in the nose, and there is increased heat loss, particularly in cold environments.

With chronic abuse, there is gastritis, cirrhosis, kidney damage, and the aggravation of ulcers and epilepsy. Fetal alcohol syndrome is characterized by impaired growth and IQ, behavior problems, and facial and joint abnormalities, but any fetus subjected to a CNS depressant may have CNS defects. (Note: the potentiation of other CNS depressants by alcohol is potentially lethal.)

The enzyme alcohol dehydrogenase converts alcohol to acetaldehyde. Some people have a slow-acting form of this enzyme due to genetic differences, and as a consequence they do not become steadily intoxicated as they drink. Consequently, they tend to continue drinking, only to experience a delayed reaction of drunkenness. Such people are more prone to alcoholism.

Methyl alcohol (wood alcohol) is metabolized into formaldehyde and then to formic acid, which causes acidosis (low blood pH), which can be fatal. If the person does not die, an accumulation of formaldehyde in the eye can cause permanent blindness, as the eye does not have the enzyme necessary to convert formaldehyde to formic acid. Other alcohols, such as isopropyl (rubbing) alcohol, are abused because they do not show up on breath tests.

Addiction to alcohol is often treated by using CNS depressants, but using other CNS depressants to treat this CNS depressant does not treat the addiction. It may ease the withdrawal, but in the long run the addiction remains.

Disulfiram (Antabuse, 12–500 mg/day as the usual dose) is often used as an adjunct to treat alcoholism since it was approved in 1951. It inhibits the conversion of acetaldehyde to acetate, and these increased acetaldehyde levels cause a severe flushing and vomiting illness. After being subjected to such a reaction, the objective is to cause the patient to avoid alcohol in order to prevent this very unpleasant reaction. Those who are not so dissuaded may, in addition to the illness described, experience respiratory depression, cardiovascular collapse, a heart attack, convulsions, and death. Antabuse is generally not an effective treatment, especially without psychotherapy.

Calcium carbimide has the same mechanism of action as does Antabuse, but may have fewer side effects as Antabuse. It is available in Canada, but not in the United States.

Naltrexone (Revia, Trexan, 30 mg/day), which was approved in 1994, actually blocks opioid receptors and is thus used for opiate addiction. It reduces alcohol cravings and the hedonistic effects of alcohol. Proponents boast of a high success rate, but the studies are short, some as little as two weeks. There are side effects such as anxiety, depression, nausea, and low energy. This drug can also cause the elevation of liver enzymes. Since most alcoholics have liver dysfunction, patients should have liver enzymes monitored during the first few months of treatment.

Nalmefene (Revex) is a mu-opioid antagonist used to reverse the effects of opioids in cases of acute intoxication or overdose. It is being used experimentally to reduce alcohol cravings in alcoholics.

Calcium bisacetylhomotaurine (Acamprosate, Campral, 2,000–3,000 mg/day), also known as calcium bisacetylhomotaurinmate, is a GABA agonist developed in France. It is the structural analog of the brain chemical taurine, which seems to reduce alcohol cravings. It may also reduce the unpleasant side effects of alcohol abstinence, but it may also have adverse fetal effects. The FDA issued a letter of non-approval in 2002, stating that the research did not adequately address the issues of efficacy and safety. But the drug did receive FDA approval two years later in 2004.

Ondansetron (Zofran, 4 mcg/kg bid) is available in pill or IV form. It is a selective blocker of the 5-HT-3 receptor, and is used to prevent nausea and vomiting caused by cancer chemotherapy or after surgery. It is being studied for the treatment of alcoholism, as it might improve underlying serotonergic abnormality in some alcoholics. It seems to reduce cravings in the early stages of alcohol dependence. Its side effects include diarrhea or constipation, headache, light headedness, drowsiness, blurred vision, and chest pain.

Anticonvulsant medications such as Tegretol, Depakote, Gabapentin, and Topamax are being used experimentally to treat alcohol withdrawal and to reduce alcohol consumption in alcoholics, and to possibly reduce withdrawal seizures. Buspar is an anxiolytic and partial serotonin agonist. It has also been researched as a possible treatment for alcoholism, but it did not reduce drinking or cravings in non-anxious alcoholics.

The studies with serotonergic antidepressants yielded mixed results. One of the more promising studies showed a reduction in alcohol consumption of 15 percent to 20 percent in alcoholics who were given SSRI medication.

Rimonabant is a cannabinoid receptor agonist that may reduce the desire to drink. However, so far the manufacturer has not shown efficacy and safety and the FDA has withheld approval. It has been shown to cause severe depression with suicidal ideation.

Gamma-hydroxy-butyrate (GHB) has a structure similar to GABA. Some European studies suggest it might be useful for the treatment of alcohol dependence, but it is unlikely that it will be approved in the US because of its widespread use as a designer drug. It suppresses DA release, and then there is a rebound increase in DA release along with the release of endogenous opioid, thus producing relaxation and euphoria. Variations of the drug are used in Europe as a surgical anesthetic, but this is limited because of the potential to induce seizure activity.

In 1990, it was distributed as a "health food" product for weight loss and muscle development, but it was banned that same year because of widespread reports of poisonings, including 71 deaths. Its adverse effects include dizziness, vomiting, weakness, tonic-clonic seizure-like activity, loss of peripheral vision, confusion, agitation, hallucinations, bradycardia, unconsciousness, coma, and potentially fatal respiratory depression.

A GHB precursor (1,4-butanediol) is available over the internet. It has toxic effects (vomiting, urinary and fecal incontinence, agitation, combativeness, labile level of consciousness, respiratory depression, and death in at least several cases. It has been listed on supplement/herbal labels as tetramethylene glycol, butylene glycol, and sucol-B. Both GHB and 11,4-butanediol are found in "natural" cleaners and solvents listed as furanone, furanone dehydro, lactone, and CBL.

"Organic" Alternatives

Kava (aka Kava Kava) is a herb that has been marketed OTC to treat anxiety and insomnia. Meta-analysis of research in the US and Germany indicates it is effective for mild to moderate anxiety, but not for panic disorder.

Larger doses can cause allergic skin rashes, yellow discoloration of hair/skin/nails, weight loss, and abnormal reflexes. Most likely, it works on GABA much like the benzodiazepines, but is only a partial agonist and so it is less effective than benzodiazepines. It had been banned by the FDA because it can cause severe liver damage, but was later reintroduced to the market. Contraindications are:

a.   other CNS depressants because of potentiation of sedation and possible coma;
b.   anesthetics antipsychotics because these would prolong sedation time; and
c.   Parkinson's patients because Kava increases the tremors and decreases the effectiveness of the anti-Parkinson's medications.

Valerian (aka Heliotrope) is a herb with mild tranquilizing effects, sold OTC for insomnia and anxiety. It is a GABA agonist, or partial agonist, that reduces the time it takes to fall asleep, but there is only limited research on the quality of that sleep. It interacts with other CNS depressants to potentiate sedation. There is some research that indicates Valerian does not potentiate the effects of alcohol, but more research is needed. It is somewhat more effective than placebo for mild anxiety, but ineffective for panic disorder. The side effects are morning sedation, headache, and there are several reported cases of liver toxicity from an OTC sleep aid containing Valerian.

Chamomile is a herb used in teas for mild insomnia. It is mildly relaxing, but it is not helpful for severe insomnia or anxiety.

Drugs of Abuse

Many of the medications previously discussed can be abused. The major prescription drugs of abuse are the CNS depressants (especially the benzodiazepines) discussed previously, as well as narcotic pain medications.

Stimulants of Abuse

The stimulants of abuse include nicotine, xanthines, amphetamines, and cocaine. Many stimulant addicts begin their careers with prescription stimulants given for ADD and ADHD (their own medications, or those given or sold by friends), and later graduate to cocaine and street versions of amphetamines.

Psychedelics and Hallucinogens

Examples include LSD (lysurgic acid) and similar compounds found in such plants as aloliuqui, ipomaca; Hawaiian baby woodrose; and some morning glory varieties. It was erroneously called a mind-expansion drug during the psychedelic era (1960s and 1970s). Further examples are tryptamine-like compounds (DMT, bufoterin, and psylocybin). Salvinorin A (from the leaves of one of 700 of the plant genus Salvia, a member of the mint family) can be made into tea or chewed like chewing tobacco. It differs from other hallucinogens in that it is not an alkaloid (i.e., organic alkaline substance from a plant).

Salvia divinorum (a Mexican plant that is a member of the sage family) contains the most powerful hallucinogen known and is sold over the Internet. Its active ingredient is Salivinorin A. Effects can vary from mild to severe, and can last from just as few minutes to an hour or more, which is enough to make even regular users wary enough not to take it while alone. Mazatecs have traditionally chewed the leaf, but American users either smoke the dried leaves or ingest extracts in order to produce intense hallucinations.

Dimethyltriptamine (DMT) comes from a variety of South American plants or it is synthesized in the laboratory. As a party drug, it is a short-acting alternative to LSD, as it takes effect more rapidly and lasts about 30 minutes. Thus, it is called the "lunch hour drug."

The mechanism of psychedelics is not fully understood, but they may involve stimulation of 5-HT receptors. The routes of administration are either oral or absorption through the membranes. The desired effects are:

a. altered perception of sensory experiences, with a clouding of consciousness or delirium and hallucinations;
b. time distortion, mysticism, sensation of artistic ability, and/or profound understanding; and
c. the hallucinations usually visual and tied to the environment.

There is also a depersonalization (the feeling of standing back and watching yourself), along with hyper-suggestibility.

Unwanted effects, called a "bad trip," are increased by higher dosages and include occasional self-injury, as well as schizophreniform psychotic reactions that may last six months and require antipsychotics. Flashbacks, or recurrent effects, may occur months later and be triggered by marijuana, antihistamines, or even darkness. There may also be brain damage as manifested by long-lasting changes in EEG, along with adrenergic side effects such as tachycardia, pupillary dilation, anorexia, and hyper-reflexia. Treatments for a bad trip range from "talking the patient down," and to antipsychotic or anti-anxiety medication.

Designer Drugs

A common example of a designer drug is Ecstasy, also known as XTC, or X (3.4-methylenedioxy-methamphetamine, or MDMA). It may kill 5-HT neurons in the central nervous system (CNS), and it will not work after about 20 doses because of the dead brain cells. Consequently, Ecstasy has become a class of drugs with very subtle variations, so most of the MDMA sold today contains little or no MDMA. It gives an increased perception of so-called "fun," but headache and clenched teeth are the result the following day.

GHB is covered in the section on CNS depressants. CBL (Gamma-butyrolactone, known as Blue Nitro, Nitro Vitality, GH Revitalizer (GHR), Remforce, Renewtrient, and Gamma G) is a GHB analog and is converted to GHB in the body. Therefore, it has been illegal since 1999, although before that it was available in health food stores. It continues to be available "underground."

Fentanyl analogs are based on fentanyl, a powerful synthetic opioid used in hospital settings. Alpha methyl fentanyl, for example, is sold on the street as White China or synthetic heroin.

2 C-B (4-bromo-2.5-dimethoxyphenethylamine), called Nexus or Eros on the street, is chemically similar to Ecstasy and mescaline, is often sold as Ecstasy. Users often become terrified as the hallucinations are much more intense than Ecstasy. Unlike Ecstasy, however, it has no energizing effect, but 10 mg promotes sexual arousal, 12 to 24 mg produces visual hallucinations, and more than 24 mg results in extremely unpleasant hallucinations. The onset is 45 to 60 minutes, the plateau lasts about three hours, with the effects subsiding after four to eight hours.

There are many other available designer drugs with slight alterations in chemical structures available, as underground chemists, or "cookers," are able to slightly alter the chemical structure when one variation becomes illegal. Thus, they create a new drug that is not illegal, and prosecution is avoided under the Controlled Substances Act. Then someone has to be the first to try the new ones, a dangerous activity as a contaminant called MPTP found in some drugs causes Parkinsonism.

Drugs of Deception

In contrast to designer drugs, which have the same psychoactive properties as a scheduled drug but have had their molecular structure altered, drugs of deception are never what they appear to be. They are usually easy-to-get substances masquerading as hard-to-get drugs. Examples are:

a.   Valium sold as Quaalude (methaqualone);
b.   PCP (Phencyclidine) sold as a variety of hallucinogens such as LSD;
c.   designer drugs sold as heroin;
d.   2 C-B sold as Ecstasy; and
e.   Klonopin (Cionazepam) sold as Rohypnol.

Dissociative Anesthetics

Examples of dissociative anesthetics are PCP (Phencyclidine), known as Angel Dust, and Ketamine, called K, Special K, or Vitamin K on the street. The desired effect is increased sensitivity to external stimuli while pain is diminished, and mood elevation, along with depersonalization, a dream-like state, altered sense of reality, and feelings of invincibility. The mechanism is not clearly understood, but it may bind to sigma receptors (which are possibly related to schizophrenia) and/or to the glutamate receptors (excitatory).

Sprinkled over parsley or in PCP-soaked cigarettes, the drug can be smoked and thus inhaled, but long-term users prefer intravenous injection. The effect lasts 4 to 5 hours, with a declining phase continuing for 24 to 32 hours. Unwanted effects include agitation, gross hallucinations, blank state, catatonia, nystagmus, flushing, and an increased sensitivity to stimuli. Therefore, there is the strong potential for self-injuries from accidents, including accidental drowning.

Higher doses can result in stupor or coma, hyper-salivation, repetitive movements, and muscle rigidity. Very high doses can induce prolonged coma up to seven days or more, along with hypertension, convulsions, decreased and even absent gag reflex, and corneal reflexes. It can precipitate psychotic episodes in schizophrenics, as well as schizophrenic-like symptoms in non-schizophrenics, and these psychotic episodes may last several weeks, with depressions lasting several months. While these drugs are in one's system, other drugs with any anticholinergic side effects must be avoided because of the potentiation of these unwanted effects.

Caution: never try to "talk down" persons experiencing a psychosis induced by these drugs because of the increased sensitivity to stimuli. Violence is often a defensive reaction brought on by the sensory overload. It is best to isolate them in a dark, quiet room.

Cannabinoids

The active ingredient in cannabinoids is THC, which produces the desired effects of mild euphoria, increased empathy and relaxation, and drowsiness. With high doses there can be altered states of time, as well as delusions and hallucinations. The mechanism is not well understood inasmuch as the government for several decades made research on cannabis illegal.

Cannabis is usually smoked, but it is often eaten, most often in baked food. The street forms are most often chopped leaves and stems, or the more potent resin (hash, hashish). Pure THC is rare because of its tar-like consistency and the fact that it breaks down easily. Pure THC on the street is usually PCP.

Unwanted side effects include tachycardia, with the heart rate often doubling so it replicates the rate found in severe stress. There can be bronchial dilation and possible rupture of the plaques in the arteries. A study conducted by Dr. Murray Mittleman at Beth Israel Hospital in Boston in 2001 indicates the risk of a heart attack increases 4.8 times greater than normal during the first hour after smoking marijuana and continues at 1.7 times the second hour. THC enhances and may even cause fetal alcohol syndrome. Decreased coordination is a problem, especially if the person is driving. Chronic use results in what has been observed as the non-motivational syndrome.

Unpleasant side effects include dry-mouth with increased appetite (the so-called "marijuana munchies"), decreased testosterone levels as well as decreased sperm count, memory impairment when under the influence, and panic reaction. Further, the smoke inhalation is damaging to the lungs much like is the use of tobacco. Withdrawal symptoms include irritability, restlessness, and depression. Furthermore, it interacts with other CNS depressants. Zyban (Bupropion) has been studied as a possible treatment for marijuana addiction, but not only has it shown no benefit, some subjects had increased symptoms of marijuana withdrawal with the medication.

A number of states have enacted medical marijuana laws, citing potential beneficial uses. It has been used to reduce glaucoma, as well as an antiemetic during chemotherapy with cancer patients. Other uses have been for reduction of seizures, alleviation of asthma, and as a muscle relaxant.

Anticholinergics

There are examples in herbs and herbal derivatives, such as Jimsonweed, Nightshade, Henbane, and Mandrake. Medications include benztropine (Cogentin), trihexaphenidyl (Artane), biperiden (Akinelon), cyrimine (Pagitone), procyclidine (Kemadrin), amantadine (Symmetrel), and OTC dephenhydramine (Benadryl).

Desired effects are increased heart rate, wild delirium, hallucinations, and occasional excitation. Unwanted side effects are blurred vision, headache, dry and hot skin, dry mouth, dilated pupils, and fever. The mechanism is the blocking of acetylcholine (ACh) receptors.

Abuse is rare, but a few people will fake antipsychotic motor effects in order to get these drugs. Sometimes it is used as an adulterant or substitute for other street drugs. It should be noted that use with other medications producing anticholinergic side effects is contraindicated.

Inhalants

Inhalants are more commonly abused by adolescents and young adults in the lower economic strata, with Chemo (pronounced "CHAY-moe") the street name for a variety of inhalants. Examples range from gasoline and airplane glue to organic solvents and anti-stick cooking spray. Marking pens along with Wite-Out® and Wite-Out® thinner are inexpensive and readily available, and for those willing to buy it on the street, where it is called "locker room," there is Amyl Nitrate, also known as "poppers." The list is almost endless as long as it can be inhaled: paints, industrial solutions, adhesives, the butane in cigarette lighters, and aerosol propellants. In fact, the average household has about 150 items which can be abused as inhalants.

The desired effects are disinhibition, lightheadedness ("rush"), occasional hallucinations, and intoxication for up to 45 minutes at the most. It is harmful to most organ systems, and other unwanted effects are brain damage, lung disease, permanent damage to the kidneys, liver and heart, leukemia, and immune deficiencies. There have been accidental deaths during disorientation or through asphyxiation from lack of oxygen.

Pouring liquid or discharging gas into a plastic bag or balloon and then inhaling it is called "bagging." Holding one's mouth over the container while it is being discharged is called "huffing," while "sniffing" involves holding a soaked rag over the mouth and nose. Finally, "torching" is the inhalation of fumes from a cigarette lighter and then igniting the exhaled fumes.

Any Port in a Storm

Some people will abuse almost anything. Drinking water constantly can cause changes in blood pH, which results in extreme intoxication. This has been noted in incarcerated settings where nothing else is available. Others combine Viagra with "poppers" (Amyl Nitrate), and even Viagra + "poppers" + amphetamine, all toward enhancing sexual performance and sensitivity. Caution is indicated, as Viagra plus Amyl Nitrate can kill due to lowered blood pressure, and adding an amphetamine makes it even more deadly.

Psychopharmacology is a Constantly Evolving Field

The difficulty with a chapter on psychopharmacology is that it will be outdated soon after it goes to press, as this chapter undoubtedly is. Not only are new drugs constantly being developed, but old drugs are often no longer useful as long-term use reveals serious, debilitating, and even deadly side effects. Lithium, now in use for 35 or 40 years, is a primary example. Once regarded as totally safe, now use beyond 12 years is likely to begin the eventual failure of bodily organs (Whitaker, 2010), along with the possibility of eventual death. But not only are new drugs being developed, new classes of drugs are being discovered.

Growing in importance is the discovery of dubious reporting of clinical trials upon which FDA approval is based, along with the pharmaceutical industry's all-too-frequent secret ghost-writing of published scientific studies rather than by the so-called authors whose names appear on the publications (Healy, 2012). The psychotherapist needs not only to be current in knowledge, but aware of the fact that far too many "authorities" are questionable inasmuch as they have fallen prey to Big Pharma's subsidization.

In keeping up with the rapidly evolving field of psychopharmacology, there are incisive, timely newsletters available:

- The Brown University *Psychopharmacology Update*, which has won awards for its excellence, is a monthly publication available through the mail or online: wileyonlinelibrary.com.
- An unbiased monthly covering all things psychiatric, and particularly psychopharmacology, is *The Carlat Report*. It is available by through the mail by subscription (phone 866-348-9279) or online: www.thecarlatreport.com.

APPENDIX I

The Nicholas A. Cummings Doctor of Behavioral Health Program, Arizona State University

Ronald O'Donnell, PhD, Director

The historic healthcare reform bill makes clear the focus of the twenty-first-century healthcare system is cost control. A major mechanism to achieve cost control is integrated care: improved cost-effectiveness by better prevention and management of chronic disease, improved delivery of these services in primary care, increased use of evidence-based practices, and new payment mechanisms such as pay-for-performance incentives to encourage best practices. Providers are urged to be more accountable for healthcare costs and results, and to demonstrate cost-effectiveness. The writing is on the wall: integrated care, accountability, and cost savings are the focus of healthcare reform.

A recent article by Cummings, O'Donohue, and Cummings (2011) concluded that the field fails to adequately prepare behavioral care providers with the clinical competencies necessary to provide integrated care or with the business skills necessary to navigate healthcare economics, finance, and reimbursement, or demonstrate cost-effectiveness. The authors concluded that the unmet education and training need in these areas results in an educational deficit for behavioral care providers from all disciplines. Radical reform in educating and training is needed to prepare a new workforce of applied, doctoral-level behavioral care providers specializing in integrated care. The key elements of education reform represented by the DBH include:

- A new applied, professional doctorate degree in integrated behavioral health.
- A new professional accreditation body for the degree and professional organization for students and alumni.
- A flexible course curriculum that eliminates courses irrelevant to practicing clinicians and adds courses essential to meet the demands of healthcare reform.

- Eliminate the dissertation and replace it with a research project that focuses on the skills needed to demonstrate cost-effectiveness and business entrepreneurship in healthcare.
- Upgrade master's level licensed clinicians for enrollment in order to deliver more doctoral level integrated care clinicians in medical settings.
- Distance learning and distance case consultation for internship training.
- Incorporate e-health and tele-health into practice training.
- Adopt the competency model recommended by the American Psychological Association (APA) task force in 2006 that embraces use of clinical outcomes, utilization, and cost of care measures to demonstrate clinician performance and accountability.

In 2008, Nicholas Cummings, in collaboration with leadership in Arizona State University (ASU), developed the Doctor of Behavioral Health (DBH) program. The ASU leadership working with Dr. Cummings included no less than President Robert Bulla of the Board of Trustees, University President Michael Crow, and Provost Elizabeth Capaldi. The DBH is a new doctoral degree in behavioral health designed to train behavioral clinicians to provide integrated care in medical settings. The program is based on models of professional training and credentialing typical of most other healthcare professions. The first cohort of students enrolled in the program in the fall, 2009 semester. The DBH program is co-sponsored by the Nicholas and Dorothy Cummings Foundation. The DBH program reform is *radical* in that it:

1. is founded on a knowledge base that incorporates clinical skills in integrated care, medical literacy, healthcare economics, and entrepreneurship;
2. relies on a small core, non-tenured faculty complemented with adjunct faculty and clinical supervisors who are practicing clinicians;
3. provides hands-on internship experience in primary care and related settings;
4. systematically collects individual and program outcome data in order to evaluate competency;
5. embraces the mission of producing behavioral care providers who have the ability to produce and document medical cost offset in their clinical practice; and
6. has received provisional accreditation by a new entity, the National Institute of Behavioral Health Quality, formed under the auspices of the National Alliance of Professional Psychology Providers.

The DBH is *traditional* in that it is designed to:

1. meet the requirements for accreditation as a program of psychology by the APA;
2. meet the guidelines on internship experience endorsed by the ASPPB; and

3. meet anticipated requirements for doctoral licensure as APA and ASPPB recommendations are adopted by state licensing boards.

The DHB program is *progressive* in that it:

1. has already incorporated a comprehensive competency assessment program;
2. replaces the dissertation with a rigorous yet relevant research project;
3. uses distance learning in order to make courses and consultation available to students around the world; and
4. incorporates innovative e-health approaches as an adjunct to treatment.

The DBH program is currently designed as an upgrade for licensed, master's level behavioral clinicians. The program requires 84 credit hours for completion, 30 of which are credited from the clinicians' master's degree program. The remaining 54 credit hours include 10 core courses, 4 elective courses, a culminating research project, and internship. The internship program begins the first semester of the program and is based on a sequential, stage-based training, with students completing an average of one, 8-hour day per week in each semester for a total of 500 hours of internship experience. The program requires two years of study post-master's degree, or may be completed in 18 months in an accelerated program that includes summer sessions.

The DBH core faculty is small and comprises clinical psychologists or DBH graduates with experience in integrated care as practitioners. Core faculty members also practice in integrated care settings. The core faculty is complemented by adjunct faculty with excellent teaching skills and full-time professional experience in the area in which they are teaching.

The Curriculum

The clinical skills necessary for effective delivery of integrated behavioral care are not the same as those necessary for traditional mental health and substance abuse treatment settings. The provider must be a generalist that is responsive to a wide range of medical and behavioral problems for diverse populations across the lifespan. Principles of population-based management and stepped care are essential yet foreign to most behavioral clinicians. The behavioral provider must be able to function as a member of a multidisciplinary medical team, usually headed by a primary care physician, and in consultation with other specialists. The shift from traditional behavioral health into the medical culture, the values, beliefs, norms, and behaviors that comprise the medical mindset, are a dramatic challenge since they run directly counter to how traditional psychotherapy is delivered: visits are brief; the therapist is on the floor interacting with the team and ready for a "hallway handoff" at any time; sessions may be interrupted for crises; verbal and written communication must be concrete, action-oriented, symptom-focused, and evidence-based.

A distinguishing feature of the DBH clinical curriculum is a clinical training on the Biodyne Model of integrated care and psychotherapy outlined in this book. The Biodyne Model is seen as critical for two key reasons. First, the model is based on efficient delivery of clinical services. Efficiency is achieved largely through the use of therapeutic strategies and techniques designed to effectively manage patient resistance and achieve rapid therapeutic alliance. The Bioydne Model includes a practice management model focused on clinician productivity and efficiency using group treatment protocols.

Second, the Biodyne Model has consistently demonstrated what Cummings and associates termed "medical cost offset." Medical cost offset is used to describe how focused, targeted behavioral interventions delivered in primary care lead to reductions in medical costs that are greater than, or offset the cost of delivering, the behavioral intervention. The reductions in medical cost are due to decreased overuse of medical services such as primary care physician visits, emergency room visits, specialist referrals, labs, and imaging. These savings are achieved by the combination of efficient provision of effective psychotherapy plus population-based management of high utilizing patients via telephonic outreach, behavioral interventions, and case management.

Medical literacy courses are designed to prepare the behavioral clinicians with a broad survey of clinical medicine and pathophysiology, psychopharmacology, and clinical neuropathophysiology. These courses are designed to present a survey of disease etiology, course and progression, medical treatment, and outcome. The objective is for the behavioral clinician to understand and consult with medical providers within a multidisciplinary team setting and converse in the language of these providers.

The curriculum includes a strong focus on healthcare business and entrepreneurship. The DBH course on healthcare systems and economics includes healthcare policy and reform, financing and reimbursement, and quality and accreditation. The behavioral entrepreneurship course includes:

1. personality factors and attitudes that contribute to success;
2. how market forces enhance or limit success;
3. steps and resources needed for a "start-up" company;
4. venture capital and investment;
5. compensation;
6. business law and regulation;
7. how to write, present, implement, and evaluate a business plan; and
8. exit strategy.

The objective is to increase the ability of the behavioral care provider to demonstrate value added to healthcare payers as a means of expanding his/her economic base.

A sequence of three courses along with a culminating project, all of which are a part of an otherwise intensive clinical training, are designed to educate the practitioner to function as an informed consumer of science rather than as a research scientist. First, the population-based health management course includes a survey of epidemiology and approaches such as disease management, screening, outcomes, medical cost offset, and return on investment. A course on research design in healthcare is focused on quality improvement, performance measurement, value-based and pay-for-performance incentive programs. The culminating research project is designed to demonstrate the students' ability to design an integrated behavioral care intervention, including a literature review, appropriate research design and analysis, reporting of results, and discussion. While the project is completed in the final semester, the student actively begins to develop the project with his/her advisor in each of the sequential courses described above. In this manner, the research project is developed as part of a comprehensive, sequential learning experience.

The DBH Internship Program

The DBH internship program affords students the opportunity to function as behavioral care providers in a functioning medical setting. The internship program is based on a sequential model that includes competency levels tied to the course curriculum progression. In the novice stage, the students learn about the culture of primary care, the role of the behavioral care provider, and the model of targeted, focused behavioral interventions. In the intermediate phase, in the first semester, the students focus on screening, assessment, and treatment of the most common behavioral conditions in primary care, such as depression, anxiety, substance abuse, and somatizers. Students then focus on co-morbid medical and behavioral chronic conditions and lifestyle interventions designed to enhance health and wellness. In the advanced phase that continues into the third semester, students integrate course material on more challenging conditions, such as schizophrenia and psychotic disorders, borderline personality disorders, and suicide prevention. In the third and fourth semesters, students move to the proficient level, with a focus on couples and family interventions, and specialization in areas such as pediatrics.

DBH Program Internship Consultants

The DBH program internship case consultation is provided by licensed psychologists or DBH graduates. Consultants are experienced in the Biodyne Model, integrated care, and trained in the DBH competency model described below. Students meet in small group consultation for 60 minutes per week. Group size is kept small to facilitate discussion, typically five to six students. Webcams enable a streaming image of each participant on the computer. Audio recordings and digital video recordings of clinician–patient sessions are reviewed routinely during the group consultation. The internship supervisor is the key liaison between the DBH program and the internship site preceptor for student performance feedback on an as needed basis and during regular student performance evaluations.

DBH Internship Sites

The DBH program contracts with primary care offices or other medical settings using an affiliation agreement that defines responsibilities of the clinic, the DBH program, and the internship student. Unlike traditional doctoral training clinics, these sites generally do not have dedicated behavioral clinicians affiliated with the office to provide consultation and oversight. These arrangements simply do not exist today, and this is the gap the DBH program aims to fill. Instead, each internship site identifies a preceptor to oversee each student and serve as liaison with the DBH program. The preceptor ideally is a medical health provider. Responsibilities of the preceptor include orientation of the student to office policy and procedures and the work environment, facilitating introduction of the student to the medical team and support staff, and facilitation of collection of measures of student performance.

Competency Assessment

The DBH program is based on a comprehensive model of competency assessment based on a developmentally informed, multi-method and multi-informant process using established evaluation tools. Assessment results are incorporated into consultation in the program and in the internship site, and reviewed with the student advisor over the course of the program. First, a rating scale of integrated care knowledge and applied competencies is completed by the DBH consultant, internship preceptor, and primary care physicians to evaluate student performance. These forms are administered, collected, analyzed, and reviewed with each student, DBH supervisor, internship supervisor, and advisor near the end of each semester.

Second, an outcomes management program is used to collect and evaluate patient progress based on measures of clinical outcome and treatment alliance. The measures are the outcome rating scale (ORS) and the session rating scale (SRS) developed by Barry Duncan and Scott Miller. Research on the ORS and SRS demonstrated that outcomes and treatment alliance feedback resulted in a significant improvement in clinical effectiveness and improved treatment retention. The DBH program contracted with the company MyOutcomes (www.myoutcomes.com) in order to provide Internet access and real-time scoring and reports that summarize treatment effect size for each student, for each internship site, and for the DBH program in aggregate.

Third, the DBH program has contracted with ProChange Behavior Systems (www.prochange.com), a company founded by James Prochaska, in order to make available to DBH students and their patients a suite of Internet-based, patient behavior change computer programs based on the transtheoretical model of behavior change. The ProChange system uses patient self-assessment based on the patient's stage of change to develop individually tailored behavior change interventions. These approaches have demonstrated significant improvement for many behavioral conditions, including diet, exercise, stress, and depression (Prochaska, Redding, & Evers, 2008). The contract with ProChange will make available program-level, aggregate reports for all users.

Credentials

The DBH program limits enrollment to master's level, licensed behavioral clinicians, such as social workers, counselors, and marital and family therapists. The rationale for this criterion is that the DBH, as a new doctoral degree in behavioral health, has not yet been recognized for licensure in any state. Requiring that each student already has a license to practice the program ensures that, upon graduation, students will have a doctoral degree from an accredited university and a master's license to practice integrated behavioral care. In addition, the supply of existing therapists far exceeds the demand for patients in traditional settings. By upgrading master's level providers to integrated doctoral care providers, we are shifting clinicians from the oversupply in traditional settings to meet the demand to treat patients who are currently not being treated in primary care. This is good for patients, the healthcare system, and DBH graduates.

The DBH program is provisionally accredited by the National Institute of Behavioral Health Quality (NIBHQ), an accreditation developed by the National Alliance of Professional Psychology Providers. The vision is that other universities or professional schools adopt the DBH as a new applied doctoral degree for behavioral providers in integrated care settings, and that the NIBHQ becomes the professional accreditation organization for these emerging programs. In addition to giving clinicians credit for their master's degree credits toward the DBH degree, the program also gives clinicians credit for between 1,500 and 3,000 hours of supervised internship experience that were part of their master's degree and master's license. The DBH is designed to build on existing competencies in psychotherapy with specific new competencies for a doctoral level behavioral care provider in an integrated care setting. The DBH internship hours (500) on top of the prior supervised internship hours are seen as sufficient for achieving proficiency, provided the student achieves the benchmarks based on assessment of competency in the program. In addition, students may choose an option to complete additional curriculum and internship requirements designed to largely meet current and emerging APA and ASPPB standards for both a doctoral psychology program and internship experience. Admittedly, it may be a long and winding trajectory from establishment and credentialing of a new program to state licensure. Designing a program that largely meets existing state license board requirements for a doctoral degree license in behavioral care is prudent and logical.

Career Opportunities for the DBH Behavioral Care Provider

The key career path for the DBH behavioral care provider is the primary care or related medical setting. However, a number of other career paths seem appropriate for the provision of integrated behavioral care:

- SAMHSA is awarding grants for pilot projects to locate primary care and nursing providers in traditional mental health and substance abuse treatment settings.
- Health plans, carve-outs, and other vendors continue to offer disease management and case management programs using telephonic outreach to engage high-cost, high-risk patients with co-morbid medical and behavioral conditions.
- Large employer groups are searching for solutions to address the high cost of lost productivity and disability due to behavioral conditions. The use of EAP services is on the rise, and a potential career path.
- There is a proliferation of companies developing e-health interventions for behavioral and medical conditions. Clinicians familiar with e-health and integrated care are likely to contribute significantly to design and evaluation of such programs.

Finally, traditional education in behavioral health leaves clinicians with the perception that their only options are to accept relatively low, fee-for-service reimbursement from payers, or to opt out of insurance panels. The DBH program emphasis on behavioral entrepreneurship is designed to help clinicians think outside of the box for new business start-up opportunities (Cummings, Pallak, & Cummings, 1996).

Summary

The Doctor of Behavioral Health represents a model for radical reform in the education of doctoral-level, behavioral care providers. The program is designed to meet the emerging needs of healthcare reform to produce clinicians who are able to provide clinical services in integrated care settings with the explicit goal of improved clinical outcome and demonstrating medical cost offset. The DBH curriculum and training progression are based on a cohesive, sequential program of study that will prepare graduates with the clinical, medical literacy, and entrepreneurial skills necessary to thrive in the twenty-first-century healthcare system (Christensen, 2009).

APPENDIX II

The Biodyne Research Model for Determining Efficacy, Effectiveness, and Efficiency

Recent years have witnessed great strides in the transformation of psychotherapy from an experience-based practice to that of an empirically supported treatment discipline. Chambless and her colleagues are distinctive among a number of academic clinicians (for a thorough application to treatments of diverse conditions, see Chambless & Hollon, 1998, and O'Donohue & Fisher, 2009). Termed *efficacy*, it identifies evidenced-based treatments, indicating proven interventions for existing conditions.

This transformation has been laudable, but as Kazdin (2008) has pointed out, it has been influenced by limitations in research design inasmuch as the EBTs (as evidence-based treatments have come to be known) that have been published are those that are easily quantified and lend themselves to our circumscribed research methods. Barlow (2004) has shown that our EBTs may or may not work outside the laboratory. He calls for research in effectiveness, meaning that the EBTs actually work in the clinic and treatment room rather than just in the lab.

The Biodyne Model calls for a third E, that of efficiency. Just because a treatment has been proven to be both efficacious and effective does not mean we should not seek to make psychotherapy more efficient. The paucity of research in effectiveness and the absence of research in efficiency is characteristic of psychology, but not medicine where interest in efficiency abounds. An excellent example is in heart surgery. When coronary bypasses were perfected, many lives were saved, but the procedure was drastic and the recovery was prolonged, with many patients becoming depressed during the months-long recovery phase. Clearly efficiency was needed, and it came with the invention of the stent, which is applicable to a large percentage of cardiac patients. With the stent, the patient is out of the hospital and back to work the next day.

The Biodyne Model for decades has committed resources not only to the first and second Es, but also the third E, insisting that psychotherapy must be rapid and incisive in both its diagnosis and treatment. The Biodyne Patient Bill of Rights, described earlier, exemplifies this. Efficiency is a neglected need in psychotherapy but it is not a new concept. Sigmund Freud, before his death, lamented that psychoanalysis was so protracted that only a relatively few people could afford it. He argued that it would be the necessary responsibility of his successors to make psychoanalysis shorter and more effective. From its inception, the Biodyne Model took this admonition seriously and began research in brief psychotherapy as early as the mid-1950s, much to the consternation of the profession which responded not only with hostility, but with unceasing criticism that psychotherapy was being diluted and even destroyed. The idea that efficient psychotherapy could also be more efficacious and effective had never occurred to the myopic critics.

The Biodyne Model incorporated the first two Es as part of its research into the third E. The research methodology was, and remains, unique in that it is proven efficacious, effective, and efficient not only outside the laboratory but with extensive verification in the real world of healthcare delivery, involving not hundreds or thousands of lives, but millions.

The Biodyne Model Research Methodology

What is now called refocused psychotherapy, or the Biodyne Model, has been subjected to an unprecedented half century of research. The medical cost offset phenomenon, which measures the effectiveness of psychotherapy by the reduction of somatization (as reflected in the rapid decline of medical/surgical utilization), was employed in the development of the interventions. Cummings and his colleagues at Kaiser Permanente early on intuitively observed that certain conditions seemed to respond better to dynamically oriented therapy, others to group therapy, still others to cognitive behavioral therapy, and still others to systems approaches. This is anathema to most practitioners in that they adhere to usually one "school" of psychotherapy, making them akin to what we have termed many years ago as "psycho-religions." It was also observed that, even within the school of psychotherapy, some conditions were more effectively treated in individual therapy, others in group therapy, and still others in psychoeducational programs. They tentatively accepted the premise that all schools and modalities had truth, but none had all-encompassing truth. The optimal truth could well be an admixture of several approaches, and they set about to test the hypothesis through outcomes research utilizing medical cost offset as the criterion of efficacy. Since in our society persons under stress somatize their stress, a greater reduction in medical utilization in an aggregate group receiving one type of psychotherapy intervention over another aggregate group receiving a different kind of intervention would be a measure of the effectiveness of the intervention.

The cost-therapeutic effectiveness ratio, also known as the efficiency-effectiveness ratio, was derived by dividing the average (mean) medical/surgical utilization for the entire group for the year prior to the intervention, by the average (mean) medical/surgical utilization plus the average (mean) psych visits for that same group in the year after the intervention:

$$r = \frac{\text{Mean (medical/surgical utilization year before)}}{\begin{array}{c}\text{Mean (medical surgical utilization year after) +}\\ \text{Mean (psychotherapy sessions)}\end{array}}$$

Differentially weighting by cost the various kinds of medical utilization, such as giving an outpatient visit a value of 1.0 and a day of hospitalization value of 10, only complicated our computations and neither added precision nor altered outcome. But weighting individual therapy, group therapy, and psychoeducational programs did add precision. The formula adopted was based on psychotherapist time to accomplish a unit. Thus, individual psychotherapy (1 therapist with 1 patient for 45 minutes) received a value of 1, while group therapy (1 therapist with 8 patients for 90 minutes) received a value of 0.25, and a psychoeducational group (1 therapist with 12 patients for 90 minutes) was given a value of 0.08. To clarify further, 10 sessions of individual therapy equals 10, the same number of group therapy sessions equals 2.5, and 10 sessions of psychoeducational programming yield less than 1. A psychotherapist responding to an emergency psychotherapy visit was given a value of 2, which means that 10 such visits had a total value of 20.

To illustrate from actual research, a group of 83 borderline personality disorder patients were placed in individual psychotherapy, with the result that medical utilization declined only slightly, but at an enormous expenditure of both individual sessions and emergency therapy visits:

$$r = \frac{163}{141 + 68} = 0.8$$

The ratio is low, indicating the interventions were neither therapeutically efficient (reduction in medical/surgical utilization) or cost-efficient (number of mental health units). The staff over time created a focused set of interventions within individual therapy with some improvement in cost efficiency but little impact on therapeutic effectiveness with another group of 73 borderline personality patients:

$$r = \frac{167}{148 + 51} = 0.7$$

The overall effectiveness–efficiency ratio actually declined. With another population of 76 patients suffering from borderline personality disorder, a great deal of care and effort was expended in designing a 20-session group therapy, augmented with 10 sessions of individual therapy, and then with monthly follow-up sessions. Emergency department visits were virtually eliminated and the ratio rose dramatically:

$$r = \frac{166}{27 + 31} = 2.8$$

Learning a great deal from this group of patients, we incorporated many of the "garlic" conceptions that were being developed, and we also shortened the series to 15 group sessions followed by 10 psychoeducational sessions, and with subsequent monthly follow-up individual sessions. That yielded a ratio and a program that were adopted as both effective and efficient:

$$r = \frac{171}{11 + 12} = 7.4$$

The research team continued to experiment with honing the program even further, but the work with borderline personality disorder, a category of resistant and highly acting-out patients, never achieved the ratio of 9.0 or higher that became the goal and standard for the other protocols. In this way, using medical cost offset, there were designed 68 focused, targeted interventions for 68 psychological/psychiatric conditions that became the methodology in what was at the time termed brief, intermittent psychotherapy throughout the life cycle, an approach that concentrates on solving the problem in the "here and now" while also giving the patient a greater repertoire of responses to stress. These findings were the backbone of the clinical training and service delivery early at Kaiser Permanente and later at American Biodyne (Cummings, 1991), as well as the eight-year, longitudinal Hawaii Project with federal employees and Medicaid recipients (Cummings et al., 1991).

REFERENCES

Balint, M. (1957). *The doctor, his patient and the illness.* New York: International Universities Press.

Barlow, D.H. (2004). Psychological treatments. *American Psychologist,* 59, 869–878.

Bray, J.H. (2011). Reforms in treating children and families. In N.A. Cummings & W.T. O'Donohue (Eds.), *Understanding the healthcare crisis* (pp. 343–366). New York: Routledge.

Budman, S.H., & Gurman, A.S. (1988). *Theory and practice of brief therapy.* New York: Guilford Press.

Carlat, D.J. (2010). *Unhinged: The trouble with psychiatry: A doctor's revelations about a profession in crisis.* New York: Free Press.

Chambless, D.L., & Hollon, S.D. (1998). Defining empirically supported therapies. *Journal of Consulting and Clinical Psychology,* 66, 7–18.

Christensen, C.M. (2009). *The innovator's prescription: A disruptive solution for health care.* New York: McGraw-Hill.

Cooper, K.H. (1995). *It's better to believe.* Nashville, TN: Thomas Nelson.

Cummings, N.A. (1977). Prolonged (ideal) versus short-term (realistic) psychotherapy. *Professional Psychology,* 8, 491–501.

Cummings, N.A. (1986). The dismantling of our health system: Strategies for the survival of psychological practice. *American Psychologist,* 41, 426–431.

Cummings, N.A. (1991). Brief, intermittent psychotherapy throughout the life cycle. In J.K. Zeig & S.G. Gilligan (Eds.), *Brief therapy: Myths, methods and metaphors.* New York: Brunner/Mazel.

Cummings, N.A. (2011). Our 50-minute hour in the nanosecond era. In N.A. Cummings & W.T. O'Donohue (Eds.), *Understanding the behavioral healthcare crisis* (pp. 19–31). New York: Routledge.

Cummings, N.A., & Cummings, J.L. (1997). The behavioral health practitioner of the future: The efficacy of psychoeducational programs in integrated primary care. In N.A. Cummings, J.L. Cummings, & J.N. Johnson (Eds.), *Behavioral health in primary care: A guide for clinical integration* (pp. 325–346). Madison, CT: Psychosocial Press (International Universities Press).

Cummings, N.A., & Cummings, J.L. (2000). *The first session with substance abusers: A step-by-step guide.* San Francisco: Jossey-Bass (Wiley).

Cummings, N.A., & Follette, W.T. (1968). Psychiatric services and medical utilization in a prepaid health plan setting: Part 2. *Medical Care*, 6, 31–41.

Cummings, N.A., & Sayama, M. (1995). *Focused psychotherapy: A casebook of brief intermittent psychotherapy throughout the life cycle.* New York: Brunner Mazel.

Cummings, N.A., & VandenBos, G.R. (1981). The twenty year Kaiser-Permanente experience with psychotherapy and medical utilization: Implications for national health policy and national health insurance. *Health Policy Quarterly*, 1, 159–179.

Cummings, N.A., & Wiggins, J.G. (2001). A collaborative primary care/behavioral health model for use of psychotropic medications with children. *Issues in Interdisciplinary Care*, 3(2), 121–128.

Cummings, N.A., Cummings, J.L., & Johnson, J.N. (1997). *Behavioral health in primary care: A guide for clinical integration.* Madison, CT: Psychosocial Press (International Universities Press).

Cummings, N.A., O'Donohue, W.T., & Cummings, J.L. (2011). *The financial dimension of the behavioral healthcare crisis.* New York: Routledge.

Cummings, N.A., O'Donohue, W.T., & Ferguson, K.E. (2002). *The impact of medical cost offset on practice and research: Making it work for you.* Foundation for Behavioral Health: Healthcare Utilization and Cost Series, vol. 5. Reno, NV: Context Press.

Cummings, N.A., Pallak, M.S., & Cummings, J.L. (Eds.) (1996). *Surviving the demise of solo practice.* Madison, CT: Psychosocial Press (International Universities Press).

Cummings, N.A., Dorken, H., Pallak, M.S., & Henke, C.J. (1991). The impact of psychological intervention on health care costs and utilization. The Hawaii Medicaid Project. *HCFA Contract Report #11-C-983344/9.*

Cummings, N.A., Dorken, H., Pallak, M.S., & Henke, C.J. (1993). The impact of psychological intervention on healthcare costs and utilization: The Hawaii Medicaid Project. In N.A. Cummings & M.S. Pallak (Eds.), *Medicaid, managed behavioral health and implications for public policy. Vol. 2: Healthcare and utilization cost series* (pp. 3–23). South San Francisco: Foundation for Behavioral Health.

Erikson, E. (1950). *Childhood and society.* New York: Norton.

Follette, W.C., & Houts, A.C. (1996). Models of scientific progress and the role of theory in taxonomy development: A case study of the DSM. *Journal of Consulting and Clinical Psychology*, 64, 1120–1132.

Follette, W.T., & Cummings, N.A. (1967). Psychiatric services and medical utilization in a prepaid health plan setting. *Medical Care*, 5, 25–35.

Fromm-Reichmann, F. (1929/1950). *Principles of intensive psychotherapy.* Chicago: University of Chicago Press.

Garfield, S.L. (1998). *The practice of brief psychotherapy.* New York: Wiley.

Greenberg, G. (2010). *Manufacturing depression.* New York: Simon & Schuster.

Haley, J. (1976). *Problem solving behavior.* San Francisco: Jossey-Bass.

Hayes, S.C. (2000). Danny: A case of panic disorder. Orientation: Acceptance/commitment therapy. In N.A. Cummings & J.L. Cummings (Eds.), *The essence of psychotherapy: Reinventing the art in the new era of data* (pp. 188–193). New York: Routledge.

Healy, D. (2012). Renewing the clinical relationship. In N.A. Cummings & W. O'Donohue (Eds.), *Restoring psychotherapy as the first line intervention in behavioral health* (pp. 63–106). Dryden, NY: Ithaca Press.

Herzberg, D. (2008). *Happy pills in America.* Baltimore, MD: Johns Hopkins University Press.

Hunter, C.L. (2010). *Integrated behavioral health in primary care: Step-by-step guidance for assessment and behavioral interventions.* Washington, DC: APA Books.

Jones, K.R., & Vischi, T.R. (1979). The impact of alcohol, drug abuse, and mental health treatment on medical care utilization: A review of the research literature. *Medical Care,* 17 (suppl.), 43–131.

Kazdin, A.E. (2008). Evidence-based treatment and practice: New opportunities to bridge clinical research and practice, enhance the knowledge base, and improve patient care. *American Psychologist,* 63, 146–159.

Kirsch, I. (2010). *The emperor's new drugs.* New York: Basic Books.

Konigsberg, R.D. (2011). *The truth about grief.* New York: Simon & Schuster.

Lee, S. (1997). Estranged bodies, simulated harmony, and misplaced cultures: Neurasthenia in contemporary Chinese society. *Psychosomatic Medicine,* 60, 448–457.

Lee, S., & Kleinman, A. (2007). Are somatoform disorders changing with time: The case of neurasthenia in China. *Psychosomatic Medicine,* 69, 846–849.

Lesse, S. (1982). The uncertain future of clinical psychiatry. *American Journal of Psychotherapy,* 37(2), 306–312.

Manaster, C.J., & Corsini, R.J. (1982). *Individual psychology: Theory and practice.* San Francisco: E.E. Peacock Publications.

May, R. (1950). *The meaning of anxiety.* New York: Norton.

May, R. (1977). *The meaning of anxiety (Rev. Ed.).* New York: Norton.

Menand, L. (2010). Can psychiatry be a science? *New Yorker,* March 10. Available at: www.newyorker.com/arts/critics/2010/03/01/100301crat_atlargw.menand?curr (accessed March 20, 2010).

Mosher, L., & Hendrix, V. (2008). *Soteria: From madness to deliverance.* Washington, DC: Authors.

O'Donohue, W.T., & Fisher, J.L. (2009). *Evidence-based treatments.* New York: Springer.

O'Donohue, W.T., Byrd, M.R., Cummings, N.A., & Henderson, D.A. (2005) *Behavioral integrative care.* New York: Routledge.

Prochaska, D.O., Redding, C.A., & Evers, C.A. (2008). The trans-theoretical model of behavior change. In K. Glanz, F.M. Lewis, B.K. Rimer (Eds.), *Health behavior and health education: Theory, research and practice* (3rd ed.) (pp. 97–121). San Francisco: Jossey-Bass.

Rosenhan, D.L., & Seligman, M.E.P. (1984). *Abnormal psychology.* New York: Norton.

Selye, H. (1956). *Stress.* New York: McGraw-Hill.

Shedler, J. (2010a). Getting to know me. *Scientific American Mind,* Nov./Dec., 52–57.

Shedler, J. (2010b). The efficacy of psychodynamic psychotherapy. *American Psychologist,* 65(2), 98–109.

Shorter, E. (2010). Why psychiatry needs therapy. *Wall Street Journal (WSJ.com).* Available at: http://online.wsj.com/artikcle_emaii?SBG1000142405274870418810457700813700 227601116 (accessed December 3, 2010).

Skinner, B.F. (1938). *The behavior of organisms.* New York: Appleton-Century.

Sullivan, H.S. (1927). Affective experience in early schizophrenia. *American Journal of Psychiatry,* 6, 468–483.

Sullivan, H.S. (1940). Research in schizophrenia. *American Journal of Psychiatry,* 9, 222–248.

Tone, A. (2009). *The age of anxiety: A history of America's turbulent affair with tranquilizers.* New York: Basic Books.

Wakefield, J., & Horwitz, A. (2007). *The loss of sadness.* New York: Oxford University Press.

Whitaker, R. (2010). *Anatomy of an epidemic.* New York: Crown Publishers.

Wright, R.H., & Cummings, N.A. (Eds.) (2005). *Destructive trends in mental health: The well-intentioned path to harm.* New York: Routledge.

Zur, O. (2005). The psychology of victimhood. In R.H. Wright, & N.A. Cummings (Eds.), *Destructive trends in mental health: The well-intentioned path to harm* (pp. 45–63). New York: Routledge.

INDEX

Note: page numbers in *italic type* refer to figures.

daily living programs 224–225
DBH (Doctor of Behavioral Health)
    Program, Arizona State University
    264–266, 271; career opportunities
    271; competency assessment 269–270;
    credentials 270–271; curriculum
    226–228; internship 268–269
death/dying counseling 112–113
defense mechanisms 70, 91–92, 92; in
    addiction 126; in anxiety 93; in
    depression 102; in hysteria/conversion
    neurosis 115; in obsessive-compulsive
    personality disorders 212; in paranoia
    193; in phobic disorders 96–97
deinstitutionalization 4, 5
delusions 157, 158; joining of 51–57,
    161–162
denial 70, 71, 126
depression 9, 14, 17, 92, 101–107, 209,
    228; anniversary depression 110–115,
    205–206, 239; bereavement 9, 91, 111,
    197, 239; chronic depression 107–115,
    238; endogenous 101, 238; major
    depression 15, 101; over-diagnosis of
    13, 14; rage depression 49, 57, 58–61;
    reactive 101, 238; tests for 209
desensitization 98–101, 207, 215
diagnosis 10–11; by consensus 14–16;
    differential 69, 70–73; and
    psychopharmacology 228
Diagnostic and Statistical Manuals of
    Mental Health Disorders see DSMs
differential diagnosis 69, 70–73
"disease mongering" 16
displacement 96–97
dopamine 17, 157
Dorken, Herbert 211
drugs of abuse 226–227, 258, 262;
    anticholinergics 261–262; cannabinoids
    261; designer drugs 259–260;
    dissociative anesthetics 260–261; drugs
    of deception 260; inhalants 262;
    psychedelics and hallucinogens
    258–259; stimulants 258; see also drugs,
    street
drugs, street 226–227; and suicide
    195–196; use by elderly 197–198; see
    also drugs of abuse
DSMs (Diagnostic and Statistical Manuals
    of Mental Health Disorders) 10–11, 16;
    DSM-I 10, 11–12; DSM-II 12; DSM-
    III 12–13, 14, 15; DSM-IV 13–14;
    DSM-V 15, 16
dysthymia 15, 101

eating disorders 84–85; case illustrations
    85–87
EBTs (evidence-based treatments) 272
elderly: changing population of 197–198;
    and suicide 196–197
EMDR (eye movement desensitization
    response) 18
emergency treatment of mentally-ill
    patients 5, 206–207
explicit contracts 26–27, 34
extreme therapy 213; and the community
    as patient 223–224; and the emergency
    room 219–220; and enforced
    homework 221–223; and high utilizer
    outreach 23–25, 218–219; and house
    calls 216–218; and the immediate
    group 220–221; jump door fever
    213–215; and phobic behavior
    215–217; and the therapeutic
    "shopping spree" 224–225
eye movement desensitization response see
    EMDR

factitious disorder 209
family therapy, and psychojudo 61–68,
    88–89
FBI 183
fecal smearing 52
Filipino community, Daly City 217–218
first session, doing something novel in 33,
    37–39
Follette, W.T. 23
food: food addiction 127–129; interaction
    with tyramine 242
Freud, Sigmund 12, 273
Fromm-Reichmann, Frieda 45, 52, 214

Garfield, S.L. 7, 29
garlic disorders 70, 91, 92; and suicidal
    patients 187–188
garlic disorders (analyzable) 92, 126;
    addiction 92, 126–133; borderline
    personality disorder 92, 145–156,
    190–191, 208; hypomania 92,
    139–141; impulse neuroses 92,
    136–139; narcissistic personality 92, 95,
    142–145; personality styles and
    disorders 92, 133–136
garlic disorders (non-analyzable) 92;
    impulse schizophrenia 182–186;
    schizophrenias controlled by attacking
    the environment 177–182
Greenberg, G. 15
Gurman, A.S. 221